# Social Cognition and Communication

Language is the essence of interpersonal behavior and social relationships, and it is social cognitive processes that determine how we produce and understand language. However, there has been surprisingly little interest in the past linking social cognition and communication. This book presents the latest cutting-edge research from a select group of leading international scholars investigating how language shapes our thinking and how social cognitive processes in turn influence language production and communication. The chapters represent diverse perspectives of investigating the links between language and communication, including evolutionary, linguistic, cognitive, and affective approaches as well as the empirical analysis of written and spoken narratives. New methodologies are presented including the latest techniques of text analysis to illuminate the psychology of individual language users and entire cultures and societies.

The chapters address such questions as how are cognitive and identity processes reflected in language? How do affective states influence language production? Are political correctness norms in language use effective? How do partners manage to accommodate to each other's communicative expectations? What is the role of language as a medium of interpersonal and intergroup influence? How are individual and cultural identities reflected in and shaped by narratives in literature, school texts, and the media?

This book is intended for students, researchers, professionals, and laypersons interested in the interplay between thinking and communication.

**Joseph Paul Forgas** Scientia Professor at the University of New South Wales, Sydney, received his doctorate from the University of Oxford. His research investigates the role of affective processes in interpersonal behavior. He has published 24 books and over 200 articles and chapters. He received the Order of Australia, as well as the APS's Distinguished Scientific Contribution Award, the Humboldt Research Prize and is Fellow of the Academy of Social Sciences in Australia, the American Psychological Society, the Society of Personality and Social Psychology and the Hungarian Academy of Sciences.

**Orsolya Vincze** was educated at the University of Pécs and received her doctorate there. Since 2004 she has been an associate professor at the Institute of Psychology at the University of Pécs. She received the award for Best Young Researcher Work in 2007 from the Committee of the Hungarian Computational Linguistic Conference for developing the narrative content analytical algorithm of narrative psychological perspective.

**János László** is scientific advisor and head of the Social Psychology Department at the Institute of Psychology of the Hungarian Academy of Sciences and a graduate of the Eötvös University, Budapest.He is also professor and chair of the Social Psychology Department at the University of Pécs. He was president of the National Doctoral Council in 2008-2010, where he is now honorary president. He is founding editor of the *Journal of Cultural and Evolutionary Psychology*. In 2011 he received the Award of the Hungarian Academy of Sciences.

# The Sydney Symposium of Social Psychology series

This book is Volume 15 in the *Sydney Symposium of Social Psychology* series. The aim of the Sydney Symposia of Social Psychology is to provide new, integrative insights into key areas of contemporary research. Held every year at the University of New South Wales, Sydney, each symposium deals with an important integrative theme in social psychology, and the invited participants are leading researchers in the field from around the world. Each contribution is extensively discussed during the symposium and is subsequently thoroughly revised into book chapters that are published in the volumes in this series. For further details see the website at www.sydneysymposium.unsw.edu.au

## PREVIOUS SYDNEY SYMPOSIUM OF SOCIAL PSYCHOLOGY VOLUMES:

**SSSP 1. FEELING AND THINKING: THE ROLE OF AFFECT IN SOCIAL COGNITION**** ISBN 0-521-64223-X (Edited by J.P. Forgas). *Contributors*: Robert Zajonc, Jim Blascovich, Wendy Berry Mendes, Craig Smith, Leslie Kirby, Eric Eich, Dawn Macauley, Len Berkowitz, Sara Jaffee, EunKyung Jo, Bartholomeu Troccoli, Leonard Martin, Daniel Gilbert, Timothy Wilson, Herbert Bless, Klaus Fiedler, Joseph Forgas, Carolin Showers, Anthony Greenwald, Mahzarin Banaji, Laurie Rudman, Shelly Farnham, Brian Nosek, Marshall Rosier, Mark Leary, Paula Niedenthal & Jamin Halberstadt.

**SSSP 2. THE SOCIAL MIND: COGNITIVE AND MOTIVATIONAL ASPECTS OF INTERPERSONAL BEHAVIOR**** ISBN 0-521-77092-0 (Edited by J.P. Forgas, K.D. Williams & L. Wheeler). *Contributors*: William & Claire McGuire, Susan Andersen, Roy Baumeister, Joel Cooper, Bill Crano, Garth Fletcher, Joseph Forgas, Pascal Huguet, Mike Hogg, Martin Kaplan, Norb Kerr, John Nezlek, Fred Rhodewalt, Astrid Schuetz, Constantine Sedikides, Jeffry Simpson, Richard Sorrentino, Dianne Tice, Kip Williams, and Ladd Wheeler.

**SSSP 3. SOCIAL INFLUENCE: DIRECT AND INDIRECT PROCESSES*** ISBN 1-84169-038-4 (Edited by J.P. Forgas & K. D. Williams). *Contributors*: Robert Cialdini, Eric Knowles, Shannon Butler, Jay Linn,

Bibb Latane, Martin Bourgeois, Mark Schaller, Ap Dijksterhuis, James Tedeschi, Richard Petty, Joseph Forgas, Herbert Bless, Fritz Strack, Eva Walther, Sik Hung Ng, Thomas Mussweiler, Kipling Williams, Lara Dolnik, Charles Stangor, Gretchen Sechrist, John Jost, Deborah Terry, Michael Hogg, Stephen Harkins, Barbara David, John Turner, Robin Martin, Miles Hewstone, Russell Spears, Tom Postmes, Martin Lea, Susan Watt.

**SSSP 4. THE SOCIAL SELF: COGNITIVE, INTERPERSONAL, AND INTERGROUP PERSPECTIVES**** ISBN 1-84169-062-7 (Edited by J. P. Forgas & K.D. Williams). *Contributors*: Eliot R. Smith, Thomas Gilovich, Monica Biernat, Joseph P. Forgas, Stephanie J. Moylan, Edward R. Hirt, Sean M. McCrea, Frederick Rhodewalt, Michael Tragakis, Mark Leary, Roy F. Baumeister, Jean M. Twenge, Natalie Ciarocco, Dianne M. Tice, Jean M. Twenge, Brandon J. Schmeichel, Bertram F. Malle, William Ickes, Marianne LaFrance, Yoshihisa Kashima, Emiko Kashima, Anna Clark, Marilynn B. Brewer, Cynthia L. Pickett, Sabine Otten, Christian S. Crandall, Diane M. Mackie, Joel Cooper, Michael Hogg, Stephen C. Wright, Art Aron, Linda R. Tropp, and Constantine Sedikides.

**SSSP 5. SOCIAL JUDGMENTS: IMPLICIT AND EXPLICIT PROCESSES**** ISBN 0-521-82248-3. (Edited by J.P. Forgas, K. D. Williams & W. Von Hippel). *Contributors*: Herbert Bless, Marilynn Brewer, David Buss, Tanya Chartrand, Klaus Fiedler, Joseph Forgas, David Funder, Adam Galinsky, Martie Haselton, Denis Hilton, Lucy Johnston, Arie Kruglanski, Matthew Lieberman, John McClure, Mario Mikulincer, Norbert Schwarz, Philip Shaver, Diederik Stapel, Jerry Suls, William von Hippel, Michaela Waenke, Ladd Wheeler, Kipling Williams, Michael Zarate.

**SSSP 6. SOCIAL MOTIVATION: CONSCIOUS AND UNCONSCIOUS PROCESSES**** ISBN 0-521-83254-3 (Edited by J.P. Forgas, K. D. Williams & S.M. Laham). *Contributors*: Henk Aarts, Ran Hassin,Trish Devine, Joseph Forgas, Jens Forster, Nira Liberman, Judy Harackiewicz, Leanne Hing, Mark Zanna, Michael Kernis, Paul Lewicki, Steve Neuberg, Doug Kenrick, Mark Schaller, Tom Pyszczynski, Fred Rhodewalt, Jonathan Schooler, Steve Spencer, Fritz Strack, Roland Deutsch, Howard Weiss, Neal Ashkanasy, Kip Williams, Trevor Case, Wayne Warburton, Wendy Wood, Jeffrey Quinn, Rex Wright and Guido Gendolla.

**SSSP 7. THE SOCIAL OUTCAST: OSTRACISM, SOCIAL EXCLUSION, REJECTION, AND BULLYING*** ISBN 1-84169-424-X (Edited by K. D. Williams, J.P Forgas & W. Von Hippel). *Contributors*: Kipling D. Williams, Joseph P. Forgas, William von Hippel, Lisa Zadro, Mark R. Leary, Roy F. Baumeister, and C. Nathan DeWall, Geoff MacDonald, Rachell Kingsbury, Stephanie Shaw, John T. Cacioppo, Louise C. Hawkley, Naomi I. Eisenberger Matthew D. Lieberman, Rainer Romero-Canyas, Geraldine Downey, Jaana Juvonen, Elisheva F. Gross, Kristin L. Sommer, Yonata Rubin, Susan T. Fiske, Mariko Yamamoto, Jean M. Twenge, Cynthia L. Pickett,

Wendi L. Gardner, Megan Knowles, Michael A. Hogg, Julie Fitness, Jessica L. Lakin, Tanya L. Chartrand, Kathleen R. Catanese and Dianne M. Tice, Lowell Gaertner, Jonathan Iuzzini, Jaap W. Ouwerkerk, Norbert L. Kerr, Marcello Gallucci, Paul A. M. Van Lange, and Marilynn B. Brewer.

**SSSP 8. AFFECT IN SOCIAL THINKING AND BEHAVIOR*** ISBN 1-84169-454-2 (Edited by J.P. Forgas). *Contributors*: Joseph P. Forgas, Carrie Wyland, Simon M. Laham, Martie G. Haselton, Timothy Ketelaar, Piotr Winkielman, John T. Cacioppo, Herbert Bless, Klaus Fiedler, Craig A. Smith, Bieke David, Leslie D. Kirby, Eric Eich, Dawn Macaulay, Gerald L. Clore, Justin Storbeck, Roy F. Baumeister, Kathleen D. Vohs, Dianne M. Tice, Dacher Keltner, E.J. Horberg, Christopher Oveis, Elizabeth W. Dunn, Simon M. Laham, Constantine Sedikides, Tim Wildschut, Jamie Arndt, Clay Routledge, Yaacov Trope, Eric R. Igou, Chris Burke, Felicia A. Huppert, Ralph Erber, Susan Markunas, Joseph P. Forgas, Joseph Ciarrochi, John T. Blackledge, Janice R. Kelly, Jennifer R.Spoor, John G. Holmes, Danu B. Anthony.

**SSSP 9. EVOLUTION AND THE SOCIAL MIND*** ISBN 1-84169-458-0 (Edited by J. P. Forgas, M.G. Haselton & W. Von Hippel). *Contributors*: William von Hippel, Martie Haselton, Joseph P. Forgas, R. I. M. Dunbar, Steven W. Gangestad, Randy Thornhill, Douglas T. Kenrick, Andrew W. Delton, Theresa E. Robertson, D. Vaughn Becker, Steven L. Neuberg, Phoebe C. Ellsworth, Ross Buck, Joseph P. Forgas, Paul B.T. Badcock, Nicholas B. Allen, Peter M. Todd, Jeffry A. Simpson, Jonathon LaPaglia, Debra Lieberman, Garth J. O. Fletcher, Nickola C. Overall, Abraham P. Buunk, Karlijn Massar, Pieternel Dijkstra, Mark Van Vugt, Rob Kurzban, Jamin Halberstadt, Oscar Ybarra, Matthew C. Keller, Emily Chan, Andrew S. Baron, Jeffrey Hutsler, Stephen Garcia, Jeffrey Sanchez-Burks, Kimberly Rios Morrison, Jennifer R. Spoor, Kipling D. Williams, Mark Schaller, Lesley A. Duncan.

**SSSP 10. SOCIAL RELATIONSHIPS: COGNITIVE, AFFECTIVE, AND MOTIVATIONAL PROCESSES*** ISBN 978-1-84169-715-4 (Edited by J.P. Forgas & J. Fitness). *Contributors*: Joseph P. Forgas, Julie Fitness, Elaine Hatfield, Richard L. Rapson, Gian C. Gonzaga, Martie G. Haselton, Phillip R. Shaver, Mario Mikulincer, David P. Schmitt, Garth J. O. Fletcher, Alice D. Boyes, Linda K. Acitelli, Margaret S. Clark, Steven M. Graham, Erin Williams, Edward P. Lemay, Christopher R. Agnew, Ximena B. Arriaga, Juan E. Wilson, Marilynn B. Brewer, Jeffry A. Simpson, W. Andrew Collins, SiSi Tran, Katherine C. Haydon, Shelly L. Gable, Patricia Noller, Susan Conway, Anita Blakeley-Smith, Julie Peterson, Eli J. Finkel, Sandra L. Murray, Lisa Zadro, Kipling D. Williams, Rowland S. Miller.

**SSSP 11. PSYCHOLOGY OF SELF-REGULATION: COGNITIVE, AFFECTIVE, AND MOTIVATIONAL PROCESSES*** ISBN 978-1-84872-842-4 (Edited by J. P. Forgas, R. Baumeister & D. M. Tice). *Contributors*: Joseph P. Forgas, Roy F. Baumeister, Dianne M. Tice, Jessica L.

Alquist, Carol Sansone, Malte Friese, Michaela Wänke, Wilhelm Hofmann, Constantine Sedikides, Henning Plessner, Daniel Memmert, Charles S. Carver, Michael F. Scheier, Gabriele Oettingen, Peter M. Gollwitzer, Jens Förster, Nira Liberman, Ayelet Fishbach, Gráinne M. Fitzsimons, Justin Friesen, Edward Orehek, Arie W. Kruglanski, Sander L. Koole, Thomas F. Denson, Klaus Fiedler, Matthias Bluemke, Christian Unkelbach, Hart Blanton, Deborah L. Hall, Kathleen D. Vohs, Jannine D. Lasaleta, Bob Fennis, William von Hippel, Richard Ronay, Eli J. Finkel, Daniel C. Molden, Sarah E. Johnson, Paul W. Eastwick.

**SSSP 12. PSYCHOLOGY OF ATTITUDES AND ATTITUDE CHANGE*** ISBN 978-1-84872-908-7 (Edited by J. P. Forgas, J. Cooper & W.D. Crano). *Contributors*: William D. Crano, Joel Cooper, Joseph P. Forgas, Blair T. Johnson, Marcella H. Boynton, Alison Ledgerwood, Yaacov Trope, Eva Walther, Tina Langer, Klaus Fiedler, Steven J. Spencer, Jennifer Peach, Emiko Yoshida, Mark P. Zanna, Allyson L. Holbrook, Jon A. Krosnick, Eddie Harmon-Jones, David M. Amodio, Cindy Harmon-Jones, Michaela Wänke, Leonie Reutner, Kipling D. Williams, Zhansheng Chen, Duane Wegener, Radmila Prislin, Brenda Major, Sarah S. M. Townsend, Frederick Rhodewalt, Benjamin Peterson, Jim Blascovich, Cade McCall.

**SSSP 13. PSYCHOLOGY OF SOCIAL CONFLICT AND AGGRESSION*** ISBN 978-1-84872-932-2 (Edited by J. P. Forgas, A.W. Kruglanski & K.D Williams). *Contributors*: Daniel Ames, Craig A. Anderson, Joanna E. Anderson, Paul Boxer, Tanya L. Chartrand, John Christner, Matt DeLisi, Thomas F. Denson, Ed Donnerstein, Eric F. Dubow, Chris Eckhardt, Emma C. Fabiansson, Eli J. Finkel, Gráinne M. Fitzsimons, Joseph P. Forgas, Adam D. Galinsky, Debra Gilin, Georgina S. Hammock, L. Rowell Huesmann, Arie W. Kruglanski, Robert Kurzban, N. Pontus Leander, Laura B. Luchies, William W. Maddux, Mario Mikulincer, Edward Orehek, Deborah South Richardson, Phillip R. Shaver, Hui Bing Tan, Mark Van Vugt, Eric D. Wesselmann, Kipling D. Williams, Lisa Zadro.

**SSSP 14. SOCIAL THINKING AND INTERPERSONAL BEHAVIOR*** ISBN 978-1-84872-990-2 (Edited by J. P. Forgas, K. Fiedler & C. Sekidikes). *Contributors:* Andrea E. Abele, Eusebio M. Alvaro, Mauro Bertolotti, Camiel J. Beukeboom, Susanne Bruckmüller, Patrizia Catellani, Cindy K. Chung, Joel Cooper, William D. Crano, István Csertő, John F. Dovidio, Bea Ehmann, Klaus Fiedler, Joseph P. Forgas, Éva Fülöp, Jessica Gasiorek, Howard Giles, Liz Goldenberg, Barbara Ilg, Yoshihisa Kashima, Mikhail Kissine, Olivier Klein, Alex Koch, János László, Anne Maass, Andre Mata, Elisa M. Merkel, Alessio Nencini, Andrew A. Pearson, James W. Pennebaker, Kim Peters, Tibor Pólya, Ben Slugoski, Caterina Suitner, Zsolt Szabó, Matthew D. Trujillo, Orsolya Vincze.

* Published by Psychology Press

** Published by Cambridge University Press

# Social Cognition and Communication

Edited by

Joseph P. Forgas, Orsolya Vincze, and János László

Psychology Press
Taylor & Francis Group
NEW YORK AND LONDON

First published 2014
by Psychology Press
711 Third Avenue, New York, NY 10017

Simultaneously published in the UK
by Psychology Press
27 Church Road, Hove, East Sussex BN3 2FA

*Psychology Press is an imprint of the Taylor & Francis Group, an informa business*



*Library of Congress Cataloging-in-Publication Data*
A catalog record for this book has been requested.

ISBN: 978-1-84872-663-5 (hbk)
ISBN: 978-1-84872-664-2 (pbk)
ISBN: 978-0-203-74462-8 (ebk)

Typeset in New Caledonia and Korinna
by Apex CoVantage, LLC

Printed and bound in the United States of America
by Edwards Brothers, Inc.

# Contents

# Contributors

**Abele, Andrea E.**
University of Erlangen-Nuremberg

**Alvaro, Eusebio M.**
Claremont Graduate University

**Bertolotti, Mauro**
Catholic University of Milan

**Beukeboom, Camiel J.**
VU University Amsterdam

**Bruckmüller, Susanne**
University of Exeter

**Catellani, Patrizia**
Catholic University of Milan

**Chung, Cindy K.**
University of Texas at Austin

**Cooper, Joel**
Princeton University

**Crano, William D.**
Claremont Graduate University

**Csertő, István**
University of Pécs

**Dovidio, John F.**
Yale University

**Ehmann, Bea**
Institute of Cognitive Neurosciences and Psychology, Hungarian Academy of Sciences

**Fiedler, Klaus**
University of Heidelberg

**Forgas, Joseph P.**
University of New South Wales

**Fülöp, Éva**
Institute of Cognitive Neurosciences and Psychology, Hungarian Academy of Sciences

**Gasiorek, Jessica**
University of California, Santa Barbara

**Giles, Howard**
University of California, Santa Barbara

**Goldenberg, Liz**
University of New South Wales

**Ilg, Barbara**
University of Pécs

**Kashima, Yoshihisa**
University of Melbourne

**Kissine, Mikhail**
Université Libre de Bruxelles

**Klein, Olivier**
Université Libre de Bruxelles

**Koch, Alex S.**
University of New South Wales and University of Cologne

**László, János**
Institute of Cognitive Neurosciences and Psychology, Hungarian Academy of Sciences

**Maass, Anne**
University of Padova

**Mata, André**
University of Heidelberg

**Merkel, Elisa M.**
University of Padova

**Nencini, Alessio**
Department of Philosophy, Education, and Psychology, University of Verona

**Pearson, Adam R.**
Pomona College

**Pennebaker, James W.**
University of Texas at Austin

**Peters, Kim**
University of Exeter

**Pólya, Tibor**
Institute of Cognitive Neurosciences and Psychology, Hungarian Academy of Sciences

**Slugoski, Ben**
University of Pécs

**Suitner, Caterina**
University of Padova

**Szabó, Zsolt**
University of Pécs

**Trujillo, Matthew D.**
Princeton University

**Vincze, Orsolya**
Institute of Cognitive Neurosciences and Psychology, Hungarian Academy of Sciences

# 1

# Social Cognition and Communication

## *Background, Theories, and Research*

JOSEPH P. FORGAS, ORSOLYA VINCZE, AND
JÁNOS LÁSZLÓ

The close interdependence between social thinking and communication has long been recognized by writers and philosophers. Indeed, much of social philosophy from Plato to Kant consists of speculations about the interdependence between mental life and social life. Several classical social theorists such as Cooley, Mead, James, and Lewin have focused on this issue, investigating the close interdependence between symbolic mental processes and strategic communication and interaction. Despite repeated claims for the importance of studying language in social psychology (e.g., Forgas, 1983, 1985; Krauss & Fussell, 1996; Moscovici, 1972; Semin, 1996; Smith, 1983), social cognition and research on language have developed relatively independently of each other in empirical psychology (Bradac & Giles 2005; Semin & Fiedler, 1992). Yet language has always been an essential part of social psychology (Strack & Schwarz, 1992), and language lies at the heart of mainstream laboratory experiments as well. As in everyday life, participants in every experiment must also follow the cooperative principle in interpreting the experimenter's messages (Strack & Schwarz, 1992; Schwarz, Strack, Hilton, & Naderer, 1991).

The objective of this book is to explore the links between the fields of social cognition and communication, and present the latest research on how social

*Author Note:* The work on this paper was supported by a Professorial Fellowship by the Australian Research Council to Joseph P. Forgas and by the research grant No. 81366 of the Hungarian National Scientific Research Council to János László; we are also grateful to Kelemen, Meszaros, and Sandor Lawyers, Budapest, for financial assistance. Correspondence regarding this article should be addressed to jp.forgas@unsw.edu.au.

thinking and communication interact (Part 1). We also discuss how narratives can be analyzed to reveal the mental life of individuals and groups (Part 2), and how thinking and communication interact in strategic dyadic encounters (Part 3). Finally, the social and political significance of linking communication and cognition is considered (Part 4). In this introductory chapter, we take a brief look at the evolutionary, social, and psychological background of this integrative enterprise.

## AN EVOLUTIONARY PERSPECTIVE AND THE SOCIAL BRAIN HYPOTHESIS

Researchers in both social cognition and communication increasingly take seriously the idea that the brain, just like the body, is rich in evolved design (Buss, 1999; Cosmides, 1989). The long history of *Homo sapiens,* living in increasingly complex social groups, required cognitive adaptations for social living. Effective communication assumes the mental capacity for representing the mental states of others, as well as representing others' mental representations about ourselves. There is now strong evolutionary evidence that social thinking and communication indeed developed hand in hand over evolutionary time.

According to the *social brain* hypothesis, neocortical processing capacity and the ability to coordinate and communicate in increasingly complex social groups have developed hand in hand in our ancestral environment, with the demands of social communication driving brain development (Dunbar, 1998, 2007). The maximum number of meaningful social relationships we can manage appears to be limited by cortical processing capacity. Regression analyses for numerous primate groups indicate that for humans, the mean manageable group size could be around 150.

It is remarkable that the size of most primary human groups throughout history, such as feudal villages and Stone Age tribes, approximated this number. There were about 150 people in a Neolithic farming village; 150 was the splitting point of Hutterite settlements, 200 is about the upper limit of the number of academics in a subspecialization, and about 150 has been the basic military unit size ever since antiquity. It seems that the computational capacity of our neocortex can support group integration and communication with up to 150 others. Indeed, language itself may have emerged as a cheap and efficient means of maintaining and coordinating such basic-size social groups, allowing early humans to collaborate and coordinate their actions (Dunbar, 1998, 2007). It is communication and cooperation that are the foundations of the impressive evolutionary success of our species, and it is the parallel evolution of language and a computational organ, the human brain, that made cooperation and social cohesion possible.

### *The Contemporary Social Context of Communication*

Although an evolutionary perspective highlights the intimate links between social cognition and communication, historical and cultural influences also play an important role in how people manage their communication strategies. Modern industrialized mass societies present their members with unprecedented cognitive and communicational challenges. As our social lives become ever more complex and impersonal, and as our social interactions increasingly involve people we know hardly at all, the cognitive challenge of making our communication strategies effective becomes ever greater (Forgas, 1985). The evolution of *Homo sapiens* shaped our mental capacity to communicate well within small face-to-face social groups (Dunbar, 2007), yet we now face a profoundly different communication environment that is far removed from the ancestral world of primary groups (Buss, 1999; Sedikides & Skowronski, 1997).

In stable, small-scale societies, relationships are highly regulated. One's place in society is largely determined by ascribed status and rigid norms, identity is socially shared and defined, and social interaction mainly occurs between people who intimately know each other. In contrast, in modern mass societies, most of the people we encounter are strangers. Our position in society is flexible and negotiable, personal anonymity is widespread, mobility is high, and identity must be constructed and negotiated (see Chapters 13, 14, and 15, this volume). This dramatic change in social life occurred very recently, since the 18th century, as a direct consequence of the philosophy of enlightenment, the emergence of individualism, and the economic and political demands of industrialization and the French Revolution. Emile Durkheim (1956), the father of modern sociology, described this realignment in social relations as a change from *mechanical solidarity* (a natural byproduct of daily interaction with intimately known others) to *organic solidarity* (based on the rule-bound cooperation of strangers (see also Toennies, 1887/1957). The challenge of communication in our modern world of strangers is further exacerbated by the rapid development of information technology, where brief verbal messages sent in cyberspace increasingly replace face-to-face interactions (Semin, 1996; see also Chapter 2, this volume).

These new modes of verbal interaction present cognitive challenges that are only beginning to be understood (Forgas & Tan, 2013; see also Part 3, this volume). It is the first time in human history that social communication—once a natural, automatic process—has become problematic, and thus, an object of concern, reflection, and study (Goffman, 1972). It is perhaps no coincidence that the emergence of psychology, and social psychology in particular, as a science of interpersonal behavior so clearly coincides with the advent of anonymous mass societies. Although much of everyday communication continues to be guided by deep-seated, embodied internal mechanisms, the role of high-level reflective and inferential cognitive processes in communication has become evermore important.

## TRADITIONAL THEORIES LINKING SOCIAL COGNITION AND COMMUNICATION

A glance at the historical origins of social psychology reveals that many pioneers were well aware of the close interdependence between social cognition and communication. However, rather interestingly from a historical perspective, the links between thinking and communication received less empirical attention than they deserve.

**Symbolic interactionism.** Symbolic interactionism emphasizes the uniquely human ability to distill symbolic representations from social experiences as the key mechanism that allows people to construct mental models that regulate interpersonal behavior and communication. Rooted in American pragmatism, the symbolic interactionist approach was developed by George Herbert Mead (1934) and his student Herbert Blumer. For Mead, social cognition and social behavior (such as communication) were not distinct, separate domains but intrinsically related. Mead argued that communication is guided by the symbolic mental representations and expectations formed by social actors based on their experience of past interpersonal episodes. Thus, cognitive models of how to communicate in any given situation are partly *given* and determined by prior experiences, and are partly the product of concurrent, constructive cognitive processes. Symbolic interactionism maintains that in order to understand communication and behavior, we have to analyze the meanings that people construct about their social world.

It is unfortunate that symbolic interactionism failed to stimulate much empirical work in social psychology, possibly due to the lack of suitable methodologies for studying individual symbolic representations at the time. The currently ascendant social cognitive paradigm has changed much of this, as it essentially addresses many of the same kinds of questions that were also of interest to Mead: How do mental and symbolic representations come to influence peoples' narratives and communicative behaviors? Recent social cognitive research has produced a range of ingenious techniques and empirical procedures that for the first time allow a rigorous empirical analysis of the links between mental processes and communication (Bless & Forgas, 2000; see also Chapters 2, 4, 5, and 7, this volume). And in turn, the empirical analysis of narratives contained in books, newspapers, and personal histories now allows us to investigate the underlying mental processes of individuals and groups (see Chapters 12, 13, 14, and 15, this volume).

**Culture and the individual.** Another important, yet often neglected historical approach that is highly relevant to contemporary theorizing about the links between social thinking and communication is associated with the name of Max Weber. Foremost among the classic sociologists, Weber was always interested in how social processes and individual cognitions interact. He assumed a close and direct link between how an individual thinks about and cognitively represents social situations, and their actual interpersonal behaviors and communications. For Weber, it was precisely these mental representations about the social world that provided the crucial link between understanding individual behaviors and the operation of large-scale sociocultural systems.

Perhaps the best example of Weber's cultural analysis is his theory linking the emergence of capitalism with the spread of the values and beliefs—and behaviors—associated with the protestant ethic. This work, linking the internal, mental and the external, social, and communicative realms, is profoundly social psychological in orientation. Its key emphasis is on individual social behaviors as they are influenced by shared ideas and social norms (see Chapters 16, 17, and 19, this volume). These mental representations in turn create and are the foundation of interpersonal relations and the operation of large-scale and enduring social systems. Weber (1947) assumes that it is the communication of individual beliefs and motives—for example, the spreading acceptance of the protestant ethic—that is the fundamental influence that ultimately shapes large-scale social structures and cultures such as capitalism.

Weber was also among the first to emphasize that a clear understanding of social interaction and communication must involve the study of externally observable behavior, as well as the subjectively perceived thoughts and meanings by the actor. This approach seeks to unify the insights derived from the social cognitive approach, with a genuine concern with real-life behavior and communication and its role in larger social systems. Weber, although he was not a social psychologist in the modern sense of the term, nevertheless pioneered a variety of ingenious techniques to obtain reliable empirical data about social cognition and communication. The careful empirical analysis of written and spoken texts is fundamentally Weberian in its approach, as Chapters 2, 12, 13, and 14, illustrate in this volume.

**The phenomenological tradition.** In discussing the links between social cognition and communication, the important work of classic phenomenological theoreticians such as Fritz Heider and Kurt Lewin deserve special emphasis. For example, Heider (1958) was among the first to explore the kind of information gathering strategies and cognitive processes on which social actors must necessarily rely as they plan and execute their interpersonal and communicative strategies. Heider's phenomenological theorizing produced some of the most productive empirical paradigms, including work on such key issues as person perception, attribution processes, balance and dissonance theories, and research on attitude organization and attitude change (see Chapters 7 and 8, this volume). Kurt Lewin's (1943) field theory represents another phenomenological framework that allows researchers to conceptualize interpersonal behavior and communication in terms of the subtle influences that occur within the subjectively defined cognitive lifespace of individuals. For Lewin, and other phenomenological theorists, what mattered was not the objectively defined and measurable social reality, but rather, the subjective situation as it was seen and interpreted by unique individuals (Forgas, 1982; see also Chapter 8, this volume). The Lewinian approach affirms the principle that the way people mentally represent and experience social interactions should be the focus of social psychological research, an approach that is nicely illustrated in this volume (for example, Chapters 6, 10, 11, and 17).

Mead, Weber, Heider, and Lewin represent just a few of the classic social science theorists for whom the internal cognitive processes and external social relations and communication of social actors were integrally related. The ideas and theories of Mead and Weber produced an exciting new approach in the 1960s, the microsociological tradition. These dramaturgical analyses linking cognition and communication by Erving Goffman (1972) and others owe much to Mead's and Weber's theories and, in turn, had a definite impact on social psychologists. Microsociologists produced some illuminating papers documenting the delicate interaction between mental representations and communication strategies in real-life situations. Goffman (1972) used the metaphor of the theater to study interpersonal behavior, and his dramaturgical account of communication, self-presentation, and facework continues as a unique tradition in the discipline. The development of narrative psychology—the empirical study of the psychological meaning revealed by written and spoken texts—partly grew out of this symbolic interactionist and phenomenological tradition, as the chapters contained in Part 3 of this book show.

**Language and culture: Personal address forms.** One of early attempts to link social cognition, communication, and culture is reported in the classic textbook of social psychology by Brown (1965), analyzing the interdependence between linguistic forms, and the cognitive and social variables that regulate their use. This work provides an excellent example of how the study of language can provide deep insights into the psychology of communicators. In many European languages (such as French, German, Hungarian—but no longer in English), personal address forms can be either polite and formal (e.g., Vous, Sie, On), or they can be direct, intimate, and informal (tu, du, te). Brown and Gilman (1960) showed that prior to the French Revolution, the use of these address forms was unambiguously regulated by a *status norm:* High status individuals were addressed using the polite form, and low status persons were addressed using the informal form.

With the philosophy of the enlightenment, the ideology of equality, and the social upheavals following the French Revolution came an explicit desire to remove the linguistic codification of status differences embodied in address forms. Indeed during the French Revolution, explicit attempts were made to reform language use to abolish the injustices associated with the ancient regime—in some ways, these moves were the historical antecedents of contemporary attempts to impose politically correct language use (see Chapter 19, this volume). The old status norm in address forms was supplanted by a new *intimacy norm,* requiring that familiar others are addressed informally, but unknown others are addressed formally. These two communication norms continue to coexist, sometimes in conflict with each other, even today (Brown, 1965). In Germany, for example, university professors are typically addressed as "Sie," and students are more likely to address each other as "du." However, when after years of contact intimacy develops, even professors may progress to addressing each other as "du," an important social transition often marked by a small ceremony and drinking a toast together.

Brown's (1965) work illustrates that the analysis of how language is used in everyday life can provide rich information about psychology and cognitions of communicators, and the culture and history of the groups they belong to. It is unfortunate that this kind of research remains rare in scientific social psychology. However, the empirical analysis of written and spoken narratives represents an important emerging field that continues the line of work that Brown (1965) began, looking at language as a repository of psychological and social meanings and influences, as the next section proposes.

## THE PSYCHOLOGY OF NARRATIVES

It is social cognition that underlies the production of all communication, and linguistic narratives in turn play an important role in defining reality and the construction of social identity. Narratives offer an important window into the mental life of individuals and communities, and their analysis gives us crucial insights into the cognitive and affective mechanisms that produced them (see Chapters 2, 12, 13, 14, and 15, this volume). The primary function of language and communication is to describe events, and the manner and characteristics of *how* narratives are constructed reveal deeply meaningful information about the communicators and their culture. Narratives may be defined as reconstructions of events, which involve some temporal and/or causal coherence. This minimal definition may be extended by additional criteria that require some goal-directed action of living or personified actors taking place over time. A full-blown narrative typically involves an initial steady state, some disturbance of this state, efforts for reestablishing the normal state, a new and often transformed state, and an evaluation in conclusion, which draws the moral of the story.

### *Narrative Thinking*

Narratives whether oral, written, or pictorial reflect *narrative thinking* that is a natural, universal, and innate capacity of the human mind. Evolutionary ideas about narrative thinking stress its capacity to encode deviations from the ordinary and its mimetic force (Donald, 1991). Ricouer (1991) even derives mankind's concept of time from our narrative capacity. Recently, brain mechanisms of narrative thinking have been identified using Functional Magnetic Resonance Imagery (fMRI) procedures. However, narrative forms, just as time concepts or languages, also show a wide cultural variety, allowing the development of different sociocultural theories of narratives, reflecting the cultural evolution of narrative forms (Turner, 1981). Accordingly, these *narrative genres* reflect the characteristic intentions, goals, and values of a group sharing a culture.

Narrative thinking differs from paradigmatic or logico-scientific thinking (Bruner, 1986). In the paradigmatic or logical-scientific mode, we work with abstract concepts, we construe truth by means of empirical evidence and methods of formal logic, and we seek causal relations that lead to universal truth conditions. In the narrative mode, we investigate human or human-like intentions and acts using anecdotal methods, and explore the stories and consequences related to them. What justifies this mode of thinking is life-likeness rather than truth, as narratives create realistic representations of life. Narratives do not depict events as they occur out there in the world but construe these events by narrative forms and categories to arrive at the meaning of the events.

Narrative theories are constructivist theories, and similar approaches have been adopted in a number of disciplines such as historiography (White, 1973, 1981). A true historical text recounts events in terms of their inherent interrelations in light of an existing legal and moral order, so it has all the properties of narrative. As a consequence, the reality of these events does not simply rest on the fact that they occurred. Rather it depends on how they are remembered and how they find a place in a chronologically ordered sequence: A "historical narrative endows reality with form and thereby makes it desirable, imposing upon its processes the formal coherency that only stories possess" (White, 1981, p. 19). Reality in a historical account relies on the use of rhetorical figures and explores dimensions of consciousness, that is, what historical figures might have known, thought, and felt. The historiographer as narrator takes up a narrative position; the origin of modern historical science itself is closely related to the need for national history that was demanded by 19th century nationalism.

## *Origins of Narrative Psychology*

Interest in stories and everyday accounts of events as data for social psychologists originated in the 1970s as a direct consequence of the crisis in the discipline at the time (Gergen, 1973). The analysis of verbal accounts (Harre, 1981), social representations (Moscovici, 1981), and naïve psychology in general (Wegner & Vallacher, 1981) was advocated as a response to what was seen as the intrinsic shortcomings of manipulative experimental social psychology. Rather than obtaining data from subjects who are kept in the dark about manipulated experimental situations, why don't we just ask them for their own subjective explanation of the social world? Although using such subjective narratives as data is not without its problems, research on verbal accounts and narratives has now become a well-established field. The term *narrative psychology* was introduced in psychology by Theodor Sarbin's (1986) influential book claiming that human conduct can be best explained through stories, and this explanation should be done by qualitative studies. Events become socially meaningful through narratives, and story-like narratives permeate our understanding of everyday life with standard features such as "beginning," "peak," "nadir," or "termination."

Another important contribution, Jerome Bruner's (1986) *Actual Minds, Possible Worlds* explored the "narrative kind of knowing" in a more empiricist manner. Around the same time, Dan McAdams (1985) developed a theoretical framework and a coding system for interpreting life narratives in the personological tradition building on the Eriksonian framework that emphasizes the close relationship between life stories and personal identity. Whereas earlier psychological research looked at story production and comprehension from a cognitivist perspective, narrative psychology also focuses on the dynamics of identity construction and functioning. The narrative approach became particularly influential in self and identity research, where the analysis of life stories offered a way of exploring the unity and coherence of the individual self (Bamberg & Andrews, 2004; Brockmeier & Carbaugh, 2001; Bruner, 1990; Freeman, 1993; Ricoeur, 1991; Spence, 1982).

## *Current Approaches to the Study of Narratives*

In contrast with earlier qualitative and interpretive forms of narrative analysis (Bruner, 1986; McAdams, 1985; Polkinghorne, 1988; Sarbin, 1986), modern narrative psychology seeks to use quantitative methods to study communication and identity (László, 2008, 2011). Narrative psychology takes seriously the interrelations between language and human psychological and cognitive processes, especially the links between narrative and identity construction. The emphasis on identity is what distinguishes this approach from earlier psychometric work that analyzed correlations between language use and psychological states (Pennebaker & King, 1999; Pennebaker, Mehl, & Niederhoffer, 2003; Tausczik & Pennebaker, 2010; see also Chapter 2, this volume). Individuals in their life stories, just like groups in their group histories, express the ways in which they organize their relations to the social world and construct their identity. Studying narratives can thus provide empirical data about human social cognition and adaptation (see Part 3 here).

Recent research on narratives also recognizes the correspondence between narrative organization and psychological organization. Features of self-narratives, for example, the characters' functions, the temporal characteristics of the story, or the speakers' perspectives, can provide information about the nature and conditions of cognitive self-representations. In this sense, scientific narrative psychology exploits the achievements of narratology (e.g., Barthes, 1977; Culler, 2001; Eco, 1994; Genette, 1980), but it is also directed at exploring how narrative composition expresses inner states of the narrator. Identifiable features of narrative construction reflect psychological processes of identity construction (see László, 2008, 2012; see also Chapter 12, this volume). This approach introduces the compositional level of analysis into the psychological study of language beyond the lexical and grammatical levels. To measure narrative categories and narrative composition, empirical methods such as the Narrative Categorical Content Analysis (NarrCat) technique have been developed, exploiting recent achievements of language technology. A unique feature of NarrCat is its capacity of Semantic Role Labeling (SRL). This function yields quantitative results about how an individual or group acts, evaluates, feels, and thinks about their social world. Thus, the output depicts the narrative (psychological) composition of interpersonal and intergroup relations that define constructions of identity. Several chapters in this volume illustrate the power of this approach (Chapters 12, 13, and 14, this volume).

## LANGUAGE AND THE CONSTRUCTION OF MEANING

A key question when analyzing the interdependence of language and cognition is how various language choices can subtly communicate latent meanings to an audience (see Chapters 4, 5, and 6, this volume). Within communication research, there has long been a distinction between language and speech (cf. De Saussure, 1914/1960; Semin, 1996). According to one approach, it is possible to study and analyze the features of language as an objective system of representations. Alternatively, we may regard language as a medium of communication that can only be properly understood as *speech* when embedded within a real-life communicative context. The key question is the location of meaning (Krauss & Fussell, 1996). Within the first approach, meaning arises from the intrinsic semantic and grammatical properties of language. According to this view, language has distinct *inference-inviting characteristics* that are independent from the context (Semin & Fiedler, 1992). However, communication does not consist merely of the encoding and decoding of the message contained in a string of words, as assumed in earlier models of communication (Shannon & Weaver, 1949). Rather, decoding the *literary* meaning of a statement is merely the first step in comprehending its full social *meaning* (see Chapters 8, 10, and 11, this volume).

### The Cooperative Principle

Communicating and understanding meanings requires active cooperation, and pragmatic models of communication assume a cooperative principle embodied in conversational maxims (Grice,1975, 1989). Conversation can only be meaningful when regulated by shared rules that both parties accept. In a sense, communication is an *inference game*, as understanding the meaning of an utterance requires inferences to be made by the conversational partners (Fiedler, 2007). The task is not simply to infer the linguistic meaning of a message; the speaker's linguistic choices or behaviors have further latent extra-communicational functions with important consequences (see Chapters 3, 6, and 18, this volume). However, communicators' adherence to Gricean maxims is not universal but depends on a variety of subtle psychological and contextual influences. For example, Chapter 5, this volume, shows that negative mood tends to reduce, and positive mood tends to increase communicators' tendency to violate conversational maxims.

The analysis of conversations proposed by Grice (1975) produced a new understanding of how fallacies and anomalies occur in survey research, rational decision making, and cognitive illusions, based on the pragmatics of cooperative communication between language participants (Schwarz, 1996). Growing interest in embodiment phenomena and in information sampling processes is also related to the role of subtle environmental and contextual influences on the way communication is constructed and interpreted (Fiedler, 1996; see also Part 1 here). In terms of Grice's (1979, 1989) cooperative principle, extracting meaning from an utterance implies the operation of a cognitive filtering mechanism before a proper interpretation can be constructed. However, some theorists (see

Chapter 6, this volume) maintain that there may be a direct mechanism (the direct perception model) for perceiving meaning.

## *Language and Implicit Causality*

Subtle changes in language choices may implicitly produce large differences in inferences about causality. For example, interpersonal verbs may trigger assumptions about implicit causality that, depending on the verb class (action verbs versus state verbs), can convey different locations of causality for action. *Action* verbs (e.g., help, attack, or give) mark the subject as cause. In contrast, *state* verbs (such as admire, like, or respect) suggest the causal status of the object (Brown & Fish, 1983). The valence of the interpersonal verbs may also have causal implications. Actors of negative actions are more likely to be perceived as the cause of the event than are actors of positive actions (Franco & Arcuri, 1990).

The linguistic category model (Semin & Fiedler, 1988; see also Chapter 3, this volume) examines the influence of the concrete-abstract status of words on their attributional consequences. Depending on the abstractness of a word, people may interpret behavior as caused by situational or dispositional factors, as more abstract terms suggest enduring, dispositional causation. The tendency to use more or less abstract descriptions may in turn be influenced by such subtle and unconscious clues as a person's affective state—positive affect seems to increase, and negative affect decrease levels of linguistic abstraction (see Chapters 4 and 5, this volume). Interpersonal verbs can also provide implicit information about the time and duration of an event, the stability of the quality ascribed to the person, and the confirmability of the action (Rothbart & Park, 1986; Semin & Fiedler, 1988).

## *Counterfactuals*

Another example of language conveying implicit meanings involves the use of conditional propositions representing alternatives to actual events, or counterfactuals (Roese & Olson, 1995; see also Chapters 3 and 16, this volume). Counterfactual communication often accompanies unexpected or undesired events, allowing communicators to mentally simulate alternative scenarios, using "If . . . then" or "If only" linguistic formulations. Counterfactuals can serve an affective function, assisting people to correct past mistakes (Roese & Olson, 1995). By means of counterfactuals, people may devalue the importance of undesirable outcomes, for example, by using downward counterfactuals (when the alternative outcome is even worse than the real one). In contrast, upward comparisons increase the perceived responsibility of the agent. Counterfactual communication has great propaganda potential allowing political actors to downplay the seriousness of negative outcomes by describing even worse counterfactual scenarios (see Chapter 16, this volume).

## Language and Discrimination

Language also allows the subtle expression of preferences. The choice of words one adopts may have tangible consequences for human interactions (see Chapters 3, 6, and 18, this volume). Ever since the French Revolution, there have been political moves to regulate the use of certain terms in order to achieve socially desirable outcomes. These attempts are consistent with theories such as the Sapir-Whorf hypothesis of linguistic relativity. As language is the medium of both communication and thought, if we can influence language use by regulating communication, surely thinking would eventually be changed as well? Alas, the historical evidence is equivocal: Even absolute dictatorships with complete control over all communication for generations (such as the Soviet Union, or the former Yugoslavia) failed to achieve lasting changes in thinking and attitudes. Although expressions of ethnic discrimination were completely taboo in these countries for several generations, the collapse of the dictatorship resulted in renewed ethnic hatred.

However, Maass, Suitner, and Merkel (Chapter 19, this volume) suggest that politically correct language use may have some beneficial consequences, as the very choice of words framing a message can convey ideological preferences (Goffman, 1986). Inevitably, when communicating, people make salient some aspects of a perceived reality and neglect others, which is reflected in their word choice. Language use also reveals the framing of how someone perceives reality. Political correctness principles provide guidelines for speakers to avoid the use of discriminative language. For instance, when a question is phrased in inclusive language (male/female form), people are more likely to think of women (Stahlberg, Sczesny, & Braun, 2001). Another political correctness principle is to avoid essentializing or labeling individuals with their characteristics and conditions (e.g., a "gay male" rather than "male"). Research stimulated by the linguistic category model also showed that using different word classes can influence causal attributions (see Chapter 3, this volume), highlighting the important cognitive consequences of linguistic choices.

## Communication Accommodation

Communication of course involves a subtle and dynamic cooperation between communicators as they move toward defining and developing a mutually shared communication context (see Part 2, this volume). Communication accommodation theory (Giles, Coupland, & Coupland, 1991; Giles & Smith, 1979) suggests that interactants may choose to accommodate or not to accommodate to the communicational styles of their partners (see Chapter 9, this volume). Accommodations may serve various motives. *Cognitive functions* include communicative devices used by interlocutors to provide a meaningful organization of events most easily available for comprehension. On the other hand, the *identity maintenance function* of communication serves the reinforcement of the communicator's ego and includes protective strategies against information that may have negative effects. In this respect, a communicative act may be convergent to facilitate comprehension and solidarity or to simply reduce interpersonal differences, but it also may take a divergent form when it serves dissociative objectives such as emphasizing status or intergroup differences (Bourhis & Giles, 1977).

Accommodative communication, the attempt of being in synchrony or congruent with the partner, is the normative way of interaction, and as such, it has many positive consequences: It enhances the speaker's attractiveness, perceived supportiveness (Berger & Bradac, 1982), or intelligibility (Triandis, 1960), and also increases the chance for future meetings. However, there are many situations when interlocutors' mutual orientation to reach a shared understanding is not successful. When communication adjustment turns out to be inappropriate, it may result in misunderstanding and may also have further social consequences such as perceived impoliteness. Even accommodative communication may be evaluated as less positive if it is perceived to serve authoritarian purposes (Bradac & Mulac, 1984; see also Chapter 9, this volume). Thus, perceived motives are critical when evaluating accommodative or non-accommodative communication.

### *Affect and Communication*

Although affect has a crucial influence on interpersonal behavior (Forgas, 2001; Zajonc, 1980, 2000), it is only in recent years that affective influences on social communication have been explored. A growing number of experiments now document the influence of affective states on various cognitive mechanisms and resulting interpersonal behaviors. These effects occur because a person's affective state can influence both the *content,* and the *process* of thinking—and these cognitive changes in turn influence communication. Informational or content effects occur as a result of affect priming (Bower, 1981) or affect-as-information mechanisms (Schwarz & Clore, 1988; see also Chapter 4, this volume). Theories of processing effects emphasize the impact of mood states on the way people think and communicate (Clark & Isen, 1982; Fiedler & Forgas, 1988). People induced to feel good tend to process in a more constructive and assimilative "style", in contrast, people in a negative affective state seem to adopt a more bottom-up and accommodative processing style (Bless & Fiedler, 2006).

These affectively induced processing differences have evolutionary roots according to Bless and Fiedler (2006) and show that both positive and negative moods function to recruit processing styles best suited to situational demands. Numerous experiments found that people in a happy mood tend to be more confident, optimistic communicators: People in a good mood are more cooperative negotiators, are more confident and less polite when formulating requests, and disclose more information about themselves (Forgas, 1998, 1999; Forgas & Eich, 2012). Negative mood in turn increases peoples' tendency to pay close attention to situational requirements, so those in a negative mood tend to be better at detecting deception, tend to be more effective persuaders, and are less likely to succumb to judgmental biases when evaluating messages (Forgas, 2011a,b,c; Forgas & Koch, in press; see also Chapter 4, this volume). Positive and negative moods can also influence the speaker's communication style, resulting in greater adherence to Gricean conversational maxims when in a negative mood, and also more concrete and less abstract messages when experiencing negative affect (Beukeboom & Semin, 2005; see also Chapter 5, this volume). Thus, subtle changes in information processing strategies can result in major differences in how a person constructs and responds to communication.

## THE PRESENT VOLUME

As we suggested, contemporary research on the links between social cognition and communication has produced a number of exciting new developments. Communication is only possible because humans possess a highly elaborate cognitive apparatus to perceive, interpret, and respond to others and manage their communication strategies accordingly. In turn, the analysis of communication outputs and language choices allows us to explore the underlying psychological mechanisms that produced these messages. In other words, communication outputs offer a reliable record reflecting the thoughts, feelings, and beliefs of those who produced these messages. The chapters in this book were selected to represent a broad cross section of outstanding contemporary research linking social thinking and communication.

The book is organized into four main sections. Following this introductory chapter, Part 1 contains chapters that document the basic interdependence of communication and social cognition, showing that subtle changes in language use can produce major cognitive consequences, and cognition in turn fundamentally influences communicative. Part 2 explores the way cognitive strategies and epistemic assumptions can promote or hinder effective communication in dyadic social encounters. The chapters in Part 3 focus on the study of narratives as a means of discovering the psychological processes underlying communicators and the construction and maintenance of social identity by individuals and social groups. Finally, the chapters in Part 4 focus on the social power and cultural consequences of communication, and the role of cognitive processes in understanding these effects.

### *Part 1. The Interdependence of Social Cognition and Communication*

Pennebaker and Chung (Chapter 2) propose that quantitative language analysis can provide a window into understanding both individual cognition and social and cultural processes. A computerized investigation of the various psychological, grammatical, and content categories in communication can yield intriguing data about the cognitive, affective, and social characteristics of the communicator. Given the explosive growth of verbal data as a result of the prevalence of cyber communication, the quantitative analysis of verbal outputs offers new insights into individual psychology as well as social and cultural processes.

In Chapter 3, Fiedler and Mata suggest that simple verbal stimuli at the lexical level are ideally suited to exert social influence, as they carry substantial semantic and causal information while effectively concealing the pragmatic purpose of the persuader. Simple lexical stimuli are effective because they trigger implicit cognitive processes, produce priming effects, imply directionality and causality, may elicit in-group–out-group biases, and trigger autobiographical memory effects. Understanding the latent, implicit communicative power and social consequences of the judicious use of lexical categories can revolutionize persuasive communication.

In Chapter 4, Forgas reviews social cognitive theories predicting that affect has both an informative (content) and also a processing effect on cognition and communication. A number of experiments show that people in a positive mood are more confident communicators, use less polite requests, and are more likely to disclose intimate personal information. Other studies found that those in a negative mood process information in a more externally focused and vigilant fashion, are better at detecting deception, use more concrete and effective persuasive messages, and are less likely to succumb to various heuristic biases when interpreting verbal messages—confirming that affective states can reliably influence social cognition and communication.

Koch, Forgas, and Goldenberg (Chapter 5) show that people in a positive mood tend to adopt more assimilative, top-down processing strategies and tend to rely more on their pre-existing knowledge in social communication. Their experiments establish that those in a positive mood spontaneously adopt more abstract and less concrete words in their written and verbal descriptions of observed events. Further, positive moods reduced and negative moods increased communicators' adherence to Gricean conversational maxims—confirming that mood states have important, subconscious, adaptive roles in regulating communication strategies.

Pearson and Dovidio (Chapter 6) look at the influence of peripheral metacognitive experiences, such as processing fluency, on intergroup cognition and communication. Processing fluency tends to promote a sense of safety, liking, and familiarity, whereas disfluency triggers feelings of suspicion, distance, and dislike. Thus, experiences of disfluency tend to have particularly debilitating consequences in dyadic communication with out-group partners. This work helps to explain the role of cognitive mechanisms in the surprising persistence of communicative difficulties when interacting with members of out-groups and minorities.

In Chapter 7, Cooper and Trujillo explore the role of communication in the elicitation and resolution of cognitive dissonance. They suggest that the almost universal psychological preference for consistency exists at the interpersonal and intergroup levels as well. Communication is crucial to the process by which people infer the degree of consistency or dissonance in a given situation. In their studies, Cooper and Trujillo demonstrate that one way that communication-induced dissonance can be resolved is by individuals perceiving a counter-attitudinal communicator as atypical.

## Part 2. Cognition and Communication in Dyadic Encounters

Kissine and Klein in Chapter 8 discuss the question of epistemic trust—in other words, how we come to believe and trust communications we receive from others. Whereas theories of conversational pragmatics imply that believing a communication requires a tortuous inferential process, Kissine and Klein suggest that believing a message occurs directly and without an inferential process. Their direct perception model, following research by Gilbert and others, suggest that comprehension and belief acceptance occur more or less automatically, and it is belief rejection that requires a secondary, effortful process. They suggest that epistemic trust—believing rather than disbelieving communications—also appears to be evolutionarily adaptive.

Giles and Gasiorek (Chapter 9) discuss communication accommodation theory, the question of how, when, and why communicators may prefer, or refuse to adjust their message and communication style in response to the expectations and characteristics of their partners. Communication accommodation does not always occur, and in this chapter, Giles and Gasiorek explore the cognitive and psychological processes involved in non-accommodation and in particular the question of how partners perceive intentionality and motivation in non-accommodative encounters.

Abele and Bruckmüller (Chapter 10) suggest that there are two fundamental dimensions of relating to others: *communion,* indicating warmth, likeability, and morality, and *agency,* featuring competence, ability, dominance, and assertiveness. These dimensions correspond to basic, universal human needs, are deeply rooted in evolution, and are anchored in language and social representations. Of the two dimensions, the first one, communion, is primary and is processed and communicated preferentially because it is this feature that reveals the warmth, benevolence, and trustworthiness of a partner. According to their double perspective model (DPM), audiences should be more focused on discerning *communal* characteristics, but actors tend to use and describe more *agentic* characteristics about themselves.

Peters and Kashima in Chapter 11 analyze the psychology of gossiping—perhaps the most common and ubiquitous kind of conversational exchange. Rather than considering gossiping as morally questionable and of no functional value, Peters and Kashima suggest that gossip fulfills an adaptive function in disseminating useful information about social actors and identifying and *outing* transgressors and freeloaders. Their empirical evidence confirms that gossip mostly influences moral evaluations rather than judgments of competence, and gossipers are evaluated more positively when they share morally relevant information.

## Part 3. The Psychology of Narratives

László and Ehmann (Chapter 12) introduce narrative psychology and use narrative categorical content analysis documenting the way aspects of Hungarian national identity are represented in the language of school books and history texts. They show that these texts reveal a highly vulnerable national identity, in which victimhood, the glorification of an illusory past, lack of cognitive elaboration, blaming outsiders for misfortunes, and an excessive sense of national pride go hand in hand. This analysis of narratives offers important insights into individual social cognitive processes, as well broad social and cultural trends in constructions of identity.

Vincze, Ilg, and Pólya (Chapter 13) explore the role of narrative perspective in the way individual and historical traumas are elaborated. For example, the differential use of temporal perspective (present versus past tense) is indicative of a speaker's ability to cope with traumatic experiences. Vincze et al. also show that the way linguistic devices are employed in school books, folk history, and in newspapers is informative about the way historical traumas are understood within a particular culture. Thus, narrative analysis reveals a great deal about how personal and historical traumas are experienced and resolved.

In Chapter 14, by Fülöp et al. explore the nature and dynamics of linguistic representations of emotional events in Hungarian history. In addition to narrative analysis, they also report experimental investigations showing that emotions characteristic of a collective victim identity dominate Hungarian narratives. They document a remarkable consistency of shared beliefs and emotions in collective memory about traumatic historical events, with collective victimhood a key feature of national identity, and feelings of fear, depression, and hostility expressed in history books, novels, and contemporary texts. This narrative tends to inhibit the cognitive and emotional elaboration of traumatic events, and the emergence of mature and adaptive sense of national identity.

Nencini in Chapter 15 reports analyses of literary texts as a means of discovering narrative representations of southern and northern Italian social identity. He documents distinct territorial differences in identity between north and south and shows that local identity was more salient in the past. In southern Italy, small group membership and regional identity is important for self-definition, but in northern Italy, more individualistic and self-oriented representations of identity are apparent. These narratives provide empirical evidence about the different ways individuals and groups think about themselves.

## *Part 4. The Political and Social Consequences of Communication and Cognition*

Catellani and Bertolotti (Chapter 16) discuss how subtle linguistic strategies can influence citizens' political judgments and choices. For example, using counterfactuals (what could have been) can influence responsibility attributions, allowing speakers to attack or blame someone without incurring negative evaluation for themselves. It seems that these linguistic devices can bypass the epistemic vigilance of an audience (see Chapter 8, this volume) even in the face of countervailing partisan biases.

Crano and Alvaro (Chapter 17) suggest that persuasive messages from minorities play a crucial role in promoting progress, and even the advance of Western civilization owes a great deal to the effective communication by cultural, scientific, and intellectual minorities. Their leniency contract model suggests that strong communicative messages from minorities may be effective if they are related to, but not identical to, the focal issue. Studies show that minority-based persuasion can result in an immediate change in nonfocal attitudes and sometimes delayed change in focal attitudes as well.

Beukeboom in Chapter 18 discusses the role of linguistic bias in maintaining stereotypic expectations. For example, people may use more abstract categories when describing positive in-group and negative out-group characteristics, they may explicitly *mark* individuals by using adjectives to note deviations from expected gender or racial stereotypes, and they may use nouns instead of adjectives to suggest that a characteristic is stable and unalterable. Thus, stereotypic expectancies can be revealed in a variety of subtle ways by the automatic and subconscious choice of words (see also Chapter 3, this volume).

Maass, Suitner, and Merkel (Chapter 19) explore the effectiveness of political correctness in language use. Language control has been part and parcel of social engineering and the propaganda armory of many regimes ever since the French Revolution to major dictatorships in the 20th century. Political correctness language norms remain controversial and Maass et al. explore if political correctness norms have any psychological and social impact. They present empirical evidence suggesting that political correctness language may have tangible and positive consequences for social cognition and, more generally, for social interaction.

## CONCLUSIONS

Understanding the relationship between mental life (social cognition) and interpersonal communication has long been one of the key issues for social philosophy, and more recently, for social psychology. For some decades now, the social cognitive paradigm has evolved without paying sufficient attention to the importance of studying language and communication. Yet, as the contributions to this volume show, language is always the product of subtle social cognitive processes, and in turn, language and narratives shape and influence our thinking and mental representations. As we suggested in this introductory chapter, there are important antecedents in social science theorizing linking communication and cognition, including the work of Mead, Weber, Lewin, Heider, Brown, and others. Several of the chapters here illustrate the close interdependence of communication and social thinking (see Part 1, this volume), as well as the importance of analyzing narratives for the psychological and social insights they can provide about the mental lives of individuals and groups (Part 3). We also suggested that language has a powerful social and political impact on the functioning of individuals and societies (Part 4), and in a sense, all interpersonal behavior involves the interaction of cognitive and communicative strategies (Part 2). As editors, we hope that readers find these contributions as exciting and intriguing as we did, and we hope that collecting them in one volume stimulates a renewed interest in the intricate relationship between social cognition and communication.

## REFERENCES

Bamberg, M., & Andrews, M. (Eds.). (2004). *Considering counter-narratives: Narrating, resisting, making sense.* Amsterdam, The Netherlands: John Benjamins.

Barthes, R. (1977). *Image, music, text.* New York, NY: Hill and Wang.

Berger, C. R., & Bradac, J. J. (1982). *Language and social knowledge.* London, England: Edward Arnold Publishers.

Beukeboom, C. J., & Semin, G. R. (2005). Mood and representations of behaviour: The how and why. *Cognition & Emotion, 19,* 1242–1251.

Bless, H., & Fiedler, K. (2006). Mood and the regulation of information processing and behavior. In J. P. Forgas (Ed.), *Affect in social cognition and behavior* (pp. 65–84). New York, NY: Psychology Press.

Bless, H., & Forgas, J. P. (Eds.). (2000). *The message within: Subjective experiences and social cognition.* Philadelphia, PA: Psychology Press.

Bourhis, R. Y., & Giles, H. (1977). The language of intergroup distinctiveness. In H. Giles (Ed.), *Language, ethnicity and intergroup relations* (pp. 119–135). London, England: Academic Press.

Bower, G. H. (1981). Mood and memory. *American Psychologist, 36,* 129–148.

Bradac, J. J., & Giles, H. (2005). Language and social psychology: Conceptual niceties, complexities, curiosities, monstrosities, and how it all works. In K. L. Fitch & R. E. Sanders (Eds.), *Handbook of language and social interaction* (pp. 201–230). Mahwah, NJ: Erlbaum.

Bradac, J. J., & Mulac, A. (1984). A molecular view of powerful and powerless speech styles: Attributional consequences of specific language features and communicator intentions. *Communication Monographs, 51,* 307–319.

Brockmeier, J., & Carbaugh, D. (Eds.). (2001). *Narrative and identity.* Philadelphia, PA: John Benjamins.

Brown, R. (1965). *Social psychology.* Boston, MA: Freeman.

Brown, R., & Fish, D. (1983). The psychological causality implicit in language. *Cognition, 14,* 237–273.

Brown, R., & Gilman, A. (1960). The pronouns of power and solidarity. In T. A. Sebeok (Ed.), *Style in language* (pp. 253–276). Cambridge, MA: MIT Press.

Bruner, J. (1986). *Actual minds, possible worlds.* Cambridge, MA: Harvard University Press.

Bruner, J. (1990). *Acts of meaning.* Cambridge, MA: Harvard University Press.

Buss, D. M. (1999). *Evolutionary psychology.* Boston, MA: Allyn & Bacon.

Clark, M. S., & Isen, A. M. (1982). Toward understanding the relationship between feeling states and social behavior. In A. H. Hastorf & A. M. Isen (Eds.), *Cognitive social psychology* (pp. 73–108). New York, NY: Elsevier.

Cosmides, L. (1989). The logic of social exchange: Has natural selection shaped how humans reason? Studies with the Wason selection task. *Cognition, 31,* 187–276.

Culler, J. (2001). *The pursuit of signs: Semiotics, literature, deconstruction.* London, England: Routledge.

De Saussure, F. (1914/1960). *Course in general linguistics.* London, England: Peter Owen.

Donald, M. (1991). *The origins of the modern mind: Three stages in the evolution of culture and cognition.* Cambridge, MA: Harvard University Press.

Dunbar, R. I. M. (1998). *Grooming, gossip, and the evolution of language.* Cambridge, MA: Harvard University Press.

Dunbar, R. I. M. (2007). The social brain hypothesis and its relevance to social psychology. In J. P. Forgas, M. G. Haselton, & W. von Hippel (Eds.), *Evolution and the social mind* (pp. 21–33). New York, NY: Psychology Press.

Durkheim, E. (1956). *The division of labor in society.* New York, NY: The Free Press.

Eco, U. (1994). *Six walks in the fictional woods.* Cambridge, MA: Harvard University Press.

Fiedler, K. (1996). Explaining and simulating judgment biases as an aggregation phenomenon in probabilistic, multiple-cue environments. *Psychological Review, 103,* 193–214.

Fiedler, K. (Ed.). (2007). *Social communication.* New York, NY: Psychology Press.

Fiedler, K., & Forgas, J. P. (Eds.). (1988). *Affect, cognition, and social behavior: New evidence and integrative attempts.* Toronto, Canada: Hogrefe.

Forgas, J. P. (1982). Episode cognition: Internal representations of interaction routines. In *Advances in experimental social psychology* (pp. 59–104). New York, NY: Academic Press.

Forgas, J. P. (1983). What is social about social cognition? *British Journal of Social Psychology, 22,* 129–144.

Forgas, J. P. (Ed.). (1985). *Language and social situations.* New York, NY: Springer.

Forgas, J. P. (1998). Asking nicely: Mood effects on responding to more or less polite requests. *Personality and Social Psychology Bulletin, 24,* 173–185.

Forgas, J. P. (1999). On feeling good and being rude: Affective influences on language use and request formulations. *Journal of Personality and Social Psychology, 76,* 928–939.

Forgas, J. P. (Ed.). (2001). *Handbook of affect and social cognition*. Erlbaum: Mahwah, New Jersey.

Forgas, J. P. & Eich, E. E. (2012). Affective Influences on Cognition: Mood Congruence, Mood Dependence, and Mood Effects on Processing Strategies. In A. F. Healy & R. W. Proctor (Eds.), *Experimental Psychology*. Volume 4 in I. B. Weiner (Editor-in-Chief), *Handbook of Psychology* (pp. 61–82). New York: Wiley

Forgas, J. P. (2011a). Affective influences on self-disclosure strategies. *Journal of Personality and Social Psychology. 100*(3), 449–461.

Forgas, J.P. (2011b). Can negative affect eliminate the power of first impressions? Affective influences on primacy and recency effects in impression formation. *Journal of Experimental Social Psychology, 47*, 425–429.

Forgas, J.P. (2011c). She just doesn't look like a philosopher . . .? Affective influences on the halo effect in impression formation. European Journal of Social Psychology, 41, 812–817.

Forgas, J.P. & Koch, A. (in press). Mood effects on cognition. In Michael D. Robinson, Edward R. Watkins and Eddie Harmon-Jones (Eds.) *Handbook of Emotion and Cognition*. Guilford: New York.

Forgas, J. P., & Tan, H. B. (2013). To give or to keep? Affective influences on selfishness and fairness in computer-mediated interactions in the dictator game and the ultimatum game. *Computers and Human Behavior, 29,* 64–74.

Franco, F., & Arcuri, L. (1990). Effects of semantic valence on implicit causality of verbs. *British Journal of Social Psychology, 29,* 161–170.

Freeman, M. (1993). *Rewriting the self: History, memory, narrative.* London, England: Routledge.

Genette, G. (1980). *Narrative discourse.* Oxford, England: Blackwell.

Gergen, K. J. (1973). Social psychology as history. *Journal of Personality and Social Psychology, 23,* 309–320.

Giles, H., Coupland, N., & Coupland, J. (1991). Accommodation theory: Communication, context, and consequence. In H. Giles, J. Coupland, & N. Coupland (Eds.), *The contexts of accommodation* (pp. 1–68). New York, NY: Cambridge University Press.

Giles, H., & Smith, P. M. (1979). Accommodation theory: Optimal levels of convergence. In H. Giles & R. St. Clair (Eds.), *Language and social psychology* (pp. 45–65). Oxford, England: Blackwell.
Goffman, E. (1972). *Strategic interaction.* New York, NY: Ballantine Books.
Goffman, E. (1986). *Frame analysis. An essay on the organization of experience.* Boston, MA: Northeastern University Press.
Grice, H. P. (1975). Logic and conversation. In P. Cole & J. L. Morgan (Eds.), *Syntax and semantics 3: Speech acts* (pp. 41–58). New York, NY: Academic Press.
Grice, P. (1989). *Studies in the way of words.* Cambridge, MA: Harvard University Press.
Harre, R. (1981). Rituals, rhetoric and social cognitions. In J. P. Forgas (Ed.), *Social cognition.* London, England: Academic Press.
Heider, F. (1958). *The psychology of interpersonal relations.* New York, NY: Wiley.
Krauss, R. M., & Fussell, S. R. (1996). Social psychological models of interpersonal communication. In E. T. Higgins & A. Kruglanski (Eds.), *Social psychology: A handbook of basic principles* (pp. 655–701). New York, NY: Guilford Press.
László, J. (2008). *The science of stories: An introduction to narrative psychology.* London, England: Routledge.
Laszlo, J. (2012). *Tortenelemtortenetek*, (in Hungarian; History stories). Budapest: Akademiai Kiado.
László, J. (2011). Narrative psychology. In D. Christie (Ed.), *The encyclopedia of peace psychology* (pp. 687–691). San Francisco, CA: Wiley-Blackwell.
Lewin, K. (1943). Defining the "field" at a given time. *Psychological Review, 50,* 292–310.
McAdams, D. P. (1985). *Power, intimacy, and the life story: Personological inquiries into identity.* New York, NY: Guilford Press.
Mead, G. H. (1934). *Mind, self, and society*. Chicago, IL: University of Chicago Press.
Moscovici, S. (1972). Theory and society in social psychology. In J. Israel & H. Tajfel (Eds.), *The context of social psychology: A critical assessment.* London, England: Academic Press.
Moscovici, S. (1981). On social representations. In J. P. Forgas (Ed.), *Social cognition: Perspectives in everyday understanding.* London, England: Academic Press.
Pennebaker, J. W., & King, L. A. (1999). Linguistic styles: Language use as an individual difference. *Journal of Personality and Social Psychology, 77,* 1296–1312.
Pennebaker, J. W., Mehl, M. R., & Niederhoffer, K. G. (2003). Psychological aspects of natural language use: Our words, our selves'. *Annual Review of Psychology, 54,* 547–577.
Polkinghorne, D. E. (1988). *Narrative knowing and the human sciences.* Albany: State University of New York Press.
Ricoeur, P. (1991). L'identiténarrative. *Revues de Sciences Humaines, 221,* 35–47.
Roese, N. J., & Olson, J. M. (1995). *What might have been: The social psychology of counterfactual thinking.* Mahwah, NJ: Erlbaum.
Rothbart, M., & Park, B. (1986). On the confirmability and discomfirmability of trait concepts. *Journal of Personality and Social Psychology, 50*(1), 131–142.
Sarbin, T. R. (Ed.). (1986). *Narrative psychology: The storied nature of human existence.* New York, NY: Praeger.
Schwarz, N. (1996). *Cognition & communication.* Mahwah, NJ: Erlbaum.
Schwarz, N., & Clore, G. L. (1988). How do I feel about it? The informative function of affective states. In K. Fiedler & J. P. Forgas (Eds.), *Affect, cognition, and social behavior* (pp. 44–62). Toronto, Canada: Hogrefe.
Schwarz, N., Strack, F., Hilton, D. J., & Naderer, G. (1991). Judgmental biases and the logic of conversation: The contextual relevance of irrelevant information. *Social Cognition, 9,* 67–84.
Sedikides, C., & Skowronski, J. A. (1997). The symbolic self in evolutionary context. *Personality and Social Psychology Review, 1,* 80–102.

Semin, G. R. (1996). Relevance of language for social psychology. In C. McGarty & A. Haslam (Eds.), *The message of social psychology: Perspectives on mind and society* (pp. 291–304). Oxford, England: Blackwell.

Semin, G. R., & Fiedler, K. (1988). The cognitive functions of linguistic categories in describing persons: Social cognition and language. *Journal of Personality and Social Psychology, 54,* 558–568.

Semin, G. R., & Fiedler, K. (Eds.). (1992). *Language, interaction and social cognition.* Thousand Oaks, CA: Sage Publications.

Shannon, C., & Weaver, W. (1949). *The mathematical theory of communication.* Champaign: University of Illinois Press.

Smith, M. P. (1983). Social psychology and language. A taxonomy and overview. *Journal of Language and Social Psychology, 2,* 163–182.

Spence, D. P. (1982). *Narrative truth and historical truth. Meaning and interpretation in psychoanalysis.* New York, NY: Norton.

Stahlberg, D., Sczesny, S., & Braun, F. (2001). Name your favorite musician: Effects of masculine generics and of their alternatives in German. *Journal of Language and Social Psychology, 20,* 464–469.

Strack, F., & Schwarz, N. (1992). Communicative influences in standardized question situations: The case of implicit collaboration. In G. R. Semin & K. Fiedler (Eds.), *Language, interaction and social cognition* (pp. 173–193). Thousand Oaks, CA: Sage Publications.

Tausczik, Y., & Pennebaker, J. W. (2010). The psychological meaning of words: LIWC and computerized text analysis methods. *Journal of Language and Social Psychology, 29,* 24–54.

Toennies, F. (1887/1957). *Community and society.* East Lansing: Michigan state University Press.

Triandis, H. C. (1960). Cognitive similarity and communication in a dyad. *Human Relations, 13,* 175–183.

Turner, J. C. (1981). The experimental social psychology of intergroup behavior. In J. C. Turner & H. Giles (Eds.), *Intergroup behavior* (pp. 66–101). Chicago, IL: University of Chicago Press.

Weber, M. (1947). *The theory of social and economic organisation.* Glencoe, IL: The Free Press.

Wegner, D. M., & Vallacher, R. R. (1981). Common sense psychology. In J. Forgas (Ed.), *Social cognition: Perspectives on everyday understanding* (pp. 225–246). London, England: Academic Press.

White, H. (1973). *Metahistory: The historical imagination in nineteenth-century Europe.* Baltimore, MD: Johns Hopkins University Press.

White, H. (1981). The value of narrativity in the representation of reality. In W. J. T. Mitchell (Ed.), *On narrative* (pp. 1–23). Chicago, IL: University of Chicago Press.

Zajonc, R. B. (1980). Feeling and thinking: Preferences need no inferences. *American Psychologist, 35*(2), 151–175.

Zajonc, R. B. (2000). Feeling and thinking: Closing the debate over the independence of affect. In J. P. Forgas (Ed.), *Feeling and thinking: The role of affect in social cognition* (pp. 31–58). Mahwah, NJ: Erlbaum.

# Part 1

# The Interdependence of Social Cognition and Communication

# 2

# Counting Little Words in Big Data

## *The Psychology of Individuals, Communities, Culture, and History*

JAMES W. PENNEBAKER AND CINDY K. CHUNG

Language can provide a window into individuals, families, their community, and culture—and, at the broadest level, into history. Words are the primary means by which we express our thoughts and feelings. They are what we use to communicate, to influence, and to archive our experience of events (see Chapter 3, this volume). Given the centrality of language, it is somewhat surprising that so few social scientists have relied on word analyses to understand basic social processes. Until the very end of the 20th century, large-scale word analyses were simply too difficult to do. With the simultaneous popularity of the desktop computer and the internet, researchers for the first time were able to explore natural language on a scale never imagined.

Our approach to language has been to count words in a number of grammatical, psychological, and content categories using a computerized software program. The program was initially developed to understand psychological processes in individuals who had provided language samples in lab and clinical studies. In recent years, it has become a widely used tool for linguistic and literary studies, and for the analysis of social media and other data sets on the scale of billions of words in many languages and across hundreds of centuries.

In this chapter, we begin by describing the development and initial applications of computerized text analysis programs in lab and clinical psychology studies. One pattern that continually arose in the first decade of these studies was that many psychological effects were associated with relative rates of function word use (Pennebaker, 2011). That is, much of the variance in language to identify psychopathologies, honesty, status, gender, or age was heavily dependent on the use of little words (e.g., articles, prepositions, pronouns, etc.)

more than on content words (e.g., nouns, regular verbs, some adjectives, and adverbs). These patterns have been replicated across a variety of data sets (see Chung & Pennebaker, 2012; Pennebaker, Mehl, & Niederhoffer, 2003; Tausczik & Pennebaker, 2010).

With growing archives of computer-mediated communication on the internet, along with curated archives within the information sciences and digital humanities, the potential uses for computerized text analysis methods have expanded beyond understanding the psychology of an individual. We review studies that have counted little words in big data to understand the psychology of individuals, communities, cultures, and history. Our review focuses on studies that have used a variety of natural language processing methods to address social science research questions more than on heavily computational or linguistic research questions. We conclude with a discussion of how analyses of both lab and real-world archives of natural language together can inform our understanding of our selves, our cultures, and our history.

## BACKGROUND: THE DEVELOPMENT OF A COMPUTERIZED TEXT ANALYSIS PROGRAM

Previous research has found that participants who write for 15 to 20 minutes about their deepest thoughts and feelings surrounding a negative or traumatic event for 3 to 4 consecutive days experience later improvements in mental and physical health relative to participants who write about nonemotional topics (Pennebaker & Beall, 1986). The effects of this experimental paradigm, termed expressive writing, have been replicated across dozens of studies, across labs, and in different countries (for reviews, see Frattaroli, 2006; Pennebaker & Chung, 2011). In an attempt to identify the salutary mechanisms of expressive writing, a computer program was developed to automatically count words relevant to psychological processes in the growing archive of hundreds of expressive writing essays.

To measure the degree to which participants were expressing emotions, lists were derived of words and synonyms denoting, say, positive emotions, such as *excited, happy, love, optimism,* and *win,* and judges voted on whether or not each word belonged in that category. The same process was repeated for other psychologically relevant categories including cognitive mechanisms, social processes, and biological processes. Content categories such as home, death, and religion were included to measure the degree to which various topics were being discussed. Finally, closed class words, otherwise known as function words or junk words, were included because these are previously established categories in the English language, and so they could easily be added to the dictionary.

Ultimately, the computer program, made up of a text processor and the aforementioned dictionary, was called Linguistic Inquiry and Word Count (LIWC2001; Pennebaker, Francis, & Booth, 2001). LIWC, pronounced "Luke," computes the percentages of words used by a speaker or author that are devoted to grammatical (e.g., articles, pronouns, verbs) and psychological (e.g., emotions, cognitive mechanism words, social words) categories. The entries and categories for the LIWC dictionary were revised in 2007 (LIWC2007; Pennebaker, Booth, & Francis, 2007) with certain categories culled, created, or expanded. The processor, which matches words in the text that it processes to the dictionary that it references, remained largely the same in the 2007 revision but with the ability to process Unicode text and phrases, and to highlight dictionary matches within the text. For a demo of LIWC, visit www.liwc.net.

LIWC was first applied to the expressive writing corpus to determine the degree to which word use along certain categories might be predictive of later improvements in health. Increases in cognitive mechanism words (e.g., *because, insight, realize, understand,* etc.) and positive emotion words, along with a moderate use of negative emotion words, were found to predict later health (Pennebaker, Mayne, & Francis, 1997). More important, the LIWC analysis suggested that participants who were able to make realizations and find benefits from their experience, although acknowledging the negative aspects of a negative event, were more likely to experience improved health in the weeks after expressive writing. That is, LIWC was able to identify language markers for a variety of processes known to be associated with adaptive psychological coping. Counting words was an effective means by which to understand how authors related to their topic, with theoretically meaningful relationships to practically important outcomes.

## LANGUAGE AS A WINDOW INTO THE INDIVIDUAL SOUL

The initial tests of LIWC suggested that the ways people used language could serve as a window into basic social and psychological processes. As outlined below, our lab and others soon discovered that the analysis of function words yielded a number of promising and oftentimes surprising effects.

### *Mood Disorders*

LIWC has been applied as a tool to understand psychological processes in a variety of texts from lab and clinical studies, with some studies seeking convergent validity from online natural language samples. A recurrent finding was that the largest associations between language and other psychological measures were found in relative function word use. That is, rates of function word use showed stronger relationships to depression, bipolar disorder, and suicide than did other LIWC categories, including categories of emotion word use. For example, a relatively higher rate of first person singular pronouns (e.g., *I, me, my*) has been found in the college essays of depressed students relative to nondepressed students (Rude, Gortner, & Pennebaker, 2004), in online bulletin board messages devoted to the discussion of depression relative to discussion of home improvement or dieting (Ramirez-Esparza, Chung, Kacewicz, & Pennebaker, 2008) and in forum comments by those with bipolar disorder relative to loved ones searching for information on the disorder (Kramer, Fussell, & Setlock, 2004). Across these studies, depression and bipolar disorder were generally found to be characterized by self-focus and not simply by attention to negative topics and emotions.

Similar effects have been found for suicide. Suicide has been characterized by social isolation (Durkheim, 1951) and heightened self-focus (Baumeister, 1990). Indeed, in the analyses of the collected works by suicidal poets relative to nonsuicidal poets (Stirman & Pennebaker, 2001), and in case studies of suicide completers (for a review, see Baddeley, Daniel, & Pennebaker, 2011), suicidal individuals tended to show increasing social isolation and heightened self-focus in their increasing rates of *I* use and decreasing rates of *we* use over time. Negative emotion use tends to increase approaching suicide, but with changes in positive emotion word use mostly limited to studies that examine short time frames (less than 1 to 2 years). Again, the links between suicide and pronoun use generally tend to be larger than the effects for emotion word use.

### Personality and Demographics

Function words have also been found to be associated with various personality traits in archival experimental studies (see Mehl, Gosling, & Pennebaker, 2006), blogs (Nowson & Oberlander, 2007; Oberlander & Nowson, 2006; Yarkoni, 2010), text messages (Holtgraves, 2011), and instant messaging chats in virtual worlds (Yee, Harris, Jabon, & Bailenson, 2011). For a demo of personality in the twittersphere, visit www.analyzewords.com. Accordingly, function words play a large role in investigations of author attribution, such as age, sex, and social class (e.g., Argamon, Koppel, Pennebaker, & Schler, 2009). It has been found, for example, that women tend to use more personal pronouns relative to men, representing women's greater attention to social dimensions. On the other hand, men tend to use more articles (i.e., *a, an, the*), representing their greater attention to more concrete details (Newman, Groom, Handelman, & Pennebaker, 2008).

There is some evidence that the relative rates of pronoun use between men and women are associated with levels of the hormone testosterone. For example, in case studies of people who were administered testosterone at regular intervals, rates of pronouns referring to others decreased in journal entries and e-mails immediately following the testosterone injections. Pronouns referring to others increased as testosterone levels dropped in the following weeks. These results suggest that testosterone may have the effect of steering attention away from others as social beings (Pennebaker, Groom, Loew, & Dabbs, 2004). Across each of these studies, although women and men may have varied in the kinds of topics they discussed, examining the relative rates of function word use is reliably informative of sex across a variety of topics.

## LANGUAGE AS A WINDOW INTO RELATIONSHIPS

### Relationship Quality

Given that function words can convey attention to others as social beings, several studies have examined the degree to which function words are markers of relationship quality and stability. Previous studies have shown that using *we* at high rates in interactive tasks in the lab predict relationship functioning and marital satisfaction (Gottman & Levenson, 2000; Sillars, Shellen, McIntosh, & Pomegranate, 1997; Simmons, Gordon, & Chambless, 2005). Another study found that the use of *we*, reflecting a communal orientation to coping by spouses in interviews about a patient's heart failure condition, was predictive of improvements in heart failure symptoms of the patient in the months following the interview (Rohrbaugh, Mehl, Shoham, Reilly, & Ewy, 2008).

However, a study of over 80 couples interacting outside of the lab with each other via instant messaging over 10 days failed to show a relationship with *we*. Rather, the more participants used emotion words in talking with each other—both positive and negative emotion words—the more likely their relationship was to survive over a 3 to 6 month interval (Slatcher & Pennebaker, 2006). Taken together, the research above suggests that although brief speech samples can be reliably related to the functioning and quality of a relationship, natural language outside of the lab can provide a different picture of what types of communication patterns are associated with long-term relationship stability.

### The Development of Intimate Relationships: Speed-Dating

Rather than looking at overall levels of function words, several studies have assessed the degree to which interactants use function words at similar rates, termed *language style matching* (LSM), is associated with relationship outcomes. For example, an analysis of speed-dating sessions showed that LSM could predict which of the interactions would lead to both parties being interested in going out on a real date (Ireland et al., 2011). The transcripts came from a series of heterosexual speed-dating sessions offered on the Northwestern University campus. Forty men and 40 women participated in 12 4-minute interactions with members of the opposite sex. Following each interaction, participants rated how attractive and desirable the other person had been.

On the day following the speed-dating sessions, each person indicated whether or not they would be interested in dating each of the partners with which they had interacted. Both parties had to agree that they were interested for a *match* to occur and only then were they given contact information to set up a potential date in the future. Matches were far more likely if LSM during the speed-dating interactions was above the median. LSM measures actually predicted successful matches better than the post-interaction ratings of the individuals. In other words, LSM was able to predict if the couples would subsequently go out on a date better than the couples themselves.

In another corpus of three speed-dating sessions, Jurafsky, Ranganath, and McFarland (2009) analyzed 991 4-minute speed-dating sessions and found, among other dialogue and prosodic features, that judgments of speakers by daters as both friendly and flirting were correlated with the use of *you* by males and *I* by females. They also found that men perceived by dates as awkward used significantly lower rates of *you*. In another study on the same corpus, the authors (Ranganath, Jurafsky, & McFarland, 2009) found that the pronoun cues were generally accurate: Men who reported flirting used more *you* and more *we* among other features; women who reported flirting used more *I* and less *we*. Note that language analyses to detect self-reported intent to flirt were much better than daters' perceptions of their speed-date's flirting.

### *Instant Messages and Other Love (and Hate) Letters*

Whereas the speed-dating project focused on strangers seeking partners, another project assessed whether LSM could also predict the long-term success of people who were already dating. In a reanalysis of an older study (Slatcher & Pennebaker, 2006), the instant messages between 86 heterosexual romantic couples were downloaded before, during, and after participation in a psychology study. LSM between the couples was computed over 10 days of instant messaging. Almost 80% of couples with high LSM (above the median) were still together 3 months later, whereas only half of the couples with low LSM (below the median) were together 3 months later. LSM was able to predict the likelihood of a romantic couple being together 3 months later over and above self-reported ratings of relationship stability.

LSM has also been applied to historical relationships based on archival records (Ireland & Pennebaker, 2010). The correspondence between Sigmund Freud and Carl Jung is famous in tracking their close initial bonds and subsequent feud and falling out. The sometimes passionate and sometimes tumultuous romantic relationships of Elizabeth Barrett-Browning and Robert Browning as well as Sylvia Plath and Ted Hughes were referred to in their poetry for years before the couples met. Across all cases, LSM reliably changed in response to times of relationship harmony (higher LSM) and in times of relationship disharmony (lower LSM). Beyond controlled laboratory studies, and even without the use of self-reports, LSM was able to reliably indicate relationship dynamics over time.

## LANGUAGE AS A WINDOW INTO A COMMUNITY

### *Talking on the Same Page: Wikipedia and Craigslist*

The current generation of text analytic tools is allowing us to track ongoing interactions for the first time. Thousands of people contribute to online sites leaving traces of their communication and social network patterns.

For example, Wikipedia, which started in 2001, is an online encyclopedia-like information source that has more than 3 million articles. Many of the articles are written by experts on a particular topic and have been carefully edited by dozens, sometimes hundreds of people. For the most commonly read articles, an elaborate informal review takes place. Often, a single person will begin an article on a particular topic. If it is a topic of interest, others will visit the site and frequently make changes to the original article. Each Wikipedia article is a repository of group collaboration. The casual visitor only sees the current final product. However, by clicking on the "discussion" tab, it is possible to see archives of conversations among the various contributors.

Wikipedia discussions are a naturalistic record of interactions among the various editors of each article. Recently, the discussion threads of about 70 Wikipedia articles (all about American midsized cities) that had been edited multiple times by at least 50 editors over several years were analyzed (Tausczik & Pennebaker, 2009 and summarized in Pennebaker, 2011). By comparing the language of each entry, it is possible to calculate an overall LSM score. Wikipedia sponsors an elaborate rating system that categorizes articles as being exemplary, very good, good, adequate, or poor.

Across the 70 Wikipedia entries, the higher the LSM of the discussions, the higher the rating for the entry, $r\ (68) = 0.29, p < .05$. The LSM levels for discussion groups were quite low relative to other data sets, averaging 0.30—likely due to the highly asynchronous communication in Wikipedia discussions. Nevertheless, the highest, mid-level, and lowest rated articles had LSM coefficients of 0.34, 0.30, and 0.27, respectively. In other words, Wikipedia discussions that indicated that the editors were corresponding in more similar ways to each other tended to develop better products.

Whereas Wikipedia discussions involve minimally organized communities of people interested in a common topic, it is interesting to speculate how broader communities tend to coalesce in their use of language. Is it possible, for example, to evaluate the overall cohesiveness of entire corporations, communities, or even societies by assessing the degree to which they use language within their broader groups?

As a speculative project, we analyzed www.craigslist.com ads in 30 midsize cities to determine if markers of community cohesiveness might correlate with language synchrony (Pennebaker, 2011). During a month-long period in 2008, approximately 25,000 ads in the categories of cars, furniture, and roommates were downloaded. For each ad category, we calculated a proxy for LSM, the standard deviation of each of LSM's nine function word categories was computed by city and then averaged to build an LSM-like variability score (the psychometrics are impressive in that the more variability for one function word category, the greater the variability for the others—Cronbach's alpha averages .75).

Overall, linguistic cohesiveness was related to the cities' income distribution as measured by the gini coefficient, $r\ (28) = 0.35, p = .05$. The gini statistic taps the degree to which wealth in a community is completely evenly distributed (where gini = 0) versus amassed in the hands of a single person (gini = 1.0). As seen in Table 2.1, linguistic cohesiveness was unrelated to racial or ethnic distribution and to the region of the country.

TABLE 2.1 Most and Least Linguistically Cohesive Cities in Craigslist Ads

| Most Linguistically Cohesive Cities (Top 10) | Least Linguistically Cohesive Cities (Bottom 10) |
|---|---|
| Portland, Oregon | Bakersfield, California |
| Salt Lake City, Utah | Greensboro, North Carolina |
| Raleigh, North Carolina | Louisville, Kentucky |
| Birmingham, Alabama | Oklahoma City, Oklahoma |
| Rochester, New York | Dayton, Ohio |
| Hartford, Connecticut | El Paso, Texas |
| New Orleans, Louisiana | Jacksonville, Florida |
| Richmond, Virginia | Columbia, South Carolina |
| Worcester, Massachusetts | Tulsa, Oklahoma |
| Tucson, Arizona | Albany, New York |

*Note:* Cohesiveness is calculated by the degree to which people in the various communities used function words at comparable levels.

The citywide data is meant to be a demonstration of a possible application of a simple text analysis approach to understanding any group. In our view, LSM is reflecting the basic social processes in groups and communities. In other words, the analysis of function words may serve as a remote sensor of a group's internal dynamics.

## *Remotely Sensing Mood, Influence, and Status*

Although the previous studies examined group engagement, many studies have aimed to examine overall mood and influence within a community. For sentiment analysis, LIWC's positive and negative emotion word categories have been used to assess the relative positivity or negativity within an online forum—see Gill, French, Gergle, and Oberlander (2008) for validation of the LIWC emotion word categories for sentiment analysis, particularly anger and joy, in blogs. For example, Chee, Berlin, and Schatz (2009) examined the use of LIWC's emotion word categories in Yahoo! Groups illness groups. They found expected changes in sentiment in response to approval by the Food and Drug Administration, media attention, and withdrawal and remarketing of particular medications, suggesting that sentiment analysis could be used to examine how a market group feels and responds to a given product.

In social media sites, there are many forums in which previously unacquainted strangers are not aware of the reputations, expertise, or clout of its members. The archives of language in social media sites then provide records of how influence and status are established. Nguyen, Phung, Adams, and Venkatesh (2011) used LIWC to compare LiveJournal bloggers with many versus few friends, followers, and group affiliations. Bloggers with fewer friends, followers, and group affiliations used nonfluencies (e.g., *er, hmm, um*) and swear words (e.g., *ass, fuck, shit*) at high rates. On the other hand, bloggers with many friends, followers, and group membership used big words (i.e., words of six letters or more) and numbers (e.g., *first, two, million*) at high rates. These results suggest that more formality and precision in language style may be a feature of larger groups, whereas an informal style tends to be associated with less popularity and influence in a social network.

Language also provides cues to status hierarchies in online communities. For example, in the analysis of e-mails among faculty, graduate students, and undergraduate students, it was shown that high status interactants tend to use more *we* and lower status interactants tend to use more *I* in their e-mails, suggesting greater self-focus by lower status interactants (Chung & Pennebaker, 2007). Similar effects have been found in other social media contexts such as online bulletin board message forums (Dino, Reysen, & Branscombe, 2009), and in instant messages between employees of a research and development firm (Scholand, Tausczik, & Pennebaker, 2010). Indeed, these pronoun effects were previously found to be robust across lab studies (Kacewicz, Pennebaker, Davis, Jeon, & Graesser, 2012), and in archival memos and documents (Hancock et al., 2010).

Beyond counts of function words, Danescu-Niculescu-Mizil, Lee, Pang, and Kleinberg (2012) examined 240,000 Wikipedia discussions and found that lower status editors changed their language more (i.e., showed higher LSM) to match their higher status counterparts. Similar effects were reported in the same paper in an analysis of over 50,000 conversational exchanges in oral arguments before the U.S. Supreme Court, in which lawyers matched their language more to the chief justice than to associate justices. In other words, the social hierarchy within a community can be mapped by the use of function words, and especially through pronouns.

## LANGUAGE AS A WINDOW INTO A CULTURE

### *Shared Upheavals and Uprisings*

The analysis of *we* words (e.g., *we*, *us*, *our*) suggests that feelings of group identity are far more complicated than one might imagine. When appropriately primed, people naturally fuse their identity with groups of importance to them. In classic experiments, Cialdini and his colleagues (1976) demonstrated that people were more likely to embrace their college football team's identity after a win than after a loss. This "we won"—"they lost" phenomenon was particularly strong if interviewed by people from another state than by people from their own community. Similarly, when groups are threatened from the outside, the use of *we* words dramatically increases.

Analyses of pronouns in 75,000 blog entries from about 1,000 bloggers in the weeks surrounding September 11, 2001, demonstrated a dramatic and statistically significant jump in *we* words and a drop in *I* words immediately after the terrorist attacks. These pronoun effects persisted in moderated form for up to a month after the attacks (reanalysis of Cohn, Mehl, & Pennebaker, 2004 data; in Pennebaker, 2011; see Figure 2.1).

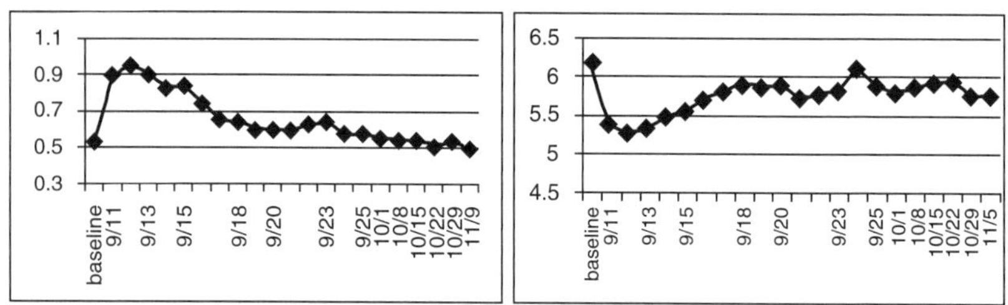


Figure 2.1 Pronoun use by bloggers before (baseline) and after September 11, 2001

*Note*: Graphs reflect percentage of *we* words (left) and *I* words (right) within daily blog entries of 1,084 bloggers in the two months surrounding September 11, 2001.

The use of social media has become an increasingly common real-time news source in tapping how a culture responds to and anticipates events. Anecdotally, more and more people are turning to their Facebook wall and Twitter feeds for news on late-breaking events than to traditional news media such as newspapers and television. Social media as a news source for tracking events in different countries has been especially prevalent in the Arab Spring, in terrorist attacks, and in natural disasters, for which the experiences of citizens, who may be inaccessible through traditional means, report on events in a local area.

For example, Elson, Yeung, Roshan, Bohandy, and Nader (2012) analyzed over 2 million Iranian tweets in a 9-month period during the contested 2009 presidential elections until the end of protests in February 2010. "Twitter users sent tweets—short text messages posted using Twitter—marked with the "IranElection" hash tag (i.e., labeled as being about the Iran election) at a rate of about 30 new tweets per minute in the days immediately following the election." (Elson et al., 2012, p. xi). Rates of LIWC's swear words rose in the weeks leading up to protests, suggesting that high levels of intense emotional expression through the use of swear words may help to predict protests. In addition, the rates of personal pronoun use, *I* and *you* in particular, were used at high rates in the protests immediately following the election and in leading up to one of the largest protests on September 18 (Quds Day in Iran). The use of these personal pronouns, and especially of *you*, which suggests that people were focused on reaching out to others, evidenced a downward trend as the government instituted unprecedented crackdowns on protests beginning in October 2009. These findings show that little words can provide a window into how a society perceives events and potentially, how they intend to respond.

## *Information and Misinformation*

In addition to being a source of social connections, much of internet traffic is devoted to people searching for information. By analyzing where people go for information, we get a sense of their interests and concerns. Only recently have we begun to make the connection between emotional experiences and people's need for specific types of information.

In late April 2009, the World Health Organization announced the potential danger of a new form of flu, based on the H1N1 virus, more commonly known as the swine flu. Over the next 10 days, a tremendous amount of media attention and international anxiety was aroused. Using a new search system, Tausczik, Faassee, Pennebaker, and Petrie (2012) identified almost 10,000 blogs that mentioned swine flu on a day-by-day basis. Analyses of the blogs revealed an initial spike in anxiety-related words that returned to baseline within a few days, followed by an increasing level of anger and hostility words. Searching for information on Wikipedia tended to lag behind the swine flu mentions on blogs by about 3 days. These results suggest that after hearing about a potentially threatening disease, most of the public lets it stew for a few days before actively searching for information about its symptoms, time course, and treatment. Note that this strategy of information-seeking complements key word search strategies reported by Google and others (Ginsberg et al., 2009) where online symptom searches actually lead diagnoses of flu across time and over regions.

Searching for information on the internet can also lead to misinformation. Accordingly, there is an increasing demand to identify misinformation on the internet, including spam (Drucker, Wu, & Vapnik, 2002), deceptive online dating profiles (Toma & Hancock, 2012), corporate scandal (Keila & Skillicorn, 2005; Louwerse, Lin, Drescher, & Semin, 2010), WikiCrimes such as Wikipedia vandalism (Harpalini, Hart, Singh, Johnson, & Choi, 2011), and deceptive product and service reviews (Ott, Choi, Cardie, & Hancock, 2011). By drawing on previous lab and forensic studies that had used LIWC to detect deception (see Hancock, Curry, Goorha, & Woodsworth, 2008; Newman, Pennebaker, Berry, & Richards, 2003), Ott and colleagues (2011) were able to develop algorithms to detect deceptive hotel reviews at rates well above chance. For a demo, visit reviewskeptic.com. Catching deviants and liars in an online community can be improved not just by the infrastructure of a given platform (e.g., spam guards, blocks, moderators, peer-rating systems, etc.) but by the ability to detect their linguistic fingerprints.

## *Sentiment Analysis: Is It Positive or Negative, and So What?*

With the potential of emotions to influence a group and to predict outcomes (see Chapter 4, this volume), there has been a growing interest within the field of natural language processing to determine whether the overall mood within social media sites is relatively positive or negative, and then to predict various outcomes such as box office sales (Asur & Huberman, 2010; Mishne & Glance, 2006), success in blogs devoted to weight loss (Chung, Jones, Liu, & Pennebaker, 2008), virality of news articles (Berger & Milkman, 2009), political activity (Tumasjan, Sprenger, Sandner, & Welpe, 2010), and stock market outcomes (Bollen, Mao, & Zeng, 2010; Gilbert & Karahalios, 2010). For a demo of mood in the twittersphere, visit www.ccs.neu.edu/home/amislove/twittermood/. For a demo of mood in the blogosphere, visit www.wefeelfine.org/.

Social psychologists have used LIWC to conduct sentiment analyses over time to characterize the prevalence of psychological constructs as a function of cultural events. DeWall, Pond, Campbell, and Twenge (2011) found that rates of LIWC's positive emotion word use decreased and rates of negative emotion word use increased from 1980 to 2007. In another project, Kramer (2010) used a dictionary-based system to assess gross national happiness across America in the status updates of 100 million Facebook users. By graphing a standardized metric of the difference in LIWC's positive and negative emotion word use across time, Kramer found that Americans were more positive on national holidays and on the culturally most celebrated day of the week, Fridays. Kramer further found that Americans were the least positive on days of national tragedy (e.g., the day Michael Jackson died) and on Mondays. In other words, the dictionary-based metric was found to be a valid indicator of happiness as a function of the cultural context. For a demo of mood in Facebook, visit apps.facebook.com/usa_gnh/.

Although the LIWC dictionary provides a previously validated measure of emotions, it should be emphasized that sentiment analysis provides only a small part of the big picture. Knowing the overall mood is informative of the degree to which a culture is celebrative, fearful, or angry about events. The literature on the narratives of nations even argues that the emotions tied to a nation's shared events become a part of that nation's identity or historical trajectory (see Chapters 12 and 14, this volume). However, there are other little words that are just as easy to assess and that may be more telling of how an author, speaker, or group is relating to their topic and to their social worlds. Pronouns tell us where and to whom people are paying attention (Pennebaker, 2011). Various prepositions tell us how complex or how precise people are thinking (Pennebaker & King, 1999). Auxiliary verbs tell us the degree to which expressions are story-like (Jurafsky et al., 2009). Going beyond sentiment analysis and analyzing function words allows us to remotely detect the social dynamics and thinking style of a culture.

## LANGUAGE AS A WINDOW INTO HISTORY

### *Searching the Past for n-grams*

Perhaps the largest analysis of cultural products has been the analysis of search terms (or n-grams, which are a continuous set of characters without spaces, in sets of *n*) in Google's digitized collection of 4% of all books ever published (Michel et al., 2011). The relative frequency of the use of particular terms indicated the degree to which those terms were prevalent over the period 1800 to 2000 and, therefore, on the minds of individuals in the culture over time. For example, the authors examined the appearance of words indicating particular widespread diseases (e.g., Spanish Flu), cuisines (e.g., sushi), political regimes (e.g., Nazis), or religious terms (e.g., God) over time. Each of the terms rose and fell when the culture was experiencing change specific to the term. The authors termed this method of investigation *culturomics*, which is a natural language processing method for observing cultural change (the concepts discussed) and linguistic change (the words used for a concept) in large corpora.

Following the culturomic approach, Campbell and Gentile (2012) examined trends in individualism and collectivism from 1960 to 2008 using Google Ngram Viewer, which is an application that reports on the relative use of search terms in the Google Books Project over time. Presuming that *I* represents individualism and *we* represents collectivism, the authors found that there was a trend for increasing individualism and a decreasing trend for collectivism in English language books in the past half century. For a demo, try this yourself at books.google.com/ngrams. Note that this pattern of findings was also found in American popular song lyrics from 1980 to 2007 (DeWall et al., 2011).

Another approach to examine what has been on the culture's mind over time is to examine word categories that represent more topic-relevant words or phrases in cultural products (see also Chapter 14, this volume). For example, Bardi, Calogero, and Mullen (2008) derived a lexicon of three words that typically tend to co-occur with each of Schwartz's value survey's 10 categories of values. The lexicon was shown to be valid, with increases in their use in American newspapers during expected times across history (e.g., the words *power, strength,* and *control* to represent the power value peaked in their collective occurrence in American newspapers during World War II, and was highly correlated with times of high military participation). Their study showed that lexicons of personal concerns can be used to examine the context in which those concerns are likely to be expressed—for example, during challenge or prosperity.

## CONCLUSIONS

Social media sites are enabling the examination of social dynamics in unprecedentedly large samples. We are creating our own records of history simply by interacting as we naturally do—by e-mail, Facebook, Twitter, instant messaging, text messages, etc. Accordingly, we have access to study our selves, relationships, communities, culture, and history through our own words. Since the turn of the century, a growing number of studies have used natural language processing methods to identify language patterns that signal even subtle psychological effects. Although some computing power, data mining, and database management are required for such large data sets, programs such as LIWC are easy to use; the dictionary that it references can be customized; and the results can easily be compared across studies. Although lab and clinical studies are vital to understanding the psychology of individuals, counting little words in big data, just as has been found in smaller sample sizes, can shed light on the greater psychological context in which we communicate—our communities, culture, and history.

On a broader level, the new language analysis methods have the potential to completely change the face of social psychology. By drawing on increasingly sophisticated, computer-based methods on data sets from hundreds of millions of people, the traditional two by two laboratory methods of the 20th century begin to have an anachronistic feel. Indeed, the study of individuals and cultures can now be done faster and more efficiently, with far larger and more valid samples than has ever been possible.

In many ways, we view this work as a call to arms. If social psychologists want to exert a powerful influence on the acquisition of knowledge about groups and social dynamics, they must break from the past. By working with experts in social media, linguistics, communications, computer science, information science, engineering, and the private sector, our discipline will become a central player in the social world. The failure to master these new technologies will result in social psychologists being co-opted by other disciplines that desperately are trying to figure out social behavior in natural settings.

## ACKNOWLEDGMENTS

Department of Psychology A8000, University of Texas at Austin, Austin, Texas 78712. Correspondence should be addressed to Pennebaker@mail.utexas.edu or CindyK.Chung@gmail.com. Order of authorship does not reflect the relative contribution of the authors. Preparation of this manuscript was aided by funding from the Army Research Institute (W91WAW-07-C-0029) and National Science Foundation (NSCC-0904913). We thank Mike Thelwall and Yla Tausczik for their helpful comments in the preparation of the manuscript.

Financial and Disclosure Notes: The LIWC2007 program, co-owned by Pennebaker, is commercially available for $89 USD (full package), $29 USD (student version), with discounts for bulk purchases on www.liwc.net. LIWC2007 demos, downloads, and products can be found on www.liwc.net. Text data for research purposes will be analyzed by Pennebaker free of charge. All profits that go to Pennebaker from LIWC2007 sales are donated to the University of Texas at Austin Psychology Department.

## REFERENCES

Argamon, S., Koppel, M., Pennebaker, J. W., & Schler, J. (2009). Automatically profiling the author of an anonymous text. *Communications of the Association for Computing Machinery, 52,* 119–123.

Asur, S., & Huberman, B. A. (2010). *Predicting the future with social media.* arXiv:1003.5699v1.

Baddeley, J. L., Daniel, G. R., & Pennebaker, J. W. (2011). How Henry Hellyer's use of language foretold his suicide. *Crisis, 32,* 288–292.

Bardi, A., Calogero, R. M., & Mullen, B. (2008). A new archival approach to the study of values and value-behavior relations: Validation of the value lexicon. *Journal of Applied Psychology, 93,* 483–497.

Baumeister, R. F. (1990). Suicide as escape from self. *Psychological Review, 97,* 90–113.

Berger, J. A., & Milkman, K. L. (2009, December 25). What makes online content viral? Retrieved from http://dx.doi.org/10.2139/ssrn.1528077

Bollen, J., Mao, H., & Zeng, X.-J. (2010). Twitter mood predicts the stock market. *Journal of Computational Science, 2,* 1–8.

Campbell, W. K., & Gentile, W. (2012). *Cultural changes in pronoun usage and individualistic phrases: A culturomic analysis.* Talk presented at the 2012 annual meeting for the Society for Personality and Social Psychology, San Diego, CA.

Chee, B., Berlin, R., & Schatz, B. (2009). Measuring population health using personal health messages. *Proceedings of the Annual American Medical Informatics Association Symposium*, 92–96.

Chung, C. K., Jones, C., Liu, A., & Pennebaker, J. W. (2008). Predicting success and failure in weight loss blogs through natural language use. *Proceedings of the 2008 International Conference on Weblogs and Social Media*, 180–181.

Chung, C. K., & Pennebaker, J. W. (2007). The psychological function of function words. In K. Fiedler (Ed.), *Social communication: Frontiers of social psychology* (pp. 343–359). New York, NY: Psychology Press.

Chung, C. K., & Pennebaker, J. W. (2012). Linguistic inquiry and word count (LIWC): Pronounced "Luke" and other useful facts. In P. McCarthy & C. Boonthum (Eds.), *Applied natural language processing and content analysis: Identification, investigation, and resolution* (pp. 206–229). Hershey, PA: IGI Global.

Cialdini, R. B., Borden, R. J., Thorne, A., Walker, M. R., Freeman, S., & Sloan, L. R. (1976). Basking in reflected glory: Three (football) field studies. *Journal of Personality and Social Psychology, 34,* 366–375.

Cohn, M. A., Mehl, M. R., & Pennebaker, J. W. (2004). Linguistic markers of psychological change surrounding September 11, 2001. *Psychological Science, 15,* 687–693.

Danescu-Niculescu-Mizil, C., Lee, L., Pang, B., & Kleinberg, J. (2012). Echoes of power: Language effects and power differences in social interaction. *Proceedings of the 21st International World Wide Web Conference.*

DeWall, C. N., Pond, R. S., Jr., Campbell, W. K., & Twenge, J. M. (2011). Tuning in to psychological change: Linguistic markers of psychological traits and emotions over time in popular U.S. song lyrics. *Psychology of Aesthetics, Creativity, and the Arts, 5,* 200–207.

Dino, A., Reysen, S., & Branscombe, N. R. (2009). Online interactions between group members who differ in status. *Journal of Language and Social Psychology, 28,* 85–93.

Drucker, H., Wu, D., & Vapnik, V. N. (2002). Support vector machines for spam categorization. *Neural Networks, IEEE Transactions on, 10*(5), 1048–1054.

Durkheim, E. (1951). *Suicide.* New York, NY: Free Press.

Elson, S. B., Yeung, D., Roshan, P., Bohandy, S. R., & Nader, A. (2012). *Using social media to gauge Iranian public opinion and mood after the 2009 election.* Santa Monica, CA: RAND Corporation. Retrieved from http://www.rand.org/pubs/technical_reports/TR1161

Frattaroli, J. (2006). Experimental disclosure and its moderators: A meta-analysis. *Psychological Bulletin, 132,* 823–865.

Gilbert, E. & Karahalios, K. (2010). Widespread worry and the stock market. *4th International AAAI Conference on Weblogs and Social Media (ICWSM)*, Washington, DC, 58–65.

Gill, A. J., French, R. M., Gergle, D., & Oberlander, J. (2008). The language of emotion in short blog texts. *Proceedings of the ACM 2008 Conference on Computer Supported Cooperative Work,* San Diego, CA, 299–302.

Ginsberg, J., Mohebbi, M. H., Patel, R. S., Brammer, L., Smolinski, M. S., & Brilliant, L. (2009). Detecting influenza epidemics using search engine query data. *Nature, 457,* 1012–1014.

Gottman, J. R., & Levenson, R. W. (2000). The timing of divorce: Predicting when a couple will divorce over a 14-year period. *Journal of Marriage and the Family, 62,* 737–745.

Hancock, J. T., Beaver, D. I., Chung, C. K., Frazee, J., Pennebaker, J. W., Graesser, A. C., & Cai, Z. (2010). Social language processing: A framework for analyzing the communication of terrorists and authoritarian regimes. *Behavioral Sciences in Terrorism and Political Aggression, Special Issue: Memory and Terrorism, 2,* 108–132.

Hancock, J. T., Curry, L., Goorha, S., & Woodworth, M. T. (2008). On lying and being lied to: A linguistic analysis of deception. *Discourse Processes, 45,* 1–23.

Harpalini, M., Hart, M., Singh, S., Johnson, R., & Choi, Y. (2011). Language of vandalism: Improving Wikipedia vandalism detection via stylometric analysis. *Association for Computational Linguistics.*

Holtgraves, T. (2011). Text messaging, personality, and the social context. *Journal of Research in Personality, 45,* 92–99.

Ireland, M. E., & Pennebaker, J. W. (2010). Language style matching in reading and writing. *Journal of Personality and Social Psychology, 99,* 549–571.

Ireland, M. E., Slatcher, R. B., Eastwick, P. W., Scissors, L. E., Finkel, E. J., & Pennebaker, J. W. (2011). Language style matching predicts relationship formation and stability. *Psychological Science, 22,* 39–44.

Jurafsky, D., Ranganath, R., & McFarland, D. (2009). Extracting social meaning: Identifying interactional style in spoken conversation. *Proceedings of the 2009 Annual Conference of the North American Chapter of the Association for Computational Linguistics—Human Language Technologies,* 638–646.

Kacewicz, E., Pennebaker, J. W., Davis, D., Jeon, M., & Graesser, A. C. (2012). *Pronoun use reflects standings in social hierarchies.* Manuscript submitted for publication.

Keila, P. S., & Skillicorn, D. B. (2005). Detecting unusual email communication. *Proceedings of the 2005 Conference of the Centre for Advanced Studies on Collaborative Research,* 238–246.

Kramer, A. D. I. (2010). An unobtrusive behavioral model of "gross national happiness." *Proceedings of the 28th International Conference on Human Factors in Computing Systems,* New York, NY, 287–290. doi:10.1145/1753326.1753369

Kramer, A. D. I., Fussell, S. R., & Setlock, L. D. (2004). Text analysis as a tool for analyzing conversation in online support groups. *Proceedings of the 23rd International Conference on Human Factors in Computing Systems: Late Breaking Results,* New York, NY, 1485–1488.

Louwerse, M., Lin, K.-I., Drescher, A., & Semin, G. (2010). Linguistic cues predict fraudulent events in a corporate social network. *Proceedings of the 2010 Annual Meeting of the Cognitive Science Society,* 961–966.

Mehl, M. R., Gosling, S. D., & Pennebaker, J. W. (2006). Personality in its natural habitat: Manifestations and implicit folk theories of personality in daily life. *Journal of Personality and Social Psychology, 90,* 862–877.

Michel, J.-B., Shen, Y. K., Aiden, A. P., Veres, A., Gray, M. K., The Google Books Team, . . . Aiden, E. L. (2011). Quantitative analysis of culture using millions of digitized books. *Science, 14,* 176–182.

Mishne, G., & Glance, N. (2006). Predicting movie sales from blogger sentiment. *Proceedings of the AAAI 2006 Spring Symposium on Computational Approaches to Analysing Weblogs.*

Newman, M. L., Groom, C. J., Handelman, L. D., & Pennebaker, J. W. (2008). Gender differences in language use: An analysis of 14,000 text samples. *Discourse Processes, 45,* 211–246.

Newman, M. L., Pennebaker, J. W., Berry, D. S., & Richards, J. M. (2003). Lying words: Predicting deception from linguistic style. *Personality and Social Psychology Bulletin, 29,* 665–675.

Nguyen, T., Phung, D., Adams, B., & Venkatesh, S. (2011). Towards discovery of influence and personality traits through social link prediction. *Proceedings of the International Conference on Weblogs and Social Media,* Barcelona, Spain.

Nowson, S., & Oberlander, J. (2007). Identifying more bloggers: Towards large scale personality classification of personal weblogs. *Proceedings of the International Conference on Weblogs and Social Media.*

Oberlander, J., & Nowson, S. (2006). Whose thumb is it anyway? Classifying author personality from weblog text. *Proceedings of the COLING Association for Computational Linguistics—Main Conference Poster Sessions,* 627–634.

Ott, M., Choi, Y., Cardie, C., & Hancock, J. (2011). Finding deceptive opinion spam by any stretch of the imagination. *Association for Computational Linguistics*.

Pennebaker, J. W. (2011). *The secret life of pronouns: What our words say about us*. New York, NY: Bloomsbury Press.

Pennebaker, J. W., & Beall, S. (1986). Confronting a traumatic event: Toward an understanding of inhibition and disease. *Journal of Abnormal Psychology, 95*, 274–281.

Pennebaker, J. W., Booth, R. J., & Francis, M. E. (2007). Linguistic Inquiry and Word Count: A Text Analysis Program (Version LIWC2007) [Computer software]. Austin, TX: LIWC.net.

Pennebaker, J. W., & Chung, C. K. (2011). Expressive writing and its links to mental and physical health. In H. S. Friedman (Ed.), *Oxford handbook of health psychology* (pp. 417–437). New York, NY: Oxford University Press.

Pennebaker, J. W., Francis, M. E., & Booth, R. J. (2001). Linguistic Inquiry and Word Count (Version LIWC2001) [Computer software]. Mahwah, NJ: Erlbaum.

Pennebaker, J. W., Groom, C. J., Loew, D., & Dabbs, J. M. (2004). Testosterone as a social inhibitor: Two case studies of the effect of testosterone treatment on language. *Journal of Abnormal Psychology, 113*, 172–175.

Pennebaker, J. W., & King, L. A. (1999). Linguistic styles: Language use as an individual difference. *Journal of Personality and Social Psychology, 77*, 1296–1312.

Pennebaker, J. W., Mayne, T. J., & Francis, M. E. (1997). Linguistic predictors of adaptive bereavement. *Journal of Personality and Social Psychology, 72*, 863–871.

Pennebaker, J. W., Mehl, M. R., & Niederhoffer, K. (2003). Psychological aspects of natural language use: Our words, our selves. *Annual Review of Psychology, 54*, 547–577.

Ramirez-Esparza, N., Chung, C. K., Kacewicz, E., & Pennebaker, J. W. (2008). The psychology of word use in depression forums in English and in Spanish. Testing two text analytic approaches. *Proceedings of the 2008 International Conference on Weblogs and Social Media*, Menlo Park, CA, 102–108.

Ranganath, R., Jurafsky, D., & McFarland, D. (2009). It's not you, it's me: Detecting flirting and its misperception in speed-dates. *Proceedings of the 2009 Conference on Empirical Methods in Natural Language Processing*, 334–342.

Rohrbaugh, M. J., Mehl, M. R., Shoham, V., Reilly, E. S., & Ewy, G. A. (2008). Prognostic significance of spouse "we" talk in couples coping with heart failure. *Journal of Consulting and Clinical Psychology, 76*, 781–789.

Rude, S. S., Gortner, E. M., & Pennebaker, J. W. (2004). Language use of depressed and depression-vulnerable college students. *Cognition and Emotion, 18*, 1121–1133.

Scholand, A. J., Tausczik, Y. R., & Pennebaker, J. W. (2010). Social language network analysis. *Proceedings of Computer Supported Cooperative Work 2010*, New York, NY, 23–26.

Sillars, A., Shellen, W., McIntosh, A., & Pomegranate, M. (1997). Relational characteristics of language: Elaboration and differentiation in marital conversations. *Western Journal of Communication, 61*, 403–422.

Simmons, R. A., Gordon, P. C., & Chambless, D. L. (2005). Pronouns in marital interaction: What do you and I say about marital health? *Psychological Science, 16*, 932–936.

Slatcher, R. B., & Pennebaker, J. W. (2006). How do I love thee? Let me count the words: The social effects of expressive writing. *Psychological Science, 17*, 660–664.

Stirman, S. W., & Pennebaker, J. W. (2001). Word use in the poetry of suicidal and nonsuicidal poets. *Psychosomatic Medicine, 63*, 517–522.

Tausczik, Y., Faassee, K., Pennebaker, J. W., & Petrie, K. J. (2012). Public anxiety and information seeking following H1N1 outbreak: Blogs, newspaper articles, and Wikipedia visits. *Health Communication, 27*, 179–185.

Tausczik, Y. R. & Pennebaker, J. W. (2009). Leadership in informal groups: A linguistic investigation of Wikipedia. Presented at the annual meeting of the Group Processes and Intergroup Relations pre-conference for Society for Personality and Social Psychology, Las Vegas, NV.

Tausczik, Y. R., & Pennebaker, J. W. (2010). The psychological meaning of words: LIWC and computerized text analysis methods. *Journal of Language and Social Psychology, 29*, 24–54.

Toma, C. L., & Hancock, J. T. (2012). What lies beneath: The linguistic traces of deception in online dating profiles. *Journal of Communication, 62*, 78–97.

Tumasjan, A., Sprenger, T. O., Sandner, P. G., & Welpe, I. M. (2010). Predicting elections with Twitter: What 140 characters reveal about political sentiment. *Proceedings of the Fourth International Conference on Weblogs and Social Media*, Menlo Park, CA, 178–185.

Yarkoni, T. (2010). Personality in 100,000 words: A large-scale analysis of personality and word use among bloggers. *Journal of Research in Personality, 44*, 363–373.

Yee, N., Harris, H., Jabon, M., & Bailenson, J. N. (2011). The expression of personality in virtual worlds. *Social Psychological and Personality Science, 2*, 5–12.

# 3

# The Art of Exerting Verbal Influence through Powerful Lexical Stimuli

KLAUS FIEDLER AND ANDRÉ MATA

## INTRODUCTION

For verbal influence to be effective, it has to master a communication trade-off (Fiedler, 2008). On one hand, influential communication must dare to state something new and informative that deviates from the communication partner's old knowledge or opinion. On the other hand, effective communication has to conceal its manipulative purpose to avoid reactance and inoculation effects (Brehm, 2000; Engelkamp, Mohr, & Mohr, 1985; McGuire, 1964). The research reviewed in the present article suggests that simple verbal stimuli at the lexical level are ideally suited to meeting this double goal, because word stimuli carry substantial semantic information while often concealing the pragmatic purpose of communication. Words constitute neutral and natural units of information that can be freely combined to produce an infinite number of communicative acts (Chapter 7, this volume). This flexibility and generative power of language (Glucksberg & Danks, 1975) is at the heart of virtually all verbal influence strategies, in politics, negotiation, scientific argumentation, advertising, deception, ingratiation, and education (Chapter 4, this volume).

Any expanded question, imperative command, or more elaborate text unit used to advertise an object or to request help may elicit reactance or suspicion. The many nice things a car dealer has to say about the qualities of a used car may be understood as a veridical description of the car, as an attempt to gain money, as an empty professional statement that is routinely repeated with each and every car, or even as plain deception. Likewise, sentence- or paragraph-like requests for help may be framed as an expression of misery, as a joke or role play, or as a reflection of the laziness of someone who might as well help him- or herself. Communication success will obviously depend on the recipient's appraisal and evaluation of the pragmatic situation. An advertisement or request for help will fail if it raises the impression of a selfish, inadequate, unfair, or provocative influence attempt.

Even when communicative acts do not run against the recipients' own pragmatic interests, the very detection of an influence attempt may be sufficient to induce reactance or an inoculation effect in the message recipient. Counterarguments are often generated spontaneously if only the recipient of a communication is aware of an influence attempt. As spelled out in Brehm's (1966) theory of reactance, any attempt to prescribe certain actions or to forego others will cause in the recipient a countertendency to regain his or her freedom of choice. It may therefore be not only necessary to let the speech act appear harmless or prosocial; it may even be necessary to fully distract the recipient from pragmatic thinking and to conceal the speech act as perfectly as possible. Thus, a useful strategy might be to make influence attempts subliminal or subtle enough to prevent the communication partner from drawing pragmatic inferences.

Lexical stimuli are ideally suited for such influence strategies. Reading or hearing the isolated word *fairness* in a football stadium or on a package of coffee just raises the meaning of morality and social exchange, and maybe activates corresponding behavioral scripts. It hardly reveals any specific speech act. People exposed to lexical stimuli will rarely start reasoning whether fairness is an arrogant imperative, an expression of a moral value, an unfair attempt to exploit others' cooperation, or a joke or irony. Likewise, lexical primes in advertising like *erotic*, *paradise*, or *wellness* will hardly raise counterarguments or critical questions about the validity or pragmatic meaning of minimal verbal communications (Hansen & Wänke, 2011; Wänke, 2007). Such modest single-word stimuli neither come as promise, nor as ingratiation, deceptive strategy, or pretentious assertion. People who are exposed to such unspecified communications will rarely engage in pragmatic reasoning about the advertiser's goals or intentions; they will be simply influenced by the meaning and associative power of the lexical stimuli.

## LEXICAL STIMULI TRIGGER IMPLICIT COGNITION

### *Verbal Influences as Priming Effects*

Using a fashionable term in contemporary social and cognitive psychology, the lexical-influence paradigm may be referred to as one-word priming. It is hardly by coincidence that words constitute by far the largest class of stimuli used in the huge research industry of priming studies. Presenting a related prime (e.g., *professor*) before a target stimulus (e.g., *intelligent*) facilitates the recognition and naming of the target (as evident in faster response latency) and the classification of the target as word or nonword in a lexical decision task, or as positive versus negative in evaluative priming (Fazio, 2001; Fiedler, 2003; Klauer & Musch, 2003). Single-word primes have also been shown to bias subsequent judgments in the direction of the prime (Srull & Wyer, 1980). For example, in an affective-misattribution task (Payne, Hall, Cameron, & Bishara, 2010), neutral targets (e.g., abstract drawing or pattern) were judged to be more pleasant or higher in aesthetic value when the preceding prime words were of positive rather than negative valence. In action priming studies (e.g., Dijksterhuis et al., 1998), priming participants with the lexical stimulus *professor* was even shown to enhance their intellectual test performance, just as priming the concept of the *elderly* served to reduce the participants' walking speed (Bargh, Chen, & Burrows, 1996).

In a similar vein, priming of achievement-related words has been shown to enhance achievement motivation (Hart & Albarracìn, 2009). Distrust-related lexical primes induce critical mindsets and more elaborate processing styles (Schul, Mayo, & Burnstein, 2004). When such words as *fairness*, *morality*, and *solidarity* were presented subliminally or remembered in an alleged verbal-learning task (Hertel & Fiedler, 1994), the rate of cooperative behavior in dilemma games increased. Conversely, words associated with aggressive meaning were shown to cause manifest aggressive behavior (Todorov & Bargh, 2002). With regard to therapy and interventions, Shalev and Bargh (2011) argue that priming-based interventions could be easily "administered by multiple providers and communication devised to regulate emotional states, increase adherence to treatment instructions, or activate mind-sets that facilitate adaptive functioning" (p. 488).

In a memorable study by Gilovich (1981), several lexical primes were used to jointly activate different historical analogies supposed to bias the participants' political judgments. The cover story of the political-judgment task described an allied country that was threatened by an aggressive neighboring country, and participants had to decide whether their own country (i.e., the United States) should intervene. A few key words in the cover story (e.g., the lecture hall named *Winston-Churchill Hall* or *Dean-Rusk Hall*) reminded participants of the Vietnam War (implying that the United States should not intervene) or of Hitler's Blitzkrieg at the beginning of World War II (implying the United States should intervene). Most participants actually voted for intervention in the latter condition but against intervention in the former condition.

A common denominator of all these impressive priming demonstrations is that the effective primes were compact word stimuli. One might quickly object that this merely reflects an artificial limitation of experimental research—namely, that the collection or construction of word stimuli is easier and causes less work than the construction of more elaborate text, scripts, film clips, or even more refined priming treatments. However, although this argument may be true, it should not be dismissed as artificial, because it provides a sound explanation of why word primes are so practical. They are freely and richly available in the lexicon. They can be easily combined in flexible ways to guide inference processes (such as historical analogies). They can be tried out (pilot-tested) quickly in reality or in mental simulations. And, last but not least, because no saccades are necessary to read a word, they can still be understood and exert their basic impact when the word primes are degraded or presented subliminally. Thus, the bias toward word priming in past research may reflect just a special case of the pragmatic bias toward word priming in verbal influence strategies.

## *Beyond Priming Paradigms*

Priming is by no means the only paradigm that highlights the power of lexical stimuli. The same could be said for the evaluative conditioning paradigm (De Houwer, 2007). In those evaluative conditioning studies in which verbal stimuli were used as unconditional stimuli to be paired with neutral conditional stimuli, the unconditional stimuli were almost always distinct words (for an overview, see Hofmann, De Houwer, Perugini, Baeyens, & Crombez, 2010). In hardly any study were sentences, paragraphs, or narratives used as unconditional stimuli. Again, one might claim that this merely reflects researchers' laziness or preference for simple and well-controlled stimuli. However, influence making in reality is also characterized by economy and the need to exert control over one's communicative acts. It is therefore not surprising that in economic and political reality most conditioning-based influence or advertising strategies rely on commonly understood, handy word labels, such as trait adjectives, affective terms, or celebrity names, rather than more complicated syntactical and pragmatic constructions.

In the false-memory paradigm (Roediger & McDermott, 1995), too, the most convenient and effective means of inducing falsely recalled or recognized stimuli has been the learning of lists of words revolving around a topical concept. For instance, exposure to a stimulus list that includes the words *dream*, *pillow*, *bed*, and *night* will typically mislead a majority of participants to remember the semantic core meaning *sleep*, although this word was in fact not presented. Likewise, in the context of applied research in the legal context, demonstrations of false memories or reconstructive memory biases are often based on the manipulation of critical words in leading questions. In Loftus and Palmer's (1974) seminal studies, for instance, participants were asked to estimate the speed of a car they had observed on video, in response to the question "How fast were the cars moving when they hit together/smashed together/bumped into each other/collided?" Speed estimates varied greatly as a function of the speed suggested by the meaning of the verb.

In psycholinguistics, the influence of language condensed in words is well known under the label of nominalization. In a frequently cited article—titled "truth is a linguistic question"—Bolinger (1973) provides various examples of nouns and composite nouns that presuppose a fact implicitly, rather than stating it explicitly. Terms like *insurance* or *defense ministry* presuppose implicitly that subscribing a contract warrants security or that the ministry is concerned with peace rather than starting war. Because these critical assumptions are not stated explicitly, the likelihood is low that the validity of the presupposition will be questioned and tested critically (Chapter 2, this volume). Nominalization is a prominent linguistic tool for presupposition strategies.

A number of recently developed instruments for the unobtrusive measurement of implicit attitudes, stereotypes, and prejudices are also built on lexical ground. As already mentioned, priming-based measures of implicit attitudes (e.g., measuring the speed required to evaluate positive or negative targets following male or female name primes) involve distinct words (unless they use pictures). The same holds for the implicit association test (IAT; Nosek, Greenwald, & Banaji, 2005), which almost always consists of simple lexical (or pictorial) stimuli, the sorting speed of which is supposed to measure attitudes, stereotypes, or self-concepts. There is hardly any IAT application involving sentences, narratives, or other complex text variants, which would greatly complicate the interpretation of test results. For the same reason, influence attempts in everyday communication should be equivocal and hard to comprehend if they clearly focus on distinct key words.

In the new communication media, we typically use word labels or nominal phrases to denote topics and subdirectories. To gather new information in Google or the encyclopedia too, we use lexical key words as search prompts. Whoever tried to google longer text prompts will probably have experienced the disadvantage and confusion resulting from misunderstandings of multiple prompts and syntactic relations.

## *Constraints and Syntactic Interactions between Word Primes*

This is not to say that syntactic information is completely ignored. For instance, the notion of identity priming refers to the finding that the impact of a prime on the processing of a target word increases when they are identical rather than just similar (cf. De Houwer, Hermans, & Eelen, 1998). Semantic-priming effects can be strengthened by letting more than one related prime precede a target (Balota & Paul, 1996), suggesting that simple syntactic rules like repetition can intensify word-priming effects.

Word ordering effects nicely illustrate the operation of simple and straightforward syntactic influences that operate on the lexical level. For instance, nouns were found to carry more weight for speakers of languages where nouns usually precede adjectives (e.g., Portuguese) than for speakers of languages where adjectives usually precede nouns (e.g., English). In two studies (Percy, Sherman, Garcia-Marques, Mata, & Garcia-Marques, 2009), American and Portuguese participants were presented with either adjective-noun phrases (e.g., *the honest chef, the honest journalist, the happy chef*—presented in their native language and in the natural word order of the language) or visual stimuli whose features could be designated by an adjective and a noun (e.g., red circle, red square, blue square). When they were subsequently asked to make noun-conditioned frequency estimates (e.g., "Of all the chefs presented, how many were honest?," "Of all the circles you saw, how many were red?") as well as adjective-conditioned frequency estimates (e.g., "Of all the happy people presented, how many were chefs?," "Of all the blue things you saw, how many were squares?"), participants from both samples were faster at making the noun-conditioned estimates than the adjective-conditioned estimates, but this noun-advantage was greater for Portuguese participants compared with American participants.

In other studies by these authors (Mata, Sherman, Percy, Garcia-Marques, & Garcia-Marques, 2012), Portuguese participants made more false recognitions than English speakers for new items that shared the noun category with old items (e.g., blue square and green square). Also, Portuguese speakers judged items that shared the noun category (e.g., blue square and green square) to be more similar than English speakers did, whereas the opposite was the case for items that shared the adjective attribute (e.g., blue square and blue circle). These studies show that the impact of words on memory and judgment can be constrained by native language word order.

Relational constraints come into play when lexical primes vary in abstractness or inclusiveness. Abstract and semantically broad primes are more likely to impact subsequent target responses than concrete and too specific primes, simply because more inclusive primes are semantically applicable to a broader range of targets. In the aforementioned research by Dijksterhuis et al. (1998), for instance, only the inclusive category label *professor* enhanced the participants' intellectual performance, but not the specific prime *Einstein*, which is probably so specific that participants themselves are excluded from the prime's domain. As a consequence, the Einstein prime caused a contrast effect, that is, a performance impairment. In a similar vein, the categorical prime *model* led to higher attractiveness self-ratings in female participants, whereas the specific name *Claudia Schiffer* led to lower self ratings. Schwarz and Bless' (2007) inclusion-exclusion model provides a sensible account for these pronounced inclusiveness effects.

The impact of word primes can also be moderated by strategic processes. As a general rule, all manipulations of the presentation or encoding context that serve to functionally separate the prime from the target will undermine the fusion of prime and target. A growing body of convergent evidence shows that priming effects are reduced, eliminated, or even reversed when the time interval between prime and target onset is too long (Hermans, Spruyt, & Eelen, 2003), when primes and targets are hard to integrate or to form a compound (Estes & Jones, 2009), and when primes are attended to and memorized as distinct entities, or actively responded to, so that primes are separately from the target-reaction task (Fiedler, Bluemke, & Unkelbach, 2011; Liberman, Förster, & Higgins, 2007; Sparrow & Wegner, 2006).

Strategic moderation is also evident in the dependence of priming on the list context. Both the relatedness-proportion effect in semantic priming (Bodner & Masson, 2003) and the congruity-proportion effect in evaluative priming (Klauer, Rossnagel, & Musch, 1997) testify to the adaptive flexibility in the way a prime is used. If there is a negative correlation between the meaning or valence of primes and targets in the stimulus context (e.g., if most targets following positive primes are negative and vice versa), participants can learn to invert the normal priming effect. In such a context, they can learn to react faster to targets that mismatch the prime in valence or semantic meaning.

Thus, a number of pronounced interactions and contextual or strategic moderation effects highlight the fact that priming effects are not under rigid stimulus control. Rather, they lend themselves to communication strategies that take such context dependencies into account. However, crucially, the "grammar of priming" (Fiedler et al., 2011) must not be equated with the strict syntactic and conversational rules that apply to higher-order text units.

## VERBAL INFLUENCE BASED ON STRATEGIC USES OF LINGUISTIC CATEGORIES

A growing number of empirical findings highlight the systematic impact of lexical stimuli on social influence processes. We believe that the reported evidence—which partly stems from studies conducted in our own lab and partly from others' work on linguistic categories and their cognitive implications—will refute the skeptical argument that lexical analysis provides an impoverished and inadequate picture of language and verbal behavior (Edwards & Potter, 1993). According to this view, counting and categorizing words can never do justice to the illocutionary and perlocutionary meaning of even the simplest speech act, to figurative language, and to the richness of elegance of narrative information.

This aesthetic argument must not be confused with scientific evidence about the reliability and validity of measurable aspects of language. Objective measures of speaker intentions, semantic ambiguities, anaphoric references, stylistic tools, hidden messages between the lines, and conscious or unconscious violations of Grice's (1975) maxims of communication are hard to find. Moreover, many of these higher-order rhetoric means are so original and idiosyncratic that they hardly lend themselves to statistical analyses. In contrast, word-based content analysis is simple and straightforward and can be easily accomplished by freely available software tools (Chapter 2, this volume; Tausczik & Pennebaker, 2010). Even though—or exactly because—lexical analysis reduces the miraculous complexity of language to a few objectively assessable aspects, it has a real chance to capture the systematic relations that hold between language and behavior across people and situations. The empirical evidence below is meant to substantiate this notion.

### *Implicit Verb Causality*

A long tradition of research on linguistic categories testifies to the strong and systematic constraints imposed by different word classes on language comprehension and cognitive inferences. In particular, the verbs and adjectives that make up the sentence predicates constrain the resulting attributions and evaluations. Numerous studies on implicit verb causality (Abelson & Kanouse, 1966; Brown & Fish, 1983; Fiedler & Semin, 1988; Garvey & Caramazza, 1974; Rudolph &

Försterling, 1997) demonstrate that some verbs like *help, attack,* or *insult* suggest a cause in the sentence subject, whereas other verbs like *admire, abhor,* or *hate* imply object causation. Within the taxonomy of Semin and Fiedler's (1988) linguistic-category model, these two verb classes are referred to as interpretive-action verbs (IAV) and state verbs (SV), respectively. If *Peter insults Mary,* the causal origin is in Peter; but if *Peter despises Mary,* then Mary appears to be the cause of the same disrespecting behavior. *The teacher rewards a student* tells us something about an encouraging teacher, whereas *the teacher admires a student* points to an unusually smart student. The semantic correlation is almost deterministic. Almost 90% of all IAV entries in the lexicon imply subject causation, whereas the vast majority of SVs suggest a cause in the sentence object.

Just by choosing an IAT or SV for the sentence predicate, one can thus exert a strong influence on the attribution and evaluation of the protagonist's behavior. Positive IAVs (help, encourage, save) and negative IAVs (hurt, cheat, insult) are appropriate means of communicating positive and negative subject intentions, respectively. SVs, in contrast, induce a reattribution from the subject to the object. Negative SVs (hate, abhor, fear) provide excuses for the subject's negative behavior by pointing to an external cause in the sentence object. Positive SVs (love, admire, long for) serve to relocate positive valence from the subject, who is only a passive patient or experiencer to the object person or stimulus who becomes the causal and evaluative origin. By choosing appropriate verbs, a journalist can improve or devalue a politician's image, a teacher can praise a student or him- or herself, prosecutors can blame, and defense attorneys excuse a defendant's behaviors (Schmid & Fiedler, 1998).

Two conditions facilitate the impact of implicit-verb causality on attributions and social judgments. First, many events and behaviors that are the topic of communicators are complex and ambiguous enough to allow for considerable variation in word use. Partners can describe their joint activities and conflicts at different verb levels; lawyers are free to use IAVs or SVs. Neither the wording of newspaper headlines nor the predicates used in personal reviews or letters of recommendation are restricted to one particular word class.

Second, and most important for the success of social influence, the grammatical verb type used in a sentence or utterance goes typically unnoticed. At the metacognitive level, neither speakers nor listeners are aware of the use of implicit verb causality as an influence strategy (Maass, 1999). These are exactly the conditions that render language both informative (by reducing the ambiguity) and subtle (by concealing the influence strategy).

Most published evidence on implicit verb causality (cf. Rudolph & Förderling, 1997) is restricted to questionnaires asking either for explicit causal ratings (Given the sentence, *Sandra praises Mary,* to what extent is the cause due to something about Peter or Mary?) or for pronoun disambiguation in a sentence completion task like *Sandra praises Mary because she . . .* Implicit causality is evident from the way in which the pronoun *she* is interpreted either as referring to Sandra or to Mary. Only very few studies have examined implicit-verb causality in the context of objectively given behaviors.

**Lexical strategies in prosecutors' and defense attorneys' final speeches.** In one of the few exceptions, Schmid and Fiedler's (1988) presented laypeople and lawyers with the evidence from court trials and asked different participants to take the perspective of either a prosecutor or a defense attorney. They were then asked to provide their final speech in a simulated court trial. These speeches were coded for the occurrence of word classes used as predicates in sentences with the defendant as the subject. In this conversational context, the SV rate was generally low, and positive IAVs were also hardly applicable to interpretations of the defendants' crimes. However, as expected, the prevalence of negative IAVs—which suggest internally caused, intentional actions—was enhanced in the final speeches of prosecutors, whose goal was to blame the defendant. Defense attorneys, whose goal was to avoid aggravating connotations, used fewer negative IAVs but resorted instead to SVs and adjectives referring to positive traits. Both laypeople and trained lawyers showed similar shifts in lexical strategies as a function of the accusing versus excusing role they were to play. Subsequent research based deliberate manipulations of the verb types in otherwise invariant speeches showed that other people's guilt judgments were actually affected by the manipulation (Schmid, Fiedler, Englich, Ehrenberger, & Semin, 1996).

**The answer is in the question.** Another paradigm, in which manifest social behavior was influenced by the implicit causality of verbs, was first developed by Semin, Rubini, and Fiedler (1995) and later refined by Semin and De Poot (1997). The basic idea guiding this approach was the notion that the verb class used in a question (asked by a journalist, interviewer, lawyer, survey researcher) can have a marked influence on the answer (given by a politician, interviewee, witness, survey respondent). For example, when asked to explain why people *read* a certain newspaper or why they *like* a certain newspaper, they referred to their own internal reasons (interest or preference) in the former condition, but came with external accounts (newspaper reputation or orientation) in the latter condition.

Semin and De Poot (1997) asked their participants to "think about a specific occasion when you *admired* somebody" (SV) or " . . . when you *defended* somebody" (IAV). They were then asked to remember as precisely as possible how this experience unfolded and then to describe the episode in their own words. These free descriptions were then coded for the implicit causality—that is, whether the verbs used in the answer assigned the causal origin to the subject or object in the episode. The autobiographical memories solicited by IAV and SV questions differed systematically. Whereas IAV questions led participants to report internally caused events, SV questions solicited many more externally caused episodes. It was also evident that the behavioral episodes generated in response to SV questions were of clearly higher duration, likelihood of recurrence, stability of the depicted social relationship, and lower in contextual dependence than the episodes prompted by IAT questions.

Further evidence reported by Semin and De Poot (1997) suggests that responders are not aware of the manipulations inherent in the questions and that the different narratives they produce when answering SV versus IAT questions affect the interpretations of others who listen to their answers (cf. Chapter 12, this volume). Altogether, these findings highlight the role of question answering in general and the question verb in particular, in the formation of self-fulfilling prophecies and confirmation biases (Nickerson, 1998).

**Constructive influences on person judgments.** Lexical influences not only affect the answers and related memories solicited by questions containing different verbs. They can also induce constructive errors and biases in memory and social judgment. Illustrative evidence comes from a series of experiments conducted by Fiedler, Armbruster, Nickel, Walther, & Asbeck (1996). Participants first saw a TV discussion dealing with a consumer topic. They were then presented with a list of 12 questions asking whether one target discussant has shown 12 behaviors. Depending on the experimental conditions, these behaviors were expressed by positive IAVs, negative IAVs, positive SVs, or negative SVs. Several minutes later, participants had to rate the target on two sets of 12 trait adjectives that were matched in meaning to the verbs used for the preceding questioning treatment (e.g., *attack* and *turn away* matched to *aggressive* and *arrogant*). The aim of the study was to find out whether merely considering possible behaviors might induce constructive biases in the final trait judgments, even when judges had denied seeing many behaviors that the target actually had not shown.

Indeed, merely construing the target in terms of possible behaviors, regardless of their truth value, resulted in strong constructive judgment biases, which were sensitive to the implicit causality of the verb prompts. Because IAVs imply subject causation, merely considering the target engaging in positive IAVs led to higher positive and lower negative trait ratings, whereas negative IAVs caused relatively more negative impressions. When the analysis was confined only to traits associated with correctly denied (actually false) behaviors, these constructive influences were similarly strong as in the overall analysis. Thus, denying that the target has attacked others led to increased, rather than decreased ratings of the trait aggressive.

It is interesting to note that when SVs were used for the questions treatment, the constructive biases pointed in the other direction. Thinking about negative target SVs (Did he *abhor* another discussant?) led to less negative target impressions, obviously because negative SVs suggest external excuses for negative behaviors. Conversely, positive SVs (e.g., *admire*) suggest external causes for positive behaviors and therefore led to less positive ratings. Again, the impact of merely considering the target in the light of different SVs was independent of the truth and semantic applicability of the verbs.

**Social exchange and fairness.** Related to implicit causality is another difference between IAVs and SVs that has important implications for social interaction. As IAVs, but not SVs, imply that the subject is accountable for his or her actions, IAVs are more likely to invoke the principle of reciprocity or social exchange (Homans, 1958). Preliminary support for this notion comes from an unpublished study (Fiedler, 1993). Participants were asked to judge the impact of given behaviors expressed in simple IAV sentences (e.g., Tom insults Walter) or SV sentences (Tom disrespects Walter) on future behaviors involving the same two persons. Reciprocity was invoked by IAVs, such that after Tom's negative action, it is now Walter's turn to treat Tom negatively, whereas Tom's subsequent behavior is less likely to be negative. Given a negative state (hate, disrespect) in Tom, however, the likelihood is high that Tom will continue to treat Walter negatively. The high endurability and external causality implied by SVs are not compatible with immediate reciprocity.

### *Linguistic Abstractness and Construal Level*

So far, we have been only concerned with two-word classes, which trigger causal inferences and attributions. Although IAVs (save, hurt) suggest a cause residing in the subject and an emotional consequence in the object, SVs (abhor, long for) suggest an emotion in the subject and a cause in the object. However, the vast majority of empirical studies motivated by the linguistic-category model (Semin & Fiedler, 1988, 1991) are not concerned with causality but with implications of abstract versus concrete language (Vallacher & Wegner, 1987). On one hand, descriptive action verbs (DAV) such as *kiss, kick,* or *nod* afford the most concrete word class. These ordinary words reveal little about the actor's character. Their meaning depends superficially on concrete physical details (lips for kissing), but their deeper meaning and evaluation is strongly dependent on the situational context (which can render kicking mean or friendly). As a consequence, the DAVs facilitate inferences that the behaviors denoted by the verb are common (high consensus), object-specific (high in distinctiveness), short-lived (low in consistency), and unlikely to raise divergent interpretations or debates. In contrast, abstract predicates involving adjectives such as *hostile, fair,* or *honest,* suggest diagnostic person attributes (low consensus) that generalize across objects, situations, and time (low distinctiveness and high consistency). Moreover, adjectives cannot be observed directly but depend on subjective interpretations, which are often the focus of debate.

In accordance with Kelley's (1967) ANOVA model of attribution, the low consensus, low distinctiveness, and high consensus that characterizes abstract adjectives is strongly suggestive of a dispositional cause within the subject of behavior. Indeed, adjectives and IAVs can be conceived as two different linguistic tools for inducing internal attribution, related to two different attribution theories. Although Kelley's attribution determinants (i.e. consensus, distinctiveness, and consistency) are wired into the semantic meaning of adjectives, a critical semantic feature of IAVs is intentional control, which is the chief mediator of subject attribution in Jones and McGillis' (1976) correspondent inference theory.

**Linguistic intergroup bias.** Drawing on strategic changes in the abstractness of language use, Maass and her colleagues have initiated an impressive research program on the linguistic-intergroup bias (LIB; Maass, 1999; Maass, Milesi, Zabbini, & Stahlberg, 1995; Maass, Salvi, Arcuri, & Semin, 1989). Language users tend to describe negative behaviors of out-groups and positive behaviors of in-groups in abstract terms, thus suggesting internal origins and high stability of in-group-serving information. In contrast, they tend to use concrete language to describe positive out-group and negative in-group behavior, thus reducing in-group-threatening information to transitory and superficial factors.

Convergent evidence for LIB has been found in such diverse contexts as political party discrimination (Anolli, Zurloni, & Riva, 2006), gender talk (Fiedler, Semin, & Finkenauer, 1993), modern racism (Schnake & Ruscher, 1998), and hostility between fan clubs and regional identity groups (Maass et al., 1989). Moreover, judgments by receivers of communications contaminated with LIB are actually biased in the direction suggested by the lexical strategies. That is, receivers arrive at more positive (negative) impressions if the target group's positive behaviors are described abstractly (concretely) and if their negative behaviors are described concretely (abstractly). It was also shown that the communicators' attitudes, motives, and affective states can be reliably diagnosed from the differential use of abstract and concrete predicates in self- and other descriptions (Chapter 18, this volume; Douglas & Sutton, 2006; Slatcher & Pennebaker, 2006).

This research program highlights the systematic consequences of lexical influence strategies, which meet the criterion of being both informative and subtle. The LIB strategy is informative because it relies on commonly understood implications of abstract and concrete words. At the same time, it is subtle because language users are unlikely and hardly able to monitor the frequency distribution of predicates belonging to different linguistic categories. Thus, influential communications need not resort to such direct strategies as lying or lopsided arguments that blatantly reveal the communicators goals and intentions. They can rather rely on the common ground of all language users' knowledge of knowledge built into the lexicon.

**Construal-level effects.** The explanatory power of linguistic abstraction is immense. One of the most fertile and successful research programs of the last decade, construal level theory (Trope & Liberman, 2003), testifies to the manifold consequences of abstract versus concrete representations. Abstract, high-level construals lead to simplified, low-dimensional judgments that highlight the idealized desirability of action goals and the global features of decision targets. Concrete, low-level construals, in contrast, result in more complex, multidimensional representations that take the feasibility of goals and local features of decision targets into account.

For example, it has been shown that the fundamental attribution error—that is, the generalized bias toward internal attributions in terms of trait-like dispositions—is more pronounced when behaviors are observed from a distant perspective, which is supposed to induce a high level of construal (Nussbaum,

Trope, & Liberman, 2003). Carrying this argument one step further, one can predict that abstraction accounts for the so-called actor-observer bias (Jones & Nisbett, 1972). When observers explain other people's behavior from a distance, they should form more abstract representations leading to more dispositional attributions than actors explaining their own behavior from a proximal perspective. Linguistic analysis of self-referent and other-referent coding of behavior descriptions support exactly this prediction (Fiedler et al., 1993; Fiedler, Semin & Koppetsch, 1991). Abstract predicates in general, and dispositional adjectives in particular, are more prevalent in free descriptions of others or out-groups compared with verbalizations of one's own or one's in-group behavior.

Another noteworthy function of abstract language is the regulation of social distance and power. Research conducted and reviewed by Semin (2007) indicates that abstract words let social relations appear more distant than concrete words and abstract terms are more applicable and considered more appropriate for distant relations than concrete words. Thus, somebody who does not follow an invitation might excuse the decline with reference to feeling *inappropriate* (keeping high distance) or having to *go to the dentist* (low distance). In a related vein, high-level construal using abstract words serves to indicate high status or power (Smith & Trope, 2006).

### *The Communicative Impact of Specific Words*

The impact of lexical stimuli is by no means confined to differences between grammatical word classes, such as DAV, IAV, SV, and adjectives, or nouns, which were recently shown to trigger even more dispositional inferences than adjectives (Carnaghi et al., 2008). Thus, saying that somebody *is a homosexual* implies even more stable and deeply anchored a disposition than saying that somebody *is homosexual.*

With regard to the power of specific words, for instance, an intriguing demonstration is that *why* and *how* questions can be used to induce high-level or low-level construals (Torelli & Kaikati, 2009), respectively, or different modes of motivation regulation (promotion versus prevention focus; Freitas, Gollwitzer, & Trope, 2004). "Why" is an invitation to think about long-term goals and essentialist reasons, whereas "How" asks for incidental details and side effects. In a similar vein, remembering how one felt happy in the past increases one's current life satisfaction, whereas reasoning about why one felt happy causes a contrast effect—that is, a decrease in current satisfaction (Strack, Schwarz, & Gschneidinger, 1985).

**Specific words trigger autobiographical memories.** In a study aimed at understanding the positive correlations between all four distance aspects distinguished in construal-level theory (i.e., temporal, spatial, social, and probability distance), Fiedler, Jung, Wänke, and Alexopoulos (2012) have discovered the key role played by verbal prompts. When specific action verbs were used as prompts to retrieve past memories or generate future construals, the verb-solicited scenarios exhibited a natural ecological correlation of all four distance aspects. Those reference events that were high (low) in temporal and probability distance also tended to be high (low) in spatial and social distance and vice versa. Moreover, the memories and construals solicited by particular verb prompts in different participants were highly similar in terms of their psychological distance. Similar findings were obtained by Fiedler and De Molière (2012) for noun prompts denoting high versus low power (e.g., father versus son), which led to high versus low distance construals, respectively. These findings highlight the possibility that lexical stimuli can determine retrieval and cognitive construction processes.

**Specific words as diagnostic tools.** Given the causal impact of verb prompts on cognitive and mnemonic inference processes, it is not too surprising that verb stimuli can also inform diagnostic inferences. As already noted, the abstractness of positive and negative words used to describe oneself and others, or in-groups and out-groups, can be used to diagnose the communicators' attitudes (Anolli et al., 2006; Douglas & Sutton, 2006). In a similar vein, the prevalence of abstract adjectives expressing stable traits in partner-related communication is predictive of relationship quality (Fiedler et al., 1991).

In an intriguing research program, Pennebaker and colleagues have recently shown that even the tiniest everyday words—called *junk words* (Chung & Pennebaker, 2007)—carry an enormous amount of diagnostic and prognostic information. The prevalence of such abundantly used words like first- or third-person pronouns, determinate and indeterminate articles, prepositions, or seemingly empty filler words was shown to be indicative of people's psychic state and the veracity of their communications. For example, an enhanced rate of the first person singular (I, me) expresses low personal distance and, therefore, indicates positive attitudes and true, nondeceptive communications. Moreover, studies dealing with specific cultural and historical events have found linguistic markers of psychological change surrounding September 11, 2001 (Cohn, Mehl, & Pennebaker, 2004) or discovered words that characterize the poetry of suicidal and nonsuicidal poets (Stirman & Pennebaker, 2001). The development of efficient and easily available computer tools for the lexical analysis of even huge text corpora greatly facilitates the growth of this promising and fruitful research on language as a useful diagnostic instrument.

## CONCLUDING REMARKS

The evidence on junk words as indicators of psychic states, optimistic versus pessimistic attitudes, deception, and self concepts (Pennebaker, Mehl, & Niederhoffer, 2003) reiterates, and complements, the central message of this chapter. Useful communications should be both informative and subtle. Apparently, this twofold condition renders communications not only effective and influential, but also informative about the communicators. The strategic use of words and word classes may be of more diagnostic value than the communicators' explicit declarations and self-referent attributions.

Throughout this chapter, we have provided evidence for lexical stimuli as a basic level of verbal influence. Analogous to Rosch's (1975) notion of basic-level categories in memory and cognitive development, lexical language units seem to provide optimal solutions for the trade-offs of social communication. Words informative enough to carry substantial meaning but elementary and flexible enough to be combined in many different ways. Words meanings are determinate enough to trigger evaluations and attributions but indeterminate enough to be more or less applicable to many different target objects and persons.

The studies we have reviewed testify to the ability of words to bring about social influence. Words afford distinct and powerful primes that trigger mental processes and manifest action. They serve as unconditional and conditional stimuli in associative and instrumental learning tasks. Lexical labels constrain the processes of causal and dispositional attribution, the formation of false memories, the retrieval of genuine information from autobiographical memory, and the construal of future plans and fantasies. And last but not least, they afford easily assessable units in diagnostic procedures of content analysis and measurement of communicator goals, intentions, and affective states.

## ACKNOWLEDGMENTS

The research and scientific work underlying this chapter was supported by a Koselleck Grant of the Deutsche Forschungsgemeinschaft awarded to the authors (Fi 294 / 23–1). Correspondence concerning this chapter should be addressed to kf@psychologie.uni-heidelberg.de.

## REFERENCES

Abelson, R. P., & Kanouse, D. E. (1966). Subjective acceptance of verbal generalizations. In S. Feldman (Ed.), *Cognitive consistency: Motivational antecedents and behavioral consequences* (pp. 171–197). New York, NY: Academic Press.

Anolli, L., Zurloni, V., & Riva, G. (2006). Linguistic intergroup bias in political communication. *Journal of General Psychology, 133,* 237–255.

Balota, D. A., & Paul, S. T. (1996). Summation of activation: Evidence from multiple primes that converge and diverge within semantic memory. *Journal of Experimental Psychology: Learning, Memory, and Cognition, 22*(4), 827–845.

Bargh, J. A., Chen, M., & Burrows, L. (1996). Automaticity of social behavior: Direct effects of trait construct and stereotype activation on action. *Journal of Personality and Social Psychology, 71*(2), 230–244.

Bodner, G. E., & Masson, M. E. J. (2003). Beyond spreading activation: An influence of relatedness proportion on masked semantic priming. *Psychonomic Bulletin and Review, 10,* 645–652.

Bolinger, D. (1973). Truth is a linguistic question. *Language, 49,* 539–550.

Brehm, J. W. (1966). *A theory of psychological reactance.* Oxford, England: Academic Press.

Brehm, J. W. (2000). Reactance. In A. E. Kazdin (Ed.), *Encyclopedia of psychology* (Vol. 7, pp. 10–12). Washington, DC: American Psychological Association.

Brown, R., & Fish, D. (1983). The psychological causality implicit in language. *Cognition, 14,* 233–274.

Carnaghi, A., Maass, A., Gresta, S., Bianchi, M., Cadinu, M., & Arcuri, L. (2008). Nomina sunt omina: On the inductive potential of nouns and adjectives in person perception. *Journal of Personality and Social Psychology, 94*(5), 839–859.

Chung, C. K., & Pennebaker, J. W. (2007). The psychological functions of function words. In K. Fiedler (Ed.), *Social communication* (pp. 343–359). New York, NY: Psychology Press.

Cohn, M. A., Mehl, M. R., & Pennebaker, J. W. (2004). Linguistic markers of psychological change surrounding September 11, 2001. *Psychological Science, 15,* 687–693.

De Houwer, J. (2007). A conceptual and theoretical analysis of evaluative conditioning. *The Spanish Journal of Psychology, 10,* 230–241.

De Houwer, J., Hermans, D., & Eelen, P. (1998). Affective and identity priming with episodically associated stimuli. *Cognition & Emotion, 12*(2), 145–169.

Dijksterhuis, A., Spears, R., Postmes, T., Stapel, D., Koomen, W., Knippenberg, A., & Scheepers, D. (1998). Seeing one thing and doing another: Contrast effects in automatic behavior. *Journal of Personality and Social Psychology, 75*(4), 862–871.

Douglas, K. M., & Sutton, R. M. (2006). When what you say about others says something about you: Language abstraction and inferences about describers' attitudes and goals. *Journal of Experimental Social Psychology, 42*, 500–508.

Edwards, D., & Potter, J. (1993). Language and causation: A discursive action model of description and attribution. *Psychological Review, 100*(1), 23–41.

Engelkamp, J., Mohr, G., & Mohr, M. (1985). Zur Rezeption von Aufforderungen [On the reception of imperatives]. *Sprache & Kognition, 2,* 65–75.

Estes, Z., & Jones, L. L. (2009). Integrative priming occurs rapidly and uncontrollably during lexical processing. *Journal of Experimental Psychology: General, 138*(1), 112–130.

Fazio, R. H. (2001). On the automatic activation of associated evaluations: An overview. *Cognition & Emotion, 15,* 115–141.

Fiedler, K. (1993). *Deontic consequences of state verbs and action verbs.* Unpublished research, University of Heidelberg.

Fiedler, K. (2003). The hidden vicissitudes of the priming paradigm in evaluative judgment research. In J. Musch & K. C. Klauer (Eds.), *The psychology of evaluation: Affective processes in cognition and emotion* (pp. 109–137). Mahwah, NJ: Erlbaum.

Fiedler, K. (2008). Language—A toolbox for sharing and influencing social reality. *Perspectives on Psychological Science, 3,* 38–47.

Fiedler, K., Armbruster, T., Nickel, S., Walther, E., & Asbeck, J. (1996). Constructive biases in social judgment: Experiments on the self-verification of question contents. *Journal of Personality and Social Psychology, 71,* 861–873.

Fiedler, K., Bluemke, M., & Unkelbach, C. (2011). On the adaptive flexibility of evaluative priming. *Memory & Cognition, 39*(4), 557–572.

Fiedler, K., & De Molière, L. (2012). *Power-related words trigger psychological distance.* Unpublished research, University of Heidelberg.

Fiedler, K., Jung, J., Wänke, M., & Alexopoulos, T. (2012). On the relations between distinct aspects of psychological distance: An ecological basis of construal-level theory. *Journal of Experimental Social Psychology.*

Fiedler, K., & Semin, G. R. (1988). On the causal information conveyed by different interpersonal verbs. *Social Cognition, 6,* 21–39.

Fiedler, K., Semin, G. R., & Finkenauer, C. (1993). The battle of words between gender groups: A language-based approach to intergroup processes. *Human Communication Research, 19,* 409–441.

Fiedler, K., Semin, G. R., & Koppetsch, C. (1991). Language use and attributional biases in close personal relationships. *Personality and Social Psychology Bulletin, 17,* 147–156.

Freitas, A. L., Gollwitzer, P., & Trope, Y. (2004). The influence of abstract and concrete mindsets on anticipating and guiding others' self-regulatory efforts. *Journal of Experimental Social Psychology, 40,* 739–752.

Garvey, C., & Caramazza, A. (1974). Implicit causality in verbs. *Linguistic Inquiry, 5*(3), 459–464.

Gilovich, T. (1981). Seeing the past in the present: The effect of associations to familiar events on judgments and decisions. *Journal of Personality and Social Psychology, 40*(5), 797–808.

Glucksberg, S., & Danks, J. H. (1975). *Experimental psycholinguistics: An introduction.* Oxford, England: Erlbaum.

Grice, H. P. (1975). Logic and conversation. In P. Cole & J. L. Morgan (Eds.), *Syntax and semantics 3: Speech acts* (pp. 41–58). New York, NY: Academic Press.

Hansen, J., & Wänke, M. (2011). The abstractness of luxury. *Journal of Economic Psychology, 32*(5), 789–796.

Hart, W., & Albarracín, D. (2009). The effects of chronic achievement motivation and achievement primes on the activation of achievement and fun goals. *Journal of Personality and Social Psychology, 97*(6), 1129–1141.

Hermans, D., Spruyt, A., & Eelen, P. (2003). Automatic affective priming of recently acquired stimulus valence: Priming at SOA 300 but not at SOA 1000. *Cognition & Emotion, 17*(1), 83–99.

Hertel, G., & Fiedler, K. (1994). Affective and cognitive influences in a social dilemma game. *European Journal of Social Psychology, 24*(1), 131–145.

Hofmann, W., De Houwer, J., Perugini, M., Baeyens, F., & Crombez, G. (2010). Evaluative conditioning in humans: A meta-analysis. *Psychological Bulletin, 136*(3), 390–421.

Homans, G. C. (1958). Social behavior as exchange. *American Journal of Sociology, 63,* 597–606.

Jones, E. E., & McGillis, D. (1976). Correspondent inferences and the attribution cube: A comparative reappraisal. *New Directions in Attribution Research, 1,* 389–429.

Jones, E. E., & Nisbett, R. E. (1972). The actor and the observer: Divergent perceptions of the causes of behavior. In E. E. Jones, D. E. Kanouse, H. H. Kelley, R. E. Nisbett, S. Valins, & B. Weiner (Eds.), *Attribution: perceiving the causes of behavior.* Morristown, NJ: General Learning Press.

Kelley, H. H. (1967). Attribution theory in social psychology. In D. Levine (Ed.), *Nebraska Symposium on Motivation* (Vol. 15, pp. 192–238). Lincoln: University of Nebraska Press.

Klauer, K. C., & Musch, J. (2003). Affective priming: Findings and theories. In J. Musch & K. C. Klauer (Eds.), *The psychology of evaluation: Affective processes in cognition and emotion* (pp. 7–49). Mahwah, NJ: Erlbaum.

Klauer, K. C., Rossnagel, C., & Musch, J. (1997). List-context effects in evaluative priming. *Journal of Experimental Psychology: Learning, Memory, and Cognition, 23,* 246–255.

Liberman, N., Förster, J., & Higgins, E. T. (2007). Completed vs. interrupted priming: Reduced accessibility from post-fulfilment inhibition. *Journal of Experimental Social Psychology, 43,* 258–264.

Loftus, E. F., & Palmer, J. C. (1974). Reconstruction of automobile destruction: An example of the interaction between language and memory. *Journal of Verbal Learning & Verbal Behavior, 13*(5), 585–589.

Maass, A. (1999). Linguistic intergroup bias: Stereotype perpetuation through language. In M. P. Zanna (Ed.), *Advances in experimental social psychology* (Vol. 31, pp. 79–121). San Diego, CA: Academic Press.

Maass, A., Milesi, A., Zabbini, S., & Stahlberg, D. (1995). Linguistic intergroup bias: Differential expectancies or in-group protection? *Journal of Personality and Social Psychology, 68,* 116–126.

Maass, A., Salvi, D., Arcuri, L., & Semin, G. R. (1989). Language use in intergroup contexts: The linguistic intergroup bias. *Journal of Personality and Social Psychology, 57,* 981–993.

Mata, A., Sherman, S. J., Percy, E. J., Garcia-Marques, L., & Garcia-Marques, T. (2012). *The effect of adjective-noun word order on perceived similarity and recognition memory.* Manuscript in preparation.

McGuire, W. J. (1964). Inducing resistance to persuasion. In L. Berkowitz (Ed.), *Advances in experimental social psychology* (Vol. 1, pp. 191–229). New York, NY: Academic Press.

Nickerson, R. S. (1998). Confirmation bias: A ubiquitous phenomenon in many guises. *Review of General Psychology, 2*(2), 175–220.

Nosek, B. A., Greenwald, A. G., & Banaji, M. R. (2005). Understanding and using the Implicit Association Test: II. Method variables and construct validity. *Personality and Social Psychology Bulletin, 31,* 166–180.

Nussbaum, S., Trope, Y., & Liberman, N. (2003). Creeping dispositionism: The temporal dynamics of behavior prediction. *Journal of Personality and Social Psychology, 84*(3), 485–497.

Payne, B., Hall, D. L., Cameron, C., & Bishara, A. J. (2010). A process model of affect misattribution. *Personality and Social Psychology Bulletin, 36*(10), 1397–1408.

Pennebaker, J. W., Mehl, M. R., & Niederhoffer, K. (2003). Psychological aspects of natural language use: Our words, our selves. *Annual Review of Psychology, 54,* 547–577.

Percy, E. J., Sherman, S. J., Garcia-Marques, L., Mata, A., & Garcia-Marques, T. (2009). Cognition and native-language grammar: The organization role of adjective-noun word order in information representation. *Psychonomic Bulletin & Review, 16,* 1037–1042.

Roediger, H., & McDermott, K. (1995). Creating false memories: Remembering words not presented in lists. *Journal of Experimental Psychology: Learning, Memory, and Cognition, 21,* 803–814.

Rosch, E. (1975). Cognitive representations of semantic categories. *Journal Of Experimental Psychology: General, 104*(3), 192–233.

Rudolph, U., & Försterling, F. (1997). The psychological causality implicit in verbs: A review. *Psychological Bulletin, 121,* 192–218.

Schmid, J., & Fiedler, K. (1998). The backbone of closing speeches: The impact of prosecution versus defense language on juridical attributions. *Journal of Applied Social Psychology, 28,* 1140–1172.

Schmid, J., Fiedler, K., Englich, B., Ehrenberger, T., & Semin, G. (1996). Taking sides with the defendant: Grammatical choice and the influence of implicit attributions in prosecution and defense speeches. *International Journal of Psycholinguistics, 12*(2), 127–148.

Schnake, S. B., & Ruscher, J. B. (1998). Modern racism as a predictor of the linguistic intergroup bias. *Journal of Language and Social Psychology, 17*(4), 484–491.

Schul, Y., Mayo, R., & Burnstein, E. (2004). Encoding under trust and distrust: The spontaneous activation of incongruent cognitions. *Journal of Personality and Social Psychology, 86*(5), 668–679.

Schwarz, N., & Bless, H. (2007). Mental construal processes. The inclusion/exclusion model. In D. A. Stapel & J. Suls (Eds.), *Assimilation and contrast in social psychology* (pp. 119–141). New York, NY: Psychology Press.

Semin, G. R. (2007). The regulation and distance. In K. Fiedler (Ed.), *Social communication* (pp. 389–408). New York, NY: Psychology Press.

Semin, G. R., & Fiedler, K. (1988). The cognitive functions of linguistic categories in describing persons: Social cognition and language. *Journal of Personality and Social Psychology, 54,* 558–568.

Semin, G. R., & Fiedler, K. (1991). The linguistic category model, its bases, applications, and range. In W. Stroebe & M. Hewstone (Eds.), *European review of social psychology* (Vol. 2, pp. 1–30). Chichester, England: Wiley.

Semin, G. R., & De Poot, C. J. (1997). You might regret it if you don't notice how a question is worded! *Journal of Personality and Social Psychology, 73,* 472–480.

Semin, G. R., Rubini, M., & Fiedler, K. (1995). The answer is in the question: The effect of verb causality on locus of explanation. *Personality and Social Psychology Bulletin, 21,* 834–841.

Shalev, I., & Bargh, J. A. (2011). Use of priming-based interventions to facilitate psychological health: Commentary on Kazdin and Blase (2011). *Perspectives on Psychological Science, 6*(5), 488–492.

Slatcher, R. B., & Pennebaker, J. (2006). How do I love thee? Let me count the words. *Psychological Science, 17,* 660–664.

Smith, P. K., & Trope, Y. (2006). You focus on the forest when you're in charge of the trees: Power priming and abstract information processing. *Journal of Personality and Social Psychology, 90*(4), 578–596.

Sparrow, B., & Wegner, D. M. (2006). Unpriming: the deactivation of thoughts through expression. *Journal of Personality and Social Psychology, 91,* 1009–1019.

Srull, T. K., & Wyer, R. S. (1980). Category accessibility and social perception: Some implications for the study of person memory and interpersonal judgments. *Journal of Personality and Social Psychology, 38*(6), 841–856.

Stirman, S. W., & Pennebaker, J. W. (2001). Word use in the poetry of suicidal and non-suicidal poets. *Psychosomatic Medicine, 63,* 517–522.

Strack, F., Schwarz, N., & Gschneidinger, E. (1985). Happiness and reminiscing: The role of time perspective, affect, and mode of thinking. *Journal of Personality and Social Psychology, 49,* 1460–1469.

Tausczik, Y., & Pennebaker, J. W. (2010). The psychological meaning of words: LIWC and computerized text analysis methods. *Journal of Language and Social Psychology, 29,* 24–54.

Todorov, A., & Bargh, J. A. (2002). Automatic sources of aggression. *Aggression and Violent Behavior, 7,* 53–68.

Torelli, C. J., & Kaikati, A. M. (2009). Values as predictors of judgments and behaviors: The role of abstract and concrete mindsets. *Journal of Personality and Social Psychology, 96*(1), 231–247.

Trope, Y., & Liberman, N. (2003). Temporal construal. *Psychological Review, 110,* 403–421.

Vallacher, R. R., & Wegner, D. M. (1987). What do people think they're doing? Action identification and human behavior. *Psychological Review, 94,* 3–15.

Wänke, M. (2007). What is said and what is meant: Conversational implicatures in natural conversations, research settings, media and advertising. In K. Fiedler (Ed.), *Social communication* (pp. 223–256). New York, NY: Psychology Press.

# 4

# Feeling and Speaking

## *Affective Influences on Communication Strategies and Language Use*

JOSEPH P. FORGAS

## INTRODUCTION

*Homo sapiens* is a gregarious species, and coordinating our interpersonal behaviors can be a demanding cognitive task. Most interpersonal communication is imbued with affect. Every social encounter can influence our affective state, and affect in turn plays an important role in how we communicate and use language (see also Chapter 5, this volume). It is surprising to note that until recently, social and cognitive psychologists have remained uninterested in the role that affect plays in interpersonal communication. The importance of affect in social life was only rediscovered in the early 1980s (Bower, 1980; Zajonc, 1980), and the past few decades saw a dramatic increase in experimental research on affect by social psychologists. This chapter reviews a series of experiments demonstrating that affective states have an important and often adaptive influence on the way people produce and respond to social communication. Further, it is argued that the communicative consequences of affect may be best understood by analyzing the cognitive information processing consequences of affective states.

Affect probably remained neglected as a result of the dominance of first the behaviorist and later the cognitivist paradigms in psychology (Hilgard, 1980). Affect has also long been considered a dangerous, invasive force that subverts rational thinking and behavior. Fortunately, the last few decades saw a radical change in our view of affect. As a result of advances in physiology and neuroanatomy, several lines of evidence now indicate that affect is often an essential and adaptive component of responding to social situations, as several of the present experiments also show (Adolphs & Damasio, 2001; Forgas, 1995, 2002; Ito & Cacioppo, 2001; Zajonc, 2000).

This chapter begins with a brief review of research of the antecedents of contemporary research on affect and social communication, followed by a summary of current theories that inform research in this area (see also Chapters 1 and 2, this volume). We then review a number of experiments demonstrating the consequences of affective states for social communication and language use, including the production of, and responding to requests, negotiation, the production of persuasive messages, and self-disclosure strategies. The role of different information processing strategies in mediating these effects receives special attention.

## BACKGROUND

Zajonc (1980) was among the first to argue that affect often constitutes the primary response to social situations, claiming that affect indeed functions as the dominant force in social behavior (Zajonc, 2000). Human beings readily and rapidly acquire an affective response toward social stimuli, and such reactions powerfully influence subsequent responses (Unkelbach, Forgas, & Denson, 2008). Affect also dominates how people represent and structure their social experiences (Forgas, 1979, 1982, 2001, 2006), as social "stimuli can cohere as a category even when they have nothing in common other than the emotional responses they elicit" (Niedenthal & Halberstadt, 2000, p. 381). Indeed, it is striking that social situations are typically "described in terms of affects (e.g., threatening, warm, interesting, dull, tense, calm, rejecting) and organized in terms of similarity of affects aroused by them" (Pervin, 1976, p. 471).

Thus, affect plays a critical role in how social situations are represented and responded to. Affective influences on social behavior and communication were also confirmed in some early experiments. For example, Feshbach and Singer (1957) found that attempts to suppress affect paradoxically increased the pressure for affect to infuse unrelated attitudes and behaviors, as fearful persons were more likely to see "another person as fearful and anxious," suggesting that "suppression of fear facilitates the tendency to project fear onto another social object" (p. 286). In another study, Razran (1940) found that people who were made to feel bad or good reported significantly more negative or positive responses toward sociopolitical messages. A similar pattern of affective conditioning was subsequently demonstrated by Byrne and Clore (1970) and Clore and Byrne (1974).

## AFFECT, MOOD, AND EMOTION

However, there is still little general agreement about how best to define terms such as affect, feelings, emotions, or mood (Fiedler & Forgas, 1988; Forgas, 1992, 1995, 2002, 2006). We have proposed elsewhere that *affect* may be used as a generic label to refer to both *moods* and *emotions.* Moods in turn could be described as "low-intensity, diffuse, and relatively enduring affective states without a salient antecedent cause and therefore little cognitive content (e.g., feeling good or feeling bad)", whereas emotions "are more intense, short-lived, and usually have a definite cause and clear cognitive content" (e.g., anger or fear; Forgas, 1992, p. 230). It appears that subtle, nonspecific moods may often have a potentially more enduring and insidious motivational influence on social cognition and communication (Fiedler, 1991; Forgas, 1992, 1995, 2002; Sedikides, 1992, 1995). Accordingly, our primary concern here is with the effects of low-intensity moods rather than distinct emotions on communication strategies.

## THEORIES OF AFFECTIVE INFLUENCES ON COMMUNICATION

Contemporary cognitive theories identify two kinds of affective influences on cognition and communication: (a) *informational effects* (e.g., affect congruence), when affective states directly influence the information people access and use in social situations and (b) *processing effects,* when affect influences the way information is processed.

### *Informational Effects*

Two theories of informational effects are considered here, *affect priming* and *affect-as-information* models. *The affect-priming account* proposed by Bower (1981) is based on associative theories of memory and argues that affect is integrally linked to an associative network of memory representations. An affective state may thus selectively prime associations previously linked to that affect, making these concepts more available to be used in subsequent constructive cognitive and communicative tasks. Several studies demonstrated such affective priming. For example, people induced to feel good or bad tend to selectively remember more mood-congruent details from their childhood and recall more mood-congruent events they had recorded in diaries for the past few weeks (Bower, 1981). Mood congruence was also observed in how people interpret social communication (Forgas, Bower, & Krantz, 1984) and how they form impressions of other people (Forgas & Bower, 1987). However, affect priming is also subject to several boundary conditions (Bower, 1991), and mood-congruent effects are most reliably obtained when tasks require a high degree of open, constructive processing, as is often the case with interpersonal communication (e.g., Bower & Forgas, 2001; Forgas, 2002).

Alternative, *affect-as-information* models (Clore & Storbeck, 2006; Schwarz & Clore, 1983, 1988) suggests that "rather than computing a judgment on the basis of recalled features of a target, individuals may . . . ask themselves: 'how do I feel about it? [and] in doing so, they may mistake feelings due to a preexisting state as a reaction to the target" (Schwarz, 1990, p. 529). Thus, affect congruence in communication is caused by an inferential error, when people misattribute their affective state.

It appears that people only rely on affect as a heuristic cue when "the task is of little personal relevance, when little other information is available, when problems are too complex to be solved systematically, and when time or attentional resources are limited" (Fiedler, 2001, p. 175). For example, Forgas and Moylan (1987) found that almost 1,000 people responded in an affect-congruent manner to an attitude survey on the sidewalk outside a cinema after watching happy or sad films, as respondents presumably had little time, interest, motivation, or capacity to engage in elaborate processing and so relied on their affect as a heuristic shortcut to infer their reactions.

### *Processing Effects*

In addition to influencing the *content* and *valence* of cognition and behavior, affect may also influence the *process* of cognition, that is, *how* people think (Clark & Isen, 1982; Fiedler & Forgas, 1988; Forgas, 2002; see also Chapter 5, this volume). Early studies indicated that people in a positive mood seemed to reach decisions faster, used less information, avoided demanding, systematic thinking, and showed greater confidence in their decisions—suggesting that positive affect might produce a more superficial, less systematic, and less effortful processing style. In contrast, negative affect seemed to trigger a more effortful, systematic, analytic, and vigilant processing style (Clark & Isen, 1982; Schwarz, 1990).

However, later research by Bless (2000; Bless & Fiedler, 2006) and Fiedler (2000) showed that the fundamental evolutionary significance of positive and negative affect is not simply to influence processing effort, but to recruit more qualitatively different processing styles. Positive affect recruits more *assimilative,* internally driven, top-down processing, whereas negative affect calls for more *accommodative,* externally oriented, bottom up processing styles. Assimilation means to impose internalized structures onto the external world, whereas accommodation means to modify internal structures in accordance with external constraints.

Numerous experiments support the affectively induced assimilative or accommodative processing dichotomy. For example, those in a positive mood use broader, more assimilative cognitive categories, use more abstract representations in their language choices (Beukeboom & De Jong, 2008; Beukeboom & Semin, 2005, 2006; see also Chapter 18, this volume), and are more likely to retrieve a generic rather than specific representation of a persuasive message (Forgas, 2007; see also Chapter 3, this volume). Thus, moods perform an adaptive function essentially preparing us to respond to different environmental challenges. Positive mood indicates that the situation is safe and familiar and that existing internal knowledge can be relied upon. In contrast, negative mood functions like a mild alarm signal, indicating that the careful monitoring of new, external information is required. Thus *both* positive and negative mood can produce processing advantages albeit in response to different situations requiring different processing styles. Given the almost exclusive emphasis on the benefits of positive affect in our culture, this is an important message with some intriguing real-life implications. Numerous studies now suggest that negative mood can produce definite processing and communicative advantages in situations when the careful and detailed monitoring of new, external information is required, as we shall see below.

## *Integrative Theories*

Thus, affect can have both an informational and a processing influence on the way people communicate. As a comprehensive explanation of these effects, the affect infusion model (AIM; Forgas, 1995, 2002) predicts that affect infusion should only occur in circumstances that promote open, constructive processing. The AIM suggests that affect infusion should be dependent on the kind of processing strategy that is used, and identifies four alternative processing strategies: *direct access, motivated, heuristic, and substantive*. The first two strategies, direct access and motivated processing, call for highly targeted information search and selection, limiting the scope for incidental affect infusion. In contrast, heuristic and substantive processing are open and constructive and thus promote affect infusion.

These four strategies also differ in terms of two basic dimensions: the degree of *effort* exerted and the degree of *openness* of the information search strategy. Thus, substantive processing involves high effort and open, constructive thinking; motivated processing involves high effort but closed, predetermined information search; heuristic processing is characterized by low effort but open, constructive thinking; and direct access processing represents low processing effort and closed information search.

The model also predicts that different processing strategies are triggered by specific features of the *task*, the *person*, and the *situation*, and affect itself can also influence processing choices. The main contribution of integrative models like the AIM is that they can predict the *absence* of affect infusion when direct access or motivated processing is used, and the *presence* of affect infusion during heuristic and substantive processing. The implications of this model have been supported in a number of experiments considered below.

There are thus good theoretical reasons to expect that affect has a significant influence on how people represent the social world, the way they plan and use communication strategies, and in particular, how they generate and respond to verbal messages. The experiments to be described below typically employ a two-stage procedure. Participants are first induced to experience an affective state, using methods such as hypnotic suggestions, exposure to happy or sad movies, music, autobiographic memories, or positive or negative feedback about performance. After mood induction, their communicative behaviors are assessed in what participants believe is a separate, unrelated experiment.

The experimental evidence is summarized in two sections: (a) affective influences on the content and valence of communication (affect congruent effects) and (b) affective influences on the process of communication (processing effects).

## AFFECT CONGRUENCE IN COMMUNICATION

As social communication typically demands open, constructive thinking, affective states may infuse our thoughts and communicative behaviors. Positive affect may prime positive interpretations and produce more confident, friendly, and cooperative approach behaviors and messages, whereas negative affect may facilitate access to negative memories and produce more cautious, circumspect, and controlled attitudes and communications (Bower & Forgas, 2001; Eich & Macauley, 2000; Forgas, 1995), especially when the situation calls for constructive, substantive processing (Forgas, 1995, 1999a,b). For example (Forgas & Gunawardena, 2001), people communicate in a much more positive manner when feeling good rather than bad after watching happy or sad films—they smile more, communicate more effectively, disclose more personal information, and behave in a more poised, skilled, and rewarding manner. In other words, slight changes in mood seem to have a significant influence on a variety of communicative behaviors.

There may also be affect-congruent distortions on the way people interpret *observed* communicative behaviors (Forgas et al., 1984). Happy subjects tend to see more positive skilled behaviors and communicative acts, although sad mood produces more critical, negative interpretations of the very same messages, even when objective, videotaped evidence is readily available. Several experiments explored mood effects on specific communicative behaviors such as request formulations, negotiation, and self-disclosure.

### *Mood Effects on Request Strategies*

Requesting is a complex communicative task characterized by uncertainty: Requests must be formulated with just the right degree of assertiveness versus politeness so as to maximize compliance without risking giving offense. Positive mood should prime a more confident, direct requesting style, and negative mood should lead to more cautious, polite requests (Forgas, 1999b). When happy or sad persons were asked to select among more or less polite requests that they would use in easy or difficult social situations (Forgas, 1999b, Exp. 1), happy participants preferred more direct, impolite requests, whereas sad persons preferred more cautious and polite requests. In a follow-up experiment, similar effects were found when participants produced their own open-ended requests, which were subsequently rated for politeness and elaboration by two independent raters. Further, mood effects on requesting were much stronger when the request situation was difficult and problematic, and thus required more extensive, substantive processing.

Do these mood effects also occur in real-life interactions? In an unobtrusive experiment (Forgas, 1999a, Exp. 2), participants first viewed happy or sad films. Next, in an apparently impromptu development, the experimenter casually asked them to get a file from a neighboring office. Their words in making the request were recorded by a concealed tape recorder, and the requests were subsequently analyzed for politeness and other communicative qualities.

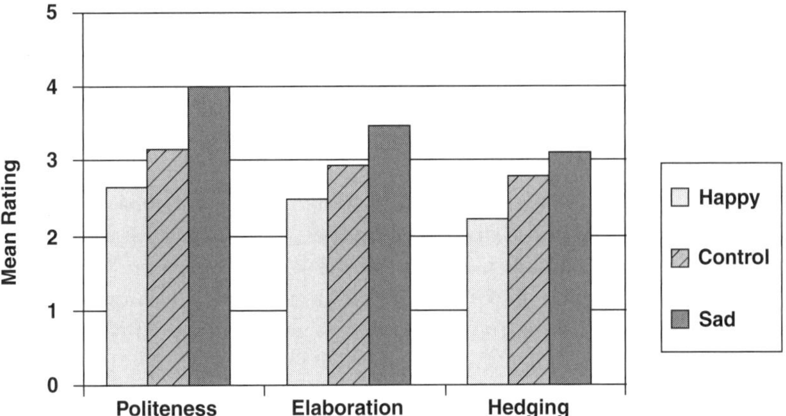


Figure 4.1 Mood effects on naturally produced requests

Positive mood increases, and negative mood decreases the degree of politeness, elaboration, and hedging in strategic communications (Forgas, 1999a).

Negative mood resulted in significantly more polite, elaborate, and hedging requests, whereas those in a positive mood used more direct and less polite strategies—shown in Figure 4.1. An analysis of participants' later recall memory for the requests they made (indicating the extent of elaborate processing) showed that more elaborately processed requests were remembered better, and were also more influenced by mood as predicted by models such as the AIM (Forgas, 2002).

## *Mood Effects on Responding to Requests*

Spontaneous, impromptu reactions to communications, such as responding to a verbal request, also require constructive processing and should also be subject to affect infusion. Several of our field experiments were carried out in a university library to confirm this prediction (Forgas, 1998a). Affect was induced by leaving folders containing funny or sad pictures (or text) on some unoccupied library desks. Students occupying the desks were surreptitiously observed as they exposed themselves to the mood induction. A few minutes later, another student (a confederate) made an unexpected polite or impolite verbal request for several sheets of paper to the unsuspecting subjects. Their responses were noted, and soon after, a second confederate asked them to complete a brief questionnaire assessing their perception and memory of the request and the requester. There was a clear mood-congruent pattern in response to the request. Sad people were less inclined to help and evaluated the request and the requester more negatively. These mood effects were greater when the request was impolite and unconventional and thus required more elaborate and substantive processing. These results confirm that affect infusion into communication behaviors is a real phenomenon that depends on how much constructive processing is required—in this case, to respond to more or less unusual, unconventional request forms.

## *Mood Effects on Communicating in Negotiations*

One of the most common and difficult communication situations occurs when people need to engage in verbal negotiation to resolve a conflict. Effective negotiation is a critical communication skill in resolving personal and relationship problems and is also routinely used in organizations. Can such carefully planned social encounters as verbal negotiation be open to affect infusion (Forgas, 1998c)? In a series of studies, mood was induced before participants engaged in highly realistic interpersonal and intergroup negotiation. We found that happy participants were more confident, formed higher expectations about their success, made more optimistic and cooperative communication plans, and actually used more positive, "integrative, trusting" messages than did control, or negative mood participants—shown in Figure 4.2. Further, happy participants also achieved better outcomes. It is interesting to note that individuals who scored high on measures such as machiavellism and need for approval were less influenced by mood. It seems that affect infusion into interpersonal communication behaviors is weaker for individuals who habitually approach interpersonal tasks from a motivated, predetermined perspective that limits the degree of open, constructive thinking they employ. These findings support the principle that mood effects on social behaviors are highly dependent on processing strategies, often linked to enduring personality traits (Ciarrochi & Forgas, 1999, 2000; Ciarrochi, Forgas, & Mayer, 2006; Forgas & Ciarrochi, 2002).

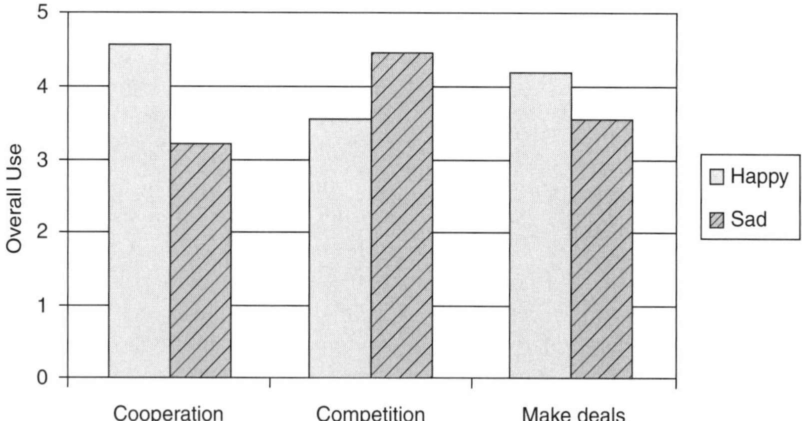


Figure 4.2 Mood congruent influences on communication in negotiation

Happy persons plan and use more cooperative and less competitive bargaining strategies, and are more likely to make and honor deals than do negotiators experiencing negative affect. (Data based on Forgas, 1998c).

In terms of the AIM, these mood effects on communication in a negotiation can be explained in terms of affect priming mechanisms. Positive mood was found to selectively prime more positive thoughts and associations, leading to the formulation and use of more optimistic, cooperative, and integrative bargaining strategies and messages. In contrast, negative mood primed more pessimistic, negative thoughts and associations, leading to less ambitious communication goals and less cooperative, more competitive, and ultimately less successful bargaining strategies.

## *Mood Effects on Self Disclosure*

Self-disclosure—revealing intimate information about the self—is a critical aspect of skilled interpersonal communication and essential for the development of rewarding intimate relationships (Forgas, 1985). Affective influences on self-disclosure strategies were demonstrated in several recent experiments (Forgas, 2010), when happy or sad participants were asked to indicate the order in which they would feel comfortable disclosing increasingly intimate information about themselves to a person they have just met. Happy people preferred significantly more intimate disclosure topics, consistent with a generally more confident and optimistic interpersonal communication style. In subsequent experiments, participants interacted with another person in a neighboring room through a computer keyboard, as if exchanging e-mails. Using this *bogus partner* method, the computer was preprogrammed to respond in ways that indicated either consistently high or low levels of self disclosure. Individuals in a positive mood produced a greater variety of more intimate, more abstract, and more positive self-disclosing messages about themselves and also formed more positive impressions about the partner, and these effects were especially marked when the partner was also disclosing—shown in Figure 4.3. Positive mood did not increase the intimacy of self-disclosure when the partner was not disclosing.

Why do these effects occur? In uncertain and unpredictable communicative situations, affect can selectively prime access to more affect-congruent thoughts, and these ideas should ultimately influence plans and behaviors. Thus, affective influences on communicative behaviors depend on how much open, constructive processing is required to deal with a more or less demanding interpersonal task. Whenever motivated, closed information processing is used, these mood effects tend to be reduced. The same mechanisms of affect infusion seem to influence the way people formulate personal requests, the way they respond to approaches by others, the way they plan and execute negotiations, and the way they produce self-disclosing messages (Forgas, 1998a,b; 1999a,b; 2010).

In addition to influencing confidence and the valence of communicative strategies (the content of cognition), affective states also have a marked effect on how people deal with social information, the *process* of cognition and message production. We shall next turn to the processing effects of mood states on social communication.

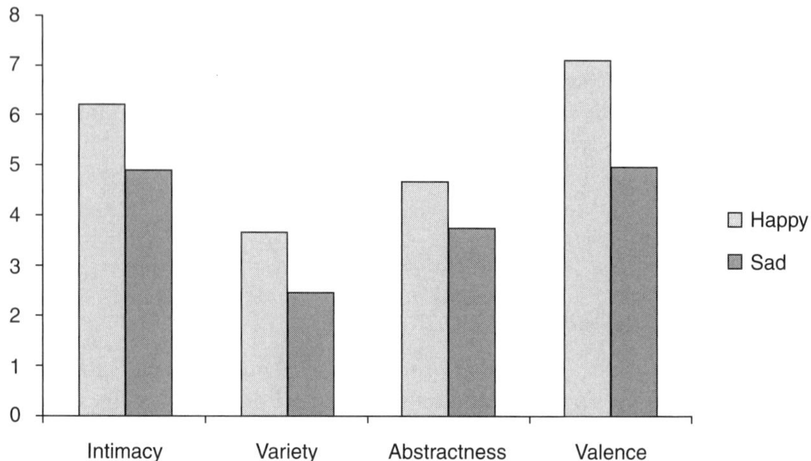


Figure 4.3 Mood effects on the intimacy, variety, abstractness, and valence of self-disclosing messages

Communicators in a positive mood reveal more intimate, more abstract, more varied, and more positive information about themselves.

## *The Processing Consequences of Affect on Social Communication*

Although it is commonly claimed that feeling good promotes better thinking in terms of creativity and flexibility (Ciarrochi, Forgas, & Mayer, 2006; Forgas, 1994, 2002), this is only part of the story. In this section, we present several experiments showing that negative affect may also produce desirable and beneficial cognitive consequences for social communication. In functional terms, negative mood may operate as an adaptive signal recruiting more attentive and *accommodative* thinking that may help people to cope with the requirements of demanding social situations (Forgas, 2007).

## *Negative Affect Improves the Accuracy of Interpreting Messages*

Interpreting the behavior of communication partners is often subject to various biases (see also Chapters 6 and 17, this volume). The *fundamental attribution error* (FAE) occurs when people see intentionality and internal causation in messages despite evidence for the influence of situational forces (Gilbert & Malone, 1995), because they focus on salient and conspicuous information—the communicator—and fail to process information about situational constraints (Gilbert, 1991). If negative mood promotes the more detailed processing of situational information, the incidence of the FAE and other judgmental biases may be reduced (Forgas, 1998b). For example, we asked happy or sad participants to read and make judgments about the verbal messages sent by the writer of an essay advocating a popular or unpopular position (for or against nuclear testing), which they were told was either assigned, or was freely chosen (e.g., Jones & Harris, 1967). Happy mood increased, and sad mood reduced the fundamental attribution error, consistent with the more attentive thinking style recruited by negative affect.

Similar effects can also occur in real life. In a field study, happy or sad participants made attributions about messages by writers of popular and unpopular essays arguing for, or against recycling (cf. Forgas & Moylan, 1987). Once again, positive mood increased and negative mood reduced the incidence of the fundamental attribution error (inferring internal causation from coerced messages). Recall memory data confirmed that these effects were due to the more attentive processing of the actual information contained in the messages when in negative mood (Forgas, 1998b, Exp. 3). These effects are consistent with the suggested evolutionary benefits of negative affect in recruiting more accommodative processing styles.

### *Affective Influences on Believing or Disbelieving Doubtful Messages*

Believing or not believing a communication partner is another crucial decision people often face in everyday life. How do we know if the messages we receive from others are accurate? Accepting invalid information as true (false positives, excessive gullibility) can be just as dangerous as rejecting information that is valid (false negatives, excessive skepticism). Negative moods might produce more critical and skeptical judgments, whereas happy people may accept interpersonal messages at face value, as genuine and trustworthy due to the information processing consequences of affect we discussed previously.

Several recent experiments found that doubtful messages (such as urban myths—e.g., power lines cause leukemia; the CIA murdered Kennedy) are more likely to be uncritically accepted by people in a positive rather than a negative mood. Induced mood states can influence credibility judgments about both factual claims (*factual skepticism*) and interpersonal representations (*interpersonal skepticism*; Forgas & East, 2008a,b).

**Mood effects on accepting factual messages.** Many messages—urban legends, anecdotes, and myths—circulate in all societies that advocate plausible, but ultimately untested claims as facts. Does mood determine the likely acceptance of such propositions? In one experiment (Forgas & East, 2008a), we asked happy or sad participants to judge the probable truth of a number of verbal messages describing urban legends and rumors. Negative mood increased, and positive mood reduced skepticism, but only for new and unfamiliar claims. A follow-up experiment manipulated the familiarity of a variety of factual claims taken from trivia games (Forgas & East, 2008a). Happy mood significantly increased the tendency to accept messages previously seen and familiar as true. Negative mood in turn produced greater skepticism, consistent with the hypothesis that negative affect triggers a more externally focused and accommodative thinking style and the more critical evaluation of communications.

In another study, participants judged the truth of 25 true and 25 false general knowledge verbal messages and were also told whether each item was actually true (Forgas & East, 2008a). Two weeks later, after a positive or negative mood induction, only sad participants were able to correctly distinguish between true and false statements they had seen previously. Happy participants were unable to remember the truth of these messages and were more likely to rate all previously seen messages as true, even if they were told previously that the information was false. This pattern confirms that happy mood increased and sad mood reduced the tendency to rely on the "what is familiar is true" heuristic. In all, negative mood conferred an adaptive advantage by promoting a more accommodative, systematic processing style in the recipients of dubious communications (Fiedler & Bless, 2001). This effect seems due to negative mood reducing and positive mood increasing the tendency to use perceived familiarity as an indication of truthfulness.

**Mood effects on interpreting interpersonal messages.** Mood may also influence people's tendency to accept or reject interpersonal communications as genuine or false. In one experiment (Forgas & East, 2008a), happy and sad participants judged the genuineness of positive, neutral, and negative facial expressions. Participants in a negative mood were significantly less likely to accept facial expressions as genuine than were those in a positive or neutral mood. In another study, instead of positive and negative facial displays, we used the six basic facial expressions of emotions as the communication targets (i.e., anger, fear, disgust, happiness, surprise, sadness). Once again, negative mood reduced and positive mood increased participants' tendency to accept the facial displays as genuine, consistent with the more attentive and accommodative processing style associated with negative moods.

### *Affective Influences on Detecting Deceptive Communication*

Can these mood effects influence the ability to detect deception? We asked happy or sad participants to evaluate the videotaped statements of people who were interrogated after a staged theft and were either guilty or not guilty (Forgas & East, 2008b). Those in a positive mood were more likely to accept denials as truthful. Sad participants in contrast were better able to see through attempts to deceive, made significantly more guilty judgments, and were significantly better at correctly detecting communications by deceptive (guilty) targets. Thus, negative affect produced a significant advantage in accurately distinguishing truths from lies. A signal detection analysis confirmed that sad judges were more accurate in detecting deception (identifying guilty targets as guilty) consistent with the predicted mood-induced processing differences (Forgas & East, 2008b)—shown in Figure 4.4. These results confirm that negative affect increased peoples' ability to pay close attention to communications, increased scrutiny, and increased skepticism. More remarkably, negative mood also improved accuracy and the ability to detect deception consistent with negative affect producing a more accommodative cognitive style.

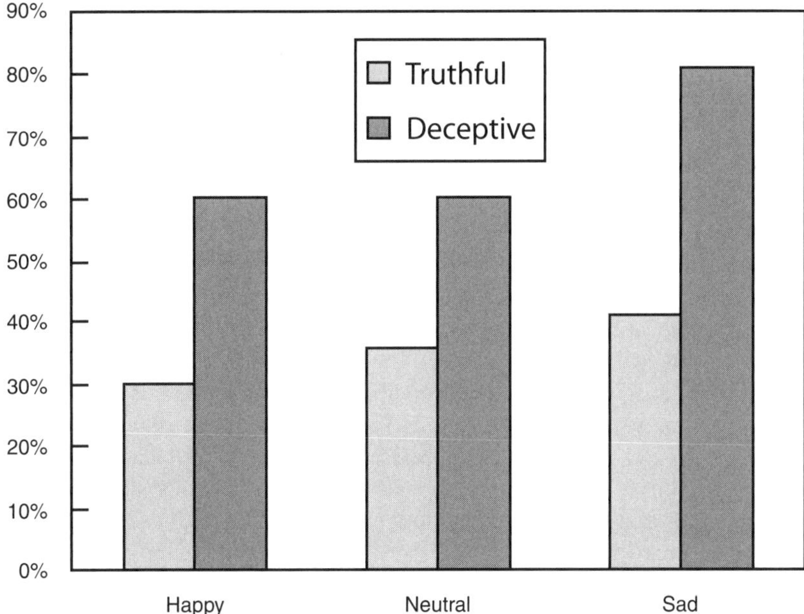


Figure 4.4 Negative mood improves the ability to detect deceptive communication and assign blame to a communicator attempting to deny a theft (Forgas & East, 2008b).

## *Affective Influences on the Quality and Efficacy of Persuasive Messages*

Producing verbal messages designed to influence others—persuasive communication—is a particularly important communication task of everyday life (see also Chapters 3, 6, and 17, this volume). We rely on verbal messages to influence others, both in our personal lives (romantic partners, children, family members), and in our working lives (colleagues, employees). We know that affect can influence information processing strategies (Bless, 2000; Fiedler, 2000; Forgas, 1998a,c), and it may be that negative affect may also improve the quality of persuasive messages by focusing increased attention on concrete, situational details (Forgas, 2007). Accommodative processing promoted by negative affect may thus result in more concrete and factual thinking and lead to the production of more successful and effective persuasive messages.

We explored this possibility (Forgas, 2007, Exp. 1) by asking happy or sad participants to produce persuasive verbal arguments for or against topical attitude issues, such as an increase in student fees and Aboriginal land rights. As predicted, negative mood resulted in the production of verbal arguments that were of significantly higher quality, more concrete and more persuasive than those produced by happy participants, as assessed by trained raters blind to the experimental conditions. A mediational analysis established that it was indeed the greater concreteness and detail of the arguments produced in negative mood that improved argument quality and effectiveness.

In a further experiment, happy or sad participants were asked to produce persuasive verbal arguments for or against other attitudes issues, such as Australia becoming a republic, and for or against a radical right-wing party. Negative mood again resulted in higher quality and more effective persuasive arguments, consistent with the prediction that negative mood should promote a more careful, systematic, bottom-up processing style and greater attention to concrete details (Bless, 2001; Bless & Fiedler, 2006; Fiedler, 2001; Forgas, 2002; see also Figure 4.5 ).

As the effectiveness of the verbal messages produced in these experiments was assessed by trained raters, we also wanted to demonstrate that arguments produced in negative mood were actually more effective in bringing about attitude change by real, naive participants. To further test the actual effectiveness of negative mood arguments, in Experiment 3 the verbal arguments produced by happy or sad participants were presented to a naive audience of undergraduate students, whose original attitudes on these issues were independently assessed at the beginning of term. Arguments written by negative mood participants in Experiments 1 and 2 were actually significantly more successful in producing a real change in attitudes than were arguments produced by happy participants, confirming that negative affect produced a real improvement in the quality of persuasive messages and the effectiveness of communication.

Finally, in Experiment 4 an interactive situation was created, where the persuasive attempts by happy and sad people were directed at a partner through a computer link-up, who were asked to volunteer for a boring experiment using

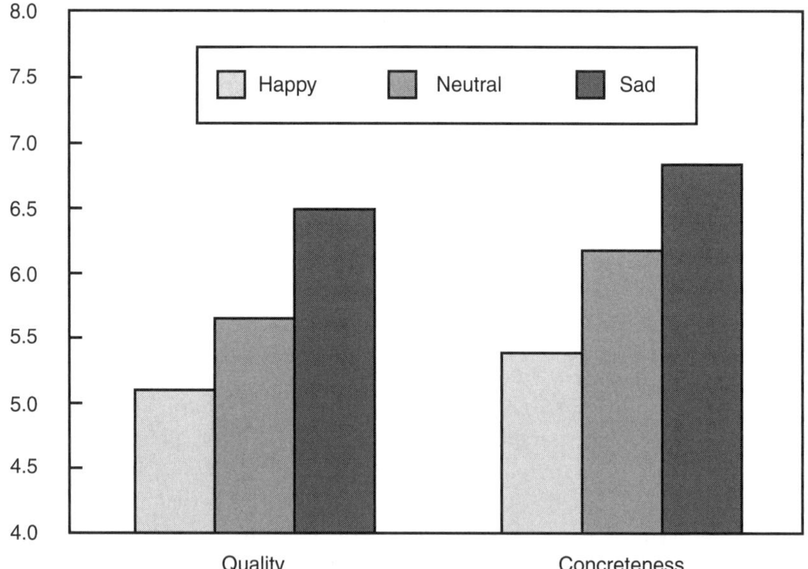


Figure 4.5 The effects of positive and negative mood on the quality and concreteness of persuasive arguments produced: Negative mood results in more concrete, higher quality, and ultimately more effective persuasive messages than positive mood.

e-mail exchanges (Forgas, 2007). The motivation to be persuasive was also manipulated by offering some communicators a significant reward if they manage to persuade their partner (movie passes). Once again, results showed that people in a negative mood produced higher quality persuasive arguments. However, the offer of a reward reduced mood effects, confirming a key prediction of the AIM (Forgas, 1995, 2002), that mood effects on information processing—and subsequent social influence strategies—are reduced by motivated processing. Mediational analyses confirmed that negative mood induced longer, and more accommodative thinking, and more concrete and specific arguments.

These experiments confirm that persuasive arguments produced in negative mood are not only of higher quality as judged by raters, but are also significantly more effective in producing genuine attitude change in people. However, when motivation is already high, mood effects tend to diminish, as predicted by the AIM (Forgas, 2002). This finding may have interesting applied implications for managing communication strategies in personal and organizational situations that also involve a great deal of persuasive communication. It is an intriguing possibility that mild negative affect may actually promote a more concrete, accommodative, and ultimately, more successful communication style in some social situations.

## CONCLUSIONS

Human beings are a moody species. Our fluctuating affective states and moods permeate everything that we think and do. In particular, moods have strong and predictable informational and processing effects on the way people produce and respond to social communication. This chapter reviewed evidence from a number of experimental studies demonstrating affective influences on the way people use requests, engage in negotiation, disclose intimate information about themselves, detect deception, and produce persuasive messages. Many social encounters elicit powerful emotional responses, and there is also growing evidence that affective influences on different information processing strategies play a critical role in explaining the presence or absence of affect infusion into social communication.

Integrative theories, like the AIM (Forgas, 1995, 2002) offer a process-based explanation of when, how, and why affect infusion occurs. Several of the experiments here indicate that, surprisingly, more extensive, substantive processing often enhances mood congruity effects on communication (Forgas, 1998a,b, 1999a,b). On the other hand, affect infusion is often absent when a communication task can be performed using either a direct access or a motivated processing strategies that limit the use of affectively primed information in producing or interpreting a message (Fiedler, 1991; Forgas, 1995). These effects are not limited to controlled laboratory environments, as unobtrusive field experiments showed that affect infusion occurs in many real-life situations.

Producing and responding to social communication requires complex and elaborate information processing strategies. It is the very richness and elaborateness of communication situations that make mood effects particularly likely, as even a minor selective priming of positive and negative memory-based information may have large consequences for what is perceived, how it is interpreted, and the kind of responses that are constructed. The messages produced and responses to messages received tend to be more assertive, confident, and optimistic when a person is in a positive mood state, and more likely to be nonassertive, negative, or critical when the person is in a dysphoric mood.

We have also seen that affective states may also influence *how* people deal with social information. It turns out that mild negative moods can have a beneficial effect by recruiting more accommodative and attentive processing styles, reducing interpretational errors, improving the quality of persuasive arguments, detecting deception, and also increasing the degree of scrutiny that incoming factual and interpersonal messages receive. The processing effects of negative mood described here seem particularly intriguing, because these studies suggest that mild dysphoria could actually improve communicative strategies and even result in superior outcomes in some situations (Forgas, 2007).

It is interesting to note that these results also challenge the common assumption in much of applied, organizational, clinical, and health psychology that positive affect has universally desirable social cognitive and communicative consequences. Together with other recent experimental studies, our findings confirm that negative affect often produces adaptive and more socially sensitive outcomes. For example, negative moods can reduce judgmental errors (Forgas, 1998b), improve eyewitness accuracy (Forgas, Vargas, & Laham, 2005), improve interpersonal communication strategies (Forgas, 1998 c; 2007), and may also increase fairness and sensitivity to the needs of others. There is much scope in future work to explore mood effects on other kinds of strategic communication behaviors, such as forgiveness.

In conclusion, evidence suggests a closely interactive relationship between affective states and social information processing strategies that determines the way people communicate and respond to communication in their daily lives. A number of contextual influences mediate and moderate these effects. Considering that most of the research on affect in social psychology is less than a few decades old, a great deal has been achieved. However, we are still far from fully understanding the multifaceted influences that affect has on social thinking, judgments, and communication in particular. It is hoped that the present chapter in particular stimulates further interest in this fascinating and rapidly developing area of inquiry.

## ACKNOWLEDGMENTS

This work was partly supported by a Special Investigator award from the Australian Research Council and the Research Prize by the Alexander von Humboldt Foundation to Joseph P. Forgas. Please address all correspondence in connection with this paper to Joseph P. Forgas, at the School of Psychology, University of New South Wales, Sydney 2052, Australia; e-mail jp.forgas@unsw.edu.au. For further information on this research project, see also the web site www.psy.unsw.edu.au/~joef/jforgas.htm.

# REFERENCES

Adolphs, R., & Damasio, A. (2001). The interaction of affect and cognition: A neurobiological perspective. In J. P. Forgas (Ed.), *The handbook of affect and social cognition* (pp. 27–49). Mahwah, NJ: Erlbaum.

Beukeboom, C. J., & De Jong, E. M. (2008). When feelings speak: How affective and proprioceptive cues change language abstraction. *Journal of Language and Social Psychology, 27*(2), 110–122.

Beukeboom, C. J., & Semin, G. R. (2005). Mood and representations of behaviour: The how and why. *Cognition & Emotion, 19*(8), 1242–1251.

Beukeboom, C. J., & Semin, G. R. (2006). How mood turns on language. *Journal of Experimental Social Psychology, 42,* 553–566.

Bless, H. (2000). The interplay of affect and cognition: The mediating role of general knowledge structures. In J. P. Forgas (Ed.), *Feeling and thinking: The role of affect in social cognition* (pp. 201–222). New York, NY: Cambridge University Press.

Bless, H. (2001). Mood and the use of general knowledge structures. In L. L. Martin (Ed.), *Theories of mood and cognition: A user's guidebook* (pp. 9–26). Mahwah, NJ: Erlbaum.

Bless, H., & Fiedler, K. (2006). Mood and the regulation of information processing and behavior. In J. P. Forgas (Ed.), *Affect in social cognition and behavior* (pp. 65–84). New York, NY: Psychology Press.

Bower, G. H. (1981). Mood and memory. *American Psychologist, 36,* 129–148.

Bower, G.H. (1991). Mood congruity of social judgments. In J.P. Forgas (Ed.), *Emotion and social judgments* (pp.31–53). Oxford: Pergamon.

Bower, G. H., & Forgas, J. P. (2001). Mood and social memory. In J. P. Forgas (Ed.), *The handbook of affect and social cognition* (pp. 95–120). Mahwah, NJ: Erlbaum.

Byrne, D., & Clore, G. L. (1970). A reinforcement model of evaluation responses. *Personality: An International Journal, 1,* 103–128.

Ciarrochi, J.V., & Forgas, J. P. (1999). On being tense yet tolerant: The paradoxical effects of trait anxiety and aversive mood on intergroup judgments. *Group Dynamics: Theory, Research and Practice, 3,* 227–238.

Ciarrochi, J.V., & Forgas, J. P. (2000). The pleasure of possessions: Affect and consumer judgments. *European Journal of Social Psychology, 30,* 631–649.

Ciarrochi, J., Forgas, J., & Mayer, J. (Eds.). (2006). *Emotional intelligence in everyday life: A scientific inquiry.* (2nd ed.). New York, NY: Psychology Press.

Clark, M. S., & Isen, A. M. (1982). Towards understanding the relationship between feeling states and social behavior. In A. H. Hastorf & A. M. Isen (Eds.), *Cognitive social psychology* (pp. 73–108). New York, NY: Elsevier-North Holland.

Clore, G. L., & Byrne, D. (1974). The reinforcement affect model of attraction. In T. L. Huston (Ed.), *Foundations of interpersonal attraction* (pp. 143–170). New York, NY: Academic Press.

Clore, G. L., & Storbeck, J. (2006). Affect as information for social judgment, behavior, and memory. In J. P. Forgas (Ed.), *Affect in social cognition and behavior* (pp. 154–178). New York, NY: Psychology Press.

Eich, E., & Macauley, D. (2000). Fundamental factors in mood-dependent memory. In J. P. Forgas (Ed.), *Feeling and thinking: The role of affect in social cognition* (pp. 109–130). New York, NY: Cambridge University Press.

Feshbach, S., & Singer, R. D. (1957). The effects of fear arousal and suppression of fear upon social perception. *Journal of Abnormal and Social Psychology, 55,* 283–288.

Fiedler, K. (1990). Mood-dependent selectivity in social cognition. In W. Stroebe & M. Hewstone (Eds.), *European review of social psychology* (Vol. 1, pp. 1–32). New York, NY: Wiley.

Fiedler, K. (1991). On the task, the measures and the mood in research on affect and social cognition. In J. P. Forgas (Ed.), *Emotion and social judgments* (pp. 83–104). Oxford, England: Pergamon.

Fiedler, K. (2000). Towards an integrative account of affect and cognition phenomena using the BIAS computer algorithm. In J. P. Forgas (Ed.), *Feeling and thinking: The role of affect in social cognition* (pp. 223–252). New York, NY: Cambridge University Press.

Fiedler, K. (2001). Affective influences on social information processing. In J. P. Forgas (Ed.), *The handbook of affect and social cognition* (pp. 163–185). Mahwah, NJ: Erlbaum.

Fiedler, K., & Bless, H. (2001). The formation of beliefs in the interface of affective and cognitive processes. In N. Frijda, A. Manstead, & S. Bem (Eds.), *The influence of emotions on beliefs.* New York, NY: Cambridge University Press.

Fiedler, K., & Forgas, J. P. (Eds.). (1988). *Affect, cognition, and social behavior: New evidence and integrative attempts.* Toronto, Canada: Hogrefe.

Forgas, J. P. (1979). *Social episodes: The study of interaction routines.* London, England: Academic Press.

Forgas, J. P. (1982). Episode cognition: Internal representations of interaction routines. In L. Berkowitz (Ed.), *Advances in experimental social psychology* (pp. 59–104). New York, NY: Academic Press.

Forgas, J. P. (1985). *Interpersonal behaviour: The psychology of social interaction.* Sydney, Australia: Pergamon Press.

Forgas, J. P. (1992). On bad mood and peculiar people: Affect and person typicality in impression formation. *Journal of Personality and Social Psychology, 62,* 863–875.

Forgas, J. P. (1994). Sad and guilty? Affective influences on the explanation of conflict episodes. *Journal of Personality and Social Psychology, 66,* 56–68.

Forgas, J.P. (1995). Mood and judgment: The affect infusion model (AIM). *Psychological Bulletin, 117,* 39–66.

Forgas, J. P. (1998a). Asking nicely? Mood effects on responding to more or less polite requests. *Personality and Social Psychology Bulletin, 24,* 173–185.

Forgas, J. P. (1998b). Happy and mistaken? Mood effects on the fundamental attribution error. *Journal of Personality and Social Psychology, 75,* 318–331.

Forgas, J. P. (1998c). On feeling good and getting your way: Mood effects on negotiation strategies and outcomes. *Journal of Personality and Social Psychology, 74,* 565–577.

Forgas, J. P. (1999a). Feeling and speaking: Mood effects on verbal communication strategies. *Personality and Social Psychology Bulletin, 25,* 850–863.

Forgas, J. P. (1999b). On feeling good and being rude: Affective influences on language use and request formulations. *Journal of Personality and Social Psychology, 76,* 928–939.

Forgas, J. P. (Ed.). (2001). *The handbook of affect and social cognition.* Mahwah, NJ: Erlbaum.

Forgas, J. P. (2002). Feeling and doing: Affective influences on interpersonal behavior. *Psychological Inquiry, 13,* 1–28.

Forgas, J. P. (Ed.). (2006). *Affect in social cognition and behavior.* New York, NY: Psychology Press.

Forgas, J. P. (2007). When sad is better than happy: Negative affect can improve the quality and effectiveness of persuasive messages and social influence strategies. *Journal of Experimental social Psychology, 43,* 513–528.

Forgas, J. P. (2010). Mood effects on self-disclosure strategies. *Journal of Personality and Social Psychology. 100*(3), 449–461.

Forgas, J. P., & Bower, G. H. (1987). Mood effects on person perception judgements. *Journal of Personality and Social Psychology, 53,* 53–60.

Forgas, J. P., Bower, G. H., & Krantz, S. (1984). The influence of mood on perceptions of social interactions. *Journal of Experimental Social Psychology, 20,* 497–513.

Forgas, J. P., & Ciarrochi, J. V. (2002). On managing moods: Evidence for the role of homeostatic cognitive strategies in affect regulation. *Personality and Social Psychology Bulletin, 28,* 336–345.
Forgas, J. P., & East, R. (2008a). How real is that smile? Mood effects on accepting or rejecting the veracity of emotional facial expressions. *Journal of Nonverbal Behavior, 32,* 157–170.
Forgas, J. P., & East, R. (2008b). On being happy and gullible: Mood effects on scepticism and the detection of deception. *Journal of Experimental Social Psychology, 44,* 1362–1367.
Forgas, J. P., & Gunawardena, A. (2001). *Affective influences on spontaneous interpersonal behaviors.* Unpublished manuscript, University of New South Wales, Sydney, Australia.
Forgas, J. P., & Moylan, S. J. (1987). After the movies: The effects of transient mood states on social judgments. *Personality and Social Psychology Bulletin, 13,* 478–489.
Forgas, J. P., Vargas, P., & Laham, S. (2005). Mood effects on eyewitness memory: Affective influences on susceptibility to misinformation. *Journal of Experimental Social Psychology, 41,* 574–588.
Gilbert, D. T. (1991). How mental systems believe. *American Psychologist, 46,* 107–119.
Gilbert, D. T., & Malone, P. S. (1995). The correspondence bias. *Psychological Bulletin, 117,* 21–38.
Hilgard, E. R. (1980). The trilogy of mind: Cognition, affection, and conation. *Journal of the History of the Behavioral Sciences, 16,* 107–117.
Ito, T., & Cacioppo, J. (2001). Affect and attitudes: A social neuroscience approach. In J. P. Forgas (Ed.), *The handbook of affect and social cognition.* Mahwah, NJ: Erlbaum.
Jones, E. E., & Harris, V. A. (1967). The attribution of attitudes. *Journal of Experimental Social Psychology, 3,* 1–24.
Niedenthal, P., & Halberstadt, J. (2000). Grounding categories in emotional response. In J. P. Forgas (Ed.), *Feeling and thinking: The role of affect in social cognition* (pp. 357–386). New York, NY: Cambridge University Press.
Pervin, L. A. (1976). A free-response description approach to the analysis of person-situation interaction. *Journal of Personality and Social Psychology, 34,* 465–474.
Razran, G. H. S. (1940). Conditioned response changes in rating and appraising sociopolitical slogans. *Psychological Bulletin, 37,* 481.
Schwarz, N. (1990). Feelings as information: Informational and motivational functions of affective states. In E. T. Higgins & R. Sorrentino (Eds.), *Handbook of motivation and cognition: Foundations of social behaviour* (Vol. 2, pp. 527–561). New York, NY: Guilford Press.
Schwarz, N., & Clore, G. L. (1983). Mood, misattribution and judgments of well-being: Informative and directive functions of affective states. *Journal of Personality and Social Psychology, 45,* 513–523.
Schwarz, N., & Clore, G. L. (1988). How do I feel about it? The informative function of affective states. In K. Fiedler & J. P. Forgas (Eds.), *Affect, cognition, and social behavior* (pp. 44–62). Toronto, Canada: Hogrefe.
Sedikides, C. (1992). Mood as a determinant of attentional focus. *Cognition & Emotion, 6,* 129–148.
Sedikides, C. (1995). Central and peripheral self-conceptions are differentially influenced by mood: Tests of the differential sensitivity hypothesis. *Journal of Personality and Social Psychology, 69*(4), 759–777.
Unkelbach, C., Forgas, J.P. & Denson, T. F. (2008). The turban effect: The influence of Muslim headgear and induced affect on aggressive responses in the shooter bias paradigm. *Journal of Experimental Social Psychology, 44,* 1409–1413
Zajonc, R. B. (1980). Feeling and thinking: Preferences need no inferences. *American Psychologist, 35,* 151–175.
Zajonc, R. B. (2000). Feeling and thinking: Closing the debate over the independence of affect. In J. P. Forgas (Ed.), *Feeling and thinking: The role of affect in social cognition* (pp. 31–58). New York, NY: Cambridge University Press.

# 5

# In the Mood to Break the Rules

## *Happiness Promotes Language Abstraction and Transgression of Conversation Norms*

ALEX S. KOCH, JOSEPH P. FORGAS, AND LIZ GOLDENBERG

## INTRODUCTION

Staying tuned to the complex state of affairs and course of events in our environment requires that we mutually engage in circulating both first-hand and second-hand information. At this, however, varied compositions of motivational, affective, and cognitive factors determine what and how we speak or write, leading to great and far-reaching differences in communication output based on the same input of information (Fiedler, 2007; Forgas, 2007). The present chapter is devoted to illustrate how *affective states* and *cognitive processing styles* may interact in influencing two fundamental aspects of communication style.

In particular, we argue that *positive* mood triggers *assimilative* thinking, that *negative* mood triggers *accommodative* thinking (Bless & Fiedler, 2006), and that this mood-induced processing dichotomy translates into meaningful and considerable differences in (a) *language abstraction* and (b) *transgression of conversation norms*. To be precise, assimilative processing in good mood is hypothesized to promote greater language abstraction and greater transgression of conversation norms than accommodative processing in bad mood.

## MOOD STATES AND COGNITIVE PROCESSING STYLES

Positive and negative mood promote qualitatively different processing styles. According to Bless and Fiedler's (2006) assimilative or accommodative processing theory, moods are informative about whether the current situation poses assimilative chances or accommodative challenges to the self, and thus subconsciously regulates whether we construe adaptive cognition as "imposing internal structures on the external world" (=assimilation) or "modifying internal structures in accordance with external constraints" (=accommodation; Bless & Fiedler, 2006, p. 66). Positive mood signals that the environment is familiar or benign, and that it is adequate to process incoming information in an internally focused, top-down, and assimilative fashion where people follow their personal goals and intuitively apply their abstract, integrated knowledge to interpret and respond to the current situation. In contrast, negative mood signals that the environment is novel or malign, and that it is necessary to process incoming information in an externally focused, bottom-up, and accommodative way where people follow social norms and deliberately attend to concrete, particular stimuli to interpret and respond to the current situation (Bless & Fiedler, 2006; Forgas, 2002, 2010).

## MOOD STATES AND COMMUNICATION STYLE

Given that happy individuals rather *transform* incoming information according to their internal goals and abstract concepts, categories, expectations, etc. (i.e., assimilation) and given that sad individuals rather *preserve* stimulus information according to external norms (i.e., accommodation; Bless & Fiedler, 2006; Chapter 4, this volume), our predictions regarding mood effects on communication style are straightforward and easy to see: Good mood should result in both greater language abstraction and greater transgression of conversation norms compared with bad mood. To test these two hypotheses, we conducted two studies.

## STUDY 1

### *Method*

**Overview, design, and participants.** Study 1 investigated whether induced affect moderates the abstraction of written communications about fictional events. We applied a between-subjects design, with mood state (positive, neutral, or negative) as the independent variable, and language abstraction as the dependent variable. A total of 100 undergraduate students (39 men, 61 women) participated for course credit.

**Procedure and materials.** Upon arrival, subjects were told that they would take part in two ostensibly unrelated studies: "evaluating film clips to be used in a later study" (in fact, the mood manipulation) and "writing three fictional stories." At first, they watched an 8-minute excerpt from *Love Actually*, a documentary on birds, or *Angela's Ashes.* After this positive, neutral, or negative mood induction, respectively, participants were presented with three ambiguous images (a captain and a passenger talking at the side of an anchored vessel, two lab-coated scientists working in a lab, and an employee sitting at an office desk) selected from the thematic apperception test (McClelland, Atkinson, Clark, & Lowell, 1953), designed to elicit idiosyncratic interpretations that also vary in terms of language abstraction. Subjects were asked "What comes to your mind when looking at the images that lie in front of you? Please generate and write down a fictional story for each of these three images, and describe: Who are these people, what is happening? What happened before, how did the story begin? What are these people thinking about, how do they feel? How will the story end?" Participants worked on this creative writing task for as long as they wanted. Finally, prior to a debriefing that concluded the experiment, they completed a questionnaire that consisted of several distracter items plus two 9-point scales (*bad-good* and *sad-happy*) asking them to indicate how they had felt after watching the affective film clip.

**Dependent variables.** Two independent coders separated all the stories written into 3,729 distinct communicative acts. Next, they numerically coded every communicative act for language abstraction on a 4-point scale, as a *trait inference* ( = 4; e.g., "he is an *evil* man"), *state inference* ( = 3; e.g., "he *hopes* the cruise goes well"), *action interpretation* ( = 2; e.g., "captain Rogers *smuggled* something on board"), or *action description* ( = 1; e.g., "he is *talking* to a businessman"), achieving a satisfactory inter-rater agreement (Cohen's $\kappa = .73$). Communicative acts referring to the context or background of a story (17.5%; e.g., "the event takes place in a high school chemistry lab") were not analyzed as we were only interested in the ones referring to the persons mentioned in the fictional stories. This operationalization of language abstraction is based on the linguistic category model (Semin & Fiedler, 1988, 1991, 1992), which defines four increasingly abstract ways of communicating about people: descriptive action verbs (e.g., *said* and *paid*) describe observable, separate *actions;* interpretive action verbs (e.g., *babbled* and *wasted*) interpret *compounds of actions* that are observable in principle; state verbs (e.g., *loved* and *craved*) infer psychological *states* that are detached from observable actions; and adjectives (e.g., *spoiled* and *impulsive*) infer completely decontextualized and thus highly abstract character *traits.* An overall score for language abstraction that ranged from 1 to 4 was calculated for each subject.

## *Results*

**Mood validation.** The sad-happy and bad-good mood scales were highly correlated ($r = 0.59$, $p < .001$) and thus were combined to form a single scale. As expected, mood was significantly better after watching the positive rather than the neutral film ($M_{positive} = 7.45$, $SD = 1.57$; $M_{neutral} = 6.09$, $SD = 1.47$), $t(65) = 3.66$, $p < .001$, $d = 0.88$, and significantly better after watching the neutral rather than the negative film ($M_{negative} = 3.57$, $SD = 0.91$), $t(64) = 8.35$, $p < .001$, $d = 2.11$, confirming the effectiveness of our mood manipulation.

**Preliminary analyses.** There was no difference between the mood conditions regarding the number of communicative acts used, *Freferences*$(2, 97) = 0.18$, NS, and the number of words written, *Fwords*$(2, 97) = 0.07$, NS. From this, it follows that any mood effect on language abstraction cannot be confounded by the amount of material communicated.

**Language abstraction.** As predicted, good mood led to greater language abstraction compared with bad mood (*Mpositive* = 2.38, *SD* = 0.14; *Mnegative* = 2.28, *SD* = 0.17), $t(65) = 2.58$, $p = .01$, $d = 0.64$. Controls fell in between the positive and negative mood conditions (*Mneutral* = 2.32, *SD* = 0.15), but neither the difference between positive and neutral mood, nor the difference between the neutral and negative mood, was found to be significant, *tpositive/neutral*(65) = 0.98, NS, *tneutral/negative*(64) = 1.64, NS.

Next, mood effects on each of the four levels of language abstraction were analyzed by means of a 2 (mood: positive versus negative) × 4 (percentage use of communicative acts referring to traits versus states versus compounds of behaviors versus separate behaviors) mixed ANOVA with repeated measures on the second factor. Results confirmed that mood made a difference to the relative frequency with which the different levels of abstraction were used, $F(3, 195) = 7.90$, $p < .001$, $\eta^2 = .11$. References to abstract traits (*Mpositive* = 6%, *SD* = 5%; *Mnegative* = 3%, *SD* = 4%) and references to rather abstract states (*Mpositive* = 40%, *SD* = 9%; *Mnegative* = 35%, *SD* = 8%) were significantly more frequent in positive rather than negative mood, *ttraits*(65) = 2.31, $p < .05$, $d = .57$, and *tstates*(65) = 2.77, $p < .01$, $d = .67$. In contrast, references to rather concrete compounds of behaviors were significantly more frequent in negative rather than positive mood (*Mpositive* = 39%, *SD* = 8%; *Mnegative* = 49%, *SD* = 11%),

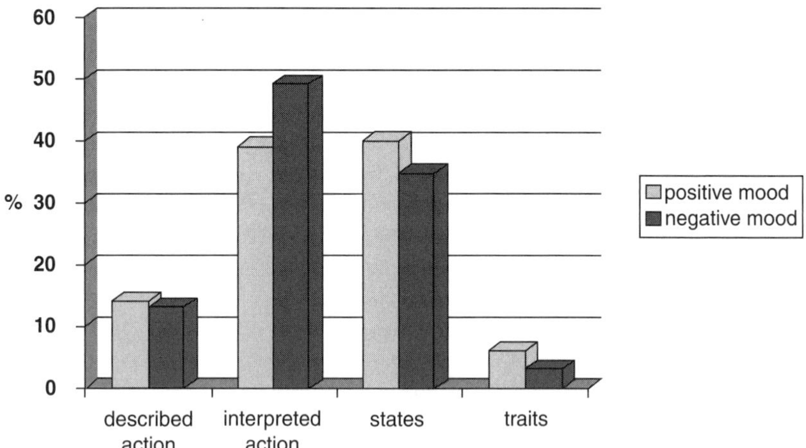


Figure 5.1 Mood effects on percentage use of increasingly abstract person descriptions in written messages

$tIA(65) = 3.96, p < .001, d = .97$. There was no difference between the positive and negative mood conditions regarding the relative frequency of references to concrete, separate behaviors (*Mpositive* = 14%, *SD* = 7%; *Mnegative* = 13%, *SD* = 11%), $tDA(65) = 0.44$, NS).

### Discussion

Consistent with the assimilative or accommodative processing theory (Bless & Fiedler, 2006), these results confirm that mood may significantly influence the level of abstraction in written communications about entirely fictional, self-generated events. Subjects in good mood mentioned more decontextualized, abstract character traits and psychological states than subjects in bad mood. In contrast, those in bad mood mentioned and interpreted or evaluated more context-embedded, concrete behaviors than those in good mood.

Study 2 aimed at confirming and extending these findings in several directions. Communicating fictional events generated on the spot, as investigated in Study 1, essentially is a creativity task that involves a great deal of *divergent,* unrestricted thought (Cropley, 2006) open to influence of mood-based processing styles (Forgas, 1995, 2002). In contrast, communicating factual events retrieved from memory is by far less likely to vary subject to assimilative versus accommodative processing (Bless & Fiedler, 2006), because recalling clearly defined information clusters calls for *convergent,* restricted thinking (Cropley, 2006). Thus, to examine the robustness and generality of mood effects on language abstraction, Study 2 aimed at replicating the findings of Study 1 in a reproductive rather than creative task where subjects were instructed to recount a recently experienced event.

Further, as writing and speaking involve substantially different cognitive processes (Casagrande & Cortini, 2008), it needs to be clarified whether the observed mood effects occur in both modalities. Thus, in Study 2 we asked participants to speak rather than write.

Also, to examine our second hypothesis that mood influences transgression of conversation norms, in Study 2 we designed and implemented transgression measures for each of the four general communication rules postulated by Grice (1975), predicting that happy, assimilative thinkers should commit more transgressions of Grice's maxims of quantity, relevance, quality, and manner than sad, accommodative thinkers.

## STUDY 2

### Method

**Overview, design, and participants.** Study 2 investigated whether mood moderates both language abstraction and transgression of conversation norms in verbal communications about factual events. We applied two between-subject designs, with mood (positive, neutral, or negative) as the independent variable, and language abstraction and transgression of conversation norms as the dependent variables. A total of 98 undergraduate students (30 men, 68 women) participated for course credit.

**Procedure and materials.** Participants were informed that the lab session would involve two ostensibly independent tasks: "evaluating film clips to be used in a later study" (in fact, the mood manipulation) and "recounting a social interaction in your own words." Then, they watched a funny, affectively neutral, or sad mood induction film (5-minute excerpts from *The Jungle Book,* a documentary on birds, or *The Shawshank Redemption,* respectively). Next, participants were presented with a highly ambiguous social interaction from *Annie Hall* (2.5 minutes). The episode showed the encounter between comedian Alvi and backstage manager Alison, who appear to be either arguing or flirting with each other. Immediately afterward, they were instructed to "recount this social interaction to a person who wants to know what happened by speaking into a microphone for between 1 and 3 minutes" in total, and their narratives were recorded. Finally, prior to a thorough debriefing, participants filled out distracter items plus two 9-point scales (*bad-good* and *sad-happy*) asking them to indicate how they had felt after watching the affective film clip.

**Dependent variables—language abstraction.** To preclude unwanted effects of paralinguistic communication features (e.g., tone and voice pitch), the recorded narratives were transcribed into text prior to the coding phase. Language abstraction was coded using the same method as described in the previous study. Two judges first identified 1,681 distinct communicative acts and then rated their abstraction on the same 4-point scale as in Study 1, achieving a satisfactory inter-rater agreement (Cohen's $\kappa$ = .68). Again, communicative acts referring to context or background of the target event were excluded (12.2% in total), leaving 1,476 communicative acts in the final analysis. Further, metacognitive remarks (e.g., *I guess* and *I don't know*), false starts, stuttering, and fillers such as *then, and, so, like, um, yeah,* etc., were also omitted (27.1% of all words spoken). As in Study 1, an average abstraction score ranging from 1 to 4 was calculated for each participant.

**Dependent variables—transgression of conversation norms.** According to Grice (1975), it is in everyone's best interest to comply with the four *conversational maxims* of *quantity, relevance, quality,* and *manner,* social norms that define the most efficient and thus expected way of sharing information. The maxim of *quantity* calls for contributions to be as informative, but not more so than required for the aim of a given conversation. The maxim of *quality* requires "do not say what you believe is false." The maxim of *relevance* demands to convey only germane information. Finally, the maxim of *manner* urges dialogue partners to "avoid obscurity and ambiguity" and to "be brief and orderly" (Grice, 1975, pp. 45–46). Altogether, these four conversation norms demand to clearly utter an appropriate amount of exclusively relevant and truthful information (Wänke, 2007; for a critical discussion of Grice's communication model, see Chapter 8, this volume). Transgressions of Grice's conversation norms were assessed by five other independent judges, who assigned ratings based on the four operationalizations described in the following sections.

As already noted by Grice himself (Grice, 1975, 2008), the relevance and quantity maxims partially overlap each other, because providing irrelevant information is tantamount to providing too much information, and failing to provide relevant information is tantamount to providing too little information. As a possible approach to clearly distinguish between transgressions of these two maxims, the quantity index was set to measure the number of relevant communicative acts that nevertheless were absent in a participant's event report, whereas the relevance index was set to measure the number of irrelevant communicative acts that nevertheless were present in a participant's event report. On average, participants used 12 distinct communicative acts to recount the target event, which is why we instructed two more independent judges to familiarize themselves with the target event, and to then split it into 12 distinct and equally relevant sub-events, yielding two very similar solutions (see Appendices). Sub-events listed and not listed in these two sub-event catalogs were

TABLE 5.1 Appendix A: Information classified as relevant for recounting the target event (*Judge 1*)

| **Background** | **Left-wing political rally with entertainers giving shows.** |
|---|---|
| 1st response | Comedian Alvi approaches backstage manager Alison and asks her when he is due to go on. |
| 2nd response | She responds that he's next. |
| 3rd response | He doesn't want to perform right after another comedian; he becomes nervous and stressed, and he has stage fright; he hectically demands to be postponed in the order of performers. |
| 4th response | She calmly insists that he performs next; she comforts and encourages him; she tells him that "everything is going to be fine." |
| 5th response | He wants to get rid of his stage fright by starting a distractive conversation; hest he starts to ask her personal questions (her last name, her thesis topic). |
| 6th response | She calmly responds to all his questions. |
| 7th response | Based on her thesis topic, he reduces her to a cultural stereotype; he is interested in her. |
| 8th response | She is not impressed, but she doesn't feel seriously insulted; she answers with a disapproving, ironic comment. |
| 9th response | He realizes that he likes her; he asks her for some encouraging words. |
| 10th response | She likes him as well; she smiles and responds that she thinks that he is cute. |
| 11th response | He goes on stage and begins to tell jokes to the audience. |

TABLE 5.2 Appendix B: Information classified as relevant for recounting the target event (*Judge 2*)

| Background | Political rally |
|---|---|
| 1st response | He (comedian Alvi) asks when he'll go on. |
| 2nd response | She (backstage manager Alison) says he's on next. |
| 3rd response | He freaks out about being next; he wants to perform sometime later. |
| 4th response | She stays calm and insists on the order of shows; she tries to reassure him. |
| 5th response | He asks her about herself. |
| 6th response | She tells him her name; she also tells him that she's writing a thesis on political commitment. |
| 7th response | He asks her an elaborate identity question; he tries to impress and charm her. |
| 8th response | She says she loves being reduced to a cultural stereotype, but she doesn't seem too offended. |
| 9th response | He says he has to go on stage and asks for encouragement. |
| 10th response | She says he's cute; she looks at him in a way that indicates that she's interested in him. |
| 11th response | He goes on stage and makes a successful entrance. |

defined as relevant and irrelevant for recounting the event, respectively. Thus, *quantity transgression* scores were higher the more relevant sub-events were failed to be conveyed by a subject ($M$ = 5.78 out of 12, $SD$ = 1.67; inter-rater agreement: $Mr$ = 0.71, $SD$ = 0.06), whereas *relevance transgression* scores were higher the more irrelevant sub-events were conveyed by a participant ($M$ = 1.10; $SD$ = 0.91; inter-rater agreement: $Mr$ = 0.34, $SD$ = 0.14; e.g., "he was wearing a brown jacket").

*Transgression of the maxim of quality* was measured by a separate scale indicating the number of obviously untrue communicative acts used by each subject ($M$ = 0.71, $SD$ = 0.67; inter-rater agreement: $Mr$ = 0.35, $SD$ = 0.11; e.g., "he didn't keep eye-contact with her"). Finally, *transgression of the maxim of manner* was measured by (a) *prolixity* as indicated by the average number of words per communicative act ($M$ = 9.22, $SD$ = 1.99), (b) *redundancy* as indicated by the number of repetitions of communicative acts ($M$ = 1.91, $SD$ = 1.31; e.g., "he keeps freaking out" and "he keeps doing this"), and (c) *discontinuity* as indicated by the number of pauses and filler words or phrases (e.g., *like, um, yeah, I don't know*, etc.) interrupting the speech flow ($M$ = 12.35, $SD$ = 5.11). Participants' prolixity, redundancy, and discontinuity scores were transformed into Z-scores and averaged within participants and across the judges, who achieved a satisfactory inter-rater agreement ($Mr$ = 0.72, $SD$ = 0.06).

The within-subject correlations between these four transgression indices were low ($M|r|$ = 0.11), confirming that we assessed distinct yet theoretically related conversation norms. Finally, averaging across the four transgression indices, we computed a Z-score indicating overall transgression of Grice's conversation norms.

## Results

Three subjects were excluded from the following analyses whose total number of words spoken was at least 3 *SD*s higher or lower than the mean ($M_{words}$ = 180, *SD* = 62), because such atypical verbosity may confound the results.

**Mood validation.** The mood self-ratings on the sad-happy and bad-good scales were highly correlated ($r = 0.95$, $p < .001$) and thus were combined to form a single scale. As expected, mood was significantly better after watching the positive rather than the neutral film ($M_{positive}$ = 7.33, *SD* = 1.83; $M_{neutral}$ = 5.05, *SD* = 1.01), $t(59) = 5.80$, $p < .001$, $d = 1.60$, and significantly better after watching the neutral rather than the negative film ($M_{negative}$ = 2.76, *SD* = 0.81), $t(59) = 9.82$, $p < .001$, $d = 2.51$.

**Preliminary analyses.** As in Study 1, we found no differences between the mood conditions regarding the number of communicative acts used, $F_{references}(2, 92) = 0.25$, NS, the number of words spoken, $F_{words}(2, 92) = 0.72$, NS, and the time taken to recount the target social interaction, $F_{time}(2, 92) = 0.34$, NS, which confirms that any mood effects on both language abstraction and transgression of conversation norms cannot be confounded by the amount of material communicated.

**Language abstraction.** Two other subjects were excluded from these analyses whose number of references to traits, states, interpreted action, or described action was at least 3 *SD*s higher or lower than the overall mean, leaving 33 happy, 27 neutral, and 33 sad subjects in the final analyses. As expected, positive mood ($M_{positive}$ = 2.05, *SD* = 0.34) resulted in greater language abstraction than negative mood ($M_{negative}$ = 1.85, *SD* = 0.29), $t(64) = 2.45$, $p < .05$, $d = 0.60$. Again, there was no difference between the positive and neutral mood conditions, $t(58) = 0.43$, NS; however, controls ($M_{neutral}$ = 2.00, *SD* = 0.33) spoke in more abstract terms than the negative mood group, $t(58) = 1.91$, $p = .06$, $d = 0.47$.

As in Study 1, we also computed a 2 (mood: positive versus negative) × 4 (percentage use of references to traits versus states versus interpreted action versus described action) mixed ANOVA with repeated measures on the second factor, which revealed a significant interaction effect, $F(3, 192) = 3.25$, $p < .01$, $\eta^2 = .08$. This effect confirms that communicators' use of the increasingly abstract communicative acts varied significantly as a function of mood. Specifically, the percentage of references to traits ($M_{positive}$ = 6%, *SD* = 8%; $M_{negative}$ = 2%, *SD* = 5%) and states ($M_{positive}$ = 34%, *SD* = 14%; $M_{negative}$ = 26%, *SD* = 13%) was greater in positive compared with negative mood, $t_{traits}(64) = 2.52$, $p < .05$, $d = 0.64$, and $t_{states}(64) = 2.47$, $p < .05$, $d = 0.61$, whereas in contrast, the percentage of references to interpreted action was greater in negative compared with positive mood ($M_{positive}$ = 16%, *SD* = 9%; $M_{negative}$ = 26%, *SD* = 11%), $t_{IA}(64) = 3.89$, $p < .001$, $d = 0.96$. However, the positive and negative mood

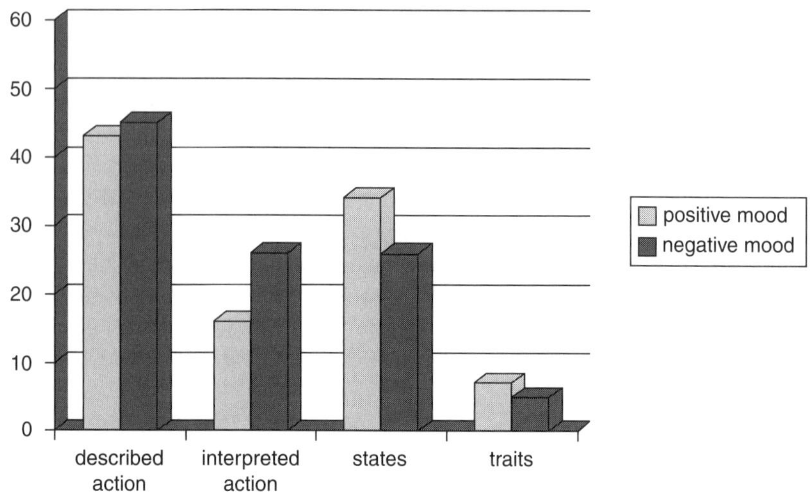


Figure 5.2 Mood effects on percentage use of increasingly abstract person descriptions in written messages

groups did not differ in the percentage of references to described action (*Mpositive* = 43%, *SD* = 16%; *Mnegative* = 45%, *SD* = 17%), *tDA*(64) = 0.65, NS).

**Transgression of conversation norms.** There was no difference between controls (*Mneutral[Z-score]* = 0.03, *SD* = 0.57) and subjects in the other mood conditions, *tpositive/neutral*(59) = 1.02, NS, and *tneutral/negative*(59) = 0.95, NS. However, as predicted, participants in good mood committed more transgressions of Grice's (1975) maxims than participants in bad mood (*Mpositive[Z-score]* = 0.18, *SD* = 0.60; *Mnegative[Z-score]* = –0.11, *SD* = 0.48), *tpositive/negative*(66) = 2.14, $p < .05$, $d = 0.52$.

Looking at transgressions of each conversation norm separately revealed that participants in good mood committed significantly more transgressions of the relevance, quality and manner maxims did subjects in bad mood (relevance: *Mpositive* = 1.26, *SD* = 0.93; *Mnegative* = 0.81, *SD* = 0.82; $t(66) = 2.06$, $p < .05$, $d = 0.51$; and quality: *Mpositive* = 0.85, *SD* = 0.83; *Mnegative* = 0.55, *SD* = 0.42; $t(66) = 1.84$, $p = .06$, $d = 0.47$; and manner: *Mpositive[Z-score]* = 0.17, *SD* = 0.46; *Mnegative[Z-score]* = –0.08, *SD* = 0.56; $t(66) = 2.02$, $p < .05$, $d = 0.49$), whereas this was not the case with the quantity maxim (*Mpositive* = 6.17, *SD* = 1.74; *Mnegative* = 5.68, *SD* = 1.62; $t(66) = 1.21$, NS).

However, controlling for the number of communicative acts used revealed the expected mood effect regarding each and every of Grice's (1975) conversation norms, *Fquantity*(1, 65) = 3.12, $p = .08$, $\eta^2 = .05$; and *Frelevance*(1, 65) = 4.54, $p < .05$, $\eta^2 = .07$; and *Fquality*(1, 65) = 3.37, $p = .07$, $\eta^2 = .05$; and *Fmanner*(1, 65) = 4.14, $p < .05$, $\eta^2 = .06$.

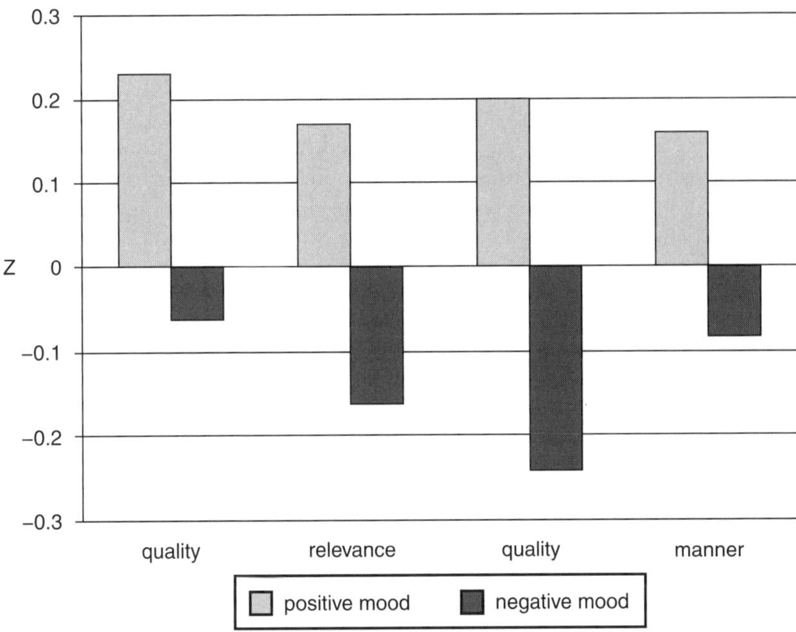


Figure 5.3 Mood and transgressions of Grice's conversational maxims in verbal messages

## Discussion

There is affect infusion on both writing and speaking about both facts and fiction, as evident from our findings that participants in a positive mood wrote about completely fabricated events (Study 1) as well as spoke about a recently experienced, real event (Study 2) in a more abstract fashion than subjects in a negative mood. In fact, these results confirm and extend earlier evidence about mood effects on language abstraction: For instance, in a study by Beukeboom and Semin (2005), happy subjects were more likely to rephrase separate actions (e.g., "reading a book") in abstract *why* terms (e.g., "acquiring knowledge"). To the contrary, sad subjects were more likely to use concrete *how* terms (e.g., "flipping pages"). Furthermore, these authors showed that mood moderates language abstraction in written communications about both private and public events of the past (Beukeboom & Semin, 2006).

Our results add to this literature by showing that mood effects on language abstraction can be traced to differential use of *inferences* about traits or states and action *interpretations*, but not to differential use of action *descriptions*. In both studies, subjects in a negative mood interpreted and evaluated more actions than participants in a positive mood, who in turn inferred more psychological states and character traits. As these three increasingly abstract ways of communicating about persons involve more *substantive, constructive* processing than straightforward descriptions of separate actions, this pattern of results is consistent with the affect infusion model (Forgas, 1995, 2002), suggesting that mood-based differences in both thinking style and language use should only emerge in task components that require a considerable amount of substantive, constructive processing (Fiedler, 2001).

Further, our data show that positive mood may result in greater transgression of conversation norms than negative mood. More specific, happy subjects communicated in a more verbose, redundant, and discontinuous fashion than sad participants, as evident from greater scores on the *manner* transgression index. Happy subjects also used more irrelevant and more untrue communicative acts than sad participants, as evident from greater scores on the *relevance* and *quality* transgression indices, respectively. These results are consistent with past research showing that happy people are less likely to distinguish between relevant and irrelevant information than sad people (Bless, Bohner, Schwarz, & Strack, 1990; Bless, Mackie, & Schwarz, 1992; Petty & Cacioppo, 1986), and recent research demonstrating that positive mood facilitates reconstructive memory processes compared with negative mood (Forgas, Laham, & Vargas, 2005; Storbeck & Clore, 2005).

However, we did not find the predicted difference between positive and negative mood regarding transgressions of the *quantity* maxim except for when controlling for the number of communicative acts used (Grice, 1975). Thus, it seems like individual differences in talkativeness overrode the mood effect on the transmission of actually relevant information. Put another way, affective influences on the amount of pertinent communicative acts seem to only hold true for people in a more or less equally talkative state.

It is interesting to note that subjects who used more abstract terms showed greater transgression of conversation norms ($r$ = 0.50, p < .001), which cannot be due to a coding artifact, as we used different groups of completely independent judges blind to hypotheses and condition. Rather, it seems like communicating in an abstract fashion entails omitting relevant information and committing untrue information, as evident from the correlations between language abstraction on the one hand and transgression of the quantity and quality maxims on the other hand ($r$[*quantity*] = 0.49, $p$ < .001; $r$[*relevance*] = 0.18, $p$ = .08; $r$[*quality*] = 0.32, $p$ < .01; $r$[*manner*] = –0.08, NS). That is, our data suggest that abstract person descriptions (i.e., lots of inferences about character traits and psychological states) should be treated with caution, as they are not only highly informative, but also incomplete and, in fact, questionable as a whole.

## GENERAL DISCUSSION

### *Limitations and Future Prospects*

First, it is advisable to replicate our findings using other types of mood inductions, such as purely auditory, purely visual, or memory-based techniques (Martin, 1990). Further, future studies may also explore language abstraction, transgression of conversation norms, and other aspects of communication style as a function of distinct emotions (e.g., pride, gratitude, fear, and anger; Lerner & Keltner, 2001; Williams & DeSteno, 2008), and personality factors that may be related to processing information in an assimilative versus accommodative way, such as agency and communion (see Chapter 10, this volume).

Also, it should be established that mood effects on language abstraction also occur in the context of indices other than the ones used here, such as the percentage use of articles, numerals, and certain other classes of function words (see Beukeboom, Tanis, & Vermeulen, in press; for a review of the manifold implications of function word use, see Chapter 2, this volume). By analogy, it should be demonstrated that mood effects on transgression of conversation norms do not hinge on Grice's (1975) conversation norms and the corresponding operationalizations implemented here.

More important, future studies should aim at identifying the processes that mediate the observed mood effects on language abstraction and transgression of conversation norms. At this point, the most parsimonious assumption is that happy subjects formed more abstract and more individualized mental representations, and sad subjects formed more concrete and more conventionalized mental representations of the event to be communicated. If so, then follow-up studies should clarify whether mood influenced subjects' event representation during encoding, retrieval, or during both phases, as suggested by the assimilative or accommodative processing model (Bless & Fiedler, 2006). The present studies do not answer this question, as mood was manipulated only before participants were presented with the social interaction to be communicated. However, in a similar set of experiments by Beukeboom and Semin (2006), participants communicated events that they had observed prior to being subjected to a mood manipulation, and the results show that mood during the encoding phase is not a necessary condition for affective influences on language abstraction. It is interesting to note that mood during the retrieval phase may not be a necessary condition either, because the assimilative or accommodative processing model also predicts that mood influences both language abstraction and transgression of conversation norms among people who encode and retrieve the very same mental representation of an event to be communicated.

In particular, it could be that happy participants *strategically shifted to higher levels* of both language abstraction and transgression of conversation norms, because they construed the communication task as a request to *explain* (the event) *in an individual way*—a reframing that is entirely consistent with assimilative thinking ("imposing internal structures on the external world"; Bless & Fiedler, 2006, p. 66). In contrast, it could be that sad subjects *strategically shifted to lower levels* of both language abstraction and transgression of conversation norms, because they construed the communication task as a request to *report* (the event) *in a conventional way*—a reframing that is entirely consistent with the original definition of accommodative thinking ("modifying internal structures in accordance with external constraints"; Bless & Fiedler, 2006, p. 66). In fact, Bless and Fiedler's model offers several reasons for predicting these strategic communication behaviors.

For instance, as positive mood signals that *the social environment is familiar or benign* (Bless & Fiedler, 2006), communicators in high spirits may get the impression that their conversation partner is an in-group member who shares their personal opinion about what information is true, clear, concise, relevant, and irrelevant, and who will appreciate their personal understanding of a matter to be discussed. As a result, they will feel encouraged to *explain* (events) *in an individual way*. In contrast, as negative mood signals that *the social environment is novel or malign* (Bless & Fiedler, 2006), communicators in low spirits may get the impression that their conversation partner is an out-group member who does not share their personal opinion about what information is evidence-based and efficient (Grice, 1975) and who will disapprove of their personal understanding of a matter to be discussed. Hence, they will reason that it is best to simply *report* (events) *in a conventional way*. In other words, it may also be that people use their mood to figure out the communication strategy that is most appropriate for finding common ground on the topic of the conversation at hand (Beukeboom, 2009; Beukeboom & De Jong, 2008).

In addition to predicting such mood-based differences in cooperative communication, the assimilative or accommodative processing model (Bless & Fiedler, 2006) also suggests that there are mood-based differences in *noncooperative communication*. That is, it could also be that speakers in a positive mood deliberately betrayed their conversation partners more often than speakers in a negative mood (i.e., by concealing relevant and conveying irrelevant, confusing, or even untrue information)—consistent with recent evidence that individuals in a positive mood focus more on selfish desires and pay less attention to fairness norms than those in a negative mood (Tan & Forgas, 2010).

In sum, future studies should assess communicators' event representations (e.g., Beukeboom & Semin, 2006) as well as interpersonal intentions to *clarify why* positive mood results in both greater language abstraction and greater transgression of conversation norms than negative mood. In this regard, there is a lot to be learned from receivers' reactions to senders' messages. For example, people who pay greater attention to Grice's (1975) maxims are perceived to be more moral (see Chapter 11, this volume), which suggests that sad communicators feel a greater need to enhance their moral standing than happy communicators. Again, this would be entirely consistent with Bless & Fiedler's (2006) affect-cognition theory, which claims that negative and positive mood signal that the social environment is novel or malign, and familiar or benign, respectively.

Having outlined a number of possible reasons for mood-based variation in both language abstraction and transgression of conversation norms, it should be noted that, naturally, more than one reason may apply at the same time, and different reasons may apply to different communication tasks and settings. To illustrate, historians may *unintentionally* use abstract and concrete language in narrations of glorious and miserable epochs, respectively, because their mental representations are less detailed for positive than for negative events (Unkelbach, Fiedler, Bayer, Stegmüller, & Danner, 2008). In contrast, storytellers may *intentionally* use abstract and concrete language in narratives about glory and misery, respectively, because they want to project that positive occurrences are the rule, whereas negative occurrences are the exception (for a review of the implications of narrative style for both personal and group identity, see Chapters 12, 13, and 14, this volume).

Finally, it is of high interest to investigate whether communicators in the same mood understand and like each other better than conversation partners in opposing moods and, if so, whether this is due to feelings of interpersonal fluency and disfluency (see Chapter 6, this volume) and/or corresponding perceptions of communication accommodation and under-accommodation (see Chapter 9, this volume) that arise from the congruence and incongruence of their language use, respectively.

### *Theoretical Implications*

The findings obtained in the present studies further increase the explanatory power of mood-based cognitive styles for variation in communication style (see Chapter 4, this volume). We conclude that positive mood results in greater language abstraction than negative mood, which is consistent with the idea that happy people focus their attention inward and tend to *transform* information in an abstract, top-down, and *assimilative* fashion where personal goals and integrated knowledge take priority (Bless, 2001; Bless & Fiedler, 2006; Fiedler, 2001). We also conclude that negative mood results in greater adherence to conversation norms than positive mood, which is consistent with the idea that sad people focus their attention outward and tend to *preserve* information in a concrete, bottom-up, and *accommodative* fashion where social norms and separated stimuli take priority (Bless & Fiedler, 2006).

### *Practical Implications*

Effective communication is a critically important skill in everyday life and is significantly related to professional and personal success. The finding that positive mood results in greater language abstraction and greater transgression of conversation norms than negative mood can be of importance in a variety of situations where abstract and individual, or concrete and conventional communicative acts are clearly better suited for the purpose of the given social interaction. Consistent with this idea, positive mood increases performance in communication tasks that mainly require assimilative processing (e.g., formulating requests and disclosing information about the self; Forgas, 1999, 2011), whereas negative mood increases performance in communication tasks that mainly require accommodative processing (e.g., bargaining and persuasion; Forgas, 1998, 2007). To give some more specific examples, politicians who intend to use *counterfactual reasoning* (in fact, transgressions of the conversational maxim of manner; Grice, 1975) to enhance the plausibility of their speeches (see Chapter 16, this volume) should benefit from low-intensity, positive affect, whereas speakers who intend to adhere to the communication norm of *politi-*

*cal correctness* to promote egalitarian values and views (see Chapter 19, this volume) should benefit from low-intensity, negative affect.

In general, the downstream effects of affective influences on language abstraction are easier to predict than the downstream effects of affective influences on transgression of conversation norms, because the interpersonal outcomes of variation in language abstraction (see Chapter 3, this volume) are better known than the interpersonal outcomes of variation in transgression of conversation norms. Using abstract and concrete language is a powerful tool to circulate and challenge stereotypic expectations about (groups of) persons, respectively (see Chapter 18, this volume; Maass, Salvi, Arcuri, & Semin, 1989; Wigboldus, Semin, & Spears, 2000), as abstract and concrete linguistic forms are known to elicit dispositional and situational attributions of responsibility, respectively (Schmid & Fiedler, 1998; Schmid, Fiedler, Englich, Ehrenberger, & Semin, 1996). Further, abstract messages about other persons also influence receivers' (*A*) impressions about the sender (*B*), and the relationship between *B* and the person mentioned (*C*). For example, *A* will like both *B* (and *C*) and will infer that *C* is part of the in-group of *B* if *B* says nice things about *C*; in contrast, *A* will dislike both *B* (and *C*) and will infer that *C* is part of the out-group of *B* if *B* says nasty things about *C* (Douglas & Sutton, 2003, 2010; see also Semin, 2007).

## CONCLUSIONS

In conclusion, the present studies were successful in showing that positive mood can result in greater language abstraction and greater transgression of conversation norms than negative mood, findings that are consistent with Bless & Fiedler's (2006) assimilative or accommodative processing theory. Much remains to be discovered about the necessary, sufficient, and boundary conditions for these effects, and about the communicative intentions and conversational outcomes that accompany mood-based differences regarding these two fundamental aspects of communication style.

## REFERENCES

Beukeboom, C. J. (2009). When words feel right: How affective expressions of listeners change a speaker's language use. *European Journal of Social Psychology, 39,* 747–756.

Beukeboom, C. J., & De Jong, E. M. (2008). When feelings speak: How affective and proprioceptive cues change language abstraction. *Journal of Language and Social Psychology, 27,* 110–122.

Beukeboom, C. J., & Semin, G. R. (2005). Mood and representations of behaviour: The how and why. *Cognition & Emotion, 19,* 1242–1251.

Beukeboom, C. J., & Semin, G. R. (2006). How mood turns on language. *Journal of Experimental Social Psychology, 42,* 553–566.

Beukeboom, C. J., Tanis, M. A., & Vermeulen, I. (in press). The language of extraversion: Extraverted people talk more abstractly, introverts are more concrete. *Journal of Language and Social Psychology.*

Bless, H. (2001). Mood and the use of general knowledge structures. In L. L. Martin & G. C. Clore (Eds.), *Theories of mood and cognition: A user's guidebook* (pp. 9–26). Mahwah, NJ: Erlbaum.

Bless, H., Bohner, G., Schwarz, N., & Strack, F. (1990). Mood and persuasion: A cognitive response analysis. *Personality and Social Psychology Bulletin, 16,* 331–345.

Bless, H., & Fiedler, K. (2006). Mood and the regulation of information processing and behavior. In J. P. Forgas (Ed.), *Hearts and minds: Affective influences on social cognition and behaviour* (pp. 65–84). New York, NY: Psychology Press.

Bless, H., Mackie, D. M., & Schwarz, N. (1992). Mood effects on encoding and judgmental processes in persuasion. *Journal of Personality and Social Psychology, 63,* 85–595.

Casagrande, M., & Cortini, P. (2008). Spoken and written dream communication: Differences and methodological aspects. *Consciousness and Cognition, 17,* 145–158.

Cropley, A. (2006). In praise of convergent thinking. *Creativity Research Journal, 18,* 391–404.

Douglas, K. M., & Sutton, R. M. (2003). Effects of communication goals and expectancies on language abstraction. *Journal of Personality and Social Psychology, 84,* 682–696.

Douglas, K. M., & Sutton, R. M. (2010). By their words ye shall know them: Language abstraction and the likeability of describers. *European Journal of Social Psychology, 40,* 366–374.

Fiedler, K. (2001). Affective influences on social information processing. In J. P. Forgas (Ed.), *Handbook of affect and social cognition* (pp. 163–185). Mahwah, NJ: Erlbaum.

Fiedler, K. (2007). *Social communication.* New York, NY: Psychology Press.

Forgas, J. P. (1995). Mood and judgment: The affect infusion model (AIM). *Psychological Bulletin, 117,* 39–66.

Forgas, J. P. (1998). On feeling good and being rude. Affective influences on language use and request formulations. *Journal of Personality and Social Psychology, 76,* 928–939.

Forgas, J. P. (1999). Feeling and speaking: Mood effects on verbal communication strategies. *Personality and Social Psychology Bulletin, 25,* 850–863.

Forgas, J. P. (2002). Feeling and doing: Affective influences on interpersonal behavior. *Psychological Inquiry, 13,* 1–28.

Forgas, J. P. (2007). When sad is better than happy: Mood effects on the effectiveness of persuasive messages. *Journal of Experimental Social Psychology, 43,* 513–128.

Forgas, J.P. (2010). Affect and local versus global processing: Affective influences on social memory, judgments and behaviour. *Psychological Inquiry. 21*, 216–224.

Forgas, J. P. (2011). Affective influences on self-disclosure strategies. *Journal of Personality and Social Psychology, 100,* 449–461.

Forgas, J. P., Laham, S. M., & Vargas, P. T. (2005). Mood effects on eyewitness memory: Affective influences on susceptibility to misinformation. *Journal of Experimental Social Psychology, 41,* 574–588.

Grice, H. P. (1975). Logic and conversation. In P. Cole & J. L. Morgan (Eds.), *Syntax and semantics: Speech acts* (Vol. 3, pp. 41–58). New York, NY: Academic Press.

Grice, H. P. (2008). Further notes on logic and conversation. In J. E. Adler & L. J. Rips (Eds.), *Reasoning: Studies of human inference and its foundations* (pp. 765–773). New York, NY: Cambridge University Press.

Lerner, J. S., & Keltner, D. (2001). Fear, anger, and risk. *Journal of Personality and Social Psychology, 81,* 146–159.

Maass, A., Salvi, D., Arcuri, A., & Semin, G. (1989). Language use in intergroup contexts: The linguistic intergroup bias. *Journal of Personality and Social Psychology, 57,* 981–993.

Martin, M. (1990). On the induction of mood. *Clinical Psychology Review, 10,* 669–697.

McClelland, D. C., Atkinson, J. W., Clark, R. A., & Lowell, E. L. (1953). *The achievement motive.* East Norwalk, CT: Appleton-Century-Crofts.

Petty, R. E., & Cacioppo, J. T. (1986). *Communication and persuasion: Central and peripheral routes to attitude change.* New York, NY: Springer.

Schmid, J., & Fiedler, K. (1998). The backbone of closing speeches: The impact of prosecution versus defense language on juridical attributions. *Journal of Applied Social Psychology, 28,* 1140–1172.

Schmid, J., Fiedler, K., Englich, B., Ehrenberger, T., & Semin, G. (1996). Taking sides with the defendant: Grammatical choice and the influence of implicit attributions in prosecution and defense speeches. *International Journal of Psycholinguistics, 12,* 127–148.

Semin, G. R. (2007). Implicit indicators of social distance and proximity. In K. Fiedler (Ed.), *Social communication: Frontiers of social psychology* (pp. 389–409). New York, NY: Psychology Press.

Semin, G. R., & Fiedler, K. (1988). The cognitive functions of linguistic categories in describing persons: Social cognition and language. *Journal of Personality and Social Psychology, 54,* 558–568.

Semin, G. R., & Fiedler, K. (1991). The linguistic category model, its bases, applications and range. In W. Stroebe & M. Hewstone (Eds.), *European review of social psychology* (Vol. 2., pp. 1–30). Chichester, England: Wiley.

Semin, G. R., & Fiedler, K. (1992). The inferential properties of interpersonal verbs. In G. R. Semin & K. Fiedler (Eds.), *Language, interaction and social cognition* (pp. 58–78). Newbury Park, CA: Sage.

Storbeck, J., & Clore, G. L. (2005). With sadness comes accuracy; with happiness, false memory: Mood and the false memory effect. *Psychological Science, 16,* 785–791.

Tan, H. B., & Forgas, J. P. (2010). When happiness makes us selfish, but sadness makes us fair: Affective influences on interpersonal strategies in the dictator game. *Journal of Experimental Social Psychology, 46,* 571–576.

Unkelbach, C., Fiedler, K., Bayer, M., Stegmüller, M., & Danner, D. (2008). Why positive information is processed faster: The density hypothesis. *Journal of Personality and Social Psychology, 95,* 36–49.

Wänke, M. (2007). What is said and what is meant: Conversational implicatures in natural conversations, research settings, media and advertising. In K. Fiedler (Ed.), *Social communication* (pp. 223–256). New York, NY: Psychology Press.

Wigboldus, D. H. J., Semin, G. R., & Spears, R. (2000). How do we communicate stereotypes? Linguistic bases and inferential consequences. *Journal of Personality and Social Psychology, 78,* 5–18.

Williams, L., & DeSteno, D. (2008). Pride and perseverance: The motivational role of pride. *Journal of Personality and Social Psychology, 94,* 1007–1017.

# 6

# Intergroup Fluency

## *How Processing Experiences Shape Intergroup Cognition and Communication*

ADAM R. PEARSON AND JOHN F. DOVIDIO

Social psychologists have long known that how people perceive, evaluate, and interpret the actions of others is highly dependent upon their immediate surroundings. Within the field of intergroup relations, this perspective has been the cornerstone of research aimed at understanding how structured forms of intergroup contact can lead to more positive intergroup attitudes and relations (Allport, 1954; Pettigrew & Tropp, 2006). However, even seemingly inconsequential aspects of the environment (e.g., weather, lighting, background music, prior moods) can have a substantial effect on social perception. In recent decades, emerging theoretical perspectives on social cognition (e.g., situated and embodied cognition approaches, Smith & Semin, 2004, 2007; feelings-as-information theory, Schwarz & Clore, 2007; affect infusion, Forgas, 1995, 2008; assimilative/accommodative processing, Bless & Fiedler, 2006; Chapters 3 and 5, this volume) have begun to highlight the role that physical environments play in shaping not only the *content* of cognition, but also the experiential *process* of thinking. *Meta*cognitive experiences, such as the subjective ease or difficulty processing information, have been shown to have a potent effect on judgments across a wide variety of domains, from stock choices to furniture preferences (for recent reviews, see Alter & Oppenheimer, 2009; Schwarz, 2004; and Schwarz & Clore, 2007). Yet, despite growing evidence of its influence, the impact of metacognition on intergroup judgments has remained largely unexplored.

In the present chapter, we first briefly review past research on the role of processing experiences in social cognition and then highlight new findings that suggest systematic effects of processing experiences on intergroup perception and communication. We conclude by considering theoretical and practical benefits of extending an experiential approach to the study of intergroup relations, more generally, and outline several avenues for future exploration.

## FROM CONTENT TO EXPERIENCE: THE POWER OF EXPERIENTIAL CUES IN SOCIAL COGNITION

Research on stereotyping and prejudice has traditionally focused on *what* comes to mind (evaluative and semantic associations) when people think about or interact with a member of their own or another social group (see Correll, Judd, Park, & Wittenbrink, 2010). These approaches typically focus on stable individual differences in not only what people think about other groups, including explicit and implicit attitudes, but also the content of group stereotypes (Blair, 2002; Fiske, Cuddy, Glick, & Xu, 2002). Methodological techniques for assessing intergroup attitudes and stereotypes have similarly focused on the measurement of presumably stable knowledge structures (or schemas)—the affective and semantic representations associated with social categories (Correll et al., 2010; Ferguson & Bargh, 2007).

Although these *content-based* approaches have been fruitful in illuminating systematic sources of bias, they often neglect peripheral features in the environment that may exert additional influences on perception. Indeed, contrary to early theoretical perspectives emphasizing the stability of implicit attitudes (e.g., Wilson, Lindsey, & Schooler, 2000), bias, as assessed by both explicit (self-report) and implicit measures, appears to be highly context-sensitive. A growing literature has now documented the sensitivity of implicit prejudice measures to a wide variety of affective states (Bodenhausen, Mussweiler, Gabriel, & Moreno, 2001), contextual variables (e.g., darkened rooms, social roles; Schaller, Park, & Mueller, 2003; for a review, see Gawronski & Sritharan, 2010) as well as to attitude change interventions (e.g., classical conditioning; Olson & Fazio, 2006).

As Schwarz (2010) recently noted, there is more to thinking than the mere content of one's thoughts. Every cognitive process is accompanied by a host of subjective experiences, from affective reactions and bodily sensations to metacognitive feelings of ease or difficulty associated with any given task. Seemingly irrelevant (or incidental in Bodenhausen's [1993] terminology) emotional and mood states influence people's judgments and actions, often outside of awareness (see Chapters 4 and 5, this volume). For instance, Bodenhausen (1993) induced happiness, sadness, or anger and had participants read about a physical assault by a student with either a Hispanic surname or without a Hispanic surname. Participants in a positive or negative emotional state (states hypothesized to constrain processing motivation) judged the defendant in stereotypic terms and were more likely to find the defendant guilty. DeSteno, Dasgupta, Bartlett, and Cajdric (2004) showed similar effects of incidental emotion on implicit evaluations. When made angry (versus a neutral or a sad emotional state) in an ostensibly unrelated task, participants in their study showed more negative automatic attitudes toward a laboratory-created out-group versus in-group.

Other types of feelings also determine people's responses to others and to elements of their environments. Situated and embodied cognition perspectives (for reviews, see Smith & Semin, 2004, 2007) have emphasized the role of bodily states and sensorimotor systems in human cognition and the emergence of social cognition as the dynamic outcome of the interaction between perceivers and their immediate physical environments. Consistent with these perspectives, proprioceptive feedback from arm flexion and extension (bodily movements associated with approach and avoidance, respectively; Kawakami, Phills, Steele, & Dovidio, 2007) and induced facial expressions (Ito, Chiao, Devine, Lorig, & Cacioppo, 2006) have also been shown to influence social judgments.

Conceptually, *affective experiences* (valenced experiences such as emotions and moods; Clore & Huntsinger, 2007) can be distinguished from *cognitive experiences* (processing experiences generated by information retrieval and integration, including the ease or difficulty of recall, thought-generation, or the ease with which new information can be processed; for a more extensive treatment of this distinction, see Greifeneder, Bless, & Pham, 2011 and Schwarz & Clore, 2007). Empirically, whereas affective experiences may often have a direct influence on judgments (Greifeneder et al., 2010), the interpretation and consequences of cognitive experiences depend upon a wide range of theories of mental processes that participants apply (e.g., that ease indicates frequency, familiarity, safety, truth, etc.; see Schwarz & Clore, 2007).

Despite the ubiquity of metacognitive experiences (indeed, every mental or physical task can be described along a continuum from effortless to effortful) and their remarkably consistent effects across a range of instantiations (Alter & Oppenheimer, 2009), their role in intergroup perception and communication has remained largely unexplored. In the following section, we present an initial framework for examining the impact of processing experiences on intergroup judgments, considering both individual and situational features that may impact processing demands, and report the results of a series of studies testing several components of this model.

## A FLUENCY APPROACH TO INTERGROUP SOCIAL COGNITION AND COMMUNICATION

*Processing fluency*, the subjective ease or difficulty of processing information, has been shown to powerfully influence judgments independent of the content that accompanies the experience (Schwarz et al., 1991). Any mental task can be described along a continuum from effortless to highly effortful, which produces a corresponding metacognitive experience that ranges from highly fluent to highly disfluent. Researchers have manipulated processing fluency using a wide range of experimental methods, including varying visual and audio clarity, frequency, and duration of exposure, and ease of word pronunciation, all producing remarkably similar effects on judgments. Across 18 instantiations, Alter and Oppenheimer (2009) found that whereas the experience of fluency when processing information tends to promote a sense of safety, familiarity, liking, and truth, the experience of disfluency promotes a sense of psychological distance, deception, and risk.

A primary route through which fluency has been proposed to influence judgments is through the *naive theories* (Schwarz, 2004), or lens of ready-made attributions, that individuals take to a given judgment context. For this reason, fluency effects are posited to be highly context-dependent. In one demonstration, Briñol, Petty, and Tormala (2006) had participants read a passage that primed either positive or negative associations with fluency (as indicating intelligence or a lack of intelligence of the reader) and then evaluate a new exam policy written in either easy or difficult-to-read font. Consistent with a naive theory account of fluency effects, the researchers found that the same fluency cue produced divergent effects on judgments depending upon the available theory (in this case, that fluency reflects either an underlying positive or negative attribute). Fluency has also been shown to spontaneously elicit a positive affective state, as captured by psychophysiological measures, which itself can influence judgments (*hedonic marking*; see Winkielman, Schwarz, Fazendeiro, & Reber, 2003). Additionally, disfluent processing can increase the use of affectively primed information during impression formation (*affect infusion*; Forgas, 1995), which can further impact judgments.

Each of the above perspectives suggest that disfluency may be particularly problematic for intergroup contexts, in which people often have more negative expectations and affective orientations (naive theories) and experience more disfluency (both cognitively and behaviorally) compared with intragroup exchanges. People spontaneously experience more positive affect toward and are more trusting of in-group than out-group members (Otten & Moskowitz, 2000; Yuki, Maddux, Brewer, & Takemura, 2005) and retain more information about the ways in which in-group members are similar to and out-group members are dissimilar to the self (Wilder, 1981). In part as a consequence of these dynamics, people generally have more pessimistic expectations for their encounters with out-group compared with in-group members (Mallett, Wilson, & Gilbert, 2008; Plant, 2004). In the United States, interracial and interethnic interactions, in particular, are often marred by uncertainty and distrust (Dovidio, Gaertner, Kawakami, & Hodson, 2002; Plant & Butz, 2006). Whites and ethnic minorities often make different attributions about the same event involving a racial in-group and out-group member (Chatman & Von Hippel, 2001) and have more negative interpretations of out-group than in-group members' intentions, even when their behaviors are identical (Hess, Adams, & Kleck, 2008; Shelton & Richeson, 2005).

Although few studies have directly examined effects of perceptual fluency on intergroup judgments, there are several reasons to suspect that disfluency may enhance intergroup biases. Consistent with the naive theory or attributional account of fluency effects (Schwarz, 2004), empirical studies have shown, for example, that people generally misattribute disfluency to a lack of familiarity (see Kelley & Rhodes, 2002) and that low processing fluency can reduce perceptions of similarity (Blok & Markman, 2005) and reduce trust (see Alter & Oppenheimer, 2009). Within the intergroup domain, Claypool, Housley, Hugenberg, Bernstein, and Mackie (2012) found that fluent faces, manipulated through exposure times and image resolution, were categorized more readily as in-group members and liked more than disfluent stimuli. To the extent people rapidly perceive category distinctions (Grill-Spector & Kanwisher, 2005; He, Johnson, Dovidio, & McCarthy, 2009), we reasoned that disfluency may, therefore, exacerbate the perception of group differences and enhance biases during impression formation.

Building on the work of Schwarz (2004) and Oppenheimer and colleagues (e.g., Alter & Oppenheimer, 2009), in a series of studies, we applied a fluency approach to the study of intergroup perception and communication, considering both individual and situational features that may impact processing demands—shown in Figure 6.1. We first describe a series of studies that explored the effects of incidental processing demands (e.g., clarity of text and images) on intergroup perception. We then extend a fluency perspective to the domain of social interactions, examining fluency processes hypothesized to have a substantial impact on dyadic intergroup relations. Together, the studies test the notion that the mere effortfulness of social perception can serve as a metacognitive cue that enhances intergroup bias. That is, disfluency not only may be more likely to be generated in intergroup, relative to within-group contexts (e.g., Vorauer, 2006 and Vrij, Dragt, & Koppelaar, 1992), but is also hypothesized to carry more evaluative potency in the intergroup domain. Below, we describe empirical studies examining this possibility.

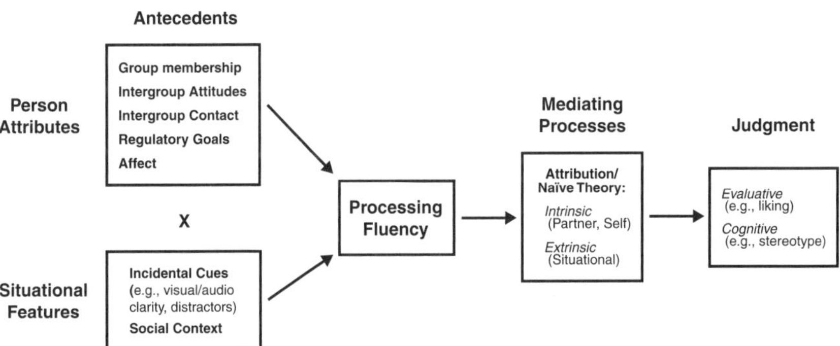


Figure 6.1 Person *x* situation model of intergroup fluency and its effects on social judgment.

Person attributes include perceiver and target influences on information processing examined in the present research. Situational features represent external demands on information processing, including incidental cues and other contextual variables.

## FLUENCY AND INTERGROUP PERCEPTION: EMPIRICAL EVIDENCE

In an initial study (Pearson & Dovidio, 2012, Study 1), we examined the impact of fluent versus disfluent communication on perceptions of *intergroup* relations. Participants were presented with declassified correspondence between two political leaders (see Sampson & LaFantasie, 1996), U.S. President John F. Kennedy and Russian President Nikita Khrushchev, during a time of heightened tension between the United States and Russia (the 1961 Cuban Missile Crisis) and asked about their perceptions of relations between the two nations and similarities between its citizens. Fluency was manipulated by presenting the text in either low or high contrast (see Hansen, Dechêne, & Wänke, 2008; Reber & Schwarz, 1999).

Based on previous fluency work, we hypothesized that processing ease in this context would serve two heuristic functions: To the extent that contentious relations (particularly major international conflicts) are generally seen as complex and difficult to understand, and similarities are typically easier to process than differences, we hypothesized that the experience of difficulty when reading about intergroup conflict would (a) heighten the salience of group differences and (b) be used as a cue to its intractability. More specifically, we, predicted that participants in the low contrast condition would perceive Americans and Russians as less similar, view the crisis as more severe and perceive greater potential for conflict between the United States and Russia in the future, relative to those in the high contrast condition.

The results were largely consistent with our predictions. As expected, participants in the disfluent condition perceived the United States and Russia more as separate groups and American and Russian citizens as being less similar and having different moral values, compared with those in the fluent condition. Additionally, participants who received the disfluent text perceived a greater likelihood of war occurring in the future between the United States and Russia compared with those receiving fluent text. Moreover, the effects of fluency on perceptions of future conflict were mediated by participants' perceptions of the differences (computed as a composite index) between the two nations. These findings offer preliminary evidence that incidental presentation variables such as the visual contrast of communications can systematically impact perceptions of intergroup relations.

In a second study (Pearson & Dovidio, 2012, Study 2), we moved beyond general perceptions of intergroup relations to examine impressions of individual stigmatized versus nonstigmatized group members. In this study, we used a race-modified version of the classic *Donald* vignette developed by Srull and Wyer (1979; see also Devine, 1989) in which participants are asked to read about an ambiguously hostile fictitious person and to rate the person on a series of traits, including stereotypic (hostile) and nonstereotypic evaluative dimensions. In our modified version of the task, the target individual was given either a stereotypically African American (Tyrone) or White-sounding name (Jack). Fluency was manipulated by presenting the vignette in either a *hard-to-read* or easy-to-read font, a manipulation that has been used extensively in fluency research (see Alter & Oppenheimer, 2009).

Our hypotheses were derived from previous work on fluency and racial bias. Prior research suggests disfluent stimuli elicit a less positive affective response, as captured by psychophysiological measures (Winkielman et al., 2003), relative to more fluent stimuli, which can reduce feelings of liking and enhance distrust (see Schwarz & Clore, 2007), and that the impact of experiential cues on impressions increases with less expertise in the domain of judgment (Kirk, Harvey, & Montague, 2011; Ottati & Isbell, 1996; Sedikides, 1995). Given that people spontaneously experience more negative affect toward members of stigmatized racial out-groups (e.g., Blacks; Amodio et al., 2003; Dovidio, Kawakami, Johnson, Johnson, & Howard, 1997; Vanman, Saltz, Nathan, & Warren, 2004) and generally have less experience evaluating them relative to members of the majority group (Bar-Haim, Ziv, Lamy, & Hodes, 2006), we hypothesized that perceptual fluency would have a stronger effect on Whites' impressions of a Black compared with a White target. In particular we hypothesized that experiencing disfluency in an impression formation task would promote more negative judgments of Tyrone but would have little or no effect on judgments of Jack.

The pattern of results largely supported our hypotheses. Participants evaluated a Black-sounding protagonist (Tyrone) more negatively when the description was presented in a difficult-to-read compared with an easy-to-read font but evaluated a White protagonist (Jack) no differently as a function of the fluency condition. No similar pattern of effects was found for participants' stereotypic judgments, suggesting that the effects of processing ease were restricted to evaluative bias. It is interesting to note that we also found evidence for the generalization of fluency effects beyond attitudes toward individual group members: Participants who read about a Black target in disfluent (versus fluent) text subsequently reported less favorable attitudes toward Blacks as a group on a thermometer measure of group attitudes, an effect that was not obtained for attitudes toward other racial/ethnic groups (e.g., Latinos, Whites) or other nonracial stigmatized groups (e.g., elderly). This finding is important because it suggests our fluency effects cannot be attributed to general self-control failure (cognitive depletion), a potential alternative explanation for effects of processing difficulty on intergroup bias (see Muraven, 2008).

Together, these studies offer preliminary evidence of systematic effects of processing experiences on intergroup perception. Specifically, the present findings suggest that, to the extent they reduce processing ease, contextual variables that are seemingly irrelevant to a judgment task may enhance biases during impression formation. In the next section, we extend a fluency framework to the study of dyadic intergroup interaction.

## FROM PERCEPTION TO ACTION: FLUENCY IN INTERGROUP EXCHANGES

Research on fluency, to date, has been a largely asocial enterprise, focusing almost exclusively on antecedents and consequences of fluency at the individual level. Intergroup interactions offer an ideal context for examining fluency processes in vivo, as there is considerable evidence to suggest that, relative to within-group interactions, these exchanges may be particularly effortful (see Shelton & Richeson, 2006; Vorauer, 2006). Indeed, disfluencies in verbal and nonverbal behavior (e.g., hesitations) that are commonly associated with anxiety have been documented repeatedly within interracial and interethnic interactions where evaluative concerns are often heightened relative to interactions with in-group members (e.g., Winkel & Vrij, 1990; Vorauer, 2006). Within interracial interactions, negative expectations often manifest as a mutual fear of rejection shared by members of both majority and minority groups. Whereas racial minorities may often be concerned with being the target of prejudice and show vigilance for cues of bias, Whites may often be concerned about appearing prejudiced (Shelton & Richeson, 2006). These rejection concerns can lead individuals to overregulate interaction behaviors ("over-accommodation," see Chapter 9, this volume), which can fuel mistrust in intergroup interactions (Mendes & Koslov, 2012; Vorauer, 2006).

Although a variety of attributes might conceivably influence processing ease during social interactions (e.g., interpersonal sensitivity; Hall & Bernieri, 2001), we focus on antecedents with demonstrated relevance to intergroup interaction (group memberships, intergroup attitudes, self-regulation; see Figure 6.1 "Person Attributes") and explore their interactive effects with incidental contextual cues (e.g., clarity of audiovisual stimuli; Figure 6.1 "Situational Features," see Alter & Oppenheimer, 2009) on intergroup judgments.

## FLUENCY AND SOCIAL INTERACTION: EMPIRICAL EVIDENCE

Pearson, Dovidio, Phills, and Onyeador (2013) investigated the effects of the ease of self-regulation on Whites' cognitive functioning and interpersonal impressions during an interracial interaction. White participants were recruited to the lab for a study on first impressions in which they engaged in a brief conversation with a Black confederate, for whom responses were scripted. Just prior to the interaction, the participants were instructed to either avoid expressing negative emotions during the interaction, avoid expressing positive emotions, or received no explicit emotion regulation instructions. Participants were told that their partner (the confederate) had been assigned to a control condition and were asked not to disclose to their partner the instructions that they had been given.

Ease of self-regulation was assessed with performance on a Stroop (1935) color-naming task, administered immediately after the interaction, followed by a questionnaire in which participants were asked to judge how friendly the confederate appeared. The interactions were videotaped and observers naive to the experimental conditions and study aims also independently rated the confederates on the same dimensions. Several studies indicate that efforts to navigate interracial interactions can be particularly taxing for Whites with stronger automatic negative associations with Blacks (Richeson & Shelton, 2003). The IAT (for implicit association test; Greenwald, McGhee, & Schwartz, 1998), in particular, has been used extensively to assess automatically activated evaluative and semantic associations with different racial categories and predicts intergroup responses often in ways independent of explicit attitudes (Greenwald, Poehlman, Uhlmann, & Banaji, 2009). Thus we also assessed participants' implicit (race IAT; Greenwald et al., 1998) and explicit (self-reported, Brigham, 1993) racial attitudes in an ostensibly separate study.

Consistent with a fluency account of the effects of regulatory demands, we expected that implicitly biased Whites would perceive their partner more negatively in the more challenging regulatory condition (as assessed by performance on the Stroop task), hypothesized here to be the negative emotion suppression condition. In contrast, because of their hypothesized differing regulatory demands, we expected that low-prejudiced Whites would find the instructions to suppress positive expressions most challenging and that these individuals would therefore perceive their partner more negatively in this condition relative to the control group.

The results were consistent with our predictions. Whereas high implicitly biased Whites showed impaired performance after suppressing negative versus positive emotional expressions during an interracial interaction, relative to a no-suppression control group, low implicitly-biased Whites showed the opposite pattern. Furthermore, the current findings reveal a social cost of more effortful self-regulation. Both high and low-implicitly biased Whites evaluated the Black confederate more negatively in the more demanding regulatory condition (i.e., after suppressing negative expressions for high biased Whites and after suppressing positive expressions for low biased Whites). These effects emerged despite no corresponding differences in observers' independent judgments of the confederates across experimental conditions, suggesting that participants' impressions were affected by the ease of self-regulation rather than the confederates' actual behavior. Together, these findings suggest that self-regulation may contribute to disfluency in social interactions and, paradoxically, may promote bias among those who are working hardest to control it (i.e., participants with stronger implicit biases; see Richeson & Shelton, 2003).

In another study (Pearson et al., 2008), we examined whether temporal disfluency in dyadic interaction (e.g., a brief delay in audiovisual feedback) can not only reflect but also *promote* tension in intergroup interaction, and subsequently undermine both Whites' and minorities' interest in continuing a cross-group exchange. Minimally acquainted White, Black, and Latino participants engaged in intergroup or intragroup dyadic conversation over closed-circuit television either in real time (the control condition) or with a subtle temporal disfluency (a 1-second delay in audiovisual feedback) present throughout the course of the interaction. After interacting, participants reported how anxious they felt, their perceptions of their partner's anxiety, and their reported interest in continuing the interaction.

Whereas previous research has focused on verbal and nonverbal disfluencies as a consequence of anxiety in intergroup interactions (e.g., Vrij et al., 1992), we investigated the role of disfluency as a potential cause of anxiety and disengagement from intergroup interaction. In addition, we examined the role of anxiety attributions (a marker of negative intergroup expectancies; Plant, 2004), as a potential mechanism for the effects of interaction fluency on intergroup (relative to intragroup) perception. More specific, we hypothesized that members of intergroup dyads would perceive their partners more negatively (as more anxious) under a delay, reflecting their more negative attributions (naive theories, Schwarz, 2004) for these exchanges, and report less interest in the interaction as a consequence, compared with those interacting in real time. In contrast, we expected that the perceptions of those in intragroup interactions would be less affected by the fluency manipulation, reflecting perceivers' more positive expectations for these exchanges.

The pattern of results was largely as predicted. We found that, relative to interactions in real time, temporal disfluency amplified felt and perceived anxiety among intergroup, but not intragroup, conversation partners, reduced perceptions that out-group partners were responsive during the interaction and systematically undermined interest in intergroup (but not intragroup) interactions. Rather surprising, intragroup dyads reported less anxiety under delay conditions than when interacting in real time, suggesting a more positive naive theory for disfluency in these exchanges (e.g., as a marker of thoughtfulness).

These findings offer experimental evidence of the differential impact of disfluency on same and cross-group interaction partners at minimal acquaintance. Thus, even well-intentioned behaviors, such as efforts to monitor one's behavior to avoid appearing prejudiced, may substantially increase anxiety and reduce mutual interest in intergroup contact to the extent they produce delays in responding. Practically, this intergroup fluency bias may help account for many stubborn racial and ethnic disparities in law enforcement, such as in vehicle searches and seizures (Engel & Johnson, 2006) and job interviews (e.g., Fugita, Wexley, & Hillery, 1974; Word, Zanna, & Cooper, 1974), during which apprehensive behavior is often used as a marker of deception (Stromwall & Granhag, 2003).

## WHAT CAN FLUENCY TEACH US ABOUT SOCIAL COGNITION AND COMMUNICATION?

Research on metacognition highlights important limitations of traditional content-based approaches to the study of social cognition and communication. Although content models have been fruitful in illuminating some systematic sources and manifestations of bias (e.g., differential emotional responses to social groups; Stereotype Content Model; Fiske et al., 2002) and processes specifying their expression (e.g., application and accessibility models; see Moskowitz, 2010), they have trouble accounting for several perplexing findings. For instance, as has long been noted (e.g., Eagly & Chaiken, 1993), attitudes are often surprisingly poor predictors of how people will behave in any given situation. Within the field of intergroup relations, a weak attitude-discrimination link has often been attributed to socially desirable responding, leading investigators to search for bona fide measures of attitudes that may be less susceptible to the deliberate motives of respondents (e.g., Fazio, Jackson, Dunton, & Williams, 1995). However, a recent meta-analysis by Talaska, Fiske, and Chaiken (2008) that incorporated both explicit and implicit measures of racial attitudes revealed a relatively modest average attitude-discrimination relationship of only $r = 0.26$, with attitudes, thus, accounting for less than 7% of the variance in discriminatory behavior in any given setting. From a content perspective, in which racial attitudes and stereotypes (particularly implicit measures) are presumed to reflect stable, context-independent constructs, this finding is particularly troublesome.

One reason for the rather weak predictive power of attitude and stereotype measures may be the multitude of other inputs—including experiential cues—that may simultaneously impact judgments at any given time. Failure to account for these other contextual inputs may substantially constrain researchers' abilities to predict behaviors, including future judgments. This perspective is suggested by Lord and Lepper's (1999) "matching principle," in which responses at an initial time point are only likely to predict responses at time 2 when the contexts are similar. The present research suggests that one systematic source of contextual information may be simple presentation variables, such as font types, text contrasts, and image resolutions, that affect the ease of processing visual information during impression formation. Future research might also consider whether processing experiences in other sensory domains (e.g., sound clarity, tactile information) or in nonsensory domains (e.g., phonemic fluency, syntactic complexity, semantic coherence; see Alter & Oppenheimer, 2009; word choice, see Chapter 3, this volume) can produce parallel effects to those of visual processing experiences on intergroup cognition.

A fluency perspective may also illuminate new cognitive mechanisms that contribute to the surprising "persistence and pervasiveness" of many contemporary forms of prejudice (Dovidio & Gaertner, 2007, p. 43). There is some evidence to suggest that individuals harboring more subtle forms of prejudice, such as aversive racists (i.e., Whites who endorse egalitarian principles but show evidence of bias on indirect measures; see Dovidio & Gaertner, 2004), may be more susceptible to the influence of processing experiences when forming impressions than those with more extreme attitudes. Indeed, attitude extremity has been shown to be a powerful moderator of fluency effects. Haddock, Rothman, Reber, and Schwarz (1999), for example, found that whereas judgments of participants with moderate attitudes toward a controversial policy (doctor-assisted suicide) were influenced by ease-of-retrieval experiences, those with more extreme attitudes were not. Within the intergroup domain, individuals scoring relatively low on self-report measures of prejudice have been shown to be more influenced by extraneous influences and processing demands (e.g., ease-of-retrieval, Dijksterhuis, Macrae, & Haddock, 1999; see also Dasgupta, DeSteno, Williams, & Hunsinger, 2009 and Kawakami et al., 2007) when judging group members than high-prejudice individuals. In one such study (Dijksterhuis et al., 1999), participants who scored relatively low on a self-report measure of gender bias (the modern sexism scale) judged women more stereotypically when they had to come up with three versus eight gender differences—an effect not observed among those with stronger explicit biases.

The above findings are consistent with growing evidence of the sensitivity of indirect measures of prejudice to a wide variety of contextual variables (see Gawronski & Sritharan, 2010) and offer an information processing explanation for the persistence of contemporary forms of prejudice. That is, those with more egalitarian attitudes on self-report measures may be particularly sensitive to processing experiences when forming impressions of out-group members. Considering the vast array of cognitive operations performed in everyday life, future research on contemporary prejudice may well benefit from additional research examining how metacognitive experiences contribute to conscious and nonconscious forms of bias.

A fluency perspective may also help to explain how simple exposure to out-groups can lead to more positive intergroup attitudes even when Allport's (1954) optimal conditions for contact are not met (Pettigrew & Tropp, 2006). For example, Tam, Hewstone, Harwood, Voci, and Kenworthy (2006) and Turner, Hewstone, and Voci (2007) assessed the effects of contact on implicit and explicit attitudes toward elderly persons and Whites' attitudes toward South Asians, respectively. In general, measures of the overall amount of intergroup contact (e.g., proportion of neighbors who are out-group members) were better predictors of lower implicit prejudice than were measures of the quality of contact (e.g., self-disclosure and emotional closeness), which better predicted explicit attitudes. Interestingly, however, in both of these studies, the effects of contact on implicit attitudes were not mediated by factors that typically mediate explicit attitudes (e.g., anxiety, perspective-taking), but, rather, showed a *direct*, positive impact on implicit attitudes, suggesting the potential value of mere contact for reducing unconscious biases. This finding is consistent with work by Zebrowitz and colleagues on the face overgeneralization hypothesis (Zebrowitz & Collins, 1997), which argues that racial prejudice derives, in part, from more negative evaluations of faces that deviate from experienced prototypes, presumably due to the lower perceptual fluency unfamiliar faces engender (Reber, Winkielman, & Schwarz, 1998).

Evidence for the prejudice-reducing benefits of mere cross-group exposure has been obtained in several studies. Zebrowitz, Weineke, and White (2008), for instance, found that both supraliminal and subliminal exposure to novel Asian and Black faces increased Whites' subsequent liking for a different set of Asian and Black faces, respectively. Similar prejudice-reduction benefits have been observed when participants are asked to simply imagine interacting with an out-group member (Crisp & Turner, 2009) and point to a potential role for processing ease as a mediator of effects of both real and simulated contact on intergroup attitudes. Moreover, with regard to the quality of intergroup contact, a fluency explanation might help account for the finding that more structured intergroup interactions tend to produce more positive intergroup outcomes (Avery, Richeson, Hebl, & Ambady, 2009). To the extent structured exchanges (e.g., behavioral scripts) lessen processing demands commonly experienced in interracial interactions, they may be particularly beneficial for facilitating rapport in these exchanges (see Richeson & Trawalter, 2005). Additional studies might examine whether inducing processing ease using the wide array of other methods available to researchers, as cataloged by Alter and Oppenheimer (2009), might have similarly beneficial effects on intergroup interactions.

A fluency perspective may also illuminate mechanisms for other well-documented findings in intergroup relations. For example, the finding that in-group faces are often better remembered than out-group faces (the *own-race bias*, Meissner & Brigham, 2001), when viewed under the lens of fluency, may reflect higher level (i.e., more abstract) encoding that has been shown to accompany disfluent processing. Alter and Oppenheimer (2008), for instance, found that participants judged cities to be more distant and described them in more abstract terms (e.g., describing New York as a civilized jungle versus a large city) when the name was printed in a difficult-to-read font. To the extent that intergroup perception is experienced as a fundamentally more disfluent process (Vorauer, 2006), out-group members may be subsequently construed and encoded in memory at a more global level of processing (see Förster & Dannenberg, 2010), potentially at the expense of individuating information.

Research on identity and stereotype threat may similarly benefit from an intergroup fluency approach. A fluency account of identity threat (Steele, Spencer, & Aronson, 2002) would suggest that identification with a particular academic domain and assessments of belonging and social fit (Walton & Cohen, 2007) may be directly shaped by the cognitive demands (Schmader & Johns, 2003) and, thus, potentially disfluent metacognitive experiences that stereotype threats evoke. Furthermore, an intergroup fluency framework would suggest that these demands may arise from at least three sources: (a) situational cues that increase or decrease identity concerns (e.g., perceived diagnosticity of exams, Steele et al., 2002), (b) specific coping strategies that people deploy to manage these concerns (e.g., emotion suppression), and (c) as well as a wide range of largely unexplored incidental variables (e.g., exam fonts, clarity of audio and visual aides used in lectures, conceptual clarity of evaluation criteria) that may also impact processing demands in educational and performance settings.

## CONCLUSIONS

The research reviewed in this chapter highlights the dynamic and constructive nature of intergroup perception. Whereas past approaches to the study of prejudice, and social cognition more generally, have typically focused on *what* comes to mind when we form an impression of a member of another social group, the present chapter underscores the importance of considering the processing experiences that accompany these cognitions and may serve as additional inputs into the social inference process. Across a variety of instantiations (e.g., text fonts, low versus high contrast images, asynchrony in video-mediated interactions), we find evidence that disfluent media can enhance intergroup biases during impression formation. These detrimental effects occur primarily in intergroup interaction, where people generally have more negative expectations and affective orientations, and experience more disfluency (both cognitively and behaviorally) compared with intragroup exchanges. Thus, knowledge of metacognitive influences can illuminate how physical and social environments sculpt communication and perception, and may ultimately shape intergroup relations.

The benefits of extending a fluency approach to the study of intergroup processes may also be reciprocal. Research on fluency has traditionally been an individual-level enterprise, focused on effects of incidental cues (text fonts, image clarity, etc.) on individual perceivers, largely removed from their social surroundings. Yet, social interactions, and intergroup interactions in particular, can impose substantial processing demands on perceivers and, thus, offer an especially promising venue for investigating the role of fluency in everyday perception and communication.

Finally, an intergroup fluency framework may also have direct practical implications. A recent survey of business practices revealed that over 96% of Fortune 1000 companies regularly use virtual communications (e.g., voice-over-IP, video conferencing) in lieu of in-person meetings (Plantronics UC Gatekeeper Study, 2010; see also Pew Research Center, 2008)—a potentially troubling statistic, given evidence that more diverse teams often underperform relative to homogenous teams when going virtual (Daim et al., 2012; Jacobs et al., 2005; but see Shachaf, 2008). Understanding how digital media enhance or attenuate bias (e.g., through the speed, familiarity, and reliability of communications) will become increasingly critical as virtual interactions rapidly replace in-person exchanges. A fluency perspective may, thus, shed light on how growing diversity and new modes of communication will shape social cognition and communication in the 21st century.

## REFERENCES

Allport, G. W. (1954). *The nature of prejudice.* Reading, MA: Addison-Wesley.

Alter, A. L., & Oppenheimer, D. M. (2008). Effects of fluency on psychological distance and mental construal (or why New York is a large city, but *New York* is a civilized jungle). *Psychological Science, 19,* 161–167.

Alter, A. L., & Oppenheimer, D. M. (2009). Uniting the tribes of fluency to form a metacognitive nation. *Personality and Social Psychology Review, 13,* 219–235.

Amodio, D. M., Harmon-Jones, E., & Devine, P. G. (2003). Individual differences in the activation and control of affective race bias as assessed by startle eyeblink responses and self-report. *Journal of Personality and Social Psychology, 84,* 738–753.

Avery, D. R., Richeson, J. A., Hebl, M. R., & Ambady, N. (2009). It does not have to be uncomfortable: Behavioral scripts in Black-White interracial interactions. *Journal of Applied Psychology, 94,* 1382–1393.

Bar-Haim, Y., Ziv, T., Lamy, D., & Hodes, R. M. (2006). Nature and nurture in own-race face processing. *Psychological Science, 17,* 159–163.

Blair, I. V. (2002). The malleability of automatic stereotypes and prejudice. *Personality and Social Psychology Review, 6,* 242–261.

Bless, H., & Fiedler, K. (2006). Mood and the regulation of information processing and behavior. In J. P. Forgas (Ed.), *Affect in social thinking and behavior* (pp. 65–84). New York: Psychology Press.

Blok, S., & Markman, A. B. (2005). Fluency in similarity judgments. Proceedings of the 27th Annual Meeting of the Cognitive Science Society, Stresa, Italy.

Bodenhausen, G. V. (1993). Emotion, arousal, and stereotypic judgments: A heuristic model of affect and stereotyping. In D. M. Mackie & D. L. Hamilton (Eds.), *Affect, cognition, and stereotyping: Interactive processes in group perception* (pp. 13–37). San Diego, CA: Academic Press.

Bodenhausen, G. V., Mussweiler, T., Gabriel, S., & Moreno, K. N. (2001). Affective influences on stereotyping and intergroup relations. In J. P. Forgas (Ed.), *Handbook of affect and social cognition* (pp. 319–343). Mahwah, NJ: Erlbaum.

Brigham, J. C. (1993). College students' racial attitudes. *Journal of Applied Social Psychology, 23,* 1933–1967.

Briñol, P., Petty, R. E., & Tormala, Z. L. (2006). The malleable meaning of subjective ease. *Psychological Science, 17,* 200–206.

Chatman, C. M., & Von Hippel, W. (2001). Attributional mediation of ingroup bias. *Journal of Experimental Social Psychology, 37,* 267–272.

Claypool, H. M., Housley, M. K., Hugenberg, K., Bernstein, M. J., & Mackie, D. M. (2012). Easing in: Fluent processing brings others into the ingroup. *Group Processes & Intergroup Relations, 15,* 441–455.

Clore, G., & Huntsinger, J. R. (2007). How emotions inform judgment and regulate thought. *Trends in Cognitive Sciences, 9,* 393–399.

Correll, J., Judd, C. M., Park, B., & Wittenbrink, B. (2010). Measuring prejudice, stereotypes, and discrimination. In J. F. Dovidio, M. Hewstone, P. Glick, & V. M. Esses (Eds.), *The SAGE handbook of prejudice, stereotyping, and discrimination* (pp. 45–62). Thousand Oaks, CA: Sage.

Crisp, R. J., & Turner, R. N. (2009). Can imagined interactions produce positive perceptions?: Reducing prejudice through simulated social contact. *American Psychologist, 64,* 231–240.

Daim, T. U., Ha, A., Reutiman, S., Hughes, B., Pathak, U., Bynum, W., & Bhatla, A. (2012). Exploring the communication breakdown in global virtual teams. *International Journal of Project Management, 30,* 199–212.

Dasgupta, N., DeSteno, D. A., Williams, L., & Hunsinger, M. (2009). Fanning the flames of prejudice: The influence of specific incidental emotions on implicit prejudice. *Emotion, 9,* 585–591.

DeSteno, D. A., Dasgupta, N., Bartlett, M. Y., & Cajdric, A. (2004). Prejudice from thin air: The effect of emotion on automatic intergroup attitudes. *Psychological Science, 15,* 319–324.

Devine, P. G. (1989). Stereotypes and prejudice: Their automatic and controlled components. *Journal of Personality and Social Psychology, 56,* 5–18.

Dijksterhuis, A., Macrae, C. N., & Haddock, G. (1999). When recollective experiences matter: Subjective ease of retrieval and stereotyping. *Personality and Social Psychology Bulletin, 25,* 760–768.
Dovidio, J. F., & Gaertner, S. L. (2004). Aversive racism. In M. P. Zanna (Ed.), *Advances in experimental social psychology* (Vol. 36, pp. 1–52). San Diego, CA: Academic Press.
Dovidio, J. F., & Gaertner, S. L. (2007). New directions in aversive racism research: Persistence and pervasiveness. In C. W. Esqueda (Ed.), *Nebraska Symposium on Motivation: Motivational aspects of prejudice and racism* (pp. 43–67). New York, NY: Springer.
Dovidio, J. F., Gaertner, S. L., Kawakami, K., & Hodson, G. (2002). Why can't we just get along? Interpersonal biases and interracial distrust. *Cultural Diversity & Ethnic Minority Psychology, 8,* 88–102.
Dovidio, J. F., Kawakami, K., Johnson, C., Johnson, B., & Howard, A. (1997). On the nature of prejudice: Automatic and controlled processes. *Journal of Experimental Social Psychology, 33,* 510–540.
Eagly, A. H., & Chaiken, S. (1993). *The psychology of attitudes.* Fort Worth, TX: Harcourt Brace Jovanovich.
Engel, R. S., & Johnson, R. (2006). Toward a better understanding of racial and ethnic disparities in search and seizure rates for state police agencies. *Journal of Criminal Justice, 34,* 605–617.
Fazio, R. H., Jackson, J. R., Dunton, B. C., & Williams, C. J. (1995). Variability in automatic activation as an unobtrusive measure of racial attitudes: A bona fide pipeline? *Journal of Personality and Social Psychology, 69,* 1013–1027.
Ferguson, M. J., & Bargh, J. A. (2007). Beyond the attitude object: Automatic attitudes spring from object–centered contexts. In B. Wittenbrink & N. Schwarz (Eds.), *Implicit measures of attitudes: Progress and controversies* (pp. 216–246). New York, NY: Guilford Press.
Fiske, S. T., Cuddy, A. J., Glick, P., & Xu, J. (2002). A model of (often mixed) stereotype content: Competence and warmth respectively follow from perceived status and competition. *Journal of Personality and Social Psychology, 82,* 878–902.
Forgas, J. P. (1995). Mood and judgment: The Affect Infusion Model (AIM). *Psychological Bulletin, 117,* 39–66.
Forgas, J. P. (2008). Affect and cognition. *Perspectives on Psychological Science, 3,* 94–101.
Förster, J., & Dannenberg, L. (2010). GLOMOsys: A systems account of global versus local processing. *Psychological Inquiry, 21,* 175–197.
Fugita, S. S., Wexley, K. N., & Hillery, J. M. (1974). Black-White differences in nonverbal behavior in an interview setting. *Journal of Applied Social Psychology, 4*(4), 343–350.
Gawronski, B., & Sritharan, R. (2010). Formation, change, and contextualization of mental associations: Determinants and principles of variations in implicit measures. In B. Gawronski & B. K. Payne (Eds.), *Handbook of implicit social cognition: Measurement, theory, and applications* (pp. 216–240). New York, NY: Guilford Press.
Greenwald, A. G., McGhee, D. E., & Schwartz, J. K. L. (1998). Measuring individual differences in implicit cognition: The Implicit Association Test. *Journal of Personality and Social Psychology, 74,* 1464–1480.
Greenwald, A. G., Poehlman, T. A., Uhlmann, E., & Banaji, M. R. (2009). Understanding and using the Implicit Association Test: III. Meta-analysis of predictive validity. *Journal of Personality and Social Psychology, 97,* 17–41.
Greifeneder, R., Bless, H., & Pham, M. T. (2011). When do people rely on affective and cognitive feelings in judgment?: A review. *Personality and Social Psychology Review, 15,* 107–141.
Grill-Spector, K., & Kanwisher, N. (2005). Visual recognition: As soon as you know it is there, you know what it is. *Psychological Science, 16,* 152–160.

Haddock, G., Rothman, A. J., Reber, R., & Schwarz, N. (1999). Forming judgments of attitude certainty, importance, and intensity: The role of subjective experiences. *Personality and Social Psychology Bulletin, 25,* 771–782.

Hall, J., & Bernieri, F. (Eds.). (2001). *Interpersonal sensitivity: Theory and measurement.* Mahwah, NJ: Erlbaum.

Hansen, J., Dechêne, A., & Wänke, M. (2008). Discrepant fluency increases subjective truth. *Journal of Experimental Social Psychology, 44,* 687–691.

He, Y., Johnson, M. K., Dovidio, J. F., & McCarthy, G. (2009). The relation between race-related implicit associations and scalp-recorded neural activity evoked by faces from different races. *Social Neuroscience, 4,* 426–442.

Hess, U., Adams, R. B., Jr., & Kleck, R. E. (2008). Intergroup misunderstandings in emotion communication. In S. Demoulin, J. P. Leyens, & J. F. Dovidio (Eds.), *Intergroup misunderstandings: Impact of divergent social realities* (pp. 85–100). New York, NY: Psychology Press.

Ito, T. A., Chiao, K. W., Devine, P. G., Lorig, T. S., & Cacioppo, J. T. (2006). The influence of facial feedback on race bias. *Psychological Science, 17,* 256–261.

Jacobs, J., Van Moll, J., Krause, P., Kusters, R., Trienekens, J., & Brombacher, A. (2005). Exploring defect causes in products developed by virtual teams. *Information and Software Technology, 47,* 399–410.

Kawakami, K., Phills, C. E., Steele, J. R., & Dovidio, J. F. (2007). (Close) Distance makes the heart grow fonder: Improving implicit racial attitudes and interracial interactions through approach behaviors. *Journal of Personality and Social Psychology, 92,* 957–971.

Kelley, C. M., & Rhodes, M. G. (2002). Making sense and nonsense of experience: Attributions in memory and judgment. In B. H. Ross (Ed.), *Psychology of learning and motivation: Advances in theory and research* (Vol. 41, pp. 293–320). New York, NY: Academic Press.

Kirk, U., Harvey, A. H., & Montague, P. R. (2011). Domain expertise insulates against judgment bias by monetary favors through a modulation of ventromedial prefrontal cortex. *Proceedings of the National Academy of Sciences, 108,* 10332–10336.

Lord, C. G., & Lepper, M. R. (1999). Attitude representation theory. In M. P. Zanna (Ed.), *Advances in experimental social psychology* (Vol. 31, pp. 265–343). San Diego, CA: Academic Press.

Mallett, R. K., Wilson, T. D., & Gilbert, D. T. (2008). Expect the unexpected: Failure to anticipate similarities leads to an intergroup forecasting error. *Journal of Personality and Social Psychology, 94,* 265–277.

Meissner, C. A., & Brigham, J. C. (2001). Thirty years of investigating the own-race bias in memory for faces: A meta-analytic review. *Psychology, Public Policy, and Law, 7,* 3–35.

Mendes, W. B., & Koslov, K. (2012). Brittle smiles: Positive biases towards stigmatized and outgroup targets. *Journal of Experimental Psychology: General.* Manuscript submitted for publication.

Moskowitz, G. B. (2010). On the control over stereotype activation and stereotype inhibition. *Social and Personality Psychology Compass, 4,* 140–158.

Muraven, M. (2008). Prejudice as self-control failure. *Journal of Applied Social Psychology, 38,* 314–333.

Olson, M. A., & Fazio, R. H. (2006). Reducing automatically-activated racial prejudice through implicit evaluative conditioning. *Personality and Social Psychology Bulletin, 32,* 421–433.

Ottati, V., & Isbell, L. (1996). Effects of mood during exposure to target information on subsequently reported judgments: An on-line model of misattribution and correction. *Journal of Personality and Social Psychology, 71,* 39–53.

Otten, S., & Moskowitz, G. B. (2000). Evidence for implicit evaluative in-group bias: Affect-biased spontaneous trait inference in a minimal group paradigm. *Journal of Experimental Social Psychology, 36,* 77–89.

Pearson, A. R., & Dovidio, J. F. (2012). *The social life of fluency: The impact of processing ease on intergroup judgments.* Manuscript in preparation, Yale University, New Haven, CT.

Pearson, A. R., Dovidio, J. F., & Phills, C. E., & Onyeador, I. N. (2013). Attitude-goal correspondence and interracial interaction: Implications for executive function and impression formation. *Journal of Experimental Social Psychology.*

Pearson, A. R., West, T. V., Dovidio, J. F., Powers, S. R., Buck, R., & Henning, R. (2008). The fragility of intergroup relations: Divergent effects of delayed audiovisual feedback in intergroup and intragroup interaction. *Psychological Science, 19,* 1272–1279.

Pettigrew, T. F., & Tropp, L. R. (2006). A meta-analytic test of intergroup contact theory. *Journal of Personality and Social Psychology, 90,* 751–783.

Pew Research Center. (2008, September 24). *Networked workers.* Retrieved from http://www.pewinternet.org/Reports/2008/Networked-Workers.aspx

Plant, E. A. (2004). Responses to interracial interactions over time. *Personality and Social Psychology Bulletin, 30,* 1458–1471.

Plant, E. A., & Butz, D. A. (2006). The causes and consequences of an avoidance-focus for interracial interactions. *Personality and Social Psychology Bulletin, 32,* 833–846.

Plantronics UC Gatekeeper Study. (2010). *Key findings from a survey of US Fortune 1000 decision makers.* Retrieved from http://ucblog.plantronics.com/ 2010/04/survey-says-fortune-1000-companies-quick-to-adopt-unified-communications/

Reber, R., & Schwarz, N. (1999). Effects of perceptual fluency on judgments of truth. *Consciousness and Cognition, 8,* 338–342.

Reber, R., Winkielman, P., & Schwarz, N. (1998). Effects of perceptual fluency on affective judgments. *Psychological Science, 9,* 45–48.

Richeson, J. A., & Shelton, J. N. (2003). When prejudice does not pay: Effects of interracial contact on executive function. *Psychological Science, 14,* 287–290.

Richeson, J. A., & Trawalter, S. (2005). Why do interracial interactions impair executive function? A resource depletion account. *Journal of Personality and Social Psychology, 88,* 934–947.

Sampson, C. S., & LaFantasie, G. W. (Eds.). (1996). *Foreign relations of the United States 1961–1963 Volume VI, Kennedy-Khrushchev exchanges* (Department of State Publication 10338). Retrieved from http://www.state.gov/www/about_state/history/volume_vi/volumevi.html

Schaller, M., Park, J. H., & Mueller, A. (2003). Fear of the dark: Interactive effects of beliefs about danger and ambient darkness on ethnic stereotypes. *Personality and Social Psychology Bulletin, 29,* 637–649.

Schmader, T., & Johns, M. (2003). Converging evidence that stereotype threat reduces working memory capacity. *Journal of Personality and Social Psychology, 85,* 440–452.

Schwarz, N. (1990). Feelings as information: Informational and motivational functions of affective states. In E. T. Higgins & R. M. Sorrentino (Eds.), *Handbook of motivation and cognition: Foundations of social behavior* (Vol. 2, pp. 527–561). New York, NY: Guilford Press.

Schwarz, N. (2004). Metacognitive experiences in consumer judgment and decision making. *Journal of Consumer Psychology, 14,* 332–348.

Schwarz, N. (2010). Meaning in context: Metacognitive experiences. In B. Mesquita, L. F. Barrett, & E. R. Smith (Eds.), *The mind in context* (pp. 105–125). New York, NY: Guilford Press.

Schwarz, N., Bless, H., Strack, F., Klumpp, G., Rittenauer-Schatka, H., & Simons, A. (1991). Ease of retrieval as information: Another look at the availability heuristic. *Journal of Personality and Social Psychology, 61,* 195–202.

Schwarz, N., & Clore, G. L. (2007). Feelings and phenomenal experiences. In E. T. Higgins & A. Kruglanski (Eds.), *Social psychology: Handbook of basic principles* (2nd ed., pp. 385–407). New York, NY: Guilford Press.

Sedikides, C. (1995). Central and peripheral self-conceptions are differentially influenced by mood: Tests of the differential sensitivity hypothesis. *Journal of Personality and Social Psychology, 69,* 759–777.

Shachaf, P. (2008). Cultural diversity and information and communication technology impacts on global virtual teams: An exploratory study. *Information and Management, 45,* 131–142.

Shelton, J. N., & Richeson, J. A. (2005). Intergroup contact and pluralistic ignorance. *Journal of Personality and Social Psychology, 88,* 91–107.

Shelton, J. N., & Richeson, J. A. (2006). Interracial interactions: A relational approach. *Advances in Experimental Social Psychology, 38,* 121–181.

Smith, E. R., & Semin, G. R. (2004). Socially situated cognition: Cognition in its social context. *Advances in Experimental Social Psychology, 36,* 53–117.

Smith, E. R., & Semin, G. R. (2007). Situated social cognition. *Current Directions in Psychological Science, 16,* 132–135.

Srull, T. K., & Wyer, R. S. (1979). The role of category accessibility in the interpretation of information about persons: Some determinants and implications. *Journal of Personality and Social Psychology, 37,* 1660–1672.

Steele, C. M., Spencer, S. J., & Aronson, J. (2002). Contending with group image: The psychology of stereotype and social identity threat. In M. P. Zanna (Ed.), *Advances experimental social psychology* (Vol. 34, pp. 379–440). San Diego, CA: Academic Press.

Stromwall, L. A., & Granhag, P. A. (2003). How to detect deception: Arresting the beliefs of police officers, prosecutors and judges. *Psychology, Crime, and Law, 9,* 19–36.

Stroop, J. R. (1935). Studies of interference in serial verbal reactions. *Journal of Experimental Psychology, 18,* 643–661.

Talaska, C. A., Fiske, S. T., & Chaiken, S. (2008). Legitimating racial discrimination: A meta-analysis of the racial attitude-behavior literature shows that emotions, not beliefs, best predict discrimination. *Social Justice Research, 21,* 263–296.

Tam, T., Hewstone, M., Harwood, J., Voci, A., & Kenworthy, J. B. (2006). Intergroup contact and grandparent-grandchild communication: The effects of self-disclosure on implicit and explicit biases against older people. *Group Processes & Intergroup Relations, 9,* 413–430.

Turner, R. N., Hewstone, M., & Voci, A. (2007). Reducing explicit and implicit outgroup prejudice via direct and extended contact: The mediating role of self-disclosure and intergroup anxiety. *Journal of Personality and Social Psychology, 93,* 369–388.

Vanman, E. J., Saltz, J. L., Nathan, L. R., & Warren, J. A. (2004). Racial discrimination by low-prejudiced Whites: Facial movements as implicit measures of attitudes related to behavior. *Psychological Science, 15,* 711–714.

Vorauer, J. D. (2006). An information search model of evaluative concerns in intergroup interaction. *Psychological Review, 113,* 862–888.

Vrij, A., Dragt, A., & Koppelaar, L. (1992). Interviews with ethnic interviewees: Nonverbal communication errors in impression formation. *Journal of Community and Applied Social Psychology, 2,* 199–208.

Walton, G. M., & Cohen, G. L. (2007). A question of belonging: Race, social fit, and achievement. *Journal of Personality and Social Psychology, 92,* 82–96.

Wilder, D. A. (1981). Perceiving persons as a group: Categorization and intergroup relations. In D. L. Hamilton (Ed.), *Cognitive processes in stereotyping and intergroup behavior* (pp. 213–258). Hillsdale, NJ: Erlbaum.

Wilson, T. D., Lindsey, S., & Schooler, T. (2000). A model of dual attitudes. *Psychological Review, 107,* 101–126.

Winkel, F. W., & Vrij, A. (1990). Interaction and impression formation in a cross-cultural dyad: Frequency and meaning of culturally determined gaze behavior in a police interview setting. *Social Behavior, 5,* 335–350.

Winkielman, P., Schwarz, N., Fazendeiro, T., & Reber, R. (2003). The hedonic marking of processing fluency: Implications for evaluative judgment. In J. Musch & K. C. Klauer (Eds.), *The psychology of evaluation: Affective processes in cognition and emotion* (pp. 189–217). Mahwah, NJ: Erlbaum.

Word, C. O., Zanna, M. P., & Cooper, J. (1974). The nonverbal mediation of self-fulfilling prophecies in interracial interaction. *Journal of Experimental Social Psychology, 10*(2), 109–120.

Yuki, M., Maddux, W. W., Brewer, M. B., & Takemura, K. (2005). Cross-cultural differences in relationship-and group-based trust. *Personality and Social Psychology Bulletin, 31,* 48–62.

Zebrowitz, L. A., & Collins, M. A. (1997). Accurate social perception at zero acquaintance: The affordances of a Gibsonian approach. *Personality and Social Psychology Review, 1,* 203–222.

Zebrowitz, L. A., Weineke, K., & White, B. (2008). Mere exposure and racial prejudice: Exposure to other-race faces increases liking for strangers of that race. *Social Cognition, 26,* 259–275.

# 7

# Multiple Meanings of Communicative Acts in the Reduction of Vicarious Cognitive Dissonance

JOEL COOPER AND MATTHEW D. TRUJILLO

The tradition of social cognition has focused on the way in which people perceive and think about their social world. One of the hallmarks of perceivers' social cognitive schemas is a preference for consistency among cognitions. To extend an example of Leon Festinger's (1957), if we find ourselves standing in the rain, we prefer being wet to being dry. Getting wet may be physically uncomfortable; viewing the world as inconsistent is psychologically intolerable. Our drive to perceive consistency among our cognitions spawned the research tradition of cognitive dissonance and gave rise to more than 50 years of research to understand the ramifications and limits of our consistency need.

Inconsistency, rather than consistency, lies at the heart of research in cognitive dissonance. The latter is the state we seek; the former is the condition that gives rise to an unpleasant motivational state that can be satisfied when the inconsistency is resolved. The signal that alerts us to possible inconsistency usually arises from a communication. We may occasionally say something we do not believe; we may urge others to act in a way that is discrepant from our own behaviors; we may state a preference for a choice alternative that is inconsistent with elements of our attitudes; we may communicate attitudes that compromise our own sense of self-esteem. In these and myriad other ways, social actors often find that their communicative acts have jeopardized their cognitive consistency and placed them in a motivational quandary. Indeed, sometimes it is the very demands of successful communication, such as the need to comply with Gricean conversational postulates (see Chapter 5, this volume), that may inadvertently set off dissonance processes. Research over the past several decades has made it clear that people respond to this quandary with cognitive changes designed to restore consistency.

In a typical research study, people are asked to make a statement that is at variance with their privately held attitude. The state of uncomfortable arousal that results from such an act (Croyle & Cooper, 1983; Elliot & Devine, 1994) motivates people to change the cognitive representation of their attitude to restore consistency with their behavior (Cooper, 2007; Festinger & Carlsmith, 1959). By changing their private attitude, discrepancy with their public communication is eliminated, and the aversive motivational state is reduced.

It has become apparent that people's need for consistency extends to their social groups (see Chapter 6, this volume). Matz and Wood (2005) showed that the anticipation that members of one's social group hold inconsistent attitude positions on a topic induces the discomfort of cognitive dissonance and subsequent efforts to reduce it. Similarly, Glasford, Dovidio, and Pratto (2004) showed that intragroup inconsistency led to efforts to reduce the dissonance through the enhancement of social identity. They further showed that when dissonance is aroused through intragroup inconsistency, only group-based strategies can effectively reduce the discomfort. McKimmie, Terry, and Hogg (2009) showed that dissonance in a group can be exacerbated by the knowledge that other group members are generally consistent in their behaviors and attitudes, and can be reduced by knowledge that other group members act inconsistently.

Recently, our program of research has examined a potent extension of communicatively induced cognitive dissonance, one that is explicitly based on group membership. Cooper and Hogg (2007) proposed that people can experience cognitive dissonance vicariously on behalf of in-group members. If a person were to be merely a witness to the counterattitudinal advocacy of another person, the witness may also experience an unpleasant tension state and be motivated to alleviate this state, often by changing his or her own attitude to bring it in line with the speaker's communication. This phenomenon of *vicarious cognitive dissonance* occurs when the witness and the communicator share membership in a meaningful social group.

In dissonance research, whether at the individual or group level, a process is set in motion by a public communication of a position or a decision. At the group level, the process becomes more complex because the cognitive elements include cognitions at multiple levels of analysis. Consistency of individual cognitions coexists with cognitions at the group level. The motivation for cognitive consistency requires attention to the individual's own positions and attitudes as well as positions adopted by fellow group members individually and the group as a whole.

Although communication is central to the dissonance process, its role has rarely been examined. Most particularly in the group context, a communication is a statement of a position and is also a statement about the essential meaning of the group. It is both an act and a higher order communication about the essence of one's group. In the current chapter, we focus on the meaning and psychological consequences of dissonant communications, especially at the group level. We examine the current state of research on group-based vicarious cognitive dissonance and then present new research on the effects of communications that simultaneously express group members' attitudinal positions and serve as multilevel communications that threaten the essence of the social group (for a discussion of how individuals may respond to an in-group member communication that threatens the in-group see also Chapter 17, this volume). We show that the typical impact of dissonance motivation on attitudes is overridden when the communication questions the essential nature of the social group.

## VICARIOUS DISSONANCE: THE EXPERIENCE OF DISSONANCE AS A FUNCTION OF SHARED SOCIAL IDENTITY

The concept of vicarious cognitive dissonance is based on the observation, frequently overlooked in early work in attitude research, that people's identities are rooted in the social groups to which they belong. The theory of social identity offers a wide-ranging perspective on the relationship between collective self-conception and both group and intergroup processes (for contemporary statements see Hogg, 2005, 2006). It incorporates Tajfel and Turner's (1979) original emphasis on intergroup relations, social comparison, and self-esteem motivation, as well as Turner and colleagues' later analysis of self-categorization and prototype-based depersonalization (Turner, Hogg, Oakes, Reicher, & Wetherell, 1987). During the past 20 years, social identity theory has had a significant impact in areas that include stereotyping (Oakes, Haslam, & Turner, 1994), social influence (Turner, 1991), group solidarity (Hogg, 1993), social cognition (Abrams & Hogg, 1999), depersonalization (Reicher, Spears, & Postmes, 1995), leadership (Hogg, 2001; Hogg & Van Knippenberg, 2003), and extremism (Hogg, 2007).

According to social identity theory, people cognitively represent groups in terms of prototypes—that is, fuzzy sets of attributes that simultaneously capture in-group similarities and intergroup differences. These attributes include beliefs, attitudes, perceptions, feelings, intentions, and behaviors—in short any and all dimensions that can be used to segment the social world into discrete categories that are distinctive and high in entitativity (Hamilton & Sherman, 1996). Prototypes describe, evaluate, and prescribe group attributes.

The process of social categorization perceptually depersonalizes other people. It transforms perceptions of other people from unique individuals into embodiments of the relevant in-group or out-group prototype. Categorization-based depersonalization underpins stereotyping and valenced perceptions of other people.

Social categorization of self operates in exactly the same way. It depersonalizes self-conception and transforms one's own perceptions, beliefs, attitudes, feelings, and behaviors to conform to the in-group prototype. Self-categorization transforms individuals into group members, individual and interpersonal self-concept into collective self-concept, personal identity into social identity, and individual behavior into group and intergroup behavior. Self-categorization generates such well-defined and heavily researched phenomena as in-group bias, intergroup discrimination, ethnocentrism, in-group cohesion and solidarity, in-group loyalty and attraction, and in-group normative attitudes, feelings, and behaviors.

Depersonalization involves assimilation of self and others to relevant prototypes. Thus, within a contextually salient group, self-categorization replaces self-other differences with in-group prototypical similarity or interchangeability. The self-other distinction is blurred into a single, collective self: Self and other are *fused* into a single entity. This fusion gives rise to *intersubjectivity,* where one experiences the other as oneself. Working from different theoretical orientations, Wright, Aron, and Tropp (2002) have also argued that self-categorization extends the self-concept to include others in the self, and research by Mackie and associates (Mackie, Maitner, & Smith, 2007) shows that self-categorization may facilitate a process whereby in-group members experience the emotions of fellow group members.

The fusing of the self with one's group and with prototypical group members requires that identification with the group be strong. The more strongly a person feels about his or her membership in the group, the more central the group is to a person's self-definition and self-concept. Fusing of self and other is heightened when the group's prototype is clear and focused and when the observed in-group member is highly prototypical of the group. Research has shown that people in groups are perceptually attuned to subtle differences among group members in how prototypical they are (e.g., Haslam, Oakes, McGarty, Turner, & Onorato, 1995)—there is a clearly perceived prototypically gradient that engenders both rejection of marginally prototypical members who threaten group integrity and strong endorsement of highly prototypical members (Hogg, 2005). Thus, the process of fusion of self and other members of one's group will be affected by the degree of perceived prototypicality of a specific other member, and moderated by perceived self-prototypicality.

Another aspect of social identity theory that is relevant to the theory of vicarious cognitive dissonance is its perspective on attitude change. The social influence process associated with social identity is referent informational influence (Abrams & Hogg, 1990; Turner & Oakes, 1989). When people identify with a group, they learn the group's normative attitudes primarily from the behaviors of highly prototypical in-group members. It is therefore not surprising that we tend to assimilate our attitudes to group standards (Turner, 1991) or that our attitudes polarize toward positions expressed by group members (Mackie, 1986; Mackie & Cooper, 1984). In short, the behavior and attitudes of in-group members have their greatest impact on those who are highly identified with the group, and it is they who are more likely to be influenced by group norms (Terry & Hogg, 1996). As we shall see shortly, a clear derivation of this fact is that people who are highly identified with their group are the ones who are most likely to experience vicarious cognitive dissonance, especially based on the communication of prototypical group members.

Attitude change as a function of communication and group membership has primarily been viewed as coldly cognitive. The intriguing possibility suggested by the theory of vicarious dissonance, is that self-categorization-based attitude change may occur by a more affectively toned dissonance process. It is an idea especially consistent with Hogg's uncertainty-identity theory—a motivational extension of social identity theory that argues that people are motivated to identify with groups, particularly high entitativity groups (Hamilton & Sherman, 1996), to reduce feelings of uncertainty about themselves and things that relate to or reflect on self (Hogg, 2000, 2007). Vicarious dissonance presumably involves vicarious uncertainty pivoting on conflict between self-relevant behaviors and beliefs.

The important idea drawn from social identity theory is that where common group membership is psychologically salient, social categorization of self and in-group others generates prototype-based depersonalization. Self and others are *fused* because they are viewed in terms of a common in-group prototype—others' attitudes, feelings, experiences, and behaviors can become one's own, particularly when the other is a highly prototypical member of a group with which we strongly identify. There emerges an empathic bond, an affective involvement, and intersubjectivity, which enable one to experience the other as oneself. Not only may this protect against harming the other (cf. Galinsky & Moskowitz, 2000)—after all, the other *is* the self—but it may also allow one to vicariously experience others' thoughts and feelings and to take the role of another in constructing a sense of who one is (see Mead, 1934).

## Dissonance Following from Shared Social Identity

Intrigued by the possibility of a theoretical marriage between dissonance and social identity, we predicted that people's shared social identity would automatically activate a shared dissonance process in communicative situations when a fellow group member is observed communicating an attitude-discrepant position. At the core of vicarious dissonance is the notion that dissonance brought about by the actions of a prototypical member of a social group will lead certain observers, fellow group members, to change their own attitude even though they have no direct responsibility for the dissonance-inducing act.

This possibility was first tested by Norton, Monin, Cooper, and Hogg (2003). In a series of three experiments, Norton et al. assessed the consequences of observing a fellow group member communicate an attitudinal position that was contrary to the speaker's and the participant's private attitude. In one study, students at the University of Queensland observed another student agree to make a speech favoring an increase in university fees, a communicative position that was contrary to the participant's and the fellow group member's private attitude. The participant witnessed the fellow student agree to make the speech favoring fee increases and also witnessed the speechmaker indicate that he or she was privately against that position. From decades of research on cognitive dissonance, we would predict that the speechmaker would have experienced dissonance and changed his or her attitude about tuition fees as a consequence of agreeing to make the speech. We also could predict that the communicator making the speech would experience dissonance if and only if he or she had been given free choice to decline the request to make the speech (Linder, Cooper, & Jones, 1967) and believed that the speech might have a potentially aversive consequence (Cooper & Fazio, 1984). However, in the Norton et al. (2003) studies, the speechmaker was a confederate and not the real participant. The real participant was the observer. Would the observer experience dissonance?

The results of the Norton et al. (2003) study showed that observer changed his or her attitude in the direction of the group member's counterattitudinal communication, but only in the conditions in which the speechmaker would have been expected to experience dissonance: under conditions of free choice and a potentially aversive consequence arising from the speech. In the absence of those two variables, the observer participant showed no attitude change.

The impact of the empathic bond, or intersubjectivity between the group members, was shown in two ways. First, the effect held only if the observer and the speechmaker were from the same social group. If the speechmaker was from a different university and thus did not share a common social identity with the observer, there was no attitude change. Second, even when the observer and the speechmaker were members of the same social group, the impact of the speech on the participant's attitude was a function of the strength of identification that the participant felt for his or her group. In the absence of strong group identification, there was no vicarious dissonance and no attitude change. In a subsequent study, Monin, Norton, Cooper, and Hogg (2004) found that the vicarious dissonance effect was correlated with the participant's degree of empathy. Vicarious dissonance, then, seems to be an empathic bonding between people sharing a common and important social identity.

The data from the Norton et al. (2003) and Monin et al. (2004) studies also revealed that the attitude change effect caused by counterattitudinal communication was accompanied by the experience of vicarious discomfort, similar to the way personal discomfort accompanies personal dissonance (Croyle & Cooper, 1983; Elliot & Devine, 1994; Losch & Cacioppo, 1990). When asked, "How would you feel if you were in the shoes of the person giving the speech?" participants in the high vicarious dissonance conditions responded with high levels of discomfort. On the basis of these data, we concluded that people indeed can experience dissonance vicariously on behalf of another person, provided they feel an empathic bond as a function of their shared social identity. Moreover, the experience of vicarious dissonance results in attitude change in the direction of the fellow group member's communication.

## DISCREPANT BEHAVIOR AS A MULTILEVEL COMMUNICATION

### *The Dilemma of Counterattitudinal Communication*

Other research traditions have examined the impact of a group member acting in ways that are discrepant from the group's position. A comparison of the phenomenological status of the situation we have studied and ostensibly similar situations in prior research reveals some interesting differences. In Schachter's (1951) seminal work on deviation and rejection, confederates serving as group members espoused positions that were at variance with the positions held by most group members. Despite the common in-group bond, group members did not show change in the direction of the deviate's position but rejected the deviant.

In more recent studies, Marques and colleagues presented evidence for a black sheep effect (Marques, 1990; Marques, Yzerbyt, & Lyens, 1988). In this research, as in Schachter's (1951), people whose opinions deviated from a normative group position were derogated and rejected following the expression of their positions (see Chapter 17, this volume). However, the black sheep effect added the further observation that counter normative deviants from one's own in-group were derogated more than were deviants from an out-group. Marques, Abrams, and Serodio (2001), for example, showed university students the opinions of in-group and out-group members concerning student initiation practices at their university. It was normative for students to support initiation practices. However, the opinions of the alleged other students varied in their degree of support for the normative position. When Marques et al. asked the participants how they felt about the students whose opinions they had been shown, they rated those students who had expressed deviant opinions as less attractive than those who had expressed attitudes consistent with the group's position. In addition, being exposed to counternormative attitudes from in-group members caused participants to narrow the range of attitudes that they found to be acceptable.

Our studies appear to show a different effect. When our participants learned that an in-group member had publicly communicated a position in favor of increased tuition fees—a clearly counternormative position—the participants rallied around, rather than rejected, the speaker. Why was there neither rejection nor derogation? The apparent difference in findings is testimony to what is special about vicarious dissonance. The in-group member simultaneously violated the group norm and the speaker's own position. At one level, the explicit communication was in favor of a position that was contrary to the group's norm. At a more subtle level, it communicated the dissonance dilemma—that is, acquiescing to the will of the experimenter who requested the pro-fee statement. For in-group members, the social pain caused by the dissonance dilemma was clearly understood. They vicariously felt his or her discomfort and expressed their attitudinal support for their fellow in-group member. Our findings support this interpretation such that participants reported experiencing vicarious discomfort prior to changing their attitude to be more in-line with communicative behavior of their fellow in-group member but not after. This finding suggests the act of attitude change in support of their fellow in-group member appeared to have alleviated the discomfort felt by the participant. In the wake of dissonance, the tendency to reject and derogate an in-group member was trumped by the experience of vicarious dissonance.

### *Counterattitudinal Communications That Threaten the Group*

The act of communication-induced attitude change is not an easy one. It may require a good deal of psychological work and reorganization. A changed attitude implies downstream changes in the cognitive architecture that supported one's original attitude (see Chapter 17, this volume). If a person formerly believed that it was wrong to raise university fees, it is likely that myriad other cognitions accompanied that attitude. There are beliefs about the role of fees in university governance, knowledge of alternate sources of income, and attitudes about egalitarianism among many other possible cognitions into which an anti-fee increase attitude comfortably fit. To change that attitude implies a change in other beliefs, values, or behaviors to accommodate the newly changed attitude.

We believe that the cognitive work in which people engage is based on the premise that maintaining coherence with the social in-group is an important source of reward and esteem for individuals. They will engage in the psychological work for either of two reasons. First, its effect is to offer support to a group member who has been placed in the dissonance dilemma. Knowing that the group member is likely to change his or her attitude following an attitude discrepant remark, people change their own position to offer the support that buttresses the esteem of the group. Second, knowing that the group member is likely to change his or her attitude provides statistical evidence that the group norm will change, albeit slightly, following the speechmaker's change. Thus, to support the in-group member and to adapt to a new in-group norm, people change their attitude.

People take a different stance when the communication suggests something more draconian. When a group member's communication indicates that an essential aspect of the group may be threatened, we suggest that group members will not support the communication or the communicator (see Chapter 17, this volume). Consider a value that lies at the heart of group identity, such as being egalitarian and nonracist. A group member who delivers a racist statement threatens the antiracist core value of the group. It is illustrative of our premise that a statement can have multiple levels of communication. At the basic level, a racist statement may be a communication about a group member's position on racial equality. At a more complex level, understanding that the group member may have acceded to a request to make a statement contrary to his or her attitude may lead to intersubjectivity and empathy, leading to increased support for the group member. However, there is still a more complex level in which a statement that strikes at the group's core values ceases to produce empathy despite the group member's assertion that he or she does not believe the position advocated in the statement.

We believe that when communications challenge important group identity values, group members must make an important initial judgment to determine whether vicarious dissonance will lead to attitude change supportive of the group member or to rejection of the member from the group. We noted earlier that group members who understand that a counternormative message is also counterattitudinal tend to experience intersubjectivity and empathy with the communicator. However, the importance of the threatened value makes this judgment all the more difficult. How credible is the protestation of a group member that he or she does not really believe what he or she has been asked to communicate when it is antithetical to a core value? We believe this a *hard sell*, and we predict that in situations in which counterattitudinal messages strike at the group's core value, the less it will be perceived as counterattitudinal and the less likely it will be for group members to offer their empathy and attitudinal support to a group member. Derogation and rejection from the group are more likely. Moreover, derogation and rejection will also be a function of group identity with those group members who feel more strongly identified with their group showing the greatest amount of rejection and derogation.

## PERCEPTIONS OF RACISM AND VICARIOUS DISSONANCE: SOME NEW EVIDENCE

To conduct research on reactions to counterattitudinal behaviors that communicate social identity threat, we first had to find a value that was perceived as important to our sample—Princeton University undergraduates. Pilot testing indicated that Princeton students view being nonracist as an important part of their Princeton identity. Prejudice, in addition to being antithetical to Princeton undergraduates' identity, is easily communicated through our behavior and language (see also Chapters 18 and 19, this volume). Thus, we set the counterattitudinal behavior used in our studies such that it could be viewed as communicating aspects of the counterattitudinal actor's racial prejudice. More specific, the domain we chose for our racialized counterattitudinal behavior was that of budget cuts to minority student organizations on campus. Our pilot tested the attitudes of Princeton students regarding cutting the budget of minority student organizations. A vast majority of Princeton students reported that they are against cutting the budget of minority student organizations, and when asked to suggest a percentage to be cut to minority student organizations, individuals suggested an average of 20%. We also asked participants to provide a percentage to be cut that they imagine someone who is racially motivated would suggest, to which they responded with 60%.

In the first study, we brought participants into the lab ostensibly for a study on *speech patterns*. The study followed the procedures used in previous vicarious dissonance research (Norton et al., 2003), where participants listened to a speech supposedly provided by another participant. The speech consisted of the other participants stating that they are against cutting the budget of minority student organizations yet later freely making arguments for such action. We instantiated aversive consequences by claiming that the dean's office would see the arguments made for cutting the budget and use them to determine if actual budget cuts should be made. Two days prior to entering the lab, we recorded the strength of the participants' Princeton identity and their support for cutting the budget of minority student organizations. After participants listened to the speech, we measured their level of self-discomfort, other-discomfort, vicarious-discomfort, and degree of attitude change in support of cutting the budget of minority student organizations. Moreover, we measured how typical the participants viewed the speechmakers to be as Princeton students and how racially motivated the participants perceived the speech to be. Consistent with previous research on vicarious dissonance, we expected participants who did not (versus did) perceive the speech as racially motivated to express greater attitude change. Alternatively, we expected participants who did (versus did not) perceive the speech as racially motivated to perceive the speechmaker as less typical. Both of these effects should be stronger for high identifiers compared with low identifiers.

Indeed, findings from the study supported of our predictions. Findings indicated that the relationship between Princeton identity and attitude change was positive whereas the relationship between perceptions of racial motivation and attitude change was negative. These findings were qualified by an identity by perceptions of racial motivation interaction such that there was a significant positive relationship between identity and attitude change for participants who did not perceive the speech as racially motivated—but, as predicted, this was not the case for participants who perceived the speech as racially motivated—see Figure 7.1. Furthermore, for participants who did not perceive the speech as racially motivated, identity was positively associated with their perceptions of speechmaker typicality and negatively associated with feelings of self-discomfort. For participants who perceived the speech as racially motivated, however, identity was negatively associated with their perceptions of speechmaker typicality and positively associated with feelings of discomfort.

Findings from this first study suggest that reactions to witnessing counterattitudinal communication from an in-group member varies as a function of what one perceives that behavior as communicating. When the counterattitudinal message is perceived as threatening to their social identity, in this case as racially motivated, individuals respond by casting out the actor rather than changing their attitude to be in agreement with the behavior as seen in previous vicarious dissonance work.

Although the first study provided good initial support for our predictions, we ran a second study to address some limitations. The results from the first study are correlational in nature, so we were unable to make causal claims regarding our findings. Second, it is important that we determine that our effects were not simply due to the fact that the counterattitudinal behavior was also counternormative. In the second study, we adapted a distinction suggested by Efron and Monin (2010) in a study on moral licensing. Efron and Monin showed

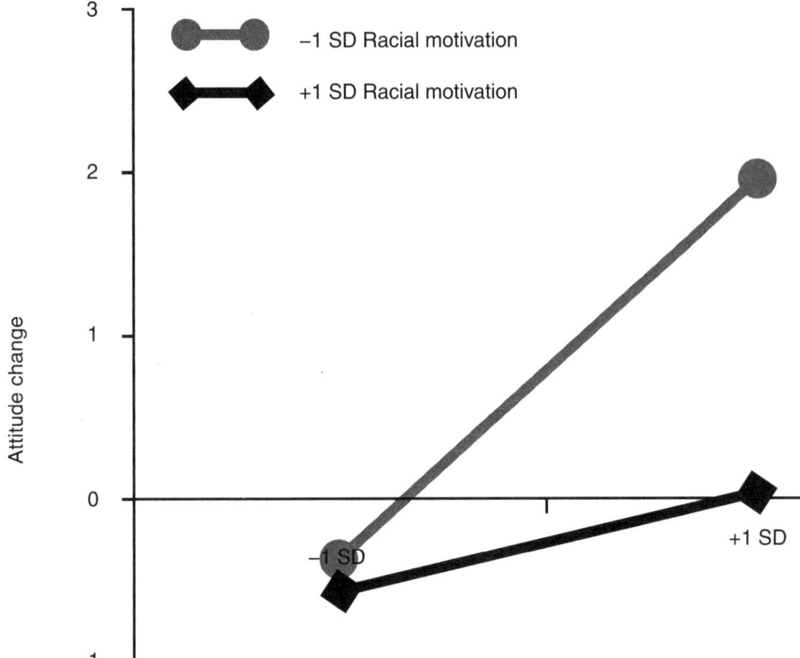


Figure 7.1 Degree of attitude change in support of cutting the budget of minority student organizations for participants who perceived the speechmaker as racially motivated One standard deviation above the mean, and participants did not perceive the speechmaker as racially motivated; one standard deviation below the mean, as a function of Princeton identity.

that people will be forgiven their trespasses, even on racist policies, if they had previously acted in a nonracist way *and* their racist communication was ambiguous. (See also Chapter 11, this volume, for a discussion of the relationship of social communication and morality.) If the statement was unambiguously racist, then no amount of prior good deeds could save them from derogation by social perceivers. In our second study, we systematically manipulated the degree of budget cuts that the speechmaker proposed to bring down upon minority organizations, ranging from those that could be considered ambiguously racist to those that were unambiguously racist.

Pilot data had indicated that the normative view of the degree to which budgets should be cut for minority organizations, in the wake of the university's fiscal shortfall, was 20%. We told our participants that the speechmaker was aware that most in-group members (Princeton University students) had suggested 20% reductions. In all conditions, the speechmaker indicated that he or she was personally against cutting the budget. At this point, the conditions varied. In the *normative control* condition, the participant heard the speechmaker agree to advocate for budget cuts and suggested a 20% reduction. In the *ambiguously racist* condition, the speechmaker agreed to give a budget-cutting speech but chose to advocate a 30% reduction. In the *unambiguously racist* condition, the speechmaker chose to advocate a 60% reduction in funds. We predicted that vicarious dissonance would cause participants in the 30% condition to support cutting the budget more than participants in the other two conditions whereas participants in the 60% condition would derogate the speechmaker by rating him or her as a less worthy and typical group member than participants in the other two conditions. We expected that both of these effects would be moderated by the participants' degree of social identity with their group.

Findings supported of our predictions. Participants who listened to the ambiguously racist speech changed their attitude to be in greater support of cutting the budget of minority student organizations more than participants who heard the other two speeches. Moreover, participants who heard the ambiguously speech, but not those who heard the other two speeches, changed their attitude as a function of their identity. Identity also negatively predicted participants' perceptions of the speechmaker's typicality, but only for participants who heard the unambiguously racist speech—who, compared with participants who heard the other two speeches, perceived the speechmakers as less typical—see Figure 7.2.

These findings provide initial support for the notion that group members respond to communications at multiple levels. Unlike other counterattitudinal communications, people respond to observing counterattitudinal behavior that communicates a social identity threat in a manner other than attitude change. Observers of threatening counterattitudinal behavior on behalf of an in-group member, rather than change their attitude, effectively treat the counterattitudinal actor as an out-group member (see Chapter 17, this volume). Compared

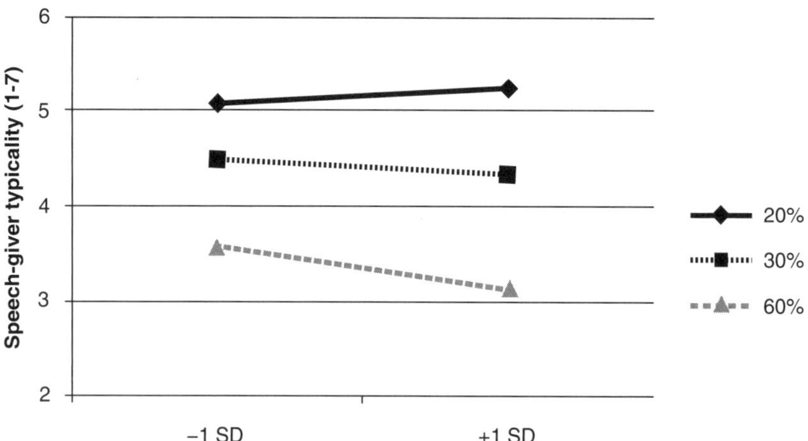


Figure 7.2 Degree to which participants perceived the normative (20%), ambiguously racist (30%), and unambiguously racist (60%) speechmakers as typical Princeton students as a function of participants' Princeton identity

with attitude change, treating an in-group member as an out-group member is a more direct means of dealing with the dissonance of the communication created by their threatening counterattitudinal behavior while simultaneously protecting the integrity of the group.

In the two studies presented above, individuals alleviated communication-induced dissonance by perceiving the counterattitudinal actor as atypical, but there may also be other dissonance reduction strategies that individuals may use. These strategies all serve as a means of protecting the group from the counterattitudinal actor and include changing the perceptions of group heterogeneity and derogating the counterattitudinal actor. Surely there is still much work to be done, primarily to ensure that the findings above are indeed dissonance findings. Future studies should test for these effects while also manipulating fundamental antecedents of dissonance such as choice or aversive consequences. We would not expect that individuals would protect their social group from an in-group member who is forced to engage in an identity threatening counterattitudinal behavior or whose behavior does not lead to aversive consequences. An another intriguing line of potential research would be to investigate how various forms of affirmation, including self, group, and other, may impact how individuals respond to witnessing social identity threatening counterattitudinal behaviors.

## CONCLUSIONS

For decades, psychology has been guided, at least in part, by the proposition that people prefer consistency among their cognitions. Although typically conceived as an intrapsychic phenomenon, recent research has made it clear that the preference for consistency exists at the interpersonal and intergroup levels as well. Communication is crucial to the process by which people infer the degree of consistency or dissonance that occurs in a social situation. We have argued in this chapter that communication is a multilevel process that can be used to infer a person's attitude, to experience intersubjectivity and therefore vicarious dissonance, or to feel threatened by the undermining of group values that lie at the heart of social identity. Understanding the level at which a communication will be perceived is key to understanding when group members will be embraced for their counterattitudinal advocacy or ostracized from their social group.

## REFERENCES

Abrams, D., & Hogg, M. A. (1990). Social identification, self-categorization and social influence. *European Review of Social Psychology, 1*, 195–228.

Abrams, D., & Hogg, M. A. (Eds.). (1999). *Social identity and social cognition*. Oxford, England: Blackwell.

Cooper, J. (2007). *Cognitive dissonance: Fifty years of a classic theory*. London, England: Sage.

Cooper, J., & Fazio, R. H. (1984). A new look at dissonance theory. In L. Berkowitz (Ed.), *Advances in experimental social psychology* (Vol. 17, pp. 229–262). Hillsdale, NJ: Erlbaum.

Cooper, J., & Hogg, M. A. (2007). Feeling the anguish of others: A theory of vicarious dissonance. In M. P. Zanna (Ed.), *Advances in experimental social psychology* (Vol. 39). San Diego, CA: Academic Press.

Croyle, R., & Cooper, J. (1983). Dissonance arousal: Physiological evidence. *Journal of Personality and Social Psychology, 45,* 782–791.

Efron, D. A. & Monin, B. (2010). Letting people off the hook: When do good deeds excuse transgressions? *Personality and Social Psychology Bulletin, 36*, 1618–1634.

Elliot, A. J., & Devine, P. G. (1994). On the motivational nature of cognitive dissonance: Dissonance as psychological discomfort. *Journal of Personality and Social Psychology, 67,* 382–394.

Festinger, L. (1957). *A theory of cognitive dissonance.* Stanford, CA: Stanford University Press.

Festinger, L., & Carlsmith, J. M. (1959). Cognitive consequences of forced compliance. *Journal of Abnormal and Social Psychology, 58,* 203–210.

Galinsky, A. D., & Moskowitz, G. B. (2000). Perspective-taking: Decreasing stereotype expression, stereotype accessibility, and in-group favoritism. *Journal of Personality and Social Psychology, 78,* 509–530.

Glasford, E. E., Dovidio, J. F. & Pratto, F. (2004). I continue to feel so good about us: In-group identification and the use of social identity-enhancing strategies to reduce intragroup dissonance. *Personality and Social Psychology Bulletin, 35,* 415–427.

Hamilton, D. L., & Sherman, S. J. (1996). Perceiving personal and groups. *Psychological Review, 103,* 336–355.

Haslam, S. A., Oakes, P. J., McGarty, C., Turner, J. C., & Onorato, S. (1995). Contextual changes in the prototypicality of extreme and moderate outgroup members. *European Review of Social Psychology, 4,* 85–111.

Hogg, M. A. (1993). Group cohesiveness: A critical review and some new directions. *European Review of Social Psychology, 4,* 85–111.

Hogg, M. A. (2000). Subjective uncertainty reduction through self-categorization: A motivational theory of social identity processes. *European Review of Social Psychology,* 223–255.

Hogg, M. A. (2001). A social identity theory of leadership. *Personality and Social Psychology Review.*

Hogg, M. A. (2005). The social identity perspective. In S. A. Wheelan (Ed.), *The handbook of group research and practice* (pp. 133–157). Thousand Oaks, CA: Sage.

Hogg, M. A. (2006). Social identity theory. In P. J. Burke (Ed.), *Contemporary social psychological theories* (pp. 111–136). Palo Alto, CA: Stanford University Press.

Hogg, M. A. (2007). Uncertainty-identity theory. In M. P. Zanna (Ed.), *Advances in experimental and social psychology* (Vol. 39, pp. 69–126). San Diego, CA: Academic Press.

Hogg, M. A., & Van Knippenberg, D. (2003). Social identity and leadership processes in groups. In M. P. Zanna (Ed.), *Advances in experimental social psychology* (Vol. 35, pp. 1–52). San Diego, CA: Academic Press.

Linder, D. E., Cooper, J., & Jones, E. E. (1967). Decision freedom as a determinant of the role of incentive magnitude in attitude change. *Journal of Personality and Social Psychology, 6,* 245–254.

Losch, M. E., & Cacioppo, J. T. (1990). Cognitive dissonance may enhance sympathetic tonus, but attitudes are changed to reduce negative affect rather than arousal. *Journal of Experimental Social Psychology, 26,* 289–304.

Mackie, D. M. (1986). Social identification effects in group polarization. *Journal of Personality and Social Psychology, 50,* 720–728.

Mackie, D., & Cooper, J. (1984). Attitude polarization: The effects of group membership. *Journal of Personality and Social Psychology, 46,* 575–585.

Mackie, D. M., Maitner, A. T., & Smith, E. R. (2007). Intergroup emotions theory. In T. D. Nelson (Ed.), *Handbook of prejudice, stereotyping, and discrimination*. Mahwah, NJ: Erlbaum.

Marques, J. M. (1990). The black sheep effect: Out-group homogeneity in social comparison settings. In D. Abrams & M. A. Hogg (Eds.), *Social identity theory: Constructive and critical advances* (pp. 131–151). London, England: Harvester Wheatsheaf.

Marques, J. M., Abrams, D., & Serodio, R. G. (2001). Being better by being right: Subjective group dynamics and derogation of the in-group deviants when generic norms are undermined. *Journal of Personality and Social Psychology, 81*, 436–447.

Marques, J. M., Yzerbyt, V. Y., & Lyens, J-P. (1988). The black sheep effect: Judgmental extremity towards in-group members as a function of group identification. *European Journal of Social Psychology, 18*, 1–16.

Matz, D. C., & Wood, W. (2005). Cognitive dissonance in groups: The consequences of disagreement. *Journal of Personality and Social Psychology, 88*, 22–37.

McKimmie, B., Terry, D. J., & Hogg, M. A. (2009). Dissonance reduction in the context of group membership: The role of metaconsistency. *Journal of Personality and Social Psychology, 13*, 103–119.

Mead, G. H. (1934). *Mind, self, and society: From the standpoint of a social behaviorist*. Chicago, IL: University of Chicago Press.

Monin, B., Norton, M. I., Cooper, J., & Hogg, M. A. (2004). Reacting to an assumed situation vs. conforming to an assumed reaction: The role of perceived speaker attitude in vicarious dissonance. *Group Processes and Intergroup Relations, 7*, 207–220.

Norton, M. I., Monin, B., Cooper, J., & Hogg, M. A. (2003). Vicarious dissonance: Attitude change from the inconsistency of others. *Journal of Personality and Social Psychology, 85*, 47–62.

Oakes, P. J., Haslam, S. A., & Turner, J. C. (1994). *Stereotyping and social reality*. Oxford, England: Blackwell.

Reicher, S. D., Spears, R., & Postmes, T. (1995). A social identity model of deindividuation phenomena. *European Review of Social Psychology, 6*, 161–198.

Schachter, S. (1951). Deviation, rejection and communication. *Journal of Abnormal and Social Psychology, 46*, 190–207.

Tajfel, H., & Turner, J. C. (1979). An integrative theory of intergroup conflict. In W. G. Austin & S. Worchel (Eds.), *The social psychology of intergroup relations* (pp. 33–47). Monterey, CA: Brooks-Cole.

Terry, D. J., & Hogg, M. A. (1996). Group norms and the attitude-behavior relationship. A role for group identification. *Personality and Social Psychology Bulletin, 22*, 776–793.

Turner, J. C. (1991). *Social influence*. Bristol, England: Open University Press.

Turner, J. C., Hogg, M. A., Oakes, P. J., Reicher, S. D., & Wetherell, M. S. (1987). *Rediscovering the social group: A self-categorization theory*. Oxford, England: Blackwell.

Turner, J. C., & Oakes, P. J. (1989). Self-categorization and social influence. In P. B. Paulus (Ed.), *The psychology of group influence* (2nd ed., pp. 233–275). Hillsdale, NJ: Erlbaum.

Wright, S. C., Aron, A., & Tropp, L. R. (2002). Including others (and groups) in the self: Self-expansion and intergroup relations. In J. P. Forgas & K. D. Williams (Eds.), *The social self: Cognitive, interpersonal, and intergroup perspectives* (pp. 343–363). New York, NY: Psychology Press.

# Part 2

# Cognition and Communication in Dyadic Encounters

# 8

# Models of Communication, Epistemic Trust, and Epistemic Vigilance

MIKHAIL KISSINE AND OLIVIER KLEIN

## INTRODUCTION

Because most social interactions involve routine use of language, one of the questions that stands prominently on the agenda of social psychology is of how people come to believe what they are told. In particular, it is the bread and butter of persuasion research. But we also come to believe many things others tell us without their necessarily pursuing a persuasive goal. When your neighbor brings up the persistent rain during his holidays in France, you will probably unquestioningly consider his description of the weather as accurate, and so even if you were yourself in Indonesia at the time. In such mundane examples, although the speaker is not pursuing any specific persuasive strategy, for the listener, believing the communicated information is a routine activity that constitutes the fabric of social interaction—and makes it possible. And yet, in spite of their importance to social life, such ordinary instances of belief validation have largely fallen out of the scope of social psychology.[1]

The most straightforward issue such unexceptional validation processes raise is that of the connection between grasping the content of a statement, and believing it. Obviously, this distinction is not only conceptual as one can mentally represent the reference of false statements (e.g., Brussels lies under the Mediterranean sun) while knowing that they are false. The question is rather how do hearers switch from one to the other. Is grasping without believing always prior to believing? Or do we automatically believe whatever we understand, such that realizing that a statement is false entails unbelieving it?

One might think this issue occupies a central place in linguistics, and more specifically in pragmatics, a subfield devoted to the study of language use. Many, if not most, linguists adhere to a dominant view, inspired by Grice's (1989), according to which verbal understanding follows a tortuous inferential route, based on assumptions about speaker's communicative intentions. As shown below, such a take on utterance interpretation entails that any communicated information has to be assessed before being translated into belief. This consequence went largely unquestioned, except by a minority who argue that, just as you (generally) believe what your eyes see, you (generally) believe what you are told until proven otherwise. Recently, however, proponents of the classic, Grice-inspired position have undertaken to actively endorse and defend the hypothesis that there are no communication-based beliefs without prior filtering (Sperber et al. 2010).

Although it remains largely unsettled, the question of validation of communicated information is thus central both to social psychology and to pragmatics. In this paper, we attempt to clarify the debate. The position that we defend is essentially the minority view. Yet, we do so in a nuanced way. The main claim of the paper is the following. Acquiring beliefs from speech is as direct as perception; however, this process may be mediated by a series of domain-specific and independent filters, so that in some cases, information is rejected without having been previously integrated among the hearer's beliefs. In the next section, we expose in more detail two competing conceptions of communication, the inferential and the direct perception models, and focus on their consequences regarding vigilance toward communicated information. The relationship between communication and epistemic vigilance can be assessed from at least two standpoints. First, there exists experimental research relevant to this issue. Second, any claim about such a link should be evolutionary plausible. In third section, we propose a critical survey of the relevant experimental evidence and argue that existing data are incompatible with the inferential model. Next, we argue that, from an evolutionary point of view, the most plausible model of communication is that of direct perception, gradually supplemented with various epistemic filters. Finally, we flag two important programs of research in social psychology that could be profitably reinterpreted in the light of the direct perception model.

## TWO MODELS OF COMMUNICATION

Let us now consider the two conflicting pragmatic models that we mentioned above. The first—and by far the most widespread one—stems from Grice (1989). The key idea is that interpretative processes can be reconstructed as an attribution of complex communicative intentions to the speaker. Although it is not clear that Grice himself conceived of this inferential mechanism as a psychologically valid model, rather than as a mere rational reconstruction of speaker's meaning (see Saul, 2002), it has been subsequently promoted as a cognitive claim. This later shift brought a very strong, albeit often unquestioned, hypothesis about interpretative processing into contemporary psychology and cognitively oriented linguistics. So, it is perhaps worth emphasizing that our aim here is not to defend any particular exegesis of Grice's work; it is rather to highlight the consequences of endorsing cognitive theories of Gricean inspiration.

The most paradigmatic transposition of Grice's ideas into a cognitive model is Sperber and Wilson's (1995) Relevance theory. According to this theory, the hearer infers the meaning communicated through a linguistic utterance (e.g., *this chair is blue*) by attributing to the speaker the informative intention to make manifest to the hearer a certain piece of information. The hearer infers this informative intention he attributed to the speaker (i.e., speaker intends hearer to believe that this chair is blue) by attributing to the speaker the communicative intention to make the speaker's informative intention manifest to the hearer (i.e., speaker intends hearer to realize that, by saying that this chair is blue, she intends to make him believe that this chair is blue). In what follows, we refer to this model of interpretation as the inferential model—IM, for short.

The IM puts communication apart from other information channels, such as perception. Visual perception is direct and devoid of any epistemic gap. When you see that there is a chair in front of you, (a) you do not come to the conclusion that there is a chair in front of you by inference from the mental processes underlying your perceiving the chair, (b) your believing that there is a chair in front of you is not preceded by an internal deliberation about your acceptance or not of this information (although you can subsequently reassess this belief in the light of other information, and, perhaps, reject it ). In other words, nothing comes between the visual experience of the chair and the belief that there is a chair over there; visual perception is direct.[2] By contrast, according to the IM, extracting meaning from an utterance is inherently indirect. From this standpoint, understanding that the content of the speaker's utterance is a piece of information amounts to grasping the speaker's informative and communicative intentions. An extra step is needed to arrive at the belief of that piece of information, as understanding that a speaker wants us to believe that piece of information does not automatically cause us to believe that piece of information. The output of the interpretation mechanism is limited to the content of the speaker's communicative intentions, and besides this, it does not provide any information about the world. Integrating communicated content within one's *belief box* would thus never be automatic. As emphasized by Sperber et al. (2010), this means that *epistemic vigilance* is part and parcel of the IM. Believing, or not believing, the content that has been communicated depends on a filtering mechanism of some sort, which checks received information for accuracy and consistency with other beliefs. In the absence of epistemic assessment, grasping the communicated content fails to lead to the belief that it is true.

The second view of information transfer through language we examine can be called the direct perception model (DPM). According to the DPM, the mechanisms allowing hearers to derive the literal meaning of an utterance are subconscious and as direct as those underlying visual perception—that is, they are not adequately modeled as inferences to what the utterance means. According to the DPM, when told that piece of information, you directly form the belief of that piece of information without any Gricean reasoning about the speaker's intentions. A central prediction of the DPM is therefore that once the contents of communicative stimuli are grasped, they do not need to go through another assessment mechanism to get into the interpreters' belief boxes. As far as the cognitive mechanisms underlying the retrieval of literal meaning go, you believe everything that you are told.

It is important to note that the DPM does not imply the absence of epistemic barrier filtering out the communicated contents that can get into the belief box. The crucial difference between the DPM and the IM is that for the IM the gap between interpretation and belief is presupposed by the very cognitive mechanisms assumed to underpin belief acquisition from linguistic stimuli. For the DPM, by contrast, any epistemic filtering of hearsay information is independent from the interpretation process.

## EXPERIMENTAL EVIDENCE

The DPM has a respectable, if somewhat minority, tradition in contemporary philosophy (see, for instance Burge, 1993; Millikan, 2004, 2005; Recanati, 2002), but there also exists an experimental side to the debate. An important set of empirical evidence that may be invoked in favor of the DPM comes from experiments by Gilbert and colleagues (Gilbert, Krull, & Malone, 1990; Gilbert, Tafarodi, & Malone, 1993). The aim of these experiments was to evaluate two competing models of belief acquisition. According to the first, dubbed "Cartesian" by Gilbert, validation of a statement is never concomitant with its comprehension: A *filter*—some kind of internal deliberation—is necessary before endorsing communicated content as a valid description of the world. The IM is very similar, at least in spirit, to this Cartesian model. The contrasting, *Spinozean*, model predicts that any belief is acquired automatically; if there is assessment, it takes place after information has been integrated within the belief box. The DPM is fully compatible with the Spinozean view.

A central prediction of the Spinozean model is that belief rejection thus operates post hoc and is an effortful process. By contrast, the Cartesian model predicts that subjects can prevent a proposition from getting within the belief box and that, if no deliberation takes place, being told that piece of information will never result in the belief of that piece of information. Because a central prediction of the DPM is that acquiring information through the communicative channel is not intrinsically mediated by epistemic filtering, results favoring the Cartesian model would disprove the DPM.

In a paradigmatic study confronting these two models (Gilbert et al., 1990, Study 1), participants read statements about the meaning of words in an unknown language (Hopi), such as, for example, *monishna is a star*. After an 8-second presentation of each statement, the words *true* or *false* appeared on the screen. For some of the statements, participants had to perform a secondary task (i.e., responding to a tone), which mobilized additional cognitive resources. In a subsequent, testing phase, participants were presented with a list of statements (some of which were true and the others false in view of the earlier statements) and asked to identify their truth-value. The variable of primary interest is the rate of correct recognition as a function of the truth of the statements and the presence of an interfering task in the learning phase. When identifying statements that had not been interrupted during the learning phase, people did not make more errors on false than on true statements. This secondary task did not influence performance on true statements either but, crucially, it led to more errors on false statements, which were more often identified as true than in the absence of such interruption. The latter result suggests that cognitive resources are necessary to correct the default endorsement of the sentence's content as true. By taxing these resources, the secondary task prevents such correction to take place. Such a pattern of findings cannot be properly explained if a Cartesian filter operates between the encoding of the statement and a (hypothetical) subsequent judgment of truthfulness.

In this initial set of studies, it is unclear whether participants' judgments reflected their memory of the information presented in the learning phase or actual belief in such information. In their second set of studies, Gilbert et al. measured more reliable indicators of actual beliefs. For example, in one experiment, they presented information about a defendant in the context of a criminal case, such that some bits of this material were explicitly tagged as false. Furthermore, the information thus communicated was either exonerating or aggravating for the defendant. In addition, half of the participants had to simultaneously perform a secondary task, whereas the other half was not interrupted. In the interrupted condition, when aggravating information was false, participants proposed a more severe penalty than when exonerating information was false. This was not the case when they were not interrupted. Thus, when interrupted, people assimilated the false information and failed to correct it. Taken together, these findings suggest not only that people encode false information as true when their cognitive resources are taxed but that they also act on it.

As is suggested by the title of the 1993 paper "You can't not believe everything you are told," Gilbert et al. seem to consider that people are incapable of suspending belief. As hearers, we would be capable of considering statements to be false only after having previously endorsed them. This—extreme—position has been challenged by Hasson et al. (2005). A straightforward concern about Gilbert's experiments is that, from the participant's point of view, false statements used in the experiment (such as the ones about the meaning of Hopi words) are uninformative. Accordingly, knowing that they are false (e.g., that it is not true that *moshina* means star in Hopi) has no informative value for the participant. But of course, being told that a statement is false may prove informative per se. For instance, when a statement like *Tom is generous* is tagged as false, the participant may directly encode the information *Tom is greedy*. That is, it is not the statement itself that would be encoded—as a strict application of the Spinozean model would suggest—but rather, an inference drawn from it being tagged as false. If this happens, the sentence *Tom is generous* should be readily identified as false in the second phase of the experiment even when cognitive resources are depleted. To test this hypothesis, Hasson et al.

replicated the first experiment of Gilbert et al. but manipulated the informativeness of false statements. They obtained the same results as Gilbert et al. when the false statements were uninformative (viz., the distracting task during the exposure phase led to consider false statements as true). However, when the false statements were informative, recognition performance was not altered by the secondary task. This result allowed Hasson et al. to conclude that recalling the truth-value—be it true or false—of informative statements is not affected by parallel cognitive overload.

Drawing on research in psycholinguistics, Richter et al. (2009) have posed another challenge to Gilbert's claims. They suggest that people routinely (i.e., in the absence of an explicit goal) and effortlessly rely on validation processes when comprehending sentences. Contrary to both the Spinozean and the Cartesian view, it would be impossible to divorce validation from comprehension. Validation, they argue, is grounded in background assumptions related to the topic at hand. Because the material used in Gilbert's experiments consisted of statements about unknown topics, lack of any relevant background may have therefore prevented the participants from performing routine validation. Richter et al. reproduced the Hopi experiment in Gilbert et al., but with statements half of which were perceived to be true or false with a high certainty in a pilot study, whereas the truth-value of the other half of the stimuli was seen as uncertain, in the same pilot study. Richter et al. replicated Gilbert's pattern for the latter group of stimuli (interruption during the learning phase yielded weaker recognition performance for false, but not true, statements). However, they also found that for statements with strong background beliefs (be they true or false), interruption did not affect performance.

In a more direct test of the presence of an implicit validation, Richter et al. (Experiments 3 and 4) relied on an *epistemic Stroop* paradigm, in which subjects had to evaluate (by rapidly clicking on one of two buttons) the spelling of words belonging to sentences that were either consistent or inconsistent with strong background beliefs. Richter et al. assume that, if belief validation is routinely triggered, it should interfere with orthographical judgments. Accordingly, people should experience difficulties both with approving the spelling of words within statements that contradict strong background beliefs and with disapproving the spelling of words within statements that conform to such beliefs. These predictions were corroborated on measures of error rates and reaction times. Participants made fewer errors and (in Experiment 4) took less time to respond when words within true sentences were correctly spelled and when words within false sentences were incorrectly spelled than in the two incongruent conditions.

These and Hasson's findings suggest that the radical version of the Spinozean view is hardly tenable. In some cases false information is not rejected a posteriori, but filtered straight at the entrance of the belief box. However, the presence of a filter in some context does not imply that it is a necessary condition for acquiring hearsay beliefs. If anything, these studies suggest boundary conditions for the operation of a filter. But this falls short of invalidating the

DPM. What remains uncontroversial about Gilbert's results is that epistemic filtering is not inherent in communication. In certain circumstances, you believe directly what you hear (or read). What the IM predicts is that there is no believing of communicated meaning without epistemic check—and this is not the case.

This line of thought receives support from data on the ontogenesis of epistemic vigilance. The capacity to assess the reliability of a communicator is quite a precocious one. From the age of four, children are capable to discriminate between a reliable and an unreliable puppet (Clément, Koenig, & Harris, 2004). Likewise, four-year-olds tend to distrust a puppet characterized as a liar (Mascaro & Sperber, 2009). Yet, this capacity is by no means part and parcel of the way communicative behavior is processed (as the IM would have it). To begin with, the same studies also revealed that at the age of three, children fail to adopt such selective trust. Furthermore, Vanderbilt, Liu, and Heyman (2011) show that explicitly identifying an adult as an unreliable deceiver in three consecutive communicative exchanges does not prevent four-year-olds from trusting the information communicated by this same person right afterward.

The point is not that young children are blindly gullible. They are not. For instance, children below five years tend to privilege first-hand, perceptual information over verbal claims made by an adult (Robinson, Mitchell, & Nye, 1995).[3] However, there is no evidence that acquisition of such *skeptic* strategies is inherent in the development of the capacity to interpret communicative stimuli.

## THE EVOLUTION OF EPISTEMIC VIGILANCE: SOME SPECULATIONS

A major finding of the neo-Darwinian paradigm has been that cooperative behavior proves evolutionarily rewarding. It is also widely accepted that such strategies must encompass a mechanism aimed at the exclusion of noncooperative *cheaters* from interaction (e.g., Axelrod, 1984; Axelrod & Hamilton, 1981; Dawkins, 1989; Kitcher, 1993). It is also widely accepted that cooperative behavior can be found, in some form or another, all over the animal kingdom, and especially among great apes (see e.g., De Waal, 2006). In this light, it is not too risky a conjecture that human communication emerged among groups whose members could already reasonably expect each other to be helpful, and from which cheaters were ostracized.

Let us indulge now in some evolutionary speculation. Imagine two hypothetical groups: the *direct perceivers* and the *inferentialists*. Members of both groups can communicate to share information, but while the former acquire information from speech in accordance with the DPM, the latter have to go through the inferential strategy posited by the IM. Assume, furthermore, that members of each group pass their interpretative strategy to their offspring.

It seems obvious that within the kind of cooperative niche just described, direct perceivers would be clearly advantaged over inferentialists.[4] Because any communicated content is directly added to the direct perceivers' belief boxes, they would acquire information much faster and in a more effortless way than inferentialists, who need, every time, to go through assessment and consistency checking before validating what they have been told. Provided that communicators are benevolent and competent, communicated information will be accurate often enough to privilege direct perceivers, because accurate information acquisition would then mobilize fewer resources than those needed by the inferentialists—resources which can thus be profitably allocated to another task. In such an environment, direct perception through speech would be evolutionary stable. Subpopulations endowed with it would rapidly take over individuals who cannot communicate altogether—and also over a hypothetical inferentialist, Cartesian subgroup.

However, being a direct perceiver makes interactions with unreliable speakers very costly. The DPM predicts there is a great risk that the contents of misleading statements will automatically get into the direct perceiver's belief box, so that an exclusion or assessment process will be necessary (at the risk of letting a false belief influence his or her decisions). But such processes take time and cognitive energy that could be better employed. Therefore, when the quantity of false utterances exceeds a certain threshold, direct perceivers become disadvantaged, and inferentialism starts to look like a more promising strategy.

Even though it is very plausible to assume that these hypothetical ancestors of ours evolved in small groups, bound by kinship and in-group cooperation links, direct perceivers were exposed to two sources of misinformation. First, encounters with out-group deceivers remained possible; second, even within their own, reliable group, direct perceivers must have had to count with benevolent but mistaken communicators. That is, direct perceivers were advantaged only if they had evolved independent means to overcome deception and unintentional misinformation.

Regarding the first type of risk, the best evolutionary strategy is clearly to supplement the mechanism that ensures quick and effortless integration of communicated information with efficient and automatic epistemic filters that activate vigilance with respect to certain speakers (or in certain conditions). Such an evolutionary scenario entails that epistemic vigilance is not of one piece—it is a patchwork of adaptive strategies, shaped by heterogeneous environmental pressures. The supplementation of interpretive mechanisms with epistemic filtering is a classical case of what Krebs and Dawkins (1984) call the *evolutionary arms race*, concomitant with the development of communication systems. The aptitude to inform begets misinformation and deception, which in turn increases the adaptability of filtering mechanisms. Such an adaptation would be hard to explain in the absence of environmental pressure to control the ingress of communicated information within the belief box. It is precisely because the cognitive processes that allow us to interpret utterances as conveying informative contents do not come with an inherent epistemic safeguard that such filtering mechanisms have been selected.

To be sure, the domain-specific epistemic filters still do not shield direct perceivers from misinformation from their benevolent fellows (viz., from being misinformed in a kind of cooperative situation where no specific vigilance should be triggered). Recall that misinformation has a higher cost for direct perceivers than for inferentialists. Therefore, the result is that, ceteris paribus, it is better for direct perceivers to avoid interaction with unreliable speakers altogether. Communicating false information, intentionally or not, should be seen as a noncooperative behavior, worthy of ostracism from the group.

At this point, it may be objected that this last feature of our evolutionary scenario renders the DPM evolutionarily implausible after all, for under such a view, speaking seems to be quite a risky business. If saying something false is assimilated to noncooperative behavior, punishable by exclusion from interaction—with all the dramatic consequences this entails—the most evolutionarily stable strategy would be to remain silent unless one is absolutely certain about the truth of her utterance (for a related discussion, see Hurford, 2007, pp. 276–277).

However, this risk may precisely be at the cornerstone of the emergence of human communication. Indeed, recent theories predict that, being prone to exchanging information—with the risk of being mistaken—has a higher evolutionary value than remaining silent in most cases, and thus avoiding any risk of being treated as a cheater. One such model is defended by Dessalles (1998), according to whom by providing reliable (and relevant) information, speakers seek to increase their social prestige, and hence, their reproductive success. Another compatible position is Miller (2000, Chapter 10), who argues that the human propensity to communication is explained in great part by sexual selection: Verbal display raises the chances for mating.

Dessalles's and Miller's rationales assume that communicating has a certain cost; otherwise, no prestige would be attached to such behavior. They both appeal to the handicap principle (Zahavi & Zahavi, 1997). Some traits that constitute a prima facie handicap can provide the organism that displays them with a higher chance of reproduction. Roughly, the idea is that by exhibiting a handicap, the individual demonstrates ability to survive despite this handicap, which, in turn indicates a high degree of fitness. For instance, male bowerbirds build elaborate bowers of twigs whose only function is to serve as a stage for courtship displays. The more adorned and the bigger this *stage* is, the more energy consuming is its construction, but also the higher is the likelihood for the *builder* to be chosen by a female. The female evolved this preference because bowers constitute a reliable indication of fitness. A male that can waste time and energy to build a big and elaborate bower, at the expense of looking for food, is likely to be more fitted to the environment than the one that cannot afford such a costly behavior.[5]

The crucial component of the handicap principle is that to be a reliable indicator of fitness, the handicap (e.g., building a complex bower) must be hard to fake—otherwise any individual, not only the fittest one, could afford it. Therefore, if, as Dessalles (1998) and Miller (2000) claim, providing information through speech benefits the speaker by increasing social prestige and sexual attractiveness, the speaker's task should not be easy.

Now, in communities of direct perceivers one such risk is obvious: Unreliable speakers run the danger of being excluded from interaction as cheaters. In other words, the DPM predicts the emergence of the policing mechanism that theories of language evolution based on the handicap principle need to get off the ground.

Another important issue, which we can only mention in passing here, is that the IM requires viewing the appearance of linguistic communication as a twofold and simultaneous evolutionary emergence of a new channel and a new way of information acquisition. Accordingly, it needs to posit a double—and simultaneous—environmental pressure to explain the emergence of linguistic communication: one factor that explains the selection of complex communicative behaviors and another that selects for an inferential acquisition strategy, with an inherent gap between understanding and believing. The DPM, by contrast, views language as a new channel to feed information into the belief box in exactly the same way as perception. This, in itself, makes the DPM more plausible from a phylogenetic point of view. To be sure, hearsay beliefs are not as reliable as perception-based ones. But, as we have argued in this section, linguistic communication proves maximally efficient when appended with domain specific epistemic filters.

## IMPACT ON SOCIAL PSYCHOLOGY

Before concluding this paper, we would like to allude to some central issues in social psychology that may benefit from a critical assessment of the IM.

A program of research that coheres with the DPM relates to the saying-is-believing effect (Higgins & Rholes, 1978). In this paradigm, participants read a description of a person (the target). This description is crafted in such a way that the statements it comprises can be interpreted as reflecting either relatively desirable or undesirable traits. Participants are then asked to describe the target to an audience (who is supposedly already acquainted with this person) to allow this audience to identify the target. Crucially, speakers are informed of the audience's attitude, which can be either favorable or unfavorable to the target. It is not surprising that communicators tend to describe the target in a more flattering light when the audience is said to hold a positive, rather than a negative, attitude. More interesting, however, is the fact that when communicators' impressions about the target are later probed, it turns out that their own memory is biased as well and in the same direction. This does not happen in a control condition in which speakers are exposed to the audience's attitude but do not have to communicate. Decades of research on this phenomenon have led to consider it as driven by a desire to establish a shared understanding of the target with the audience (shared reality; Echterhoff, Higgins, & Levine, 2009). This shared reality is contingent on trust in the audience, and especially in its capacity to form an accurate opinion of the target. When this trust is present, there seems to be no barrier to simply incorporating the audience's attitude into one's own. In other words, when trusting an audience, the latter's view of the target seems to translate into believing that this view is correct. However, this process seems to be mediated by the active construction of an understanding of this target through communication. In other words, everything happens as if once verbalized, descriptions of the target influenced by the audience's attitude come to be perceived as true. This is a very reasonable prediction that can be made from the DPM; presumably, no filter is activated for one's own statements, which, therefore, automatically end up in the speaker's belief box.

Another phenomenon that speaks to the DPM is belief perseverance (Anderson, Lepper, & Ross, 1980). In research on this topic, people are presented with facts which are later discredited. Yet, people keep believing in these facts to a greater extent than control subjects who have not been exposed to them. Obviously, this effect is not necessarily incompatible with an inferential model because what is at stake here is not belief validation but how one can come to disbelieve information that has been initially accepted as true. However, the difficulty in undoing such beliefs suggests that they are incorporated relatively automatically, without conscious control (as a Spinozean model would rather suggest).

## GRICEAN INFLUENCES IN SOCIAL PSYCHOLOGY

Grice's theory of meaning is probably the most important influence from pragmatics on social psychology (cf. Wänke, 2007; for an illustration, see Chapter 11, this volume). Especially, it has been used to (re)interpret research on a variety of cognitive biases. As we have argued in favor of the DPM against the limitations of the IM, which was deeply inspired by Grice's theory, the question naturally arises: Doesn't this work precisely show the superiority of the IM?

To address this question, we shall consider one bias that has been extensively studied under a Gricean light: base rate neglect (Kahneman & Tversky, 1973). Let us first illustrate how this bias has been experimentally demonstrated. Participants receive information regarding a person displaying traits typical of a social category A (e.g., engineers) or of a stereotypically opposite category B (e.g., lawyers). For example, *Jack loves mathematical puzzles* would be construed as more typical of engineers than lawyers. Participants are asked to estimate the likelihood that the target person belongs to category A. In addition, the target is presented as drawn from a sample containing either a majority of members of social category A (e.g., 70% engineers versus 30% lawyers) or only a minority (e.g., 30% engineers versus 70% lawyers). Typically, people's estimations of the target's membership are little affected by this statistical information. Rather, it is the stereotypicality of the target that explains most of the variance. Tversky and Kahneman (1974) famously analyzed such biases as the effects of simple heuristics (e.g., representativeness) by opposition to more elaborate and *rational* calculations. However, Schwarz (1994) pointed out that the conversational context in which these biases arose had been neglected. Conversational moves are governed by certain expectations—among which the ones Grice identified as "conversational maxims"—and these are often implicitly violated in experimental settings. Typically, hearers expect speakers' contribution to be relevant, but in the *base-rate paradigm* described above, a central part of the experimenter's contribution (viz., target's stereotypical traits) should not be relevant if participants were to behave rationally. This effect can be eliminated, or attenuated, when conversational expectations are neutralized. Thus Schwarz, Strack, Hilton, and Naderer (1991) showed that when information about the target was presented as selected by a computer, rather than a psychologist, participants' estimation of the target's membership is more influenced by statistical information. This is so because we usually do not expect computers to be sophisticated enough to select all, and only, relevant information about the psychological profile of a person; hence, not every bit of information is automatically taken to be relevant.[6] This kind of Gricean explanation has been conclusively applied to a great number of other experimental paradigms (for reviews, see Holtgraves, 2010; Schwarz, 1994).

Although Gricean in spirit, this analysis of cognitive biases is actually consistent with our rejection of the IM. In the foregoing, we claimed that epistemic vigilance is not inherent in our capacity to retrieve information from speech. What Schwarz's results reveal is that how communicated information is integrated, and hence influences other beliefs and decisions, depends on the context (e.g., the nature of the problem, the identity of the speaker, etc.). That some information selected by a computer is not taken into account does not show that when the same information is provided by a psychologist, and is used within a decision process, it necessarily undergoes inferential epistemic filtering. The DPM does not deny the influence of contextual factors such as expectations of relevance and of cooperation (and therefore allows the applications of Grice's maxims as is typically done in social psychology); what it does reject is the view that such factors are necessarily mediated by the attribution of complex, communicative intentions to the speakers.

## CONCLUSIONS

Social psychologists tend to consider comprehension and validation as two independent processes and are actually much more interested in validation than in comprehension, which is best left to (psycho)linguists. What we hope to have shown above is that it is impossible to remain agnostic about the cognitive processes underlying utterance interpretation if one undertakes to explain how communication-based beliefs are formed. Grice's work helped researchers to realize that communication is an intersubjective activity, whose many aspects are influenced by an expectation of cooperativeness. However, it is a mistake to adopt the reconstruction of speaker's meaning in terms of intention attribution, operated by Grice, as a monolithic model of language comprehension. Such a theoretical choice forces one to posit that no belief can be drawn from linguistic stimuli without having gone through an epistemic filter. We have argued that this consequence is hard to accommodate with available experimental data.

Much more plausible, both from an empirical and an evolutionary point of view, is the direct perception through language model. Contrary to the extreme position some proponents of this model might advocate, it does not compel us to assume that no information can be rejected without having been previously held as true. The cognitive equipment that allows us to acquire hearsay beliefs is supplemented with a variety of epistemic filters, which may be easily and automatically activated under certain conditions. A promising direction for future research is to understand better the typology of these filters. Meanwhile, it seems fair to conclude that epistemic vigilance is not inherent in our capacity to understand others' statements.[7]

## ACKNOWLEDGMENTS

We would like to thank Philippe De Brabanter, Marc Dominicy, Mark Jary, the members of the Linguistics reading workshop, and the members of the ULB social psychology unit for their feedback on an earlier version of this chapter.

## NOTES

1. An exception is the work on communicational grounding (Clark 1996), which considers how people elaborate a *common ground* to pursue cooperative projects. However, in this kind of research, the focus is more on an interpersonal level of analysis, viz. on how people manage to incorporate new knowledge through communicational behavior. The cognitive underpinnings of this *incorporation*, by contrast, are hardly considered.
2. To be sure, with some optical illusions—those that you recognize as such—you do not believe what you see. But note that conscious effort is needed: You eliminate the belief you acquired. Moreover, understanding that what you see is an illusion requires explicit training or at least, a time-consuming, detailed examination of the stimulus from different points of view and/or through different perceptual modalities.
3. Children below four are selective about informational medium (visual or tactile perception, or hearsay), and in cases where two sources provide contradicting information, they favor the most reliable one; however, they have difficulties in reporting correctly the source of their beliefs, which suggests that once a belief is acquired no trace of its provenance subsists (Gopnik & Graf, 1988; Mitchell, Robinson, Nye, & Isaacs, 1997; Whitcombe & Robinson, 2000; for a related discussion, see Millikan, 2005, p. 209–210).
4. Of course, the hypothesis here is not that two such groups coexisted at some point; the idea is rather to speculate how each group would have fared.
5. Handicaps may also serve to deter predators; see Zahavi and Zahavi (1997, Chapter 1).
6. Furthermore, the opposite pattern of results was obtained when the problem was presented as statistical, and not psychological (presumably, computers are better with statistical tasks than psychologists).
7. Origgi and Sperber (2000) and Sperber et al. (2010) invoke massive contextual dependence of the literal meaning to discard the DPM and argue that verbal understanding necessarily conforms to IM. However, there are very strong reasons, mostly from typical and atypical language and cognitive development, to dismiss the idea that all such pragmatic processes require the complex mind reading posited by IM (see, Breheny, 2006; Kissine, 2012, 2013, Chapters 3 and 5; Recanati, 2002).

# REFERENCES

Anderson, C. A., Lepper, M. R., & Ross, L. (1980). Perseverance of social theories: The role of explanation in the persistence of discredited information. *Journal of Personality and Social Psychology, 39,* 1037.

Axelrod, R. M. (1984). *The evolution of cooperation*. New York, NY: Basic Books.

Axelrod, R., & Hamilton, W. D. (1981). The evolution of cooperation. *Science, 211,* 1390–1396.

Breheny, R. (2006). Communication and folk psychology. *Mind and Language, 21,* 74–107.

Burge, T. (1993). Content preservation. *The Philosophical Review, 102,* 457–488.

Clark, H. H. (1996). Using language. Cambridge, England: Cambridge University Press.

Clément, F., Koenig, M., & Harris, P. (2004). The ontogenesis of trust. *Mind and Language, 19,* 360–379.

Dawkins, R. (1989). The selfish gene (2nd ed.). Oxford, England: Oxford University Press.

Dessalles, J-L. (1998). Altruism, status, and the origin of relevance. In J. R. Hurford, M. Studdert-Kennedy, & C. Knight (Eds.), *Approaches to the evolution of language: Social and cognitive bases* (pp. 130–147). Cambridge, England: Cambridge University Press.

De Waal, F. (2006). *Primates and philosophers.* How morality evolved. Princeton, NJ: Princeton University Press.

Echterhoff, G., Higgins, E. T., & Levine, J. M. (2009). Shared reality. *Perspectives on Psychological Science, 4,* 496–521.

Gilbert, D. T., Krull, D. S., & Malone, P. S. (1990). Unbelieving the unbelievable: Some problems in the rejection of false information. *Journal of Personality and Social Psychology, 59,* 601–613.

Gilbert, D. T., Tafarodi, R. W., & Malone, P. S. (1993). You can't not believe everything you read. *Journal of Personality and Social Psychology, 65,* 221–233.

Gopnik, A., & Graf, P. (1988). Knowing how you know—Young children's ability to identify and remember the sources of their beliefs. *Child Development, 59,* 1366–1371.

Grice, P. (1989). *Studies in the way of words.* Cambridge, MA: Harvard University Press.

Hasson, U., Simmons, J. P. and Todorov, A. (2005). Believe it or not: On the possibility of suspending belief. *Psychological Science, 16,* 566–571

Higgins, E. T., & Rholes, W. S. (1978). "Saying is believing": Effects of message modification on memory and liking of the person described. *Journal of Experimental Social Psychology, 14,* 363–378.

Holtgraves, T. (2010). Social psychology and language: Words, utterances, and conversations. In S. T. Fiske, D. T. Gilbert, & G. Lindzey (Eds.), *Handbook of social psychology* (Vol. I, pp. 1386–1422). New York, NY: Wiley.

Hurford, J. R. (2007). *The origins of meaning.* Oxford, England: Oxford University Press.

Kahneman, D., & Tversky, A. (1973). On the psychology of prediction. *Psychological Review, 80,* 237–251.

Kissine, M. (2012). Sentences, utterances, and speech acts. In K. Allan & K. M. Jaszczolt (Eds.), *Cambridge handbook of pragmatics* (pp. 169–190). Cambridge, England: Cambridge University Press.

Kissine, M. (2013). *From utterances to speech acts.* Cambridge, England: Cambridge University Press.

Kitcher, P. (1993). The evolution of human altruism. *Journal of Philosophy, 90,* 497–516.

Krebs, J. R., & Dawkins, R. (1984). Animal signals: Mind-reading and manipulation. In J. R. Krebs & N. B. Davies (Eds.), *Behavioural ecology. An evolutionary approach* (2nd ed., pp. 380–402). Oxford, England: Blackwell.

Mascaro, O., & Sperber, D. (2009). The moral, epistemic, and mindreading components of children's vigilance towards deception. *Cognition*, 112, 367–380.

Miller, G. (2000). *The mating mind: How sexual choice shaped the evolution of human nature*. London, England: Heinemann.
Millikan, R. G. (2004). *Varieties of meaning*. Cambridge, MA: MIT Press.
Millikan, R. G. (2005). *Language: A biological model*. Oxford, England: Oxford University Press.
Mitchell, P., Robinson, E. J., Nye, R., & Isaacs, J. E. (1997). When speech conflicts with seeing: Young children's understanding of informational priority. *Journal of Experimental Child Psychology, 64*, 276–294.
Origgi, G., & Sperber, D. (2000). Evolution, communication and the proper function of language. In P. Carruthers & A. Chamberlain (Eds.), *Evolution and the human mind: Language, modularity and social cognition* (pp. 140–169). Cambridge, England: Cambridge University Press.
Recanati, F. (2002). Does linguistic communication rest on inference? *Mind and Language*, 17, 105–126.
Richter, T., Schroeder, S. and Wöhrmann, B. 2009: You don't have to believe everything you read: Background knowledge permits fast and efficient validation of information. *Journal of Personality and Social Psychology, 96*, 538–558.
Robinson, E. J., Mitchell, P., & Nye, R. (1995). Young children's treating of utterances as unreliable sources of knowledge. *Journal of Child Language, 22*, 663–685.
Saul, J. M. (2002). What is said and psychological reality: Grice's project and relevance theorists' criticisms. *Linguistics and Philosophy, 25*, 347–372.
Schwarz, N. (1994). *Judgment in a social context: Biases, shortcomings, and the logic of conversation*. San Diego, CA: Academic Press.
Schwarz, N., Strack, F., Hilton, D., & Naderer, G. (1991). Base rates, representativeness, and the logic of conversation: The contextual relevance of irrelevant information. *Social Cognition, 9*, 67–84.
Sperber, D., Clément, F., Heintz, C., Mascaro, O., Mercier, H., Origgi, G., & Wilson, D. (2010). Epistemic vigilance. *Mind and Language, 25*, 359–393.
Sperber, D., & Wilson, D. (1995). *Relevance: Communication and cognition*. Oxford, England: Blackwell.
Tversky, A., & Kahneman, D. (1974). Judgment under uncertainty: Heuristics and biases. *Science*, 185, 1124–1131.
Vanderbilt, K. E., Liu, D., & Heyman, G. D. (2011). The development of distrust. *Child Development, 82*, 1372–1380.
Wänke, M. (2007). What is said and what is meant: Conversational implicatures in natural conversations, research settings, media and advertising. In K. Fiedler (Ed.), *Social communication* (pp. 223–256). New York, NY: Psychology Press.
Whitcombe, E. L., & Robinson, E. J. (2000). Children's decisions about what to believe and their ability to report the source of their belief. *Cognitive Development*, 15, 329–346.
Zahavi, A., & Zahavi, A. (1997). *The handicap principle. A missing piece of Darwin's puzzle*. New York, NY: Oxford University Press.

# 9

# Parameters of Nonaccommodation

## *Refining and Elaborating Communication Accommodation Theory*

HOWARD GILES AND JESSICA GASIOREK

Adjusting for our fellow interactants is a fundamental part of successful interaction. We do not speak to our colleagues in the same way we do to our spouses, or to our parents in the same way we do to our children. Rather, we adapt our communication to our present circumstances and the ways in which others respond to us (Beukeboom, 2009). However, and unfortunately, the adjustments we make for each other are not always experienced as adequate or appropriate. Problems with communicative adjustment may take a range of forms across a variety of contexts and can have serious consequences. The prospects for miscommunication are particularly rife when people breach intercultural and intergroup divides (e.g., Dubé-Simard, 1983; Hewstone & Giles, 1986). Failing to adapt to local communicative or behavioral norms—not using polite forms, for example, in a high power distance culture—could lead to speakers' committing social or cultural faux pas, resulting in their being labeled as rude, offensive, or worse. In general, when communicative adjustments are felt to be lacking or inappropriate, interaction is experienced as dissatisfying and/or problematic (e.g., Williams, 1996).

To avoid detrimental outcomes such as these, it is important to understand how poorly adjusted communication occurs, as well as what determines individuals' responses to it. Within the framework of communication accommodation theory (CAT; Gallois, Ogay, & Giles, 2005; Giles, 1973; Giles, Willemyns, Gallois, & Anderson, 2007), this chapter seeks to develop conceptually and theoretically the construct of *nonaccommodation,* defined as communicative behaviors that are inappropriately adjusted for the participants in an interaction. With particular consideration for the nature of poorly adjusted communication, we first propose a specification and elaboration of the theory's definition of *communication* (the "C" in CAT). We then consider the processes by which nonaccommodation is perceived and evaluated, proposing a model of how perceived intentionality and motive, perspective-taking, and initial orientation directly and indirectly influence our evaluations of nonaccommodation and related interactional outcomes.

## COMMUNICATION ACCOMMODATION AND NONACCOMMODATION

CAT is premised on the assumption that communication mediates and maintains interpersonal *and* intergroup relationships (Gallois & Giles, 1998). As such, it seeks to explain speakers' linguistic and behavioral choices in interaction as they relate to communicative adjustment, and to model how others in the interaction perceive, evaluate, and react to these choices. In short, CAT suggests that speakers come to interactions with an initial orientation, which is informed by such factors as relevant interpersonal and intergroup histories, as well as the prevailing sociohistorical context. In interaction, speakers adjust their communicative behavior based on evaluations of their fellow interactants' communicative characteristics in context, as well as their desire to establish and maintain a positive personal and social identity (Gallois et al., 2005). Each speaker evaluates and makes attributions about the encounter as well as the other speaker on the basis of their perceptions of that other speaker's behavior (i.e., adjustments). These attributions and evaluations then affect the quality and nature of the present interaction between these speakers, as well as speakers' intent to engage in future interaction with each other—see Figure 9.1.

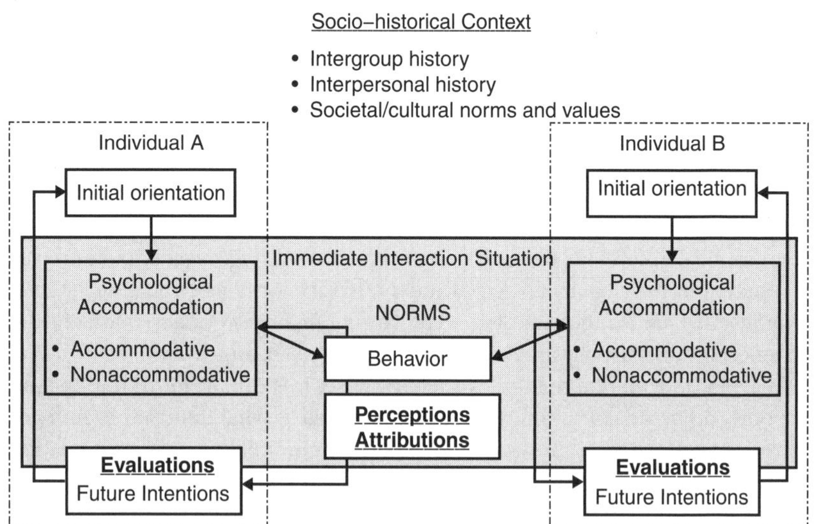


Figure 9.1 The communication accommodation theory model (adapted from Giles et al., 2007, p. 139)

Theorizing on CAT has proposed two distinct functions for accommodation: first, managing social distance and related identity concerns (*affective function*), and second, facilitating comprehension (*cognitive function*; see Gallois et al., 2005; Street & Giles, 1982). Within the first (*social regulation*) function, a number of more specific social effects of accommodation have been put forward, among them identifying or appearing similar to others, maintaining face, maintaining a relationship, and maintaining interpersonal control as it relates to power or status differentials (see Chapter 19, this volume). Within the second (*facilitating comprehension*) function, in turn, specific effects include the extent which speakers are understood, and relatedly, how discourse is directed and managed (Gallois et al., 2005).

To fulfill these two functions, there are several different *adjustment strategies* we can implement (Coupland, Coupland, Giles, & Henwood, 1988; Cretchley, Gallois, Chenery, & Smith, 2010). First, we may adjust verbal and nonverbal behavior to be more similar or different to our conversational partners' (*approximation strategies*). Recent work on mimicry (for an overview, see Chartrand & Van Baaren, 2009) has documented the myriad ways in which individuals unconsciously synchronize their verbal and nonverbal behavior with each other when they interact. Consistent with CAT, this research suggests that people regulate social distance through these adjustments: mimicry (i.e., behavioral convergence) has been found to increase empathy, liking, and rapport. Conversely, individuals mimic less when they feel neutral about or seek to (actively) disaffiliate themselves with another (Babel, 2010).

We may also adapt the manner in which information is presented with an eye to making it more or less comprehensible to our audience, according to our judgment of the audience's capacities (*interpretability strategies*). Altering speech rate, the complexity of a message's lexicon or syntax, volume, tempo, repetition, prosody, and/or content (topic choice) are all potential forms interpretability strategies may take (Giles & Coupland, 1991). Although most adjustments along the approximation axis are primarily made nonconsciously (e.g., Lineweaver, Hutman, Ketcham, & Bohannon, 2011), interpretability adjustments may be made either consciously or unconsciously.

Communicative behavior may also be adapted on a more macro level, as when we adjust our communication to guide the conversation in specific ways (*discourse management strategies*) through turn management, topic selection, topic sharing, and backchanneling (Cretchley et al., 2010; Shepard, Giles, & LePoire, 2001).

Finally, we may make adjustments to address the social dynamics at play in an encounter (*interpersonal control strategies*); for example, adjusting communication to either reaffirm or subvert power or status differentials (e.g., acting deferential or assuming a leadership style), or behaving in ways associated with formal or institutional roles and their accompanying communicative expectations (see Chapter 18, this volume).

When communicative adjustments are made appropriately in the eyes of both interactants, the result is *accommodative* communication, which is usually (although not always) experienced as successful and positive. However, when they are not seen as crafted appropriately, *nonaccommodation* is the result.

## UNPACKING NONACCOMMODATION

Although some work using CAT chooses to consider actions and outcomes in terms of an accommodative versus nonaccommodative dichotomy (e.g., Giles et al., 2007), *nonaccommodation* may in fact describe a wide variety of perceived behaviors, including divergence, maintenance, overaccommodation, and underaccommodation. Divergence is defined as individuals' altering their speech (or communication more generally) to move away and distance themselves from their conversational partners' communicative habits (e.g., Bourhis, Giles, Leyends, & Tajfel, 1979). Maintenance is the absence of accommodative adjustments by individuals, that is, maintaining their *default* way of communicating without taking into account the characteristics of their fellow interactants. It can, however, be a strategic statement about preserving one's social identity in certain intergroup contexts (Giles, Reid, & Harwood, 2010) and, as such, is an active statement about not wishing to accommodate (Bourhis, 1979). Overaccommodation, in turn, is defined as the perception that a speaker is exceeding or overshooting the level of a given communicative behavior necessary for a successful interaction. Underaccommodation, finally, is the perception that a speaker is not doing enough to implement a given communication behavior, relative to the level needed or desired by others in the interaction (Coupland et al., 1988).

To date, overaccommodation has been the primary focus of research on nonaccommodation. Variants of overaccommodation that have received considerable scholarly attention include patronizing talk (Hummert & Ryan, 2001) and so-called elderspeak, the use of overly simplified speech in interactions with older adults (for an overview of relevant studies, see Giles & Gasiorek, 2011). Overaccommodation's counterpart, underaccommodation, however, has not received comparable attention. However, and interestingly there is some evidence that underaccommodation is in fact more prevalent, at least for young adults in a college setting, than a survey of the present CAT literature would suggest. In a recent study by Gasiorek (2010) of American young adults' experiences of nonaccommodation, *under*accommodative experiences outnumbered experiences of overaccommodation by ratio of more than nine to one. It is interesting to note that underaccommodation is generally evaluated more negatively than overaccommodation in analogous situations (Gasiorek & Giles, 2012; Jones, Gallois, Barker, & Callan, 1994).

A critical distinction between the types of nonaccommodation outlined here is that of subjectivity (Thakerar, Giles, & Cheshire, 1982). Divergence and maintenance are constructs that came out of early CAT (then, speech accommodation theory) studies that were primarily concerned with dialect, accent, and related *speech* variables (see Giles, Coupland, & Coupland, 1991). As such, they are typically discussed and analyzed in relatively objective terms:

Past empirical studies have reliably measured variables like speech rate, pause length, and pitch. Over- and underaccommodation, in contrast, are inherently subjective phenomena. It is the recipient's *perception* of a behavior—not objective qualities of the behavior itself—that determine whether or not the behavior is considered over- or underaccommodative. Thus, there is the potential for overlap between these two types of nonaccommodation: Speech that is objectively divergent (in terms of qualities such as speed or pitch), for example, may also be experienced as a distancing move, and as such underaccommodating. However, under certain circumstances—for example, an instructor explaining difficult or unfamiliar material to a student asking a question—it could instead be experienced as accommodative.

The subjective nature of these constructs has two important implications. First, as over- and underaccommodation are evaluations made by the recipient of the communication in question, a speaker's *actual* motive or intentions are not strictly relevant to labeling an action as over- or underaccommodative. Rather, it is a recipients' experience of that communication that matters. Thus, communication that is intended to be appropriately adjusted may be perceived as nonaccommodative and therefore problematic; similarly, talk intended to be nonaccommodative (for example, to emphasize a particular social identity or disaffiliate with another), may be experienced as appropriate and, therefore, unproblematic for the recipient, as well as for other (in-group) peers present.

The second main implication of the subjective nature of over- and underaccommodation is that these phenomena are ultimately social attributions (Ytsma & Giles, 1997), not objective behaviors or sets of communicative features per se (see Ryan, Hummert, & Boich, 1995). Thus, they can take a wide variety of forms depending on the situation in question, with the experiences and social roles of observers and interactants affecting perceptions of accommodation (Jones et al., 1994) and what one individual perceives as over- or underaccommodative may not be perceived as such by another interactant. A number of studies in the area of intergenerational communication studies have provided support for the subjective nature of nonaccommodation and related evaluations. For example, Edwards and Noller (1993) found that overaccommodative interactions between an older adult and a caretaker were evaluated as less patronizing by the participants in the interactions, as compared with outside observers (nursing students or psychology students). Sachweh (1998) reported comparable findings in her study involving German nursing home residents. Of course, these subjective perceptions of appropriateness are generally guided by social norms (see Gallois & Callan, 1988) and, hence, there are many situations where certain communicative behaviors are predictably perceived as nonaccommodative. For instance, it is normative to answer a direct question; under the vast majority of circumstances, failing to acknowledge or address a direct question in conversation would be perceived as underaccommodative.

Given the subjective and individual nature of the phenomenon, the next question of interest becomes, what influences our evaluations of nonaccommodation and, by extension, our reactions to it?

## COMMUNICATION AS AN INFERENCE PROCESS

Early models of communication treated communication as a simple transmission of messages. More recent work has suggested that it may better be understood as a joint effort in inferential problem-solving by its interactants (e.g., Berger, 2001; for an alternative perspective, however, see Chapter 8, this volume). In this conceptualization, the function of communication is to reach some form of shared understanding between those communicating, particularly as individuals generally come to encounters with different perspectives, past experiences, and expectations, an observation integral to CAT.

In interaction, we are working with incomplete information: We know what we perceive but not necessarily what our fellow interactants actually have in mind. To make sense of others' behavior, we must make inferences about their reasons for acting, and thus their mental states (e.g., Malle & Hodges, 2005). Interaction essentially requires of making inferences about what others are thinking on the basis of the verbal and nonverbal signals sent (Levinson, 2006; Schober, 2005). It has even been suggested that "all communication requires intentionality attributions because . . . formal coding rules alone are not sufficient to determine a speaker's meaning" (Sillars, 1998, p. 85), and that such intentionality attributions are so automatic that they are essentially experienced as observations. At a general level, this conceptualization of communication is consistent with Grice's (1957) classic definition of *meaning* as a speaker's intended effect of an utterance on an audience through the audience's recognition of that intention (see again, Chapters 8 and 16, this volume).

This notion of shared understanding as well as its centrality to communication also has connections to Clark's concept of *grounding*, defined as working with fellow interactants to reach the mutual belief that each party understands each other well enough for current purposes (Clark & Brennan, 1991; Clark & Krych, 2004). In general, to allow for interaction to function, we presume that the concepts we hold match others' (the *presumption of interpretability*; Clark & Schober, 1992) and consider it the speaker's responsibility to clarify or elaborate if they mean something other than what the recipient is likely to initially interpret or understand. Attempting to reach this threshold of (perceived) shared understanding is one of the major reasons why we make adjustments for each other in social interaction using the strategies outlined earlier (i.e., *approximation, interpretability, discourse management,* and *interpersonal control*).

However, it is clear that such shared understanding is not successfully achieved in all interactions. This failure of shared understanding is often labeled *misunderstanding* or *miscommunication* when it occurs at the content level; when it takes place on a social or cultural level, the outcome may be labeled as impoliteness, faux pas, or even social deviance (see Dorjee, Giles, & Barker, 2011). All of these are, arguably, instances of nonaccommodation. As noted above, such labels are judgments or evaluations of a communicative experience; as such, they are inherently subjective.

Given the centrality of this conceptualization of communication to key CAT processes, the first refinement of CAT we propose is a more formal, elaborated definition of *communication* as part of the theory. Although it has been made clear that CAT considers communication to be both a means of exchanging information and negotiating social category memberships (Giles & Ogay, 2006), how this is done is, at present, unspecified. We suggest that CAT formally conceptualize communication (referential or social) as an inference process, the goal of which is a mutual belief of shared understanding sufficient for the purposes of interaction.

In making such inferences to determine meaning, one is essentially trying to explain a speaker's behavior. Traditionally, and indeed within CAT's extant framework, this is considered *making attributions*, and the processes involved draw on a substantial body of literature in the area of attribution theory (e.g., Heider, 1958; Hewstone, 1983; Trope & Gaunt, 2003; see also, Chapter 10, this volume). However, recent theoretical and empirical work in social psychology (e.g., Malle, 1999, 2004; Reeder, 2009) has suggested alternative models for both behavior explanations and related trait inferences. These new models provide a number of insights of particular interest to understanding how we react to nonaccommodation.

## BEYOND ATTRIBUTION THEORY: INTENTIONALITY AND MOTIVES

Traditional research in the area of attribution theory has emphasized the distinction between internal (person) and external (situational) causality. However, as Malle (1999, 2004) contends, this dichotomy is better suited to explaining the causes of unintentional actions, rather than deliberate behavior. When we are seeking to understand something intentional, we are much more concerned with what the actor is thinking, planning, and intending *at that moment,* and how it relates to the behavior we are observing and experiencing. In this case, the question becomes not whether the act can be attributed to the person or the situation—because, as in an intentional act, we know the person is the cause—but rather what reason or *motive* the person had for acting the way they did.

Thus, our first and primary concern in interpreting behavior is not determining whether the cause is internal or external, but determining whether the behavior is intentional or unintentional (Heider, 1958; Malle, 2004, 2011). Inferences about intentionality have been shown to be relatively automatic: People answer questions about intentionality more quickly than they answer questions about person or situational causality (Smith & Miller, 1983), suggesting that we may have a predisposition to process behavior in terms of intentionality, as opposed to reasoning about persons or situations. Recent theoretical and empirical work by Malle (1999, 2004, 2011) and Reeder (2009) support the assertion that we engage in different cognitive processes of explanation when we perceive a behavior as unintentional compared with intentional.

When we see something as *unintentional,* both Malle and Reeder propose we consider the internal and external forces at play in a given situation (*causes,* in the terminology of Malle's folk theory of behavior explanations), as Heider's

(1958) attribution theory suggests. (We then make dispositional inferences about actors accordingly). Thus, when behavior is seen as unintentional, the context or situation speakers are in becomes the major focus for understanding why they did what they did and thus, by extension, what—if anything—was *meant* by it.

However, when a behavior is perceived as *intentional,* then we look to actors' mental states to understand why they did what they did. Here, Malle (2004) proposes several different possible ways we can explain behavior: *reasons* (mental states: beliefs, desires, values), *causal history factors* (sources of reasons), and *enabling factors* (situational circumstances facilitating action). In all of these explanation modes, we then use both behavioral and situational information to make inferences about their motives; according to Reeder (2009) our evaluations of motives then influence our trait inferences. In general, motive is arguably a central consideration in social interaction: Understanding individuals' motives not only allows us to explain their behavior—helping us comprehend the events taking place—but also allows us to predict future behavior, which potentially confers a survival advantage (Reeder & Trafimow, 2005).

These processes are entirely cognitive and, as such, risk being interpreted as passive or quiescent. However, interactions are (as their name suggests) interactive in nature and, therefore, dynamic. Individuals have the chance to seek information (directly or indirectly) in conversation and talk through their understanding of what others are intending and doing in real time; as such, understandings of intentionality and motive are subject to negotiation. Such negotiation is particularly likely to occur if intentions are ambiguous or otherwise difficult to discern.

The inferences (attributions) and subsequent evaluations individuals make in dynamic interaction are central considerations of CAT: Per the theory (see Figure 9.1), speakers' perceptions of each others' behavior lead to attributions and then to evaluations. These evaluations both feed back into the ongoing interaction, affecting accommodative behavior in real time, and affect individuals' desire and intention to engage in future interactions. However, at present, the role of intentionality and perceived motives in this process has not been fully elaborated.

## ADDITIONAL CONSIDERATIONS: PERSPECTIVE-TAKING AND INITIAL ORIENTATION

Research in the area of perspective-taking (e.g., Galinsky, Ku, & Wang, 2005) also has potentially interesting implications for outcomes associated with non-accommodation. Perspective-taking is the experience of imagining the world from another person's point of view; when we engage in perspective-taking, we are essentially seeing things through (what we imagine to be) others' eyes. As Bazarova and Hancock (2010) and Malle (2011) point out, when perceivers provide an explanation for another's behavior, they are engaging in perspective-taking to make inferences about intentionality and motive. Galinsky et al. (2005) contend that attempting to take another's perspective increases the overlap in mental representations of the other, and the self has been increasing the "psychological sense of similarity and a feeling of behavioral and mental connectedness" (p. 110) between individuals (see also Chapter 13, this volume). This, in turn, facilitates behavioral coordination and therefore social bonding. Seeing more of themselves in others affects how people describe and evaluate each other: For example, overlap between the other and the self has been associated with decreased stereotyping (mediating the relationship between this outcome and perspective-taking; Galinsky & Moskowitz, 2000) and feelings of oneness with helping and altruistic behavior (again, mediating the relationship between this outcome and perspective-taking; Cialdini, Brown, Lewis, Luce, & Neuberg, 1997). Aron, Aron, and Smollan's (1992) *inclusion of other in the self* scale is often used as a measure of self-other overlap in research on perspective-taking.

Clearly, these findings underscore the importance of the influence that our perceptions of what others are thinking have on our own thoughts and behaviors. However, research in this area has focused primarily on outcomes and implications relating to prejudice, stereotypes, social bias, and social bonding (e.g., Cialdini et al., 1997; Galinsky et al., 2005; Galinsky & Moskowtiz, 2000). The consequences of perspective-taking on interpersonal, as opposed to strictly intergroup, relationships and related outcomes of interest, such as evaluation of an interaction, or intent to engage in future interaction, has received less attention (although Aron and colleagues' work on self-other overlap was originally situated in an interpersonal context).

Based on the aforementioned findings, it is reasonable to suggest that perspective-taking should affect interpersonal relations as well, and in similar ways. We often interpret others' words and actions in line with our own values (e.g., see the presumption of interpretability above in Clark & Schober, 1992). When these do not align, perspective-taking should, in theory, help attenuate some of these differences. By engaging in perspective-taking, we should be increasing the perceived overlap between ourselves and others, which is associated with decreased stereotyping (making an encounter less "us versus them" and more just "us") and increased social bonding. By understanding where the other party is coming from, we have the opportunity to perhaps reframe problematic behavior in more positive terms. If greater overlap between conceptions of the self and the other facilitates bonding, this in turn should result in greater perceived accommodation, more positive evaluations of an interaction and of the speaker, and consequently a greater desire to engage in future interaction.

Finally, our initial orientation toward our interactional partner—which may be affected by our goals for the interaction, psychological states, as well as past experiences with our fellow interactants and their respective social group(s)—are likely to inform our interpretations of their behavior, and by extension, our reactions to it (as evident in some theoretical models of language attitudes; see Cargile, Giles, Ryan, & Bradac, 1994; Giles & Marlow, 2011; Gluzsek & Dovidio, 2010). Broadly speaking, CAT considers both intergroup and interpersonal history to be part of the sociohistorical context that informs an interaction (see Figure 9.1 again; also Chapter 17, this volume). We propose that, more specifically our initial orientation will influence our interpretation of others' motives and, by extension, of their behavior.

Considering interpersonal and intergroup history, it is logical to suggest that the better we know someone, the more likely we are to accurately gauge their goals and motives. Research by Ickes and colleagues on empathic accuracy—defined as an individual's "ability to accurately infer the specific content of another person's thoughts and feelings" (Ickes, 1993, p. 588)—has that the better participants know each other, the higher their empathic accuracy (with respect to each other); those who knew each other better were more accurate in their inferences of each others' thoughts than those who did not.

It is interesting to note that there is also evidence that the more familiar we are with someone, the more likely we are to explain behavior in terms of goals, needs, and other mediating factors (Idson & Mischel, 2001). For instance, if we saw a person we did not know interrupting another, we might think of them as rude or pushy (trait inference). However, if we were actually quite familiar with that person, we might instead explain the interruption as the speaker trying to make an important point (goal) and/or making sure everyone else was aware of a key piece of information (need). In general, when interpreting negative or problematic behavior (as nonaccommodation is experienced), explanations involving mediating factors are likely to result in less negative evaluations of a speaker than are explanations involving trait inferences (i.e., we would evaluate a speaker we see as trying to make an important point more positively than we would a speaker we see as having a rude disposition).

Past interpersonal and intergroup experiences—and associated emotions (Smith & Mackie, 2008)—may also color the lens through which we see and interpret the present. If we have been treated badly by someone (or a representative member of some group) in the past, we are likely to approach new encounters with our guard up, ready to see malfeasance and nonaccommodation in any marginally suspicious move. However, positive past experiences may predispose us to experience others' behavior as more accommodative, and to read the best possible intentions in another's (or a representative member of another group's) behavior (e.g., Murray & Holmes, 1997).

Additionally, past experiences provide a basis for judging whether a given behavior is (idiosyncratically) normative—that is, whether the behavior is normal for that particular actor (cf. *covariation;* Kelley, 1973; Kelley & Michela, 1980). This, in turn, should affect our evaluations of and responses to that behavior: For example, if a couple we have just met speaks loudly and cuts us off when we talk, we might think they are rude and come away offended. However, if we get to know them better and see that they *always* speak loudly and cut off *everybody* that they talk with (including each other), we are less likely to be offended by the behavior. Thus, as outlined here, interpersonal and intergroup histories have the potential to influence not only evaluations of our interaction and fellow interactants—as CAT currently posits—but also our inferences about the content and nature of others' intentions, and therefore the meaning we draw from a given interaction.

In sum, when seeking to understand the meaning of others' behavior, we make inferences about intentionality and motive, and in doing so engage in perspective-taking, and both these processes may be influenced by our initial orientation toward the actor in question. Whatever meaning that we ultimately attribute to our fellow interactants' behavior then becomes the basis for the evaluations we make of the interaction as well as its participants.

## A MODEL FOR INTERPRETING NONACCOMMODATION

Although initial orientation has been a central construct in CAT for years, the constructs of intentionality, motive, and perspective-taking are quite new to the theory. Building on an initial model put forward by Gasiorek and Giles (2012), we propose that perceived motive, as well as perspective-taking, be formally incorporated into CAT's theoretical framework as factors directly and indirectly affecting participants' evaluations of encounters and speakers, and by extension, intent to engage in future interaction.

As outlined in Gasiorek and Giles (2012), accommodation is generally evaluated positively and nonaccommodation negatively (e.g., Giles, 1973; Harwood, 2000; Jones et al., 1994). However, there is empirical work demonstrating that attributions influence these judgments (e.g., Simard, Taylor, & Giles, 1976) such that when behavior is perceived as intentional and positively motivated, accommodative behavior was evaluated more positively than when it was seen as unintentional. Conversely, nonaccommodative behavior was evaluated *less* negatively when perceived as unintentional.

Other language studies provide additional evidence for the importance of motive attributions in the evaluation of accommodative behavior: Polite forms of speech were viewed more positively when attributed to a speaker's desire to be sociable than when attributed to a speaker's desire to be authoritative (Bradac & Mulac, 1984). Brown, Giles, and Thakerar (1985), in turn, found in their experimental design that a slow speech rate—which has been found across many studies to be unfavorably construed—could be contextually attributed to a benevolent motive (attempting to explain unfamiliar material to a group of students). In intergenerational encounters, patronizing talk that could be attributed to caring motives (i.e., was construed as protective or parental, attempting to help) was seen as more polite and more appropriate than patronizing talk attributed to negative motives (i.e., disapproval, exerting authority; Giles & Williams, 1994; Harwood & Giles, 1996). Relatedly, Williams (1996) found that young adults were more tolerant of underaccommodative conversations with older adults than with peers, likely because young adult participants perceived older adults as relatively well-meaning in their lack of accommodation.

In sum, these findings support the assertion that speakers' *perceived* intentionality and motives are an important factor in determining how we understand their behavior and, by extension, the valence and nature of our evaluation of that behavior. Taken together with theorizing on the factors influencing these inferences (as discussed above), we propose a model in which the relationship between perceived accommodation and evaluations of nonaccommodation is mediated by recipients' perceptions of speakers' intentionality and motives, which are, in turn, informed by recipients' initial orientation and degree of perspective-taking. Figure 9.2 illustrates these proposed relationships.

Essentially, the model suggests that, confronted with nonaccommodation of some kind, a recipient considers the intentionality of the speaker's behavior in context (Was it purposeful or not? If so, what motivated it?) and makes an inference about a speaker's motives (positive/negative/none) accordingly. This inference, in turn, affects recipients' evaluation of the encounter and of the speaker they are interacting with, and these evaluations affect their intent to engage in future interaction. In general, when nonaccommodation is perceived as either unintentional or intentional and positively motivated, it should be viewed less negatively than if it is perceived as intentional and negatively motivated. Recipients' degree of perspective-taking may affect both their initial perceptions of nonaccommodative behavior (such that greater perspective-taking is associated with lower levels of perceived nonaccommodation) and their inferences about intentionality and motive (with perspective-taking associated with less negative perceptions of motive). To the extent that it is related to perceived overlap between ourselves and others, perspective-taking may also have direct effects on evaluations of the encounter and the other speaker. Finally, perceptions of nonaccommodation, perspective-taking, motive inference processes, and subsequent evaluations and intentions to engage in future interaction are all informed by the recipient's initial orientation. Greater familiarity between interactants and more positive past interpersonal and/or intergroup histories should increase the accuracy of motive inferences, as well as influence inference and evaluation processes and outcomes.

Part of this model has received empirical support in initial tests. In two studies, Gasiorek and Giles (2012) examined the effects of perceived intentionality and motive on evaluations of nonaccommodative encounters and speakers. As the model predicts, inferring a negative motive for others' nonaccommodation resulted in significantly less positive evaluations of both the interaction and the speaker than inferring either a positive motive or a lack of intentionality. As noted by Gasiorek and Giles (2012), this part of the model also helps explain why underaccommodation is evaluated more negatively than overaccommodation. Here, we may look to the nature of the two constructs in question to help determine motive: Underaccommodation is, by definition, a *lack* of sufficient adjustment, from which a lack of caring (about the interaction or its participants—negative motive) might be inferred. Overaccommodation, in contrast, is overcompensation in terms of interactional adjustment (e.g., being overly helpful—which could be seen as a positive motive). Although overaccommodation may be unpleasant, interactants may still view it as an attempt to be helpful (positive motive)—albeit poorly executed, interactionally—and, therefore, be more forgiving in their evaluation of it, and its source than they would of underaccommodation.

As a final note, we would like to emphasize that as interaction is a dynamic experience, the processes proposed in this model are neither singular nor static:

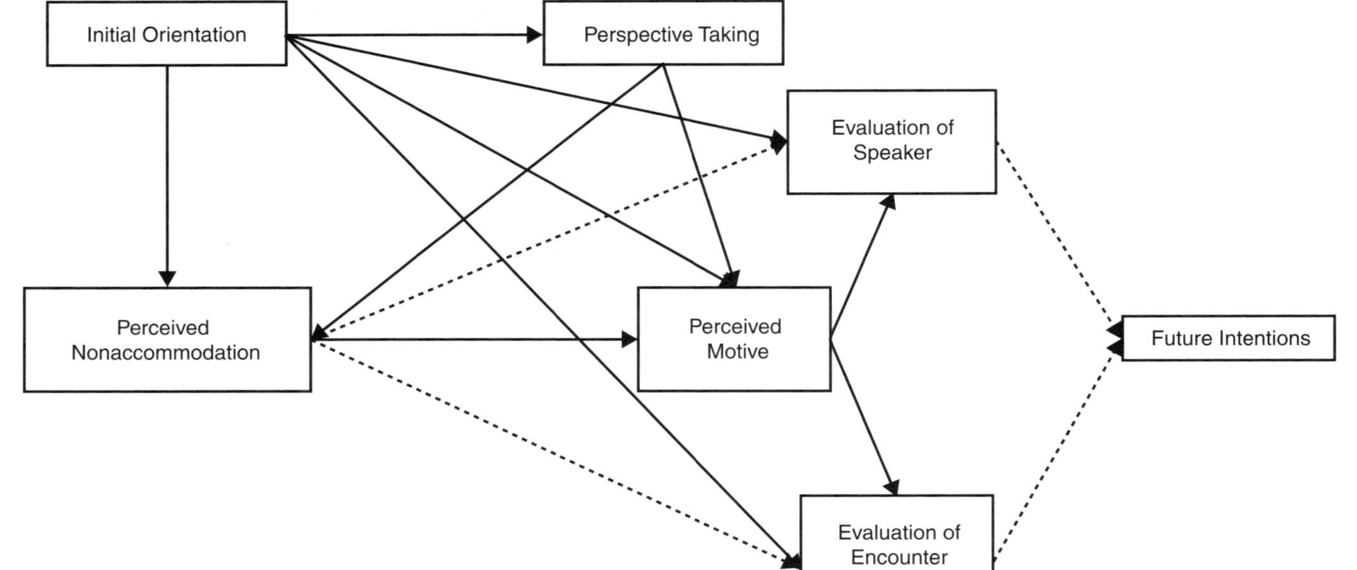


Figure 9.2 A proposed model for interpreting nonaccommodation

Dotted lines indicate paths predicted by the present framework of CAT (direct relationship between perceived accommodation and evaluations).

They are repeated again and again through the course of an encounter and are interactive. To test our inferences about intentionality and motive, for example, we may ask direct or indirect questions, or see what kind of reaction a particular statement garners. The information we gather at each step of this interactive process informs the evaluations we make on an ongoing basis, with our final impression of an encounter (and its participants) as a function of the cumulative experience across the entire interaction.

## CONCLUSIONS

In this chapter, we have sought to elaborate the construct of nonaccommodation within the framework of CAT. We proposed two major refinements to the theory: First, a more precise definition of communication as part of its framework and, second, a model for how three key factors—intentionality and motive, perspective-taking, and initial orientation—influence our evaluations of nonaccommodation, nonaccommodative speakers, and related interactional outcomes. This model aims to provide a more specific set of guidelines predicting our interpretations of and subsequent responses to nonaccommodation.

As specific, measurable, and manipulable variables (initial orientation, perspective-taking, perceived intentionality, perceived motive, evaluations of the encounter and of the speaker, and intent to engage in future interaction) are outlined in the model, their proposed relationships should be the object of systematic empirical testing. Whether the strength or pattern of these relationships is different for different types of nonaccommodation (i.e., over- versus underaccommodation) is also an open—and interesting—empirical question. The application and testing of these issues in specific settings (e.g., intercultural encounters, intergenerational encounters, situations involving law enforcement, educational contexts) is another exciting direction for work in this area. Many additional, interesting questions beyond the scope of this model also remain: For example, what is the role of emotion (see Chapter 4, this volume) in shaping our inferences about motive? Do we make different inferences about motive when using different cognitive processing styles (e.g., accommodative versus assimilative; Fiedler, 2001; Kiefer, Schuch, Schenck, & Fiedler, 2007)? To what extent are these processes unconscious and automatic versus conscious and controlled? What role might fluency (see Chapter 6, this volume) have in our perceptions of communication as (non)accommodative, and our subsequent evaluations of it?

Although much work remains to be done, it is our hope that at the very least, the ideas elaborated here may both encourage and serve as a basis for future efforts to better understand nonaccommodation and, by extension, problematic communication more generally.

## ACKNOWLEDGMENTS

We would like to gratefully acknowledge Scott Reid and Dave Seibold for their input on earlier versions of the material presented here, as well as Jeffrey Robinson for his helpful feedback and suggestions on a previous draft of this paper.

# REFERENCES


Aron, A., Aron, E. N., & Smollan, D. (1992). Inclusion of the other in the self scale and the structure of interpersonal closeness. *Journal of Personality and Social Psychology, 63,* 596–612.

Babel, M. (2010). Dialect divergence and convergence in New Zealand English. *Language in Society, 39,* 437–456.

Bazarova, N. N., & Hancock, J. T. (2010). From dispositional attributions to behavior motives: The folk-conceptual theory and implications for communication. In C. Salmon (Ed.), *Communication yearbook* (Vol. 34, pp. 62–91). Mahwah, NJ: Erlbaum.

Berger, C. R. (2001). Miscommunication and communication failure. In W. P. Robinson & H. Giles (Eds.), *The new handbook of language and social psychology* (pp. 177–192). Chichester, England: Wiley.

Beukeboom, C. J. (2009). When words feel right: How affective expressions of listeners change a speaker's language use. *European Journal of Social Psychology, 39,* 747–756.

Bourhis, R. Y. (1979). Language in ethnic interaction: A social psychological approach. In H. Giles & B. Saint-Jacques (Eds.), *Language and ethnic relations* (pp. 117–141). Oxford, England: Pergamon.

Bourhis, R. Y., Giles, H., Leyends, J. P., & Tajfel, H. (1979). Psychological distinctiveness: Language divergence in Belgium. In H. Giles & R. St.-Clair (Eds.), *Language and social psychology* (pp. 158–185). Oxford, England: Blackwell.

Bradac, J. J., & Mulac, A. (1984). A molecular view of powerful and powerless speech styles: Attributional consequences of specific language features and communicator intentions. *Communication Monographs, 51,* 307–319.

Brown, B. L., Giles, H., & Thakerar, J. N. (1985). Speaker evaluations as a function of speech rate, accent, and context. *Language and Communication, 5,* 207–220.

Cargile, A. C., Giles, H., Ryan, E. B., & Bradac, J. J. (1994). Language attitudes as a social process: A conceptual model and new directions. *Language and Communication, 14,* 211–236

Chartrand, T. L., & Van Baaren, R. (2009). Human mimicry. *Advances in Experimental Social Psychology, 41,* 219–274.

Cialdini, R. B., Brown, S. L., Lewis, B. P., Luce, C., & Neuberg, S. L. (1997). Reinterpreting the empathy-altruism relationship: When one into one equals oneness. *Journal of Personality and Social Psychology, 73,* 481–494.

Clark, H. H., & Brennan, S. A. (1991). Grounding in communication. In L. B. Resnick, J. M. Levine, & S. D. Teasley (Eds.), *Perspectives on socially shared cognition* (pp. 127–149). Washington, DC: APA Books.

Clark, H. H., & Krych, M. A. (2004). Speaking while monitoring addressees for understanding. *Journal of Memory and Language, 50,* 62–81.

Clark, H. H., & Schober, M. F. (1992). Asking questions and influencing answers. In J. M. Tanur (Ed.), *Questions about questions: Inquiries into cognitive bases of surveys* (pp. 15–48). New York, NY: Russell Sage Foundation.

Coupland, N., Coupland, J., Giles, H., & Henwood, K. (1988) Accommodating the elderly: Invoking and extending a theory. *Language in Society, 17,* 1–41.

Cretchley, J., Gallois, C., Chenery, H., & Smith, A. (2010). Conversations between carers and people with schizophrenia: A qualitative analysis using Leximancer. *Qualitative Health Research, 20,* 1611–1628.

Dorjee, T., Giles, H., & Barker, V. (2011). Diasporic communication: Cultural deviance and accommodation among Tibetan exiles in India. *Journal of Multilingual and Multicultural Development, 32,* 343–359.

Dubé-Simard, L. (1983). Genesis of social categorization, threat to identity, and perception of social injustice: Their role in intergroup communication. *Journal of Language and Social Psychology, 2,* 183–206.

Edwards, H., & Noller, P. (1993). Perceptions of overaccommodation used by nurses in communication with the elderly. *Journal of Language and Social Psychology, 12,* 207–223.

Fiedler, K. (2011). Affective states trigger processes of assimilation and accommodation. In L. L. Martin & G. L. Clore (Eds.), *Theories of mood and cognition* (pp. 85–98). New York, NY: Psychology Press.

Galinsky, A. D., Ku, G., & Wang, C. S. (2005). Perspective-taking and self-other overlap: Fostering social bonds and facilitating social coordination. *Group Processes and Intergroup Relations, 8,* 109–124.

Galinsky, A. D., & Moskowitz, G. B. (2000). Perspective-taking: Decreasing stereotype expression, stereotype accessibility, and ingroup favoritism. *Journal of Personality and Social Psychology, 78,* 708–724.

Gallois, C., & Callan, V. J. (1988). Communication accommodation and the prototypical speaker: Predicting evaluations of status and solidarity. *Language and Communication, 8,* 271–284.

Gallois, C., & Giles, H. (1998). Accommodating mutual influence in intergroup encounters. In M. Palmer & G. A. Barnett (Eds.), *Mutual influence in interpersonal communication: Theory and research in cognition, affect, and behavior* (pp. 135–162). New York, NY: Ablex.

Gallois, C., Ogay, T., & Giles, H. (2005). Communication accommodation theory. In W. Gundykunst (Ed.), *Theorizing about intercultural communication* (pp. 121–148). Thousand Oaks, CA: Sage.

Gasiorek, J. (2010). *Nonaccommodation: Forms, perceptions, and consequences* (Unpublished master's thesis). University of California, Santa Barbara.

Gasiorek, J., & Giles, H. (2012). Effects of inferred motive on evaluations of nonaccommodative communication. *Human Communication Research, 38,* 309–332.

Giles, H. (1973). Accent mobility: A model and some data. *Anthropological Linguistics, 15,* 87–105.

Giles, H., & Coupland, N. (1991). *Language: Contexts and consequences.* Buckingham, England: Open University Press.

Giles, H., Coupland, N., & Coupland, J. (1991). Accommodation theory: Communication, context, and consequence. In H. Giles, J. Coupland, & N. Coupland (Eds.), *The contexts of accommodation* (pp. 1–68). New York, NY: Cambridge University Press.

Giles, H., & Gasiorek, J. (2011). Intergenerational communication practices. In K. W. Schaie & S. Willis (Eds.), *Handbook of the psychology of aging* (7th ed., pp. 231–245). New York, NY: Elsevier.

Giles, H., & Marlow, M. L. (2011). Theorizing language attitudes: Existing frameworks, an integrative model, and new directions. In C. Salmon (Ed.), *Communication yearbook* (Vol. 35, pp. 161–197). Mahwah, NJ: Erlbaum.

Giles, H., & Ogay, T. (2006). Communication accommodation theory. In B. Whaley & W. Samter (Eds.), *Explaining communication: Contemporary theories and exemplars* (pp. 293–310). Mahwah, NJ: Erlbaum.

Giles, H., Reid, S. A., & Harwood, J. (Eds.). (2010). *The dynamics of intergroup communication.* New York, NY: Peter Lang.

Giles, H., Willemyns, M., Gallois, C., & Anderson, M. C. (2007). Accommodating a new frontier: The context of law enforcement. In K. Fiedler (Ed.), *Social communication* (pp. 129–162). New York, NY: Psychology Press.

Giles, H., & Williams, A. (1994). Patronizing the young: Forms and evaluations. *International Journal of Aging and Human Development, 39,* 33–53.

Gluszek, A., & Dovidio, J. F. (2010). A social psychological perspective on the stigma of non-native accents in communication. *Personality and Social Psychology Review, 14,* 214–237.

Grice, H. P. (1957). Meaning. *Philosophical Review, 66,* 377–388.

Harwood, J. (2000). Communicative predictors of solidarity in the grandparent-grandchild relationship. *Journal of Social and Personal Relationships, 17,* 743–766.

Harwood, J., & Giles, H. (1996). Reactions to older people being patronized: The roles of response strategies and attributed thoughts. *Journal of Language and Social Psychology, 15,* 395–421.

Heider, F. (1958). *The psychology of interpersonal relations.* New York, NY: Wiley.

Hewstone, M. (1983). Attribution theory and common-sense explanations: An introductory overview. In M. Hewstone (Ed.), *Attribution theory: Social and functional extensions* (pp. 1–26). Oxford, England: Blackwell.

Hewstone, M., & Giles, H. (1986). Social groups and social stereotypes in intergroup communication: Review and model of intergroup communication breakdown. In W. B. Gudykunst (Ed.), *Intergroup communication* (pp. 10–20). London, England: Edward Arnold.

Hummert, M. L., & Ryan, E. B. (2001). Patronizing. In W. P. Robinson & H. Giles (Eds.), *The new handbook of language and social psychology* (pp. 253–269). Chichester, England: Wiley.

Ickes, W. (1993). Empathic accuracy. *Journal of Personality, 61,* 587–610.

Idson, L. C., & Mischel, W. (2001). The personality of familiar and significant people: The lay perceiver as a social-cognitive theorist. *Journal of Personality and Social Psychology, 80,* 585–596.

Jones, E., Gallois, C., Barker, M., & Callan, V. (1994). Evaluations of interactions between students and academic staff: Influence of communication accommodation, ethnic group, and status. *Journal of Language and Social Psychology, 13,* 158–191.

Kelley, H. H. (1973). The process of causal attribution. *American Psychologist, 28,* 107–128.

Kelley, H. H., & Michela, J. L. (1980). Attribution theory and research. *Annual Review of Psychology, 31,* 457–501.

Kiefer, M., Schuch, S., Schenck, W., & Fiedler, K. (2007). Emotion and memory: Event-related potential indices predictive for subsequent successful memory depend on the emotional mood state. *Advances in Cognitive Psychology, 3,* 363–373.

Levinson, S. C. (2006). On the human "interaction engine." In N. J. Enfield & S. C. Levinson (Eds.), *Roots of human sociality: Culture, cognition and interaction* (pp. 39–69). Oxford, England: Berg.

Lineweaver, T. T., Hutman, P., Ketcham, C., & Bohannon, J. N., III. (2011). The effect of comprehension feedback and listener age on speech complexity. *Journal of Language and Social Psychology, 30,* 46–65.

Malle, B. F. (1999). How people explain behavior: A new theoretical framework. *Personality and Social Psychology Review, 3,* 23–48.

Malle, B. F. (2004). *How the mind explains behavior: Folk explanations, meaning, and social interaction.* Cambridge, MA: MIT Press.

Malle, B. (2011). Time to give up the dogmas of attribution: An alternative theory of behavior explanation. *Advances in Experimental Social Psychology, 44,* 297–352.

Malle, B. F., & Hodges, S. D. (Eds.). (2005). *Other Minds: How humans bridge the divide between self and others.* New York, NY: Guilford Press.

Murray, S. L., & Holmes, J. G. (1997). A leap of faith? Positive illusions in romantic relationships. *Personality and Social Psychology Bulletin, 23,* 586–604.

Reeder, G. D. (2009). Mindreading: Judgments about intentionality and motives in dispositional inference. *Psychological Inquiry, 20,* 1–18.

Reeder, G. D., & Trafimow, D. (2005). Attributing motives to other people. In B. F. Malle & S. D. Hodges (Eds.), *Other Minds: How humans bridge the divide between self and others* (pp. 26–42). New York, NY: Guilford Press.

Ryan, E. B., Hummert, M. L., & Boich, L. H. (1995). Communication predicaments of aging: Patronizing behavior toward older adults. *Journal of Language and Social Psychology, 14,* 144–166.

Sachweh, S. (1998). Granny darling's nappies: Secondary babytalk in German nursing homes for the aged. *Journal of Applied Communication Research, 26,* 52–65.

Schober, M. F. (2005). Conceptual alignment in conversation. In B. F. Malle & S. D. Hodges (Eds.), *Other Minds: How humans bridge the divide between self and others* (pp. 239–252). New York, NY: Guilford Press.

Shepard, C. A., Giles, H., & Le Poire, B. A. (2001). Communication accommodation theory. In W. P. Robinson & H. Giles (Eds.), *The new handbook of language and social psychology* (pp. 33–56). Chichester, England: Wiley.

Sillars, A. L. (1998). (Mis)Understanding. In B. H. Spitzberg & W. R. Cupach (Eds.), *The dark side of personal relationships* (pp. 73–102). Mahwah, NJ: Erlbaum.

Simard, L., Taylor, D. M., & Giles, H. (1976). Attribution processes and interpersonal accommodation in a bilingual setting. *Language and Speech, 19,* 374–387.

Smith, E. R., & Mackie, D. M. (2008). Intergroup emotions. In M. Lewis, J. Haviland-Jones, & L. Feldman Barrett (Eds.), *Handbook of emotions* (3rd ed., pp. 428–439). New York, NY: Guilford Press.

Smith, E. R., & Miller, F. D. (1983). Mediation among attributional inferences and comprehension processes: Initial findings and a general method. *Journal of Personality and Social Psychology, 86,* 530–544.

Street, R. L., & Giles, H. (1982). Speech accommodation theory: A social cognitive approach to language and speech behavior. In M. E. Roloff & C. R. Berger (Eds.), *Social cognition and communication* (pp. 33–53). Belmont, CA: Wadsworth.

Thakerar, J. N., Giles, H., & Cheshire, J. (1982). Psychological and linguistic parameters of speech accommodation theory. In C. Fraser & K. R. Scherer (Eds.), *Advances in the social psychology of language* (pp. 205–255). Cambridge, England: Cambridge University Press.

Trope, Y., & Gaunt, R. (2003). Attribution and person perception. In M. A. Hogg & J. Cooper (Eds.), *The Sage handbook of social psychology* (pp. 190–208). London, England: Sage.

Williams, A. (1996). Young people's evaluations of intergenerational versus peer underaccommodation: Sometimes older is better? *Journal of Language and Social Psychology, 15,* 291–311.

Williams, A., & Giles, H. (1996). Intergenerational conversations: Young adults' retrospective accounts. *Human Communication Research, 23,* 220–250.

Ytsma, J., & Giles, H. (1997). Reactions to patronizing talk: Some Dutch data. *Journal of Sociolinguistics, 1,* 259–268.

# 10

# The Big Two of Agency and Communion in Language and Communication

ANDREA E. ABELE AND SUSANNE BRUCKMÜLLER

Whereas most social cognition research interested in the processing of social information has implicitly presumed that the investigated processes are more or less the same across different types of content, there is also a tradition of approaches that have recognized the importance of content (cf. Dunning, 2004). Based on Asch's (1946) classic finding that certain traits are more *central* than others, Reeder and Brewer (1979), for instance, demonstrated that content pertaining to morality receives a higher weight in social judgments than content pertaining to ability.

More recently, different strands of research have resulted in a convergence regarding the two most important dimensions of content. These two dimensions have been referred to under different names. Research on person perception has most commonly used the denominations of *morality* versus *ability* (Reeder & Brewer, 1979); research on stereotypes has mostly been concerned with the related concepts of *warmth* and *competence* (Fiske, Cuddy, & Glick, 2007; Judd, James-Hawkins, Yzerbyt, & Kashima, 2005); other research has been concerned with the distinction between *other-profitable* and *self-profitable* traits (Peeters, 1992, 2008) or between *social desirability* and *social utility* traits (Beauvois & Dubois, 2009); other research traditions use the denominations introduced by Bakan (1966), namely *agency* and *communion* (Abele & Bruckmüller, 2011; Abele & Wojciszke, 2007; Cislak & Wojciszke, 2008; Eagly, 1987; Wiggins, 1991; Ybarra et al., 2008). Despite these differences in names and slight variations in their conceptualization, all these two-dimensional approaches share a common core in content (cf. Abele & Wojciszke, 2007; Judd et al., 2005). Hence, they have been called *fundamental dimensions* (Abele, Cuddy, Judd, & Yzerbyt, 2008) or the *Big Two* (Paulhus & Trapnell, 2008).

In our research we use the denominations of communion and agency because of two reasons. First, we think that these denominations are broad enough to cover sub-components like morality and warmth in case of communion, or sub-components of competence or ability and dominance or assertiveness in case of agency. Second, we chose these denominations because both terms are more or less artificial and less loaded with lay conceptualizations like, for instance, ability or warmth. Hence, it might be easier to define a common scientific understanding of the respective concepts. Traits and behaviors related to warmth, friendliness, or trustworthiness (and their opposites) are examples of the content dimension of communion. The content dimension of agency comprises traits and behaviors like ambitious, competent, or self-confident (and their opposites).

These two fundamental content dimensions have not emerged incidentally, but they reflect basic human needs, namely forming and maintaining social connections (communion/ warmth/ morality/ other-profitability/ social desirability) and pursuing goals and manifesting skills and accomplishments (agency/ ability/ competence/ self-profitability/ social utility; Fiske et al., 2007; Ybarra et al., 2008).

Such two-dimensional conceptualizations are not only found in research on traits or interpersonal perception but inherent in many other psychological theories. Research on leadership, for instance, distinguishes between *initiating-structure* (i.e., task-orientation; agency) versus *consideration* (i.e., person-orientation; communion; Halpin & Winer, 1957). Research on group behavior distinguishes between *instrumentality* (task-orientation; agency) and *expressiveness* (social-orientation; communion; Parsons & Bales, 1955). Research on cultures distinguishes between *individualism* (agency) and *collectivism* (communion; Hofstede, 1980). Personality traits can be reduced to the circumplex of dominance (agency) versus nurturance (communion; Wiggins, 1991). Self-serving biases are subsumed under the headings of *superhero* (agency) versus *saint* (communion; Paulhus & Trapnell, 2008). Even Osgood's three-dimensional semantic differential can be reduced to two dimensions (Osgood, Suci, & Tannenbaum, 1957).

In this chapter, we give an overview of research on the Big Two with a special focus on their importance in language and communication. We then outline one study in greater detail before we relate our approach to some of the other chapters in this volume.

## AGENCY AND COMMUNION IN LANGUAGE AND COMMUNICATION

One of the first studies analyzing the fundamental content dimensions in language was conducted by Rosenberg, Nelson, and Vivekananthan (1968). They asked their participants to sort 64 trait words into piles of traits that go together, for example because they often co-occur in a person. Using a multidimensional scaling procedure to map the perceived similarity between these various traits, they found a two-dimensional structure; they interpreted these dimensions as comprising *intellectual desirability* (ranging from *foolish* to *scientific*) and *social desirability* (ranging from *dishonest* to *sociable*).

More recently, Abele and Wojciszke (2007; Study 1) asked their participants to rate 300 trait names with respect to a number of different criteria. They then factor-analyzed these ratings and found a clear two-dimensional structure in which the first factor that explained 66% of item variance was unambiguously interpretable as the communion factor; the second factor, explaining an additional 23% of item variance clearly represented agency.

In an international study, Abele, Uchronski, Suitner, and Wojciszke (2008) asked participants in different countries to rate the extent to which 69 traits expressed agency and communion (based on given definitions of these two dimensions). Comparing these ratings across five European languages (English, French, German, Italian, and Polish) they found very similar patterns of ratings, indicating a similar understanding of these two dimensions across research settings. Ybarra et al. (2008) reported similar findings for Asian languages.

In sum, these studies show that agency and communion are deeply rooted in language: They structure the words we use to describe ourselves and others (i.e., trait words) and are conceptualized similarly in different languages.

## The Primacy of Communion

Research also suggests that the content dimension of communion is the primary one of the two. In the study by Abele and Wojciszke (2007) described above, the communion factor explained much more item variance than the agency factor. It is even more universally conceptualized in different languages than the agency dimension (Abele et al., 2008; Ybarra et al., 2008), and in our own research, we found that despite extensive pretesting to ensure equivalence with regard to a number of relevant factors, participants still agreed more in their judgments of communal content than of agentic content (Abele & Bruckmüller, 2011, Studies 2 and 3).

We also found that information pertaining to the content dimension of communion is processed preferentially on various levels of social information processing. We based this *preferential processing hypothesis* (Abele & Bruckmüller, 2011) on a functional approach to person perception according to which "perceiving is for doing" (Fiske, 1992) and the primary purpose of social perception is to guide people in their actions (Dunning, 2004; Heider, 1958; Zebrowitz & Collins, 1997). Perceivers first of all want to know whether another person is benevolent and whether it is safe to approach this person. Warmth, friendliness, and trustworthiness (and their opposites) provide relevant information on whether it is safe to approach a potential interaction partner or whether a person should better be avoided. Of course another person's agency—that is, his or her competence and determination in pursuing intentions towards the perceiver—is also important, but its relevance critically depends on the person's benevolence or malevolence toward the perceiver—that is, his or her communion (see also Fiske et al., 2007).

Employing a lexical decision task, our first study (Abele & Bruckmüller, 2011, Study 1) demonstrated that people recognize communal trait words faster than agentic trait words (see also Ybarra, Chan, & Park, 2001). In Study 2 (Abele & Bruckmüller, 2011), we predicted and found that, compared with agentic trait words, participants categorized communal trait words faster with regard to valence. In Study 3, participants read behavior descriptions that had been pretested as expressing a communal and an agentic trait to a similar degree (e.g., *X organizes a successful surprise party for a friend*, which had been rated as equally *helpful* and *determined*; and *X simply keeps on walking when someone asks for the way because he or she does not know it either*, which had been rated as equally *(un-)friendly* and *(in-)competent*). Although these behavior descriptions always expressed a communal and an agentic trait to the same extent, participants were faster to infer the communal traits when reading these sentences than they were to infer the agentic traits.

These findings fit well with research on person perception that has shown that in more deliberate impression formation and judgments of others, perceivers place a higher weight on information regarding others' communion than others' agency. For instance, when participants in a study by De Bruin and Van Lange (2000) were given the choice what kind of information they wanted to receive about a later interaction partner, they chose to see the communal information first in 84% of cases and decided in only 16% of cases to see the agentic information first. Participants also spent more time reading the communal than the agentic information. Ames and Bianchi (2008) found that agreeableness (which is related to the communion dimension, cf. Wiggins, 1991) was the most commonly inferred trait when participants described various targets.

## *Agency and Communion and the Perspectives of Actor and Observer*

In our DPM (for dual perspective model), we have recently proposed that in addition to this general primacy of communion, the basic dimensions of agency and communion are differently linked to the perspectives of *actor* (a person performing an act—or, in communication, a speaker) and *observer* or *recipient* (a third person observing the actor or a person toward whom the action is directed—or the recipient of a communication), or to the perspective of self versus other, respectively (Abele, Bruckmüller, & Wojciszke, 2012; Abele & Wojciszke, 2007; Wojciszke & Abele, 2008; Wojciszke, Baryla, Parzuchowski, Szymkow, & Abele, 2011).

In the observer perspective, that is, in the perception and judgment of others' behavior or communicative acts, people first of all want to know whether a target can be approached or should be avoided (Fiske et al., 2007; Peeters & Czapinski, 1990). Hence, they direct their attention toward others' communal behaviors and traits (Abele & Bruckmüller, 2011). In the actor perspective, that is, in the perception and judgment of one's own behavior, communal content matters as well, because communal traits are essential to establish and maintain benevolent relationships with others. However, in the actor or self-perspective, people usually focus on the achievement of current action goals and on efficiently pursuing these goals. Hence, agentic content is more important in this perspective than in the observer perspective. In other words, observers first of all want to *get along* with the other; actors also want to get along, but they especially want to *get ahead* in pursuing their aims and goals. The DPM, therefore, states that agentic content is more important in the actor or self-perspective than in the observer or other-perspective; communal content is primary in either perspective but is relatively more important in the observer or other-perspective than in the actor or self-perspective.

The DPM allows predictions for a number of phenomena in the related areas of social cognition, interpersonal perception, and communication. Below, we describe one empirical example in more detail and then outline some additional predictions and ideas for future research that illustrate the value and potential of the DPM in conceptualizing and understanding social cognition and communication.

## AN EMPIRICAL EXAMPLE: AGENCY AND COMMUNION IN THE DESCRIPTION OF SELF AND OTHERS

One straightforward prediction based on the DPM concerns people's perception and description of themselves and of others. Although perceptions and, as a consequence, descriptions of others should be dominated by communal content, agentic content should figure more prominently in people's self-descriptions than in their descriptions of others.

To test these predictions, we asked 118 student participants (77 women, 41 men; mean age 22 years) to describe themselves and a friend, that is, a person that they knew well but did not feel very close to, with up to eight characteristic traits. Self-descriptions and friend-descriptions were separated by a week, and we counterbalanced between participants whose description (self or friend) they provided first. These descriptions were later content-analyzed by two independent coders unaware of the hypotheses of the study and unaware of the target (description of self or of a friend).

Coders categorized the traits listed by participants with regard to both content and valence (similarly see Abele & Bruckmüller, 2011; Uchronski, 2008). In addition to rating traits as positive or negative (or neutral) and as pertaining to agency or communion (or neither), we added a further distinction based on Peeters (2008). This author suggested not only that traits are self-profitable or other-profitable (as well as positive and negative), but that self-profitable and other-profitable traits can express this characteristic to a high or a low degree. Traits can be self-profitable (e.g., *dominant*) or other-profitable (e.g., *helpful*) or they can *lack* self-profitability (e.g., *indecisive*) or other-profitability (e.g., *rude*), respectively. This distinction is different from the distinction between positive and negative traits because there are a *lack of* traits that may be regarded as valence neutral or positive (e.g., *cautious*) and *high degree* traits that may be evaluated as neutral or negative (e.g., dominant). Our hypotheses mostly pertained to high degree agentic and communal traits, but in an exploratory fashion, we also analyzed participants' self- and other-descriptions using lack of traits.

The two coders thus categorized each trait as positive, negative, or neutral and additionally categorized each trait as *high agency* (e.g., smart), *high communion* (e.g., friendly), *lack of agency* (e.g., shy), *lack of communion* (e.g., withdrawn), or *other* (e.g., pretty, sportive) based on given definitions of agency and communion.

The definition of communion was: "Communion refers to a person's striving to be part of a community, to establish close relationships, and to give up individual needs for the common good. Communion manifests itself in empathy and understanding, in caring and cooperation, as well as in moral behavior." *Lack of communion* was defined as traits that denominate negative interpersonal behavior both with respect to sociability and with respect to morality. Examples given were *impatient* or *unreliable*.

The definition of *agency* was: "Agency refers to a person's striving to express one's individuality, to assert oneself, to attain individual goals, and to control the environment. Agency manifests itself in assertiveness and leadership behavior, in achievement, in a striving for success, and in autonomy." *Lack of agency* was defined as traits that denominate insecurity, external control, and a lack of goal orientation. Examples given were *chaotic* or *indecisive*.

The two coders agreed on 83% of the content categorizations and on 92% of the valence categorizations. Disagreements were resolved by discussion. Participants generated $M$ = 13.61 ($SD$ = 2.10) traits overall, and generated similar numbers of traits describing the self ($M$ = 6.78, $SD$ = 1.26) and describing a friend ($M$ = 6.83, $SD$ = 1.25), $t < 1$. Coders classified 51.4% of these traits as communal (including both high and lack of variants), 33.3 % as agentic (including both high and lack of variants), and 15.4% as other, again illustrating the primacy of communion. Participants listed more positive than negative (than neutral) traits; they also listed more positive traits for the friend ($M$ = 4.94, $SD$ = 1.57) than for themselves ($M$ = 4.56, $SD$ = 1.51), $t$ (117) = 2.32, $p$ = .02, and listed less negative traits for the friend ($M$ = 1.05, $SD$ = 1.10) than for themselves ($M$ = 1.43, $SD$ = 1.11), $t$ (117) = 3.20, $p < .01$.

A repeated-measures ANOVA with target (self versus friend) and trait content (agentic versus communal traits) as within participants factors revealed a highly significant content effect, $F$ (1, 117) = 45.46, $p < .001$, with more communion traits ($M$ = 2.92, $SD$ = 1.44) than agency traits listed ($M$ = 1.81, $SD$ = 1.22). This main effect was qualified by a significant target by content interaction, $F$ (1, 117) = 22.02, $p < .001$. As predicted by the DPM, participants listed more agency traits in their self-descriptions ($M$ = 2.02, $SD$ = 1.21) than in their descriptions of a friend ($M$ = 1.60, $SD$ = 1.23), $t$ (117) = 3.06, $p < .01$, and listed more communion traits for the friend ($M$ = 3.25, $SD$ = 1.56) than for themselves ($M$ = 2.59, $SD$ = 1.33), $t$ (117) = 4.47, $p < .001$. Figure 10.1 summarizes these findings.

Parallel analyses for the traits describing a lack of communion or agency also revealed a significant perspective (self versus other) by content interaction,

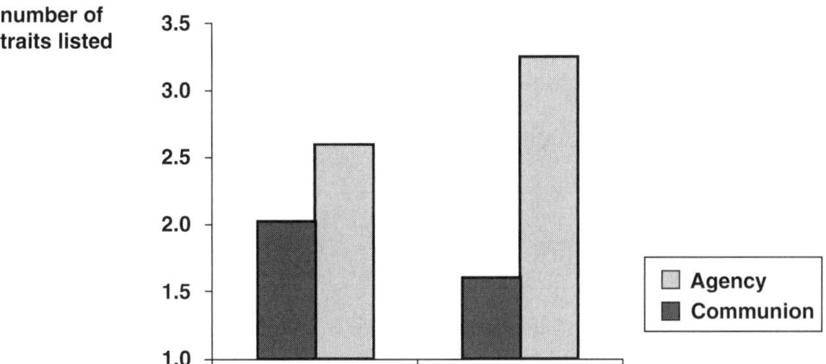


Figure 10.1 Number of traits listed for self and friend in both categories

$F$ (1, 117) = 4.49, $p$ < .04. Participants described themselves with more traits expressing a lack of communion ($M$ = .70, $SD$ = 0.87) than the friend ($M$ = 0.45, $SD$ = 0.79), $t$ (117) = 2.68, $p$ < .01, and described themselves with more attributes expressing a lack of communion than with attributes expressing a lack of agency ($M$ = 0.43, $SD$ = 0.69), $t$ (117) = 2.42, $p$ < .02. There were no differences between self- and friend-descriptions in the number of lack of agency traits mentioned, $t$ < 1, and no differences in the description of a friend with lack of traits, $t$ < 1. Thus, the observed pattern for traits expressing a lack of communion or agency paralleled participants' descriptions with traits expressing a high degree of communion or agency. However, cautious interpretation is warranted because the number of lack of traits was very low overall.

A second study, in which 45 female and 29 male student participants (mean age 24 years) rated the extent to which a number of given traits described themselves and a friend by conventional Likert-scale ratings yielded very similar findings.

Both the agency scale and the communion scale comprised 12 items that were carefully pretested with respect to valence and typicality for the respective dimension (agency: *self-confident, consistent, determined, intelligent, rational, independent, assertive, competent, persistent, active, efficient, energetic*; communion: *generous, helpful, affectionate, empathic, sincere, likeable, understanding, supportive, caring, moral, tolerant, emotional*).

We again found a significant content effect, $F$ (1, 73) = 4.31, $p$ < .05, with higher communion ($M$ = 5.21) than agency ratings ($M$ = 5.05), and a significant two-way interaction of content by target, $F$ (1, 73) = 8.79, $p$ < .01. Participants' ratings of their own agency ($M$ = 5.13, $SD$ = .68) and communion ($M$ = 5.11, $SD$ = 0.86) did not differ, $t$ < 1, but they rated their own communion lower than their friend's communion, $t$ (73) = 2.80, $p$ < .01, which is in accord with the DPM. Further supporting the DPM, they rated their own agency higher than their friend's agency, $t$ (73) = 1.83, $p$ = .07 ($p$ < .04, one-tailed), and they rated the friend's communion higher ($M$ = 5.32, $SD$ = 0.85) than the friend's

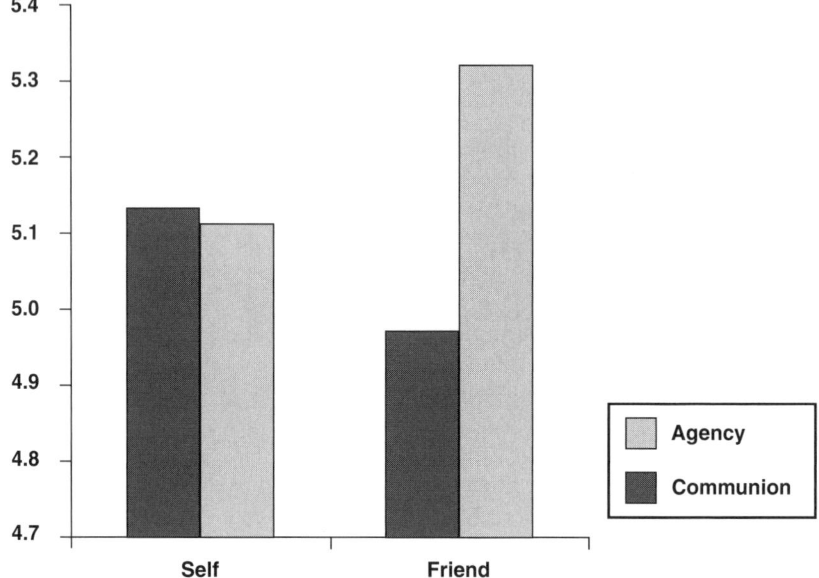


Figure 10.2 Mean ratings of agency and communion for self and friend

agency ($M$ = 4.97, $SD$ = 0.78), $t$ (73) = 3.21, $p$ < .01. Figure 10.2 summarizes the findings.

In summary, two studies that employed different operationalizations (free responses versus trait ratings) support central predictions based on the DPM, such as the primacy of communion, the closer link of agency to the actor perspective, and the closer link of communion to the observer perspective.

## THE PRESENT APPROACH AND OTHER RESEARCH ON SOCIAL COGNITION AND COMMUNICATION

So far, we have introduced the fundamental content dimensions of agency and communion, their prevalence and importance in language, the primacy of the communion dimension, and the DPM, that describes the relation of the fundamental dimensions to the basic perspectives in social interaction—that is, the perspective of an actor who performs a certain behavior and the perspective of an observer who watches the behavior or is the recipient of the actor's behavior. We think that the fundamental dimensions and the DPM represent a promising framework for approaching questions of social cognition and communication, such as the ones discussed in this volume. Below, we outline future research questions and illustrate some of the many possible connections to other chapters in this volume.

## Future Research Questions

One future research question concerns (mis-)understandings in social interaction and communication (see also Chapter 9, this volume). If observers focus mostly on communion while actors focus on both agency and communion, actors should think that they are displaying and communicating more agency than observers will actually perceive. This might cause misunderstandings, for example when one person (as actor) thinks that he or she has been asserting a standpoint in a discussion whereas the other person's dominant impression (as observer) could be that the actor was unfriendly. Likewise, one could imagine a situation in which one person (as observer) thinks that the other person has been very polite and helpful, whereas this person's own interpretation of the situation may be that he or she has been too accommodating to the other person and might not have adequately pursued his or her own action goals. Abele et al. (2012), for instance, conducted two studies in which two previously unacquainted persons had a short encounter and then rated both their own behavior and the other person's behavior. We found that one and the same behavior was differently interpreted by actors versus observers. Participants saw themselves (as actors) as more agentic and less communal than their interaction partners (as observers) perceived them. In addition to providing further support for the DPM, this research is also a continuation of the old actor-observer differences in attribution research (Jones & Nisbett, 1971) with a focus behavior on descriptions and trait inferences rather than on causal attributions.

Another research question relates to self-disclosure as perceived by actors and observers. It is well known that relationship development needs self-disclosure—that is, both partners must be willing to share intimate information about themselves with the other person (Levinger, 1980). It might well be that the communicating person (the actor) perceives a communication as more (or less) self-disclosing than the receiver of the communication (the observer) does. The fundamental dimensions might be a good starting point for analyzing such differences. The DPM would predict that actors perceive information regarding their own agentic behavior as more self-disclosing whereas observers should perceive information on another person's communal behavior as more self-disclosing.

Further questions concern how the way we communicate about others might influence the perception of these others in terms of agency and communion. A recent study by Bruckmüller and Abele (2010) has, for instance, shown that when two groups are compared, the framing of this comparison matters for how the two groups are perceived by others. When group X is compared with group Y, then Y is the standard against which X is compared (when Y is compared with X, then X is the standard). Bruckmüller and Abele (2010) showed that the framing of comparisons between both artificial groups and real groups influenced perceptions of the groups' agency and communion. The group representing the comparison standard was seen as more agentic but as less communal than when it was compared with the respective other group.

### Promising Connections to Other Research

Beyond these specific research questions, we see promising ways in which our approach can be combined with other research on language and communication discussed in this volume. Both Pennebaker's approach with the LIWC (for linguistic inquiry and word count) program (see Chapter 2, this volume) and Semin and Fiedler's LCM (for linguistic category model; see Chapter 3, this volume) could be fruitfully combined with a fundamental dimensions perspective. Including agency and communion as broader categories in the LIWC opens possibilities to investigate many interesting questions regarding the Big Two in natural language use, such as the analysis of texts written about the self and texts written about others with regard to agentic and communal content, or the investigation of psychological factors related to a focus on agentic versus communal content in a text. Concerning the LCM, research on how the fundamental dimensions relate to different abstraction levels in language use also seems like a promising approach.

In addition to these broader questions, we see direct connections of our approach to other chapters in this volume. For instance, Catellani and Bertolotti (see Chapter 16, this volume) illustrate the importance of perceived morality (communion) and leadership (agency) in the evaluation of politicians. Peters and Kashima (Chapter 11, this volume) in their investigation of the social functions of gossip demonstrate the importance of gossip content related to morality versus competence for the evaluation of the gossiper. Furthermore, our fundamental dimensions approach can also be connected to research on attitude change as presented by Cooper and Trujillo (Chapter 7, this volume) and by Crano and Avaro (Chapter 17, this volume): Communicators' agency and communion might represent important moderators of the impact of a persuasive massage.

We could continue this list, but the important point is that all these different connections to such a variety of research endeavors in social cognition and communication illustrate the fundamental character of communal and agentic content and the relevance of these dimensions in social cognition and communication. We hope that this chapter helps to facilitate fruitful combinations between a Big Two perspective and many of the other approaches and research questions addressed in this volume.

## REFERENCES

Abele, A. E., Bruckmüller, S. (2011). The bigger one of the "Big Two": Preferential processing of communal information. *Journal of Experimental Social Psychology, 47*, 935–948.

Abele, A. E., Bruckmüller, S., & Wojciszke, B. (2012). *Actor—observer differences in behavior interpretations. A new look from the "Big Two."* Manuscript submitted for publication.

Abele, A. E., Cuddy, A. J., Judd, C. M., & Yzerbyt, V. Y. (2008). Special issue: Fundamental dimensions of social judgment. *European Journal of Social Psychology, 38*, 1063–1224.

Abele, A. E., Uchronski, M., Suitner, C., & Wojciszke, B. (2008). Towards an operationalization of the fundamental dimensions of agency and communion: Trait content ratings in five countries considering valence and frequency of word occurrence. *European Journal of Social Psychology, 38,* 1202–1217.

Abele, A. E., & Wojciszke, B. (2007). Agency and communion from the perspective of self vs. others. *Journal of Personality and Social Psychology, 93,* 751–763.

Ames, D., & Bianchi, E. (2008). The agreeableness asymmetry in first impressions: Perceivers impulse to (mis)judge agreeableness and how it is moderated by power. *Personality and Social Psychology Bulletin, 34,* 1719–1736.

Asch, S. E. (1946). Forming impressions of personality. *Journal of Abnormal and Social Psychology, 41,* 258–290.

Bakan, D. (1966). *The duality of human existence. An essay on psychology and religion.* Chicago, IL: Rand MacNally.

Beauvois, J.-L., & Dubois, N. (2009). Lay psychology and the social value of persons. *Social and Personality Compass, 3,* 1082–1095.

Bruckmüller, S., & Abele, A. E. (2010). Comparison focus in intergroup comparisons: Who we compare to whom influences who we see as powerful and agentic. *Personality and Social Psychology Bulletin, 36,* 1424–1435.

Cislak, A., & Wojciszke, B. (2008). Agency and communion are inferred from actions serving interests of self or others. *European Journal of Social Psychology, 38,* 1103–1110.

De Bruin, E., & Van Lange, P. (2000). What people look for in others: Inferences of the perceiver and the perceived on information selection. *Personality and Social Psychology Bulletin, 26,* 206–219.

Dunning, D. (2004). On the motives underlying social cognition. In M. Brewer & M. Hewstone (Eds.), *Emotion and Motivation* (pp. 137–164). Oxford, England: Blackwell.

Eagly, A. H. (1987). *Sex differences in social behavior: A social-role interpretation.* Hillsdale, NJ: Erlbaum.

Fiske, S. T. (1992). Thinking is for doing: Portraits of social cognition from Daguerreotype to laserphoto. *Journal of Personality and Social Psychology, 63,* 877–889.

Fiske, S. T., Cuddy, A., & Glick, P. (2007). Universal dimensions of social cognition: Warmth and competence. *Trends in Cognitive Science, 11,* 77–83.

Halpin, A. W., & Winer, B. J. (1957). A factorial study of the leader behavior descriptions. In R. M. Stogdill & A. E. Coons (Eds.), *Leader behavior: Its description and measurement* (pp. 39–51). Columbus, OH: Bureau of Business Research.

Heider, F. (1958). *The psychology of interpersonal relations.* New York, NY: Wiley.

Hofstede, G. (1980). *Culture's consequences.* Beverly Hills, CA: Sage.

Jones, E. E., & Nisbett, R. E. (1971). *The actor and the observer: Divergent perceptions of the causes of behavior.* Morristown, NJ: General Learning Press.

Judd, C. M., James-Hawkins, L., Yzerbyt, V., & Kashima, Y. (2005). Fundamental dimensions of social judgment: Understanding the relations between judgments of competence and warmth. *Journal of Personality and Social Psychology, 89,* 899–913.

Levinger, G. (1980). Toward the analysis of close relationships. *Journal of Experimental Social Psychology, 16*(6), 510–544.

Osgood, C. E., Suci, G. J., & Tannenbaum, P. H. (1957). *The measurement of meaning.* Urbana, IL: University of Illinois Press.

Parsons, T., & Bales, R. (1955). *Family, socialization, and interaction processes.* Glencoe, Scotland: Free Press.

Paulhus, D. L., & Trapnell, P. D. (2008). Self-presentation of personality: An agency-communion framework. In O. P. John, R. W. Robins, & L. A. Pervin (Eds.), *Handbook of personality psychology: Theory and research* (3rd ed., pp. 492–517). New York, NY: Guilford Press.

Peeters, G. (1992). Evaluative meanings of adjectives in vitro and in context: Some theoretical implications and practical consequences of positive-negative asymmetry and behavioral-adaptive concepts of evaluation. *Psychologica Belgica, 32,* 211–231.

Peeters, G. (2008). The evaluative face of a descriptive model: Communion and agency in Peabody's tetradic model of trait organization. *European Journal of Social Psychology, 38,* 1066–1072.

Peeters, G., & Czapinski, J. (1990). Positive–negative asymmetry in evaluations: The distinction between affective and informational negative effects. In W. Stroebe & M. Hewstone (Eds.), *European review of social psychology*, Vol. 1. (pp. 33–60). London: Wiley.

Reeder, G. D., & Brewer, M. B. (1979). A schematic model of dispositional attribution in interpersonal perception. *Psychological Review, 86,* 61–79.

Rosenberg, S., Nelson, C., & Vivekananthan, P. (1968). A multidimensional approach to the structure of personality impressions. *Journal of Personality and Social Psychology, 9,* 283–294.

Uchronski, M. (2008). Agency and communion in spontaneous self-descriptions: Occurrence and situational malleability. *European Journal of Social Psychology, 38,* 1093–1102.

Wiggins, J. S. (1991). Agency and communion as conceptual coordinates for the understanding and measurement of interpersonal behaviour. In W. Grove & D. Ciccetti (Eds.), *Thinking clearly about psychology: Essays in honour of Paul Everett Meehl* (pp. 89–113). Minneapolis: University of Minnesota Press.

Wojciszke, B., & Abele, A. E. (2008). The primacy of communion over agency and its reversals in evaluation. *European Journal of Social Psychology, 38,* 1139–1147.

Wojciszke, B., Baryla, W., Parzuchowski, M., Szymkow, A., & Abele, A. E. (2011). Self-esteem is dominated by agentic over communal information. *European Journal of Social Psychology, 40,* 1–11.

Ybarra, O., Chan, E., & Park, D. (2001). Young and old adults' concerns about morality and competence. *Motivation and Emotions, 25,* 85–100.

Ybarra, O., Chan, E., Park, H., Burnstein, E., Monin, B., & Stanik, C. (2008). Life's recurring challenges and the fundamental dimensions: An integration and its implications for cultural differences and similarities. *European Journal of Social Psychology, 38,* 1083–1092.

Zebrowitz, L., & Collins, M. (1997). Accurate social perception at zero acquaintance: The affordances of a Gibsonian approach. *Personality and Social Psychology Review, 1,* 204–223.

# 11

# Gossiping as Moral Social Action

## *A Functionalist Account of Gossiper Perceptions*

KIM PETERS AND YOSHIHISA KASHIMA

> Gossip is a sort of smoke that comes from the dirty tobacco-pipes of those who diffuse it: It proves nothing but the bad taste of the smoker.
>
> George Eliot

Eavesdrop on the average conversation and you are unlikely to find the participants discussing the state of the economy, the American election, the upcoming Olympics, or indeed any of the very many worthy topics that occupy the broadsheets. Instead, chances are that you will catch the participants enthusiastically exchanging stories about other people. In other words, most of the time, most people are sharing gossip. Although there are some disagreements in the literature over the specific characteristics of gossip and the settings within which it should occur, most researchers agree that gossip is the transmission of information about the actions or attributes of some absent person (e.g., Dunbar, 1996; Foster, 2004). In other words, it is any communication that instantiates a triadic social structure involving a gossiper, their audience, and the social target at the heart of their discussion. So, for instance, it can include a manager's discussion of a subordinate's performance with a colleague, a husband's disclosure of an acquaintance's peccadilloes to his wife, and a columnist's divulgence of the latest drunken exploits of a Hollywood starlet.

Estimates that we spend the majority of our conversational life exchanging gossip of one form or another (e.g., Dunbar, Marriott, & Duncan, 1997; Emler, 1994; Marsh & Tversky, 2004) are particularly startling when we consider that gossiping is widely viewed with opprobrium— in Eliot's view, above, gossiping is a disgusting habit that merely serves to pollute our social surroundings. Further evidence of the general disapproval of gossip comes from an examination of the 129 unique gossip quotes compiled in four popular web sites of aphorisms (further details available on request). Of these, a full 60% were concerned with condemning gossip for its wicked nature and harmful effects (e.g., When of a gossiping circle it was asked "what are they doing?" the answer was "swapping lies"). Although another 23% of the quotes did acknowledge positive aspects of gossip—such as being informative and entertaining—they nevertheless tended to do so in ways that served to reinforce its immorality (e.g., Never trust the teller, trust the tale; If you haven't got anything nice to say about anyone, come sit next to me).

Fortunately—particularly for the more voracious gossipers among us—it appears that sharing gossip may not be the universally immoral act that folk wisdom implies. In particular, some scholars have recently suggested that gossip may actually make possible the generally high levels of cooperation that are observed in human communities (e.g., Smith, 2010). The reasoning here is that gossip can help people to gain a better understanding of others in their environment by allowing them to gather information about the actions of these individuals even when they are not able to directly observe their behaviors. This becomes increasingly important as groups become larger and members more mobile as under these circumstances direct observation becomes increasingly rare (e.g., Dunbar, 2004). Although by its very nature it may be difficult to ascertain the quality of an individual gossip item (gossipers may convey inaccurate information, either inadvertently or deliberately), it is argued that—at least on average—gossip will help people to track the trustworthy and untrustworthy individuals in their environment, and consequently, allow communities to avoid the cheats and free riders that pose a threat to cooperation within groups (e.g., Kniffin & Wilson, 2005; Smith, 2010; see also Peters & Kashima, 2007; Peters, Kashima, & Clark, 2009). At this point, it is worth noting that a number of other adaptive functions have been attributed to gossip, including entertainment, group boundary maintenance, and social comparison (Foster, 2004; Rosnow, 2001; Wert & Salovey, 2004). Although these are undoubtedly important, and we do touch on them again in passing, our focus in this review is on the implications of gossip for free rider detection.

If, in line with the claims above, gossip does increase the capacity of communities to identify and control free riders, then it seems unlikely that people will universally obey societal exhortations to judge gossipers negatively: After all, why would individuals share useful information about the behaviors of others if they were punished for doing so? In this chapter, we present our functionalist account of gossiper perceptions, which argues that because gossipers can affect the well-being of the audience (by helping them to successfully negotiate the social world) and the target (by affecting their reputation), gossiping is an action that is intrinsically located in the morality domain (i.e., it is an action with the capacity to help or harm others). This account further argues that gossipers will only be perceived to be immoral when they share gossip that neither improves the well-being of the audience nor the target. This functionalist account is therefore distinct from the existing valence account of gossiper perceptions, which argues that gossipers will be perceived negatively for sharing any negative social information (e.g., Wyer, Budesheim, & Lambert, 1990). In what follows, we present evidence that supports our functionalist account of gossiper perceptions.

## GOSSIPING AS MORAL SOCIAL ACTION

It appears that sharing gossip—information about the actions and attributes of absent parties—is one of our more frequent social actions (e.g., Dunbar et al., 1997; Hess & Hagen, 2006). For instance, in a diary study looking at students' daily conversations, 60% of the reported conversations consisted of retelling social events, telling stories about academics and romances, and sharing pure descriptions of family or other people (Marsh & Tversky, 2004). Similarly, when researchers surreptitiously listened to conversations in public spaces, they classified approximately 65% as concerning social topics, including talk about explicitly social activities, personal relationships, and likes or dislikes (Dunbar et al., 1997; see also Emler, 1994). Further, when the topics of 2,000 conversations between the Zinacantan indians in Mexico were analyzed, almost 78% of them concerned social topics (Haviland, 1977).

Social scientists have been slow to recognize the importance of gossip in social life. In particular, traditional perspectives have considered gossip to be trivial or *cheap* talk. The small cost of sending a piece of gossip is argued to increase the chance that a particular piece of gossip is inaccurate or misleading and hence disregarded in any future interactions with the target of the gossip (e.g., Aumann, 1990). However, when we consider that gossip is typically exchanged between participants who have an ongoing relationship, then it is clear that there are incentives for sharing accurate information; specifically, audiences may punish gossipers who share information that is revealed to be untrue or unhelpful (this aligns with findings that in infinitely repeating games, the optimal strategy is one of cooperation). Moreover, there is evidence that even in one-off interactions, where the incentives for sharing accurate information are absent, participants do take each other's signals of their intentions into account when choosing how to behave (Skyrms, 2002).

With the realization that gossip can provide an accurate signal of the characteristics and behaviors of others and that audiences are sensitive to these signals, views of gossip have started to change. In particular, more recently a number of scholars have suggested that because gossip is able to improve people's understanding of their social environment, it may help groups to counter the threats posed by free riders and other cheats, and so achieve high levels of cooperation (Baumeister, Zhang, & Vohs, 2004; Rosnow, 2001). In particular, if gossip improves people's understanding of the trustworthiness of the individuals around them, then it should help audiences to regulate their interactions in adaptive ways, for instance by helping them to seek out trustworthy others for cooperation and avoid possible cheats and free riders (e.g., Dunbar, 2004; Nowak & Sigmund, 1998; Smith, 2010).

There is some evidence that is consistent with this claim. In particular, Enquist and Leimar (1993; see also Nowak & Sigmund, 1998) used a computer simulation to show that whereas free riders were initially more successful in an environment where people were required to collaborate to survive, honest members were more successful when they were able to exchange a modest amount of information about free riders and used this to inform one another of their behavior. Although behavioral evidence that gossip is able to shore up cooperation is to date very limited, Ahn, Esarey, and Scholz (2009) demonstrated that when populations who were playing repeated mixed motives games were allowed to learn about the characteristics of others indirectly (i.e., through information exchange), they achieved higher levels of cooperation than when they relied on their direct experience alone.

In this experiment, players were provided with an initial financial endowment that they were able to invest to play a prisoner's dilemma game with another participant. The payoff structure for a prisoner's dilemma game is such that although mutual cooperation is rewarded more than mutual defection, unilateral defection (where one player defects and the other cooperates) provides a large incentive to cheat, as in this case the defector gets the largest payoff and the cooperator the smallest. This incentive tends to erode mutual cooperation and thus reduce payoffs. Players were able to nominate any number of the other 13 players in their population with whom to play the prisoner's dilemma in the next round, although the fixed costs for playing rose exponentially with each extra game that was played. It is important to note that games were only played when both players nominated each other. This meant that across the 20 experimental rounds, players could keep profitable partnerships and break off unprofitable ones. A baseline condition, where participants learned on the basis of their direct experience with other players, was compared with two information conditions, where participants were additionally able to learn through indirect experience. Of these two information conditions, the *local information* condition provides an analogy for gossip, as participants were able to solicit recommendations about other players from their current partners. The vast majority (95%) of these recommendations were found to be truthful, so that players positively referred cooperators and negatively referred defectors. More important, players in the local information condition significantly outperformed the other conditions, thus supporting the suggestion that gossip may have a beneficial impact in communities where members have long-term relationships and the capacity to selectively interact with one another.

Another interesting point about this study is that it provided some evidence that individuals value gossip, as they were required to make a small payment to either request or provide recommendations about other players. This corresponds with other findings that people perceive gossip to provide useful information. In particular, Baumeister, Zhang, and Vohs (2004) asked students to recall the most interesting gossip that they had heard in the past week, month, and year, and (among other things) to then indicate whether they had learned a lesson from the gossip. Participants responded affirmatively for approximately two-thirds of gossip items that they had heard. Similarly, Baxter, Dun, and Sahlstein (2001) concluded that gossip helped people to learn rules about appropriate behavior in interpersonal relationships, as university students, who completed daily diaries recording their learning of relationship rules, reported learning about 18% through gossip. Although these instances speak particularly to social comparison functions of gossip, in that individuals may use this information for self-evaluation and self-improvement purposes (Festinger, 1954; Wert & Salovey, 2004), it does demonstrate that individuals are prepared to base their behaviors on the gossip that they hear.

Further evidence that people value gossip comes from a finding that people will use gossip about a potential partner's behaviors to inform their interactions with others even if they have directly witnessed the behaviors in question. In particular, participants in Sommerfeld, Krambeck, Semmann, and Milinski's (2007) experiment had the opportunity to engage in a repeated indirect reciprocity game with other members of their 9-member groups. In particular, in each round, participants were partnered with one other player and given the opportunity to donate part of their endowment to this player. This donation was multiplied so that it was worth more to the recipient than to the donor. More important, at set points in the session, participants were presented with information about their next partner's previous behaviors either through direct observation (i.e., a factual summary of these previous decisions), indirect observation (i.e., the gossip that another player wrote describing these previous decisions), or both. Impressively, when participants had access to both sources of data, their decisions were still influenced by the content of the gossip. In 44% of cases, participants changed their decisions as a consequence of the gossip; in the vast majority of these cases (79%), their decision corresponded with the content of the gossip. This finding may speak to the ambiguity inherent in the interpretation of even very simple behaviors, which motivates individuals to conform to the evaluations of others in the interests of establishing some shared understanding.

It appears that the functional aspects of gossip are not unrecognized by defectors, and that one reason that gossip can increase levels of cooperation is by reducing defection levels. Evidence for this is provided by Feinberg, Willer, Stellar, and Keltner (2012, Study 4; see also Piazza & Bering, 2008). In this study, participants played a trust game (Berg, Dickhaut, & McCabe, 1995). This is a two-player game that provides one player (the donor) with an endowment and the opportunity to give any amount of this endowment to the second player (the recipient). The recipient receives three-times the amount that was gifted by the donor and then has the opportunity to return any of this to the donor. Under high levels of trust, donors should give more of their endowment to the recipient, maximizing joint payoffs. Participants in this study were assigned to the role of the recipient and either were (or were not) led to believe that a third party who observed their behavior in one set of games would be able to share gossip about their behavior to the individuals that they were due to play in a subsequent set of games. In line with the findings above, participants returned more to donors under the threat of gossip.

In sum, there are a number of lines of evidence that are consistent with claims that gossip is functional and may play a role in facilitating group cooperation. The utility of gossip comes from the fact that in most circumstances (i.e., those where it is not possible to directly observe a large proportion of an individual's behavior), it is the foremost means of obtaining vital information about other actors in the social world. As the studies above have shown, gossiping has implications for the well-being of both the audience (by helping them to negotiate their social world) and the target (by manipulating their reputation). This suggests that gossip is a behavior that will be perceived by audiences to fall in the moral domain, which concerns an individual's social intentions, their trustworthiness, honesty, and goodness (Leach, Ellemers, & Barreto, 2007). By implication then, audiences will not perceive gossip to fall into the second major behavioral domain—that of competence, which concerns an individual's ability to realize their intentions. By this, we do not mean that gossipers do not use gossip to try to achieve their own personal goals and that they may be more or less capable in this regard. Rather, we mean that what will be most salient to perceivers will be the possible social impact of a piece of gossip rather than what this piece of gossip may reveal about a gossiper's capability.

Evidence for the moral nature of gossip comes from recent findings that prosocial motives may drive the sharing of gossip when this gossip may protect a vulnerable audience from an untrustworthy target. In particular, across three studies, Feinberg et al. (2012) found that participants who witnessed another participant defect in a social dilemma game almost without exception chose to share gossip that contained a warning about this person's likely behavior to their future partner. They further demonstrated that more prosocially oriented participants were more likely to share this gossip and were willing to pay more to do so.

Therefore, because gossip is motivated by moral concerns and has social consequences, we expect that perceptions of gossipers will mainly fall in the moral domain; there is no reason to suppose that people will be judged as more or less competent on the basis of the gossip that they share. This supports our first hypothesis:

> Hypothesis 1: *The gossip that gossipers share will affect evaluations of their morality rather than their competence.*

Further, in line with our arguments above, we expect this to occur because gossip has the potential to indirectly help or harm the audience by providing them with information that allows the audience to protect him- or herself from a potentially harmful other. This leads to our second hypothesis:

> Hypothesis 2: *Judgments of gossiper morality will be positively related to the perceived utility of the gossip with regard to allowing the audience to form a more accurate understanding of the target.*

TABLE 11.1 Peters, Kashima, Cann, and Everett (2012) Gossip Items

| Target | Gossip Item |
|---|---|
| Honest Student | My friend Nicholas recently got a distinction in his final year of university marks; he later realized that this was a mistake. He had done badly and didn't work hard over the three years, even failing a big assignment. But he contacted the administrator of the department to let them know of the error. |
| Dishonest Seller | My friend Katherine recently sold her polo car to a family friend. But the meter that shows the mileage was broken and read less miles than had actually been driven. It read almost half the mileage that the car had done. The car looked in good condition, so she didn't tell the family friend this. |
| Academic Achiever | A girl in my class, Helena, is leaving next year to study in New York because she won a Rhodes scholarship for graduate study. She's studying theoretical physics and then wants to finish her doctoral dissertation in renomalon calculus at MIT. |
| Scam Victim | My housemate's friend Phil got an e-mail, supposedly from Nigerian royalty, which asked for help moving money out of the country. Phil was told he would get 10 grand for doing this, so he sent his bank details. However, he was scammed and had three grand stolen from his bank. |
| Dating Failure | Someone named Jack in my class has never had a long-term relationship, apparently it's because he can't have sex. |

We have recently collected data that provides provisional evidence for H1 and H2 (Peters, Kashima, Cann, & Everett, 2012). In this study, 75 participants (54 females, $M = 20.45$, $SD = 1.23$ years of age) were brought into the laboratory in groups of 3 or 4 individuals and led to believe that they would each write a story describing an event in the life of someone who they knew and then swap this story with another participant in their group. In fact, in exchange for their story, all participants were given a sheet containing one of five different pieces of gossip handwritten in a colloquial style—see Table 11.1.

Participants were then asked to rate the impressions that they formed on the basis of this story on identical 7-point Likert scales (1 = strongly disagree; 7 = strongly agree). Following Leach et al. (2007), participants first rated the gossiper's morality with three traits: This student is *honest*, *sincere*, and *trustworthy* (= .84); they then rated the gossiper's competence with an additional three items: This student is *skilled*, *competent*, *intelligent* (= .74). Finally, as a measure of gossip utility, participants rated the ability of the gossip to help them regulate their relationship with the target: *This story gives me an idea of what the target is like*; *This story gives me useful information for knowing how to behave toward the target* ($r = .59$, $p < .001$).

Figure 11.1 depicts average ratings of gossiper morality and competence as a function of the gossip item. In line with H1, we found that gossiper morality ratings (dark bars) did vary significantly more than gossiper competence ratings (light bars). Further, in line with H2, there was a significant positive correlation

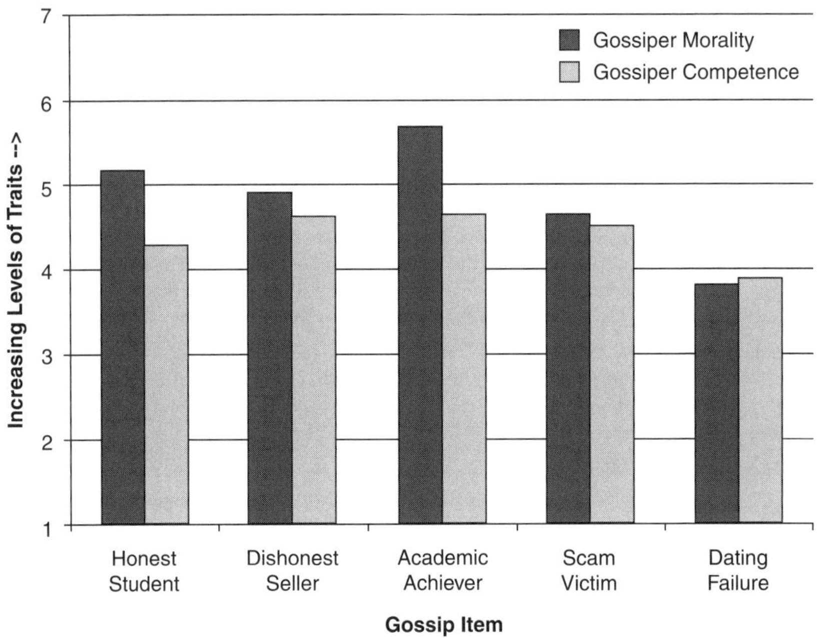


Figure 11.1 Ratings of gossiper morality and competence

between perceptions of the ability of the gossip item to help the audience regulate their relationship with the target and judgments of the gossiper's morality, indicating that gossipers were evaluated as being more moral when they shared gossip that was perceived by the audience to be useful. In contrast, perceptions of the utility of the gossip item had no impact on judgments of the gossiper's competence.

In sum, this study supports the first claim of our functionalist account of gossiper perceptions—namely, that gossiping is a behavior that falls primarily in the moral domain. This study also supports the second claim of our functionalist account of gossiper perceptions—namely, that judgments of gossiper morality (but not competence) will vary with perceptions of the regulatory functions of gossip, so that gossipers, who share gossip that helps an audience to regulate their relationship with the target, will be perceived to be more moral.

## THE MORALITY OF SHARING MORALITY AND COMPETENCE GOSSIP

So far, we have focused on morality rather than competence. Not only have we claimed that gossipers will be perceived as more or less moral (rather than more or less competent) as a consequence of the gossip that they share, but in our review of research examining the beneficial consequences of gossip, the majority of studies examined morality gossip—gossip that discussed a target's defection or cooperation—rather than competence gossip—gossip concerning a target's ability to achieve their goals. We suggest that this latter focus is not a mere oversight, and that the utility of gossip largely resides in morality gossip.

More specific, we argue that gossip that pertains to the morality of the target will have greater implications for the audiences' ability to regulate their own behavior toward this target than gossip that pertains to the competence of the target (Fiske, Cuddy, & Glick, 2007; Peeters, 1992; Ybarra et al., 2008). In other words, information about a person's morality is essential for effective social action in a way that information about their competence is not. This is not to say that an individual's competence does not matter for how we relate to him or her; rather it is that, for the most part, people pay attention first and foremost to the individual's morality because of the capacity that untrustworthy individuals—free riders and cheats—have for harming others. Evidence for this claim comes from research demonstrating that morality information has primacy in social cognition: People base their social judgments more strongly on morality information and preferentially seek out this information about others (for an excellent discussion of these issues, see Chapter 10, this volume).

For instance, Brambilla, Sacchi, Rusconi, Cherubini, and Yzerbyt (2011) measured participants' global evaluations of a fictional immigrant group as a function of whether they received positive or negative information about the group's morality, competence, or sociability (a third dimension that is sometimes distinguished from morality under a broader dimension of warmth). In two studies, they found that although positively valenced information generally led to more positive group evaluations, this effect was most marked when the information pertained to morality. In a final study, they examined whether the relative importance of morality information for group evaluations was due to the social implications of morality by examining whether the effect of morality on judgments was mediated by perceptions that the group was threatening. As expected, they found that morality (but not competence or sociability) information was related to threat perceptions, and that this could account for the impact of morality on judgments.

There is also evidence that perceivers are most interested in obtaining information about a person's morality (Wojciszke, 2005). For instance, Brambilla, Rusconi, Sacchi, and Cherubini (2011) presented participants with traits related to morality, competence, and sociability and asked how important it would be to gather information related to each trait to form a global impression of a person or to make a decision that was relevant to this person's morality (i.e., tell them a secret), competence (i.e., employ them), or sociability (i.e., invite them to a party). Although participants emphasized the importance of morality, sociability, or competence traits when the decision was specifically relevant to that domain, they prioritized information related to morality when forming a global impression of the person.

This concern with morality information appears to also apply to gossip. For instance, Wilson, Wilczynski, Wells, and Weiser (2000) found that although participants indicated that they disapproved of gossip that they saw to be self-serving, where the gossip concerned an individual's immoral actions and thus would allow the detection of free riders, they would actually punish those who did not pass the gossip on. These same concerns are evident in people's responses to gossip concerning their own behaviors. In particular, Ybarra, Park, Stanik, and Lee (2012) presented Korean and U.S. university students with a scenario that asked them to imagine that gossip was circulating that either claimed that they had failed an exam (evidence of incompetence) or that they had cheated on it (evidence of immorality). Across both cultures, participants reported higher levels of distress at the possibility that others doubted their morality than their competence.

Most interesting, this strong concern for morality may even extend into task-based interactions in work settings, where a person's competence could be expected to be the primary consideration. In particular, Casciaro and Sousa Lobo (2008) examined the impact of an individual's liking for another individual and their perceptions of this individual's competence on their work-related engagement with that individual (such as approaching the individual for advice or problem solving assistance). Across three different organizations and different types of task-related interactions, they found that individuals were more likely to engage with more likeable, less competent colleagues than less likeable, more competent colleagues. In other words, it appears that people need to like others before they will seek to exploit their competence. Although this study did not examine morality specifically, their findings are impressive for demonstrating that concerns about competence may be secondary to more social concerns, even in explicitly task-oriented settings. (It is worth noting that high perceiver power may at least weaken this effect—presumably because high power individuals are less vulnerable to the immoral actions of low power others; Ames & Bianchi, 2008).

On the basis of this research, it seems that gossip that provides diagnostic information about a target's morality—allowing audiences to identify those individuals who should be approached and those who should be avoided—will be most useful to audiences as they navigate their social world. As a consequence, we expect that audiences will evaluate gossipers who share extreme morality gossip (gossip that concerns very moral or immoral actions) as especially moral. This leads to the third hypothesis of our functionalist account of gossiper perception:

> Hypothesis 3: *Gossipers will be evaluated as more moral when they exchange extreme information about a target's morality (i.e., there will be a positive quadratic relationship between target morality and gossiper morality).*

Although we have argued that gossip that concerns a target's competence has few implications for the audience, it is still possible that the audience will perceive it to have implications for the target's well-being by contributing positively or negatively to the target's reputation, or at least communicating an intention on the part of the gossiper to affect the target's reputation in these ways. Therefore, when the gossip concerns the competence of the target, we expect that audiences will base their perceptions of the gossiper's morality on the extent to which the gossip presents the target in a positive light. This, therefore, leads to the fourth hypothesis of our functionalist account of gossiper perception:

> Hypothesis 4: *Gossipers will be evaluated as more moral when they exchange positive information about a target's competence (i.e., there will be a positive linear relationship between target competence and gossiper morality).*

In distinguishing between the consequences of morality and competence gossip, our functionalist account of gossiper perception differs from the existing *valence* account of gossiper perception, which argues that gossipers who share positively valenced gossip (regardless of content) will be liked more than gossipers who share negatively valenced gossip. Essentially, this perspective assumes that perceptions of a gossiper are entirely driven by perceptions of the gossiper's intentions toward the target, so that gossipers who say positive things about a target are seen to have friendly intentions toward this target, and as a consequence, will be perceived as warm and likeable. This perspective neglects the functionalist considerations that drive our distinction between morality and competence gossip. It is only when the gossip does not help the audience to negotiate their social world (i.e., when the gossip concerns competence) that we expect the gossiper to be judged solely on the basis of their intentions toward the target; when the gossip does affect the audience's well-being (i.e., when it concerns morality), then gossipers should largely be judged on this basis. Although these two accounts have congruent expectations for evaluations of competence and positive morality gossipers, they differ in their expectations for negative morality gossipers where the audience's concerns for their own well-being should override their concern for that of the target.

However, there is evidence that supports the valence account. For instance, Wyer, Budesheim, and Lambert (1990) found that participants who listened to a recording of two individuals gossiping about a target liked gossipers more when they described the target favorably than when they described the target unfavorably. Similarly, Wyer, Budesheim, Lambert, and Swan (1994) found that participants who listened to a recording of two individuals reflecting on one of these individual's behaviors liked gossipers who discussed this individual's positive behaviors more than gossipers who discussed this individual's negative behaviors.

The mechanism proposed by the valence account has received some empirical support. In particular, Gawronski and Walther (2008) were able to show that participants' greater liking of individuals who were said to like multiple target individuals was a function of a propositional mechanism—such as the conscious inference of the source's intentions toward the target—rather than an associative one—that is, the mistaken association of the concept *likeable* with sources who liked others (see Carlston & Skowronski, 2005). Although this study was not strictly speaking a communication study, it does suggest that judgments of gossipers are based on some propositional evaluation of the information that they communicate.

Although the valence account implies that the content of gossip should not matter, the preceding studies did not explicitly examine any content effects. In contrast, Ames, Bianchi, and Magee (2010) have shown that valence drives judgments of a gossiper's agreeableness whether they share competence or sociability gossip. More specific, participants were presented with an e-mail that had been purportedly written by a coworker discussing the sociability or competence of a new work colleague. In two studies, they found that participants evaluated gossipers who expressed positive evaluations of a target as more agreeable than gossipers who expressed negative evaluations of the target. More important, they found some evidence that this effect occurred in part because positive gossipers were seen to have positive social intentions, for instance by taking pleasure in being nice to others.

Although these studies do provide support for the valence account, it is important to note that they were not designed to distinguish between the valence and functionalist accounts. In particular, with the exception of Ames et al. (2010), these studies did not distinguish between different kinds of gossip content, or different aspects of gossiper evaluations. Further, although Ames et al. (2010) show that whether gossip concerns agreeableness or competence does not affect judgments of a gossiper's agreeableness, there is evidence that agreeableness (i.e., sociability) related information is not perceived to have the utility of morality information, and is thus processed differently (Brambilla et al., 2011). As a consequence, to test whether our functionalist account provides a better account of gossiper perceptions, it is necessary to examine the relationship between target morality and competence perceptions, and gossiper morality perceptions.

In a series of three studies, Peters, Kashima, Muir, and Tavenor (2012) have done precisely that. Participants were presented with 1 (Study 1), 4 (Study 2), or 8 (Study 3) gossip scenarios that described how an in-group member approached them and told them a piece of gossip about another group member. The gossip items were designed to describe the moral, immoral, competent, or incompetent behavior of another individual—see Table 11.2. After reading through each scenario, participants were asked to rate the competence and morality of the gossip target and the gossiper. In all three studies, participants' judgments of the target's competence and morality were found to affect their perceptions of the gossiper's morality, but not the gossiper's competence, providing further evidence that gossiping is an intrinsically moral action (see H1).

In addition, these studies demonstrated that the content of the gossip did affect perceptions of the gossiper's morality in the specified ways. In particular, hierarchical linear regression revealed that target morality had a positive quadratic relationship with gossiper morality (in line with H3), and target competence had a positive linear relationship with gossiper morality (in line with H4). In other words, gossipers who shared diagnostic morality gossip and positive competence gossip were perceived to be especially moral. These findings, therefore, provide support for our functionalist account of gossiper perceptions rather than the valence account. Figure 11.2 depicts the form of these relationships by graphing the estimated regression lines in Study 3.

TABLE 11.2 Peters, Kashima, Muir, and Tavenor (2012) Gossip Items

| Dimension | Valence | Gossip Item |
|---|---|---|
| Morality | Positive | When Alice received her end of the year university marks, she realized that they had made a mistake, as she was awarded a distinction for a subject that she had performed very poorly in—failing the major assignment. She contacted the administration to let them know their error. |
| | Negative | One of Alice's colleagues was fired because her boss believed that she was leaking organizational secrets to a member of a rival organization. It turns out that Alice had invented this gossip entirely. |
| Competence | Positive | Alice has just finished building a computer. She ordered all of the components from a catalog and assembled it herself. Because she couldn't find a fast processer, she also had to build that herself. |
| | Negative | Alice decided to follow a well-known walk on the moor. She managed to get herself lost very quickly; the police say that no one has ever managed to get lost on that walk before, as it is very well marked. |

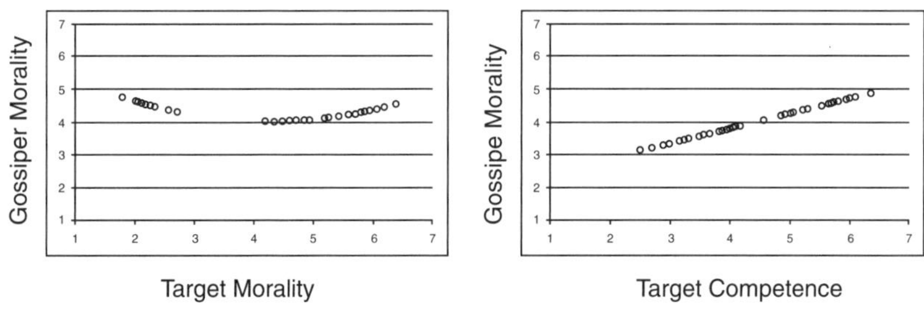


Figure 11.2 Relationship between target ratings and gossiper ratings

Study 3 provided further support for our functionalist account of gossiper perceptions as participants were asked to indicate whether the item of gossip performed a number of different functions, including (a) helping them to regulate their relationship with the target by improving their understanding of the target and his or her likely behaviors and allowing them to alter their relationship accordingly, (b) maintaining group boundaries, (c) providing entertainment, or (d) meeting Gricean conversational rules (i.e., assessing whether the gossip is seen to be relevant, appropriate, and truthful; see Chapter 5, this volume). Mediation analysis demonstrated that the quadratic relationship between target morality and gossiper morality was mediated by the ability of the gossip to regulate the participant's relationship with the target; the linear relationship between target competence and gossiper morality was instead mediated by Gricean conversational rules.

This study, therefore, demonstrated that gossip that conveys morality and competence information is seen to fulfill different functions, and judgments of gossipers are based on these functions. Moreover, in line with H2, gossipers who share diagnostic morality gossip are seen to be more moral because this gossip contributes to the audience's well-being. In sum, these studies provide convincing support for our functionalist account of gossiper perceptions.

## FUTURE RESEARCH

It is interesting to note that two frequently mentioned functions of gossip—entertainment and group boundary maintenance—were unrelated to perceptions of the gossiper's morality or competence in Study 3. In addition, although we did not assess the capacity of this gossip to facilitate social comparisons, our finding that individuals evaluated negative competence gossipers negatively is inconsistent with the possibility that one of the functions of gossip is to provide the opportunity for at least one particular kind of social comparison: downward comparisons (Wert & Salovey, 2004). Had this been the case, gossipers who allowed audiences to make favorable downward comparisons in the domain of competence, which has been shown to make an especially strong contribution to self-esteem (Wojciszke, 2005), should arguably have been evaluated most positively. In future work, therefore, it is important to ascertain the circumstances under which gossip performs these other functions and what their consequences may be for social perception.

We have argued strongly in this chapter that the gossip that serves these important functions is diagnostic morality gossip—gossip that concerns the trustworthy and untrustworthy behaviors of another—rather than competence gossip. If so, this raises a number of interesting possibilities. First, to the extent that social information has been shown to disseminate more readily through communication chains than nonsocial information (Mesoudi, Whiten, & Dunbar, 2006), we would expect to observe differences in the spread of social information as a function of its content. More specific, morality-related social information should travel further and faster than competence-related social information. In line with this idea, a number of studies have found that the moral emotion of disgust is a particularly strong driver of dissemination (Heath, Bell, & Sternberg, 2001; Peters, Kashima, & Clark, 2009).

Second, it begs the question of whether negative competence gossip could ever be perceived to affect the audience's well-being and therefore lead to favorable judgments of the gossiper's morality. Indeed, Brambilla et al.'s (2011) finding that people did have a preference for competence related information when performing a task in the competence domain, suggests that it should. Using Schweder, Much, Mahapatra, and Park's (1997) trichotomy of moral actions, we suggest that gossipers who share gossip that concerns incompetence may be judged positively if the target's incompetence (a) has implications for another's autonomy or well-being, (b) violates community norms around roles and structures, or (c), degrades another's spiritual purity. These possibilities are just a few that await investigation in this rich and burgeoning field of research into the social dynamics and consequences of gossip.

## CONCLUSIONS

Folk wisdom about gossip appears to be less than wise, highlighting the feelings of the target above the possibility that he or she may do others harm. Indeed, the functionalist accounts of gossip and gossiper perceptions suggests that if people yielded to the exhortations of popular culture and resisted sharing gossip, not only society's capacity for contributing to the common good but also their capacity for maintaining high levels of social integration (i.e., strong connections between individuals, and between individuals and their groups) would be eroded. This is because it is only by knowing who is trustworthy and who is not that community members have some chance of outsmarting the free riders and cheats that pose such a threat to their ability to cooperate. It is also because gossiping—as a behavior that instantiates a social triad of gossiper, target, and audience (see Peters & Kashima, 2007)—has the capacity to simultaneously regulate the relationships between the audience and target, and the audience and the gossiper. Therefore, we suggest that George Eliot could not have been more wrong: Where gossip serves these functions, it acts as the filter that keeps in check the immoral behaviors that pollute our social environment.

## REFERENCES

Ahn, T. K., Esarey, J., & Scholz, J. T. (2009). Reputation and cooperation in voluntary exchanges: Comparing local and central institutions. *Journal of Politics, 71*(2), 298–413.

Ames, D. R., & Bianchi, E. (2008). The agreeableness asymmetry in first impressions: Perceivers' impulse to (mis)judge agreeableness and how it is moderated by power. *Personality and Social Psychology Bulletin, 34,* 1719–1736.

Ames, D. R., Bianchi, E. C., & Magee, J. C. (2010). Professed impressions: What people say about others affects onlookers' perceptions of speakers' power and warmth. *Journal of Experimental Social Psychology, 46,* 152–158.

Aumann, R. (1990). Nash-equilibria are not self-enforcing. In J. Gabszewicz, F. Richard, L. Wolsey (Eds.), *Economic decision making: Games, econometrics and optimisation* (pp. 201–206). Amsterdam, The Netherlands: North-Holland.

Baumeister, R. F., Zhang, L., & Vohs, K. D. (2004). Gossip as cultural learning. *Review of General Psychology, 8,* 111–121.

Baxter, L. A., Dun, T., & Sahlstein, E. (2001). Rules for relating: Communication among social network members. *Journal of Social and Personal Relationships, 18,* 173–199.

Berg, J., Dickhaut, J., & McCabe, K. (1995). Trust, reciprocity and social history. *Game and Economic Behavior, 10,* 122–142.

Brambilla, M., Rusconi, P., Sacchi, S., & Cherubini, P. (2011). Looking for honesty: The primary role of morality (vs. sociability and competence) in information gathering. *European Journal of Social Psychology, 41,* 135–143.

Brambilla, M., Sacchi, S., Rusconi, P., Cherubini, P., & Yzerbyt, V. Y. (2011). You want to give a good impression? Be honest! Moral traits dominate group impression formation. *British Journal of Social Psychology.*

Carlston, D. R., & Skowronski, J. J. (2005). Linking versus thinking: Evidence for the different associative and attributional bases of spontaneous trait transference and spontaneous trait inference. *Journal of Personality and Social Psychology, 89,* 884–898.

Casciaro, T., & Sousa Lobo, M. (2008). When competence is irrelevant: The role of interpersonal affect in task-related ties. *Administrative Science Quarterly, 53,* 655–684.

Dunbar, R. I. M. (1996). Gossip, grooming and the evolution of language. London: Faber & Faber.

Dunbar, R. I. M. (2004). Gossip in evolutionary perspective. *Review of General Psychology, 8,* 100–110.

Dunbar, R. I. M., Marriott, A., & Duncan, N. D. C. (1997). Human conversational behavior. *Human Nature, 8,* 231–246.

Emler, N. (1994). Gossip, reputation, and social adaptation. In R. F. Goodman & A. Ben-Ze'ev (Eds.), *Good gossip* (pp. 117–138). Lawrence: University Press of Kansas.

Enquist, M., & Leimar, O. (1993). The evolution of cooperation in mobile organisms. *Animal Behaviour, 45,* 747–757.

Feinberg, M., Willer, R., Stellar, J., & Keltner, D. (2012). The virtues of gossip: Reputational sharing as prosocial behavior. *Journal of Personality and Social Psychology.*

Festinger, L. (1954). A theory of social comparison processes. *Human relations*, *7*(2), 117–140.

Fiske, S. T., Cuddy, A. J., & Glick, P. (2007). Universal dimensions of social cognition: Warmth and competence. *Trends in cognitive sciences*, *11*(2), 77–83.

Foster, E. K. (2004). Research on gossip: Taxonomy, methods, and future directions. *Review of General Psychology, 8*(2), 78–99.

Gawronski, B., & Walther, E. (2008). The TAR effect: When the ones who dislike become the ones who are disliked. *Personality and Social Psychology Bulletin, 34,* 1276–1290.

Haviland, J. B. (1977). Gossip as competition in Zinacantan. *Journal of Communication, 27*(1), 186–191.

Heath, C., Bell, C., & Sternberg, E. (2001). Emotional selection in memes: The case of urban legends. *Journal of Personality and Social Psychology, 81,* 1028–1041.

Hess, N. H., & Hagen, E. H. (2006). Sex differences in indirect aggression: Psychological evidence from young adults. *Evolution and Human Behavior, 27,* 231–245.

Kniffin, K., & Wilson, D. S. (2005). The effect of non-physical traits on the perception of physical attractiveness: Three naturalistic studies. *Evolution and Human Behavior, 25,* 88–101.

Leach, C. W., Ellemers, N., & Barreto, M. (2007). Group virtue: The importance of morality (vs. competence and sociability) in the positive evaluation of in-groups. *Journal of Personality and Social Psychology, 93,* 234–249.

Marsh, E. J., & Tversky, B. (2004). Spinning the stories of our lives. *Applied Cognitive Psychology, 18*(5), 491–503.

Mesoudi, A., Whiten, A., & Dunbar, R. (2006). A bias for social information in human cultural transmission. *British Journal of Psychology, 97,* 405–431.

Nowak, M. A., & Sigmund, K. (1998). Evolution of indirect reciprocity by image scoring. *Nature, 393,* 573–577.

Peeters, G. (1992). Evaluative meanings of adjectives in vitro and in context: Some theoretical implications and practical consequences of positive-negative asymmetry and behavioural-adaptive concepts of evaluation. *Psychologica Belgica, 32,* 211–231.

Peters, K., & Kashima, Y. (2007). From social talk to social action: Shaping the social triad with emotion sharing. *Journal of Personality and Social Psychology, 93,* 780–797.

Peters, K., Kashima, Y., Cann, R., & Everett, A. (2012). *Judging gossipers.* Unpublished manuscript. University of Exeter, South West England.

Peters, K., Kashima, Y., & Clark, A. (2009). Talking about others: Emotionality and the dissemination of social information. *European Journal of Social Psychology, 39*, 207–222.

Peters, K., Kashima, Y., Muir, V., & Tavenor, A. (2012). *Gossiping as moral social action: An extended functionalist account.* Unpublished manuscript. University of Exeter, South West England.

Piazza, J., & Bering, J. M. (2008). Concerns about reputation via gossip promote generous allocations in an economic game. *Evolution and Human Behavior, 29*, 172–178.

Rosnow, R. L. (2001). Rumor and gossip in interpersonal interaction and beyond: A social exchange perspective. In R. M. Kowalski (Ed.), *Behaving badly: Aversive behaviors in interpersonal relationships* (pp. 203–232). Washington, DC: American Psychological Association.

Schweder, R. A., Much, N. C., Mahapatra, M., & Park, L. (1997). The "big three" of morality (autonomy, community, divinity) and the "big three" explanations of suffering. In A. Brandt & P. Rozin (Eds.), *Morality and health.* New York, NY: Routledge.

Skyrms, B. (2002). Signals, evolution and explanatory power of transient information. *Philosophy of Science, 69*(3), 407–428.

Smith, E. A. (2010). Communication and collective action: Language and the evolution of human cooperation. *Evolution and Human Behavior, 31*, 231–245.

Sommerfeld, R. D., Krambeck, H., Semmann, D., & Milinski, M. (2007). Gossip as an alternative for direct observation in games of indirect reciprocity. *Proceedings of the National Academy of Sciences, 104*, 17435–17440.

Wert, S. R., & Salovey, P. (2004). A social comparison account of gossip. *Review of General Psychology, 8*(2), 122–137.

Wilson, D. S., Wilczynski, C., Wells, A., & Weiser, L. (2000). Gossip and other aspects of language as group-level adaptations. In C. Heyes & L. Huber (Eds.), *The evolution of cognition* (pp. 347–365). Cambridge, MA: The MIT Press.

Wojciszke, B. (2005). Morality and competence in person- and self-perception. *European Review of Social Psychology, 16*(1), 155–188.

Wyer, R. S., Budesheim, T. L., & Lambert, A. J. (1990). Cognitive representation of conversations about persons. *Journal of Personality and Social Psychology, 58*, 218–238.

Wyer, R. S., Budesheim, T. I., Lambert, A. J., & Swan, S. (1994). Person perception judgment: Pragmatic influences on impressions formed in a social context. *Journal of Personality and Social Psychology, 66*, 254–267.

Ybarra, O., Chan, E., Park, H., Burnstein, E., Monin, B., & Stanik, C. (2008). Life's recurring challenges and fundamental dimensions: An integration and its implications for cultural differences and similarities. *European Journal of Social Psychology, 38*, 1083–1092.

Ybarra, O., Park, H., Stanik, C., & Lee, D. S. (2012). Self-judgments and reputation monitoring as a function of the fundamental dimensions, temporal perspective, and culture. *European Journal of Social Psychology, 42*, 200–209.

# Part 3

# The Psychology of Narratives

# 12

# Narrative Social Psychology

JÁNOS LÁSZLÓ AND BEA EHMANN

Social psychologists argue that people's past weighs on their present (e.g., Liu & Hilton, 2005). The present chapter intends to show that language, particularly narrative language, is an extremely useful device so as to trace the impact of past experiences on current psychological conditions. We first review some basic tenets of narrative psychology. In the next section, we contrast the social cognitive approach to language with that of the narrative approach emphasizing that whereas social cognition conceives language as mediator of social perception, narrative psychology in general and narrative social psychology in particular, are interested in linguistic expressions of individual and group identity. We also demonstrate that current studies on group-based emotions—intergroup emotions (e.g., Smith, 1993) or collective emotions (e.g., Doosje, Branscombe, Spears, & Manstead, 1998)—can also be placed in the framework of narrative-linguistic analysis. A contrast between the universalistic social cognitive approach to self and self-categorization and the more relativistic stance of the narrative social psychology to narratively constructed personal identity and historically constructed group identity also is discussed. The forthcoming section outlines the concepts and methods we have developed for studying quantitatively the processes and states of personal and group identity. Finally, an application of the analytic devices to the Hungarian national identity with particular respect to the elaboration of historical traumas is presented.

## LANGUAGE AND SOCIAL PSYCHOLOGY

Although most of the social psychological experiments have used verbal material, mainstream social psychology has shown a traditional neglect toward language. With some notable exceptions (e.g., Brown, 1958, 1965; Giles, 1977), language and language use has escaped social psychologists' attention until

Semin and Fiedler's (1988) seminal paper on the LCM (for linguistic category model). Starting from Brown and Fish's (1983) insight in the implicit causality of interpersonal verbs, Semin and Fiedler (1988, 1991) have developed an attributional model for verbal accounts on behavioral events. Recently, Carnaghi, Maass, Gresta, Bianchi, Cadinu, and Arcuri (2009) included also nouns into the model, which represent an even higher level of abstraction than adjectives.

The LCM has been proven very productive in studies on intergroup relations and stereotyping. Maass, Salvi, Arcuri, and Semin (1989) discovered the phenomenon of LIB (for linguistic intergroup bias), a linguistic expression of ingroup favoritism. This phenomenon has been demonstrated not only in experimental settings, but also in media texts (Maass, Milesi, Zabbini, & Stahlberg, 1995).

Wigboldus, Semin, and Spears (2000) have also shown that language plays a subtle, but crucial role in the interpersonal transmission of stereotypes in communication. Accounting for stereotype-consistent information with more abstract people, as opposed to stereotype-inconsistent information with more concrete linguistic categories, implicitly suggests that stereotypical behavior is dispositional, whereas stereotype-inconsistent behavior is caused by less permanent situational factors. Consistency of information with stereotypes is reflected in other linguistic biases. The negation bias (Beukeboom, Finkenauer, & Wigboldus, 2010; Chapter 18, this volume) entails that the use of negations (e.g., *not stupid,* rather than *smart*) is more pronounced in descriptions of stereotype-inconsistent behaviors compared with stereotype-consistent behaviors.

The Stereotypic Explanatory Bias (Sekaquaptewa, Espinoza, Thompson, Vargas, & Von Hippel, 2003) pertains to the tendency to provide relatively more explanations in descriptions of stereotype-inconsistent, compared with consistent behavior. Learning that an individual shows behavior that is incongruent with the stereotype of the person's category instigates explanatory processing, which is reflected in an explanation to make sense of the incongruity

Not only lexical choice may convey implicit information about actors. As Turnbull (1994) has pointed out, thematic structure of a sentence (i.e., grammatical forms may shift responsibility for an action from one character to another). For example, when accounting for an interpersonal quarrel situation, we use the "Peter argued with Mary" form; recipients of this communication will perceive Peter as more responsible for the quarrel. In the case of "Mary argued with Peter," however, responsibility relations change to the opposite and Mary will carry more responsibility (see also Semin, 2000b). Responsibility for an event is derived from agency in the event. What sentence structure can manipulate is the implicit agency attached to thematic roles of the sentence. This subtle communicative mean, similar to LIB, can be employed in intergroup relations, when people tend to use less agentic forms (passive voice, general subject, etc.) or when describing socially undesirable deeds of their own group, as opposed to when they use active forms when speaking about bad deeds of the outgroups. Banga, Szabó, and László (2012) have termed this tendency syntactic agency bias.

Coming closer to our main topic (i.e., narrative social psychology), we should notice that not only sentence structure, but more general communicative structures are also susceptible to convey information about the characters. Narratives are not privilege of literature; instead they are ordinary forms of everyday communication. Narratologists coming from literary tradition (Barthes, 1977; Culler, 2001; Eco; 1994) have uncovered several structural devices by which authors shape literary meaning construction in readers. One of these compositional devices is the narrative perspective—that is, the point of view from which narrator tells the events (Bal, 1985; Cohn, 1984; Uspensky, 1974). People often tell stories about their personal experiences. Pólya, László, and Forgas (2005) assumed that in stories when narrators tell about stressful events in which they felt their identity threatened, the spatiotemporal perspective they use conveys information about their actual inner state—that is, to what extent they were able to elaborate the emotional shock and reintegrate their identity. In a social perception experiment where subjects had to assess narrator's inner state with the help of adjective checklists and identity state scales, they have provided evidence that using retrospective narrative perspective (looking back to the past from the present situation in an ordered temporal sequence) suggests much more balanced and integrated identity state, than experiencing or reexperiencing perspective not only for experts such as psychologists or psychiatrists, but also for laypeople

What we see in the above approaches and results is that social psychologists conceive language as a subtle mediator in communication that has the capacity to modulate messages (Semin, 2000), and thereby convey social psychologically relevant information to perceivers. But looking at the LIB paradigm, where group membership is a central determinant of the ongoing process or phenomenon, we should also note that prevalence of LIB in communication, through expressing certain qualities of intergroup relations, may reflect certain characteristics of the group identity. For instance, heavily versus not at all used LIB suggests that for the ingroup's identity, it is important to have hostile versus friendly relations with the target outgroup (i.e., presence or absence of identity threats). This double—that is, message modulation versus identity expression potential of linguistic communication—is even more salient in the Pólya, László, and Forgas (2005) study, where the results can be considered as a validity test for the assumed correlation between linguistic markers of the narrative perspective and emotional stability and integration of personal identity. In the next section, we discuss some functional aspects of self and identity.

## INDIVIDUAL AND GROUP IDENTITY

Following Erikson (1959, 1968), we conceive personal identity a person's experience of sameness, autonomy, continuity, and coherence (see also Ricoeur, 1991). Identity evolves in an interaction with the social environment through identifications. As Marcia (1966, 1980) convincingly argues, identity may have different states in different life stages, and, in turn, each identity state can be more or less functional, from the point of view of adaptation. Antonovsky (1987) claims that the general health condition of a person depends on the coherence of her life story which is in turn equated with identity by Antonovsky. For analyzing group identity, we borrow the identity state approach of Marcia with an important limitation. Given that groups do not have life cycles in the sense as individuals do, accordingly, they do not have *developmental tasks*. Therefore, instead of identity statuses that Marcia uses for describing individual personality development, such as achieved, moratorium, foreclosed, and diffuse, we use more general terms of emotional stability-instability or integration-disintegration. Moreover, specific states of group identity can also be grasped in this way. In the course of their history, groups get often victimized by other groups, and they may be exposed to traumatic experiences. These experiences may become part of the group identity and lead to specific forms of identity construction—such as, for example, adopting the collective victim role (Bar-Tal, Chernyak-Hai, Schori, & Gundar, 2009; Baumeister & Hastings, 1997; Klar, Schori, & Roccas, 2011; Spini, Elcheroth, & Fasel, 2008; see Chapter 14, this volume).

From the approaches that interrelate life story with personal identity (Antonovsky, 1987; Erikson, 1959; McAdams, 1985; McLean & Pratt, 2006), we also borrow analogous concepts for utilizing the group history-group identity interrelations with certain limitations. In accord with Halbwachs (1941) and several other students of collective memory (e.g., Assmann, 1992; Wertsch, 2002), we assume that group (national, ethnic) identity is constructed by genuinely narrative group history (see László, 2003, 2008; Liu & László, 2007). Although this assumption may sound novel for many social psychologists working on the field of social identity, it is almost a truism for historians engaged in studying national identity (Hobsbowm, 1992; Stearns & Stearns, 1985; White, 1981). To avoid group fallacy (Allport, 1924), however, apart from the mechanisms of narrative construction, we must also assume concepts and mechanisms that make narratively constructed group identity relevant and effective for individuals belonging to the particular group. In this vein, we accept social identity theory (Tajfel, 1978, 1981; Tajfel & Turner, 1979) and self-categorization theory (Turner, 1999; Turner, Hogg, Oakes, Reicher, & Wetherell, 1987), which outline the psychological consequences and mechanisms of belonging to a group for individuals. Nevertheless, the psychological content of the identity transmitted by the mechanisms of social identification and self-categorization still remain an open question (see Condor, 2003). These contents have earlier been grasped by discourse analytic methods (Reicher & Hopkins, 2001). Here is where language and communication comes into play. What we suggest is that states and characteristics of group identity that govern people's behavior when they act as group members, just as elaboration of traumatic experiences that affected the group as a whole, can be traced objectively—that is, empirically in the narrative language of different forms of group histories (see also Nencini, 2011).

We should note that analyzing national character used to be a central topic at the birth of our discipline; however, it has been replaced soon by studies on group perception and stereotyping, partly for avoiding the risk of group fallacy

(Allport, 1924) and partly for sound scientific methodologies that were made available only for the social perception studies. Current studies on collective memory and collective identity (László, 2003; Liu & László, 2007) have built a bridge between individual and group processes, which enables the analysis of historical narratives at both individual and group level without implying a group mind. Content analytic methodologies, particularly NarrCat, which has been developed for the purpose of analyzing life narratives and historical narratives from an identity perspective, provide a methodological tool kit for the empirical study of national identity beyond often unreliable survey and other self-report methodologies.

Before presenting the analytic devices and turning to the empirical demonstrations of the above claim, however, remaining at the level of the conceptual analysis, we discuss some aspects of group identity that matter from the angle of functionality or adaptation. We also locate our theory in the array between psychology, which strives to uncover universally valid causal relations, and history, which interprets the meaning of past events through narratives in locally relevant contexts.

## IDENTITY-RELEVANT PSYCHOLOGICAL PROCESSES IN GROUP NARRATIVES

### *Intergroup Agency*

Agency seems to be a major category in narrative construction. At the same time, it is one of the basic dimensions underlying judgments of self, persons, and groups. It refers to task functioning and goal achievement, and involves qualities like *efficient, competent, active, persistent,* and *energetic* (Wojciszke & Abele, 2008; Chapter 10, this volume). Agency has a wide range of psychological forms (e.g., *capacity, expansion, power, dominancy, separation,* and *independence*). Harter (1978) defines the desire to control our environment or have an effect on it as *effectance motivation*. Deci (1975) attributes inner control of actions to intrinsic motivation. The definition of DeCharms (1968) holds personal causation to be human disposition, which means intentional action for the sake of change. The psychological phenomena mentioned above all refer to the intention and desire to shape our physical and social environment. Bandura's (1989, 1994) definition of self-efficacy or personal efficacy expresses the belief or idea that individuals are able to achieve their proposed aims and can keep control of the actions happening in their life. The expectations of individuals about their own efficacy have a relationship with their ability to cope: Our belief in our own efficacy inspires us to invest more effort in achieving our aims, and in a situation of stress, we feel less pressure or discomfort.

Not only individuals but also groups are seen as agents as they are capable of performing goal-directed behavior and also have an effect on their environment. Hamilton (2007) distinguishes between two approaches to agency in group-perception research: One perceives agency as the capacity of efficient action (Abelson, Dasgupta, Park, & Banaji, 1998; Brewer, Hong, & Li, 2004), the other approach emphasizes the function of the mental states (Morris, Menon, & Ames, 2001). The perception of a group's agency was measured by Spencer-Rogers, Hamilton, and Sherman (2007) with four items, the group is able to: *influence others, achieve its goals, act collectively,* and *make things happen* (produce outcomes). Kashima et al. (2005) assessed perceptions of agency with nine items mapping mental states (beliefs, desires, and intentions), which, according to him, are the basis of the group-agency.

At least in Western cultures, agency is an important component of personal and social identity. To arrive at a well-organized and adaptive adult identity, people have to acquire autonomy, which is reflected in their agency in life events (McAdams, 2001). Current narrative models of identity reconstruct personal identity from life stories (Bamberg & Andrews, 2004; Brockmeier & Carbaugh, 2001; Freeman, 1993; McAdams, 1985). Similar to individual identity, group identity can also be reconstructed from narratives about the group's past. Representations of history reflect psychological characteristics of national identity such as stability or vulnerability, strength or weakness, autonomy or dependency, etc. (László, 2008; Liu & László, 2007). Distribution of agency between ingroup and outgroup appears to be a sensitive indicator for the above identity states. High level of agency in negative events reflects accepting responsibility for past failures, whereas assigning agency in these events only to outgroups indicates defensive identity and low level of elaboration of historical traumas. If ingroup agency is prevalent in both positive and negative events, it indicates a stable, well-organized, and autonomous identity and a progress in trauma elaboration. On the contrary, high level ingroup agency in positive, victorious events, and low level outgroup agency in the same events accompanied with a low level of ingroup agency in negative events, suggests inflated but instable identity.

## Intergroup Evaluation

Intergroup evaluation is an essential linguistic tool for narrative identity construction that organizes the narrated historical events and its characters into a meaningful and coherent representation. Intergroup evaluations are explicit social judgments that evaluate the groups concerned in the event or their representatives. These evaluations can be (a) positive and negative attributions (assigned to them or to their actions; e.g., *wise, unjust*), (b) emotional reactions and relations to them (e.g., *admire, scorn*), (c) evaluative interpretations referring to their actions (instead of or beside factual description; e.g., *excel, exploit*), and (d) acts of rewarding and punishment or acknowledgement and criticism (e.g., *cheer, protest*).

Intergroup evaluation plays an important role in the maintenance of positive social identity. Social identity theory (Tajfel, 1981; Tajfel & Turner, 1979) is based on the proposition that individuals obtain their identities to a great extent from those groups which they are members of. A positively evaluated group membership provides positive self-evaluation and the feeling of safety for the individual. However, social identity is not an absolute category but a relational one: The ingroup gains its value by the positive distinction from similar outgroups. At the same time, an individual is always a member of multiple groups, and it always depends on the current social situation that social category forms the basis for distinction. The demand for positive social identity leads to intergroup comparison and bias, that is, overvaluation of the ingroup and devaluation of the outgroup.

Thus, in an intergroup context, interpersonal and intergroup evaluation shows bias both on the behavioral and on the linguistic level whose motivational basis is the demand for a positive social identity. The evaluation bias intensifies in extreme intergroup conflicts. If this bias is intensively persistent in contemporary historical narratives, it suggests that the group still experiences historical conflicts as identity threats and strengthens its positive identity and cohesion by enhancing its historical greatness.

Pennebaker (1993) found that successful coping is indicated by an increase of words referring to cognitive mechanisms during the repeated reconstruction of the traumatic event, whereas emotional words are important in the initial stage of elaboration when the catharsis enables the release of the paralyzing emotional stress. In group historical narratives about a collective trauma, a similar tendency is expected within the evaluative perspective of the present, that is, within narrator's evaluations. Initially, the rate of emotionally loaded evaluations is relatively high as opposed to that of cognitive, rational evaluations that pattern reflects an emotional focus in the appraisal of the event. During the elaboration process, the rate of emotionally loaded evaluations decreases as opposed to that of cognitive, rational evaluations that implies the improvement of emotional control and rational insight; a more objective perspective is applied in the narrative, treating the event as a subject (and not experiencing it).

## *Emotions*

Another important aspect of identity states and elaboration of group traumas is emotion regulation. Emotions have become a fashionable topic in social psychology in the past two decades (Forgas, 1995). Cognitive theories of interpersonal emotions (e.g., Leary & Baumeister, 2000; Roseman, 1984; Smith & Ellsworth, 1985) and group based emotions (e.g., Doosje et al., 1998; Smith, 1993; Mackie, Devos, & Smith, 2000) have also been developed. It is assumed in these theories that group based emotions are felt when people categorize themselves as group members in situations when emotionally relevant stimuli affect the whole group. There is however another tradition in social psychology looking back to early cultural anthropology (Benedict, 1946; Mead, 1937), which claims that certain emotions and emotional patterns are characteristic to certain cultures. This tradition has been further developed in contemporary cultural psychology (e.g., Markus & Kitayama, 1991; Rozin, Lowery, Imada, & Haidt, 1999; Shweder, Much, Mahapatra, & Park, 1997). Not culturally, but socially conditioned, relatively stable emotional orientations are currently also assumed (Bar-Tal, 2001; Bar-Tal, Halperin, & De Rivera, 2007). Being a member of and identified with a group, people think and feel in accord with the group's characteristic emotional orientation. One of the emotional orientations that has been researched in more detail is the collective victimhood orientation (Bar-Tal et al., 2009), which means that the group turns to intergroup situations with emotions of an innocent victim (see also Chapter 14, this volume).

There are two interrelated but equally relevant questions concerning these kinds of emotions that stand at the core of group identity. How to uncover them empirically and how to explain their evolvement and transmission? Our answer to both questions is group narratives (i.e., history). Emotions that the ingroup experiences as well as emotions assigned to outgroups in narratives about the group's past carry the emotions that are characteristic to the group by being an undetachable part of the identity of the group. In turn, these emotions derive from the representations of the past. Master narratives of nations that clearly have emotional entailments are called narrative templates by Wertsch (2002), or charters by Liu and Hilton (2005) following Malinowski (1926). We prefer to call them historical trajectories (László, 2011; see also Chapter 14, this volume), because emotions can be related best to the different sequential patterns of the nation's victories and failures as they became preserved in its collective memory.

A more immediate functional aspect of the emotional content of a nation's historical narratives is trauma elaboration (see also Chapter 14, this volume). In the 20th century, masses of people experienced trauma as an ethnic or national group. Genocides and ethnic cleansings swept over mainly the European, but also the Asian and the African continent, and many countries were forced to shrink or move in the geographic space as a consequence of massive military defeats. Because traumatic group experiences can be and are, if at all, elaborated in the public sphere, parsing the emotional content of historical narratives over time provides information about the stages and processes of group trauma elaboration. According to this assumption, a progress in trauma elaboration is prevalent if a decrease can be observed in hostile, negative emotions toward outgroups, in self-enhancing emotions and depressive emotions of the ingroup, and the overall extremity of the emotions diminishes.

## *Cognitive States and Perspectives*

The most common interpretation of cognitive states in accounts of traumatic or stressful events is related to trauma elaboration. According to this interpretation, the more cognitive states and processes appear in both ingroup and outgroup, the further the trauma elaboration has progressed (Paez, Basabe, & Gonzales, 1997; Pennebaker, 1993; see also Chapter 13, this volume). In this sense, frequency of cognitive states in historical narratives on ethnic or national traumas indicates the process of trauma elaboration toward a coherent, emotionally stable group identity. There are, however, other possibilities of the interpretation of the presence of cognitive states in historical narratives. For instance, Vincze and Rein (2011) have shown that the propositional content of cognitive states may overwrite the trauma elaboration interpretation. In these cases, negative propositional contents of the perpetrator outgroup's cognitive states serves assigning deliberation and thereby even more responsibility to outgroups for bad deeds. These maneuvers probably do not promote the reconciliation with the traumatic loss, rather add to maintaining the emotionally disturbing experience.

Another aspect of cognitive (and emotional) states in narrative is psychological perspective taking. This function is also related to identity states in as much it allows for entering the outgroup's perspective in historical narrative. It is obvious that people having a stable, emotionally balanced, future oriented ethnonational identity can afford to appear the perspective of former enemies in their historical accounts.

As we have already noted when discussing intergroup evaluations, historical narratives always have at least three perspective forms. There is the ingroup (internal) perspective represented by ingroup members taking part in the events, the outgroup (external) perspective, represented by outgroup members, and the perspective of the narrator, who is usually, but not necessarily, a member of the ingroup and sees the events from a physical and temporal distance. The narrator's perspective prevails in most historical accounts, and this fact strengthens the categorical empathy of the group members who are exposed to these narratives in as much as the group is affected in the story. Given that cognitive process attributed to outgroups, as a whole or individual, outgroup members introduce an outgroup perspective, which in turn may set into motion a different form of empathy, that is situational—that is, leads to a more balanced representation of the events (Hogan, 2003). Propositional content of the cognitive processes and outcome valence of the event—that is, whether it was good or bad for the ingroup or the outgroup cannot be neglected in this analysis either. Enhanced situational empathy as a consequence of perspectivization through cognitive processes and a better understanding of the historical event, which may contribute to improving intergroup relations through abolishing stereotypes (Galinsky & Moskowitz, 2000; Chapter 13, this volume) will only occur if outgroup enemies are endowed with cognitive (and emotional) processes that go beyond the hostility and the unanimously negative consequences for the ingroup in their propositional content. Such an analysis of cognitive processes and perspectivization from the angle of group identity, which also considers relations to different outgroups in a wider historical span—that is, numbers and types of outgroups who are endowed with their own perspective in a historical period, provides information on group identity with respect to its stability, plasticity, and future orientation.

## NARRATIVE CATEGORICAL CONTENT ANALYSIS (NARRCAT)

The computerized content analytic methodology we have developed rests on the psychologically relevant features of narrative composition or narrative categories. It is not the psychological correlates of words, word types (e.g., function words versus content words), or grammatical features (e.g., past tense) that interests us. Instead, following the principles of narrative composition, we are interested in the spatiotemporal perspective structure, the internal versus external perspective, the self-other and ingroup–outgroup emotion structure, evaluation structures, distribution of cognitive processes between characters and groups, etc. Similar to other computerized content analytic devices—for example, LIWC (Pennebaker, Francis, & Booth, 2001), RID (Martindale, 1975), General Inquirer (Stone, Dunphy, Smith, & Oglivie, 1966)—NarrCat also has lexicons. Because of the complex morphology of the Hungarian language and the need for disambiguation, lexicons are endowed with local grammar that perform the task of disambiguation and enable further grammatical analysis. So as to arrive at psychologically relevant hits, two other language processing tasks have to be completed. A grammatical parser solves the anaphors by putting the proper name in place of personal pronouns, because we need to identify characters in each sentence. In the next step, a semantic role analyzer connects each psychological content to a particular semantic role (agent or patient, stimulus, or experiencer, etc.). These usually correspond to the sentence's subject-object roles. The program outputs a quantitative measure on who feels, acts, evaluates, and thinks what, toward whom—that is, the psychological composition of interpersonal and intergroup relations that are relevant for identity construction becomes transparent.

*Agency* has two ingredients: active and passive verbs (e.g., occupy, achieve, and choose versus become, sleep, or grow up) and expressions of intention versus constraint. For agency measures, frequencies of activity are divided by passivity, and intentions are divided by constraint. The overall agency index is calculated by averaging the two ratios.

*Evaluations* can be (a) positive and negative attributions (assigned to characters or to their actions; e.g., *wise, unjust*), (b) emotional reactions and relations to characters (*admire, scorn*), (c) evaluative interpretations referring to characters' actions (instead of or beside factual description; *excel, exploit*), and (d) acts of rewarding and punishment or acknowledgement and criticism (*cheer, protest*).

*Emotion* subcategories are positive and negative emotions (joy versus sadness); primary and secondary emotions (fear versus guilt); moral emotions, within this self-critical and other-critical emotions (regret versus despise). Furthermore, the module is able to detect the control of spatial emotional distance (approaching and distancing, and ambivalence thereof) in individual and group narratives.

*Cognition* includes two kinds of content: verbs with word-level cognitive meaning (generalizes, ponders) and idioms thereof (take an idea, immerses in the past).

Further modules of the NarrCat are *spatio-temporal perspective, self and we reference, negation,* and *subjective time experience.*

## SOME ASPECTS OF THE HUNGARIAN NATIONAL IDENTITY EXPRESSED IN THE NARRATIVE LANGUAGE OF SCHOOLBOOKS AND FOLK HISTORY TEXTS

In a series of studies (Csertő & László, 2011; Fülöp, 2010; Fülöp, Péley, & László, 2011; László, Ehmann, & Imre, 2002; László & Fülöp, 2011a, 2011b; László, Szalai, & Ferenczhalmy, 2010; László & Vincze, 2004; Szalai, 2010; Vincze & László, 2011; Vincze, Tóth, & László, 2007), we have examined characteristics of the Hungarian national identity in a series of historical text corpora including history textbooks, folk history stories, historical novels, and newspaper texts.

Here we summarize some results gained with NarrCat on intergroup agency, intergroup evaluations, emotions, and cognitive processes in the folk story corpus, the schoolbook corpus, and the newspaper corpus. The folk story corpus consists of brief narratives about the most positive and the most negative Hungarian historical events that were solicited from a stratified sample of 500 subjects. Ten events were chosen with the highest frequency. Three of them were in the positive domain (conquest of homeland in 896, establishing an independent state in 1000, and the system's change in 1990). Four negative events were named with high frequency, among them three in the 20th century: Mongolian invasion in 1241, the Paris Peace treaty in 1920, World War II from 1941 (when Hungary entered the war) to 1945 and the Holocaust, which affected Hungary in 1944 to 1945. Most interesting, there were three events that were chosen in both positive and negative domains. Hungary's occupation by the Ottoman Empire in 1526 and the Turkish rule that lasted until 1686 took place among the negative events, but temporary victories against the Turks were celebrated as highly positive events. Similarly, the bourgeois revolution and freedom fight against the Habsburg Empire in 1848 to 1849 was selected with high frequency among the positive events, but suppression of the revolution was a negative event. The beginning of the 1956 revolution against dictatorship and the Soviet occupation and the suppression of the revolution were chosen with almost equally high frequency, but the former among the positive, the latter among the negative events. Without any further commentaries, we only note that in the line of salient historical events, we do not find a sequence where the first part or initiation was represented as negative and the second part, or climax, as positive.

The subjects were asked to give a brief account on the chosen historical events both for positive and negative. The full text corpus consists of 104,011 words.

The schoolbooks text corpus (223,740 words) has been selected from a wide range of secondary school and high school history books published after 2000. From each textbook, those text parts were sampled that dealt with the positive

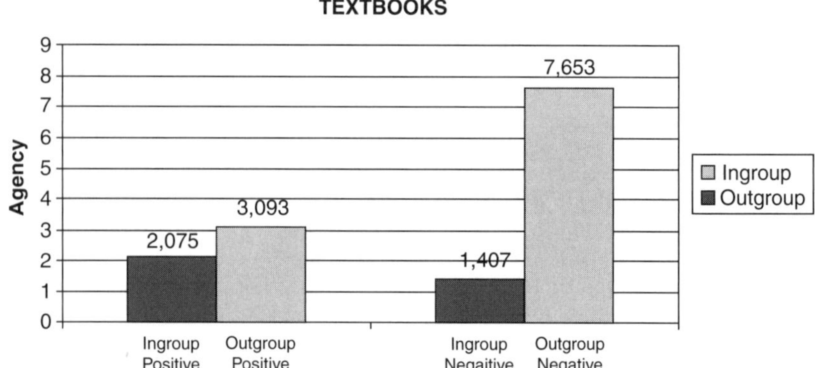


Figure 12.1 Ingroup and outgroup agency in positive versus negative historical events as presented by history textbooks (adapted from László, Szalai, & Ferenczhalmy, 2010)

or negative historical event or period that had been chosen in the folk history survey (altogether 13 events).

## *Schoolbooks and Folk History Results Concerning Agency*

Results concerning ingroup–outgroup agency—see Figures 12.1 and 12.2—show that agency of the Hungarian ingroup is much lower than the agency of the outgroups. The pattern of results is very similar in the history school textbooks and folk narratives. The figures also show that folk narratives tend to depict both ingroup and outgroups as having more agency than textbooks do,

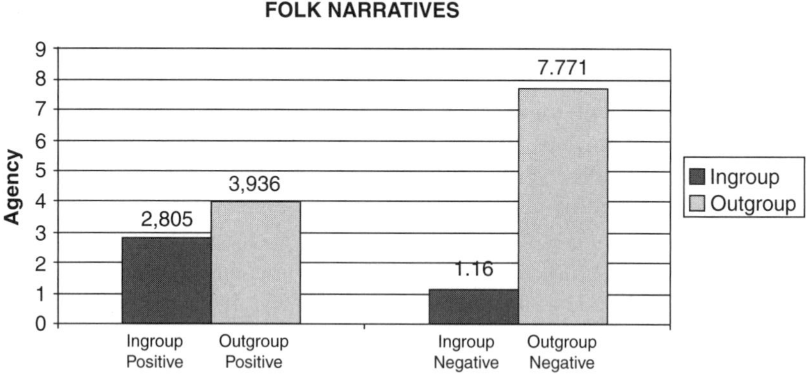


Figure 12.2 Ingroup and outgroup agency in positive versus negative historical events as presented by folk narratives (adapted from László, Szalai, & Ferenczhalmy, 2010)

except the Hungarian ingroup in the negative events, where the agency level is extremely low.

### Schoolbooks and Folk Story Results Concerning Intergroup Evaluation

Intergroup evaluation results are seen in Figures 12.3 and 12.4. For the sake of simplicity and comparability, only narrators' evaluations are considered. The figures show a similar pattern to the results obtained with agency. Ingroups are evaluated much higher than outgroups both in positive and negative events, but there is a statistically significant interaction with event valence: Hungarians are evaluated even more positively in positive events, and outgroups are evaluated even lower in negative events. Comparing folk stories and textbooks, these effects are prevalent in folk stories even more markedly.

### Schoolbook and Folk Story Results Concerning Emotions

What are the characteristic emotions of the Hungarians in the historical events, and what does this emotion pattern suggest for the Hungarian national identity? In the whole corpus, we have found 57 emotion types with 918 tokens. We considered *Hungarian* emotion when frequency of a particular emotion differed significantly. According to the data, sadness and hope are the emotions that most distinguish Hungarians from other nations. A similar pattern can be observed in the folk history texts, except enthusiasm, which adds to the Hungarian emotions in this corpus. Hope and enthusiasm are more prevalent in positive events, whereas sadness and disappointment are in negative events. There is an emotion, which does not differ significantly between Hungarians and outgroups, but reaches the highest frequency in the Hungarian texts both in schoolbooks and folk stories: It is fear with a 78 (one-sixth of the total) and 32 (one-fifth of the total) frequency, respectively. We compared this pattern of emotions (sadness, disappointment, fear, hope, and enthusiasm) between Hungarians and the outgroups in both text corpora and found highly significant differences between the two groups in both cases ( 2 (1) = 10.02, $p < .01$) and 2 (1) = 10.61, $p < .001$, respectively. (See also Chapter 14, this volume).

### Schoolbook and Folk Story Results Concerning Cognitive Processes

Frequency of cognitive processes does not follow the usual parallel between schoolbooks and folk history—see Figure 12.5. This correspondence still can be observed in the positive events, where Hungarians are endowed with more cognitive states and processes. Whereas the differences are significant between Hungarians and outgroups for the positive events in both corpora, significant difference can be observed in negative events only in the folk history corpus with higher frequency of cognitive states and processes of the outgroups.

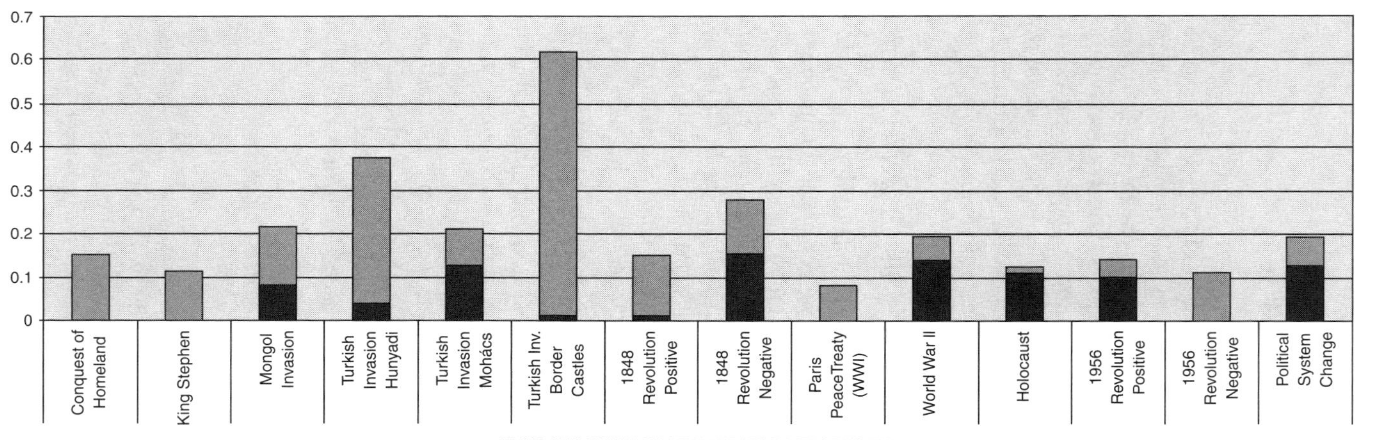


Figure 12.3 Narrator's positive (green) and negative (red) evaluations of the ingroup (adapted from Csertő & László, 2012)

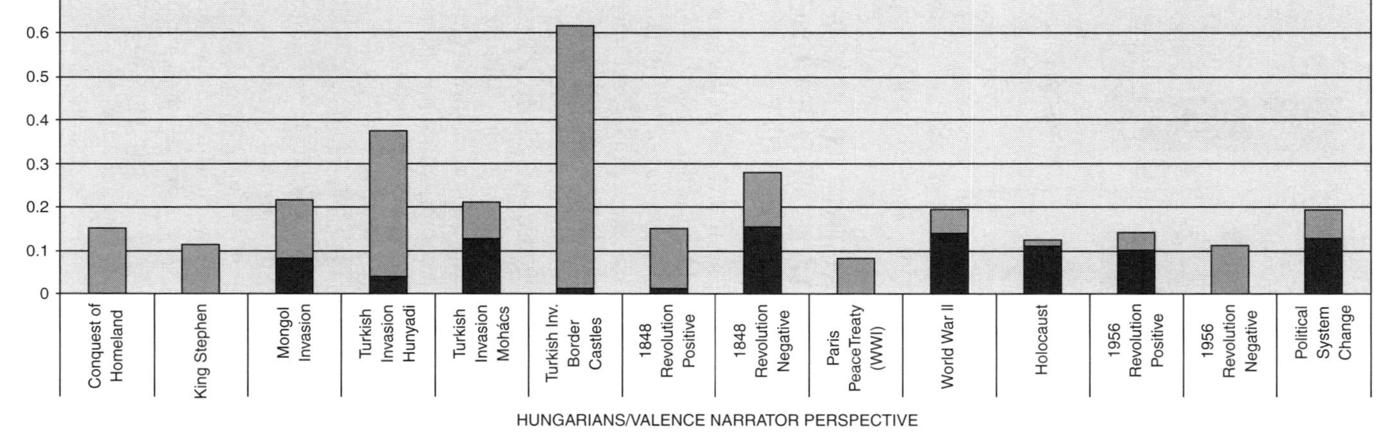


Figure 12.4 Narrator's positive (green) and negative (red) evaluations of the outgroup (adapted from Csertő & László, 2012)

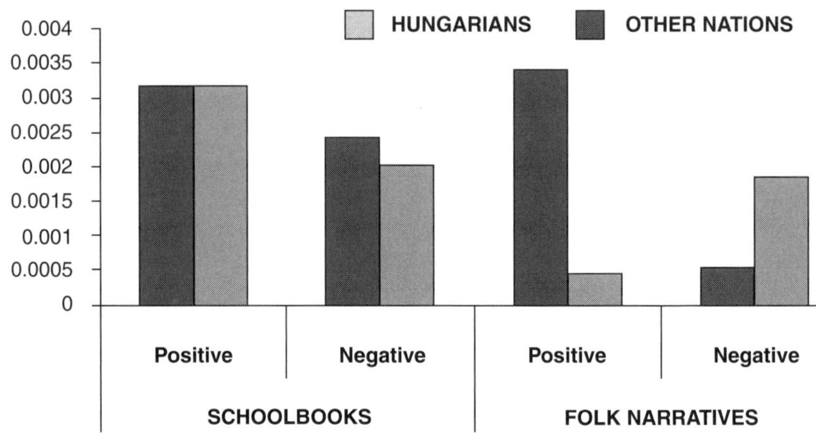


Figure 12.5 Distribution of cognitive processes in schoolbooks and folk stories according to the valence of the events (adapted from Vincze & Rein, 2011)

## SUMMARY AND INTERPRETATION OF THE RESULTS FROM THE PERSPECTIVE OF THE HUNGARIAN NATIONAL IDENTITY

The results that have been sampled from several studies converge in portraying a vulnerable Hungarian national identity and suggest a long-term adoption of the collective victim role. Although the public image of Hungarians may be different from both internal and external angle, emotional and cognitive organization of the Hungarian national identity as it is expressed in historical narratives show a deep attachment to the glorious past and a relatively low level of cognitive and emotional elaboration of the 20th century and earlier traumas. The very fact that collective memory splits history into glorious distant past followed by a series of defeats and losses and occasional heroic revolts are represented as starting with celebrated victories, but ending with suppression and subjugation suggests that this historical trajectory is not the most favorable ground to build an emotionally stable identity around. As we saw, emotions that are implied in this trajectory are fear, sadness, disappointment, enthusiasm, and hope.

Results with agency-, evaluation-, and cognitive processes-measures show a picture that is consistent with that of the emotion regulation. Inflated self-evaluation accompanied with devaluation of the outgroups, low ingroup agency in negative events—particularly in events when Hungarians were clearly perpetrators (e.g., Holocaust), assigning a very high rate of cognitive process to the outgroups in the negative events and thereby passing even more responsibility onto them—all remind us of what Bar-Tal et al. (2009) has termed an identity state of collective victimhood. According to the concept of collective victimhood, when ethnic groups or nations experience repeated traumas, losses, repressions, and failures, these experiences render difficult to maintain beliefs that the group is competent, strong, and capable to tackle with conflicts; moreover, they threaten integrity or survival of the collective. Developing identity with embedded experiences of victimhood may function as protection of positive group image through perceiving moral superiority of the ingroup, refusing of responsibility, evoking sympathy of other groups, and avoiding criticism of them (see Chapter 14, this volume). A Hungarian political thinker, István Bibó (1991) not long after World War II, interpreted Hungarian national identity very similarly. According to him, recurrent historical traumatization, and the permanent threat to the existence of the state, led to pervasive fear that in turn led to cognitive and emotional regression. Traumatic collective experiences have distorted perception of reality, and have resulted in political illusions and a psychological state resembling collective victimhood—what he termed *political hysteria*.

As a concluding remark to this section, we should warn that trauma elaboration not only is a function of time, but it proceeds (or is thwarted) in political context. If narratives about collective traumas are suppressed in the public sphere, the likelihood of carrying them on increases.

## SCHOOLBOOKS AND FOLK STORIES AS TOOLS FOR CONSTRUCTING NATIONAL IDENTITY

There are two different, but as we shall show, related modes relating past experiences. History aspires to provide an accurate representation of the past or, in other words, to give the true story of past events (Carr, 1986). In doing this, historiography often neglects or brackets subjective experiences that have been shared by the participants of the events. Current historical approaches to history of mentality (e.g., Goldhagen, 1997; La Capra, 2001; Schievelbush, 2001) try to rectify this neglect. In contrast, in collective remembering, the past is represented so that group identity is sustained. American historian Nowick contrasts the two modes as follows:

> To understand something historically is to be aware of its complexity, to have sufficient detachment to see it from multiple perspectives, to accept the ambiguities, including moral ambiguities, of protagonists' motives and behaviour. Collective memory simplifies; sees events from a single, committed perspective; is impatient with ambiguities of any kind; reduces events to mythic archetypes. (Novick, 1999, pp. 3–4)

School history textbooks stand somewhere between the two modes. They transfer *objective*, for the distant past culturally settled knowledge. Several authors claim that they are primary sources of historical awareness of a nation's past (e.g., Angvik & Von Borries, 1997; Roediger, Zaromb, & Butler, 2009). On the other hand, they are also mediating identity patterns, as our results clearly suggest. An interesting finding of our investigations that supports the distinction between history and collective memory is that folk history compared with historically oriented schoolbooks expresses national identity in more extreme psychological features. But in tendency, it is important to stress, they are consistent.

Narrative identity construction and trauma elaboration thus proceeds on at least three channels. History writing pretends to depict events objectively, but ingroup biases frequently permeate these historical accounts. Even canonical or mythological interpretations, belonging to cultural memory (Assmann, 1992) may be characterized by this biased perspective. Collective memory, which is objectified in diaries, family accounts, oral histories, etc., exists in relation with history but unfolds, in part, independently from historiography and carries more from emotions and thoughts that are important for group identity. It corresponds more what Assmann (1992) has termed communicative memory. Between the two forms of group remembering, there are the history representations presented by schoolbooks, representations of the past presented by art and literature, and public memory presented by the media. The role of the latter two forms is evidenced by several authors (e.g., Bar-Tal, 2001; Bar-Tal & Antebi, 1992; Fülöp et al., 2011; László & Vincze, 2004; László, Vincze, & Kővárine Somogyvári, 2003; see also Chapters 14 and 15, this volume).

Given that telling history even in pictural form is genuinely a narrative genre, narrative social psychology and narrative categorical content analysis (NarrCat) seem to be adequate tools for tracing empirically how ethnonational groups are constructing their collective identity by shaping their collective memory, how they are elaborating their traumatic experiences, and what are the factors that influence these processes. Moreover, results gained with this conceptual and methodological equipment can serve not only explaining the past or the present, but also predicting future coping behavior of ethnonational groups and the potential success of this coping.

## ACKNOWLEDGMENTS

The authors are grateful to the Hungarian National Research Foundation for the support by grant No. 81366 to János László.

## REFERENCES

Abelson, R. P., Dasgupta, N., Park, J., & Banaji, M. R. (1998). Perception of the collective other. *Personality and Social Psychology Review, 2*, 243–250.

Allport, F. H. (1924). *Social psychology*. Boston, MA: Houghton Mifflin

Angvik, M., & Von Borries, B. (1997). *A comparative European survey on historical consciousness and political attitudes among adolescents*. Hamburg, Germany: Korber-Stiftung.

Antonovsky, A. (1987). *Unraveling the mystery of health*. San Francisco, CA: Jossey-Bass.

Assmann, J. (1992). *Das kulturelle Gedachtnis*. Munich, Germany: C. H. Beck.

Bal, M. (1985). *Narratology: Introduction to the theory of narrative*. Toronto, Canada: University of Toronto Press.

Bamberg, M., & Andrews, M. (2004). Introduction. In M. Bamberg & M. Andrews (Eds.), *Considering counter-narratives: Narrating, resisting, making sense*. Amsterdam, The Netherlands: John Benjamins.

Bandura, A. (1989). Perceived self-efficacy in the exercise of personal agency. *The Psychologist: Bulletin of the British Psychological Society, 2*, 411–424.

Bandura, A. (1994). Self-efficacy. In V. S. Ramachaudran (Ed.), *Encyclopedia of human behavior* (Vol. 4, pp. 71–81). New York, NY: Academic Press.
Banga, Cs., Szabó, Zs. P., & László, J. (2012). Implicit measures of ingroup favoritism. In E. Matanovi , A. Milardovi , D. Paukovi , D. Vidovi , N. Jožanc, & V. Raos (Eds.), *Series of political science research centre forum book 10: Confronting the past: European experiences* (pp. 67–81). Zagreb, Croatia: Political Science Research Centre.
Bar-Tal, D. (2001). Why does fear override hope in societies engulfed by intractable conflict, as it does in the Israeli society? *Political Psychology, 22,* 601–627.
Bar-Tal, D., & Antebi, D. (1992). Siege mentality in Israel. *Ongoing Production in Social Representations, 1*(1), 49–67.
Bar-Tal, D., Chernyak-Hai, L., Schori, N., & Gundar, A. (2009, June). A sense of self perceived collective victimhood in intractable conflicts. *International Review of the Red Cross.*
Bar-Tal, D., Halperin, E., & De Rivera, J. (2007). Collective emotions in conflict situations: Societal implications. *Journal of Social Issues, 63*(2), 441–460.
Barthes, R. (1977). *Image, music, text.* New York, NY: Hill & Wang.
Baumeister, R. F. & Hastings, S. (1997). Distortions of collective memory: How groups flatter and deceive themseves. In: Pennebaker, J. W. Paez, D. Rimé, B. (eds.) *Collective Memory and Political Events. Social Psychological Perspective.* Mahwah, NJ: Lawrence Erlbaum Associates. 277–293.
Benedict, R. (1946). *The chrysanthemum and the sword.* Boston, MA: Houghton Mifflin.
Beukeboom, C. J., Finkenauer, C., & Wigboldus, D. H. J. (2010). The negation bias: When negations signal stereotypic expectancies. *Journal of Personality and Social Psychology, 99*(6), 978–992.
Bibó, I. (1991). *Democracy, revolution, self-determination selected writings.* New York, NY: Columbia University Press.
Brewer, M. B., Hong, Y., & Li, Q. (2004). Dynamic entitativity: Perceiving groups as actors. In V. Yzerbyt, C. Judd, & O. Corneille (Eds.), *The psychology of group perception: Perceived variability, entitativity, and essentialism* (pp. 25–38). New York, NY: Psychology Press.
Brockmeier, J., & Carbaugh, D. (Eds.). (2001). *Narrative and identity.* Philadelphia, PA: John Benjamins.
Brown, R. (1958). *Words and things.* New York, NY: Simon & Schuster.
Brown, R. (1965). *Social psychology.* London, England: Collier-Macmillan.
Brown, R., & Fish, D. (1983). The psychological causality implicit in language. *Cognition, 14,* 237–273.
Carnaghi, A., Maass, A., Gresta, S., Bianchi, M., Cadinu, M., & Arcuri, L. (2009). Nomina sunt omina: On the inductive potential of nouns and adjectives in person perception. *Journal of Personality and Social Psychology, 94*(5), 839–859.
Carr, D. (1986). Narrative and the Real World: An Argument for Continuity. *History and Theory, 25,* 2, 117–131.
Csertő, I., & László, J. (2011). Exploration of group identity processes by a narrative analysis of intergroup evaluation. In *EASP 2011—16th European Association of social psychology general meeting,* Stockholm, Sweden.
Cohn, D. C. (1984). *Transparent minds.* Princeton, NJ: Princeton University Press.
Condor, S. (2003). The least doubtful promise for the future? In L. László & W. Wagner (Eds.), *Theories and controversies in societal psychology.* Budapest, Hungary: New Mandate.
Culler, J. (2001). *The pursuit of signs: Semiotics, literature, deconstruction.* London, England: Routledge.
DeCharms, R. (1968). *Personal causation.* New York, NY: Academic Press.
Deci, E. L. (1975). *Intrinsic motivation.* New York, NY: Plenum.

Doosje, B., Branscombe, N. R., Spears, R., & Manstead, A. S. R. (1998). Guilty by association: When one's group has a negative history. *Journal of Personality and Social Psychology, 75,* 872–886.

Eco, U. (1994). *Six walks in the fictional woods.* Cambridge, MA: Harvard University Press.

Erikson, E. H. (1959). Identity and the life cycle: Selected papers. *Psychological Issues, 1*(1), 5–165.

Erikson, E. H. (1968). *Identity: Youth and crisis.* New York, NY: Norton.

Forgas, J. P. (1995). Mood and moral judgment: The affect in fusion model (AIM). *Psychological Bulletin, 117,* 39–66.

Freeman, M. (1993). *Rewriting the self: History, memory, narrative.* London, England: Routledge.

Fülöp, É. (2010). *A történelmi pálya és a nemzeti identitás érzelmi szervez dése* [*Hungarian historical trajectory and the emotional organization of the Hungarian national identity*]. Unpublished doctoral thesis.

Fülöp, É., Péley, B., & László, J. (2011). A történelmi pályához kapcsolódó érzelmek modellje magyar történelmi regényekben [Historical trajectory emotions in Hungarian historical novels]. *Pszichológia, 31, 1,* 47–67.

Galinsky, A. D., & Moskowitz, G. B. (2000). Perspective-taking: Decreasing stereotype expression, stereotype accessibility, and ingroup favouritism. *Journal of Personality and Social Psychology, 78,* 708–724.

Giles, H. (1977). *Language, ethnicity, and intergroup relations.* New York, NY: Academic Press.

Goldhagen, D. J. (1997). *Hitler's willing executioners: Ordinary Germans and the Holocaust.* New York, NY: Springer.

Halbwachs, M. (1941). *La topographic légendaire des évangilesen Terre Sainte.* Paris, France: Presses Universitaires de France.

Hamilton, D. L. (2007). Agenda 2007: Understanding the complexities of group perception: Broadening the domain. *European Journal of Social Psychology, 37,* 1077–1101.

Harter, S. (1978). Effectance motivation reconsidered: Toward a developmental model. *Human Development, 6,* 34–64.

Hobsbowm, E. (1992). *Nations and nationalism since 1780: Programme, myth, reality* (2nd ed.). Cambridge, England: Cambridge University Press.

Hogan, P. C. (2003). *The mind and its stories. Narrative universals and human emotion.* Cambridge, England: Cambridge University Press.

Kashima, H. Y., Kashima, E., Chiu, C., Farsides, T., Gelfand, M., Hong, Y., . . . Yzerbyt, V. (2005). Culture, essentialism, and agency: Are individuals universally believed to be more real entities than groups? *European Journal of Social Psychology, 35,* 147–169.

Klar, Y., Schori, N., & Roccas, S. (2011). *Effects of group past trauma on current intergroup reconciliation.* Paper presented at the 16th general meeting of the European Association of Social Psychology.

La Capra, D. (2001). *Writing history, writing trauma.* Baltimore, MD: Johns Hopkins University Press.

László, J. (2003). History, identity and narratives. In J. László & W. Wagner (Eds.), *Theories and controversies in societal psychology.* Budapest, Hungary: New Mandate.

László, J. (2008). *The science of stories: An introduction to narrative psychology.* London, England: Routledge.

László, J. (2011). Narrative psychology. In *Daniel Christie: The encyclopedia of peace psychology* (pp. 687–691). San Francisco, CA: Wiley-Blackwell.

László, J., Ehmann, B., & Imre, O. (2002). Les representations sociales de l'histoire: La narration populaire historique et l'identité nationale. In S. Laurens & N. Roussiau (Eds.), *La Mémoire sociale. Identités et representations sociales.* Rennes, France: Université de Rennes.

László, J., & Fülöp, É. (2011a). Nemzeti identitás és kollektív áldozati szerep [National identity and collective victim role]. *Pszichológia, 31*(3), 295–315.
László, J., & Fülöp, É. (2011b). Érzelmek a valós csoportközi konfliktusokban [Emotions in real intergroup conflicts]. *Magyar Pszichológiai Szemle, 66*(3), 467–485.
László, J., Szalai, K., & Ferenczhalmy, R. (2010). Role of agency in social representations of history. *Societal and Political Psychology International Review, 1,* 31–43.
László, J., & Vincze, O. (2004). Coping with historical tasks. The role of historical novels in transmitting psychological patterns of national identity. *Spiel, 21*(1), 76–88.
László, J., Vincze, O., & K váriné Somogyvári, I. (2003). Representation of national identity in successful historical novels. *Empirical Studies of the Arts, 21*(1), 69–80.
Leary, M. R., & Baumeister, R. F. (2000). The nature and function of self-esteem: Sociometer theory. In M. Zanna (Ed.), *Advances in experimental social psychology* (Vol. 32., pp. 1–62). San Diego, CA: Academic Press.
Liu, J. H., & Hilton, D. J. (2005). How the past weighs on the present: Social representations of history and their impact on identity politics. *British Journal of Social Psychology,* 537–556.
Liu, J. H., & László, J. (2007). A narrative theory of history and identity: Social identity, social representations, society and the individual. In G. Moloney & I. Walker (Eds.), *Social representations and identity: Content, process, and power.* Basingstoke, England: Palgrave-Macmillan.
Maass, A., Milesi, A., Zabbini, S., & Stahlberg, D. (1995). The linguistic intergroup bias: Differential expectancies or ingroup protection? *Journal of Personality and Social Psychology, 68,* 116–126.
Maass, A., Salvi, D., Arcuri, L., & Semin, G. R. (1989). Language use in intergroup contexts: The linguistic intergroup bias. *Journal of Personality and Social Psychology, 57*(6), 981–993.
Mackie, D. M., Devos, T., & Smith, E. R. (2000). Intergroup emotions: Explaining offensive action tendencies in an intergroup context. *Journal of Personality and Social Psychology, 79,* 602–616.
Malinowski, B. (1926). *Myth in primitive psychology.* London, England: Kegan Paul, Trench, Trubner.
Marcia, J. E. (1966). Development and validation of egoidentity status. *Journal of Personality and Social Psychology, 5,* 551–558.
Marcia, J. E. (1980). Identity in adolescence. In J. Adelson (Ed.), *Handbook of adolescent psychology.* New York, NY: Wiley.
Markus, H., & Kitayama, S. (1991). Culture and the self: Implications for cognition, emotion, and motivation. *Psychological Review, 98,* 224–253.
Martindale, C. (1975). *Romantic progression: The psychology of literary history.* New York, NY: Wiley.
McAdams, D. P. (1985). *Power, intimacy, and the life story: Personological inquiries into identity.* New York, NY: Guilford Press.
McAdams, D. P. (2001). The psychology of life stories. *Review of General Psychology, 5*(2), 100–122.
McLean, K. C., & Pratt, M. W. (2006). Life's little (and big) lessons: Identity statuses and meaning-making in the turning point narratives of emerging adults. *Developmental Psychology, 42*(4), 714–722.
Mead, M. (1937). *Cooperation and competition among primitive peoples.* New York, NY: McGraw-Hill.
Morris, M. W., Menon, T., & Ames, D. R. (2001). Culturally conferred conceptions of agency: A key to social perception of persons, groups, and other actors. *Personality and Social Psychology Review, 5,* 169–182.
Nencini, A. (2011). Social representations of national history: Stability and changeability between different generations of Italians over a period of three years. *Societal and Political Psychology Review, 2*(1), 111–126.

Novick, P. (1999). *The Holocaust in American life.* New York, NY: Mariner Books.

Paez, D., Basabe, N., & Gonzales, J. L. (1997). Social processes and collective memory: A cross-cultural approach to remembering political events. In J. W. Pennebaker, D. Paez, & B. Rimé (Eds.), *Collective memory of political events.* Mahwah, NJ: Erlbaum.

Pennebaker, J. W. (1993). Putting stress into words: Health, linguistic and therapeutic implications. *Behavior Research and Therapy, 31*(6), 539–548.

Pennebaker, J. W., Francis, M. E., & Booth, R. J. (2001). *Linguistic inquiry and word count (LIWC).* Mahwah, NJ: Erlbaum.

Pólya, T., László, J., & Forgas, J. P. (2005). Making sense of life stories: The role of narrative perspective in communicating hidden information about social identity and personality. *European Journal of Social Psychology, 35,* 785–796.

Reicher, S., & Hopkins, N. (2001). *Self and nation.* London, England: Sage.

Ricoeur. (1991). L'identiténarrative. *Revues de Sciences Humaines, 221,* 35–47.

Roediger, H. L., Zaromb, F. M., & Butler, A. C. (2009). The role of repeated retrieval in shaping collective memory. In P. Boyer & J. V. Wertsch (Eds.), *Memory in mind and culture* (pp. 138–170). New York, NY: Cambridge University Press.

Roseman, I. (1984). Cognitive determinants of emotions: A structural theory. In P. Shaver (Ed.), *Review of personality and social psychology* (Vol. 5, pp. 11–36). Beverly Hills, CA: Sage.

Rozin, P., Lowery, L., Imada, S., & Haidt, J. (1999). The CAD triad hypothesis: A mapping between three morale motions (contempt, anger, disgust) and three moral codes (community, autonomy, divinity). *Journal of Personality and Social Psychology, 76,* 574–586.

Schievelbush, W. (2001). *The culture of defeat: On national trauma, mourning, and recovery.* New York, NY: Picador.

Sekaquaptewa, D., Espinoza, P., Thompson, M., Vargas, P., & Von Hippel, W. (2003). Stereotypic explanatory bias: Implicit stereotyping as a predictor of discrimination. *Journal of Experimental Social Psychology, 39,* 75–82.

Semin, G. R. (2000a). Agenda 2000-communication: Language as an implementational device for cognition. *European Journal of Social Psychology, 30,* 595–612.

Semin, G. R. (2000b). Language as a cognitive and behavioral structuring resource: Question-answer exchanges. In W. Stroebe & M. Hewstone (Eds.), *European review of social psychology* (pp. 75–104). Chichester, England: Wiley.

Semin, G. R., & Fiedler, K. (1988). The cognitive functions of linguistic categories in describing persons: Social cognition and language. *Journal of Personality and Social Psychology, 54,* 558–568.

Semin, G. R., & Fiedler, K. (1991). The linguistic category model, its bases, applications and range. In W. Stroebe & M. Hewstone (Eds.), *European review of social psychology* (Vol. 2). Chichester, England: Wiley.

Shweder, R. A., Much, N. C, Mahapatra, M., & Park, L. (1997). The "Big Three" of morality (autonomy, community, divinity) and the "Big Three" explanations of suffering. In A. Brandt & P. Rozin (Eds.), *Morality and health* (pp. 119–169). New York, NY: Routledge.

Smith, E. R. (1993). Social identity and social emotions: Toward new conceptualizations of prejudice. In D. M. Mackie & D. L. Hamilton (Eds.), *Affect, cognition, and stereotyping: Interactive processing group perception* (pp. 297–315). San Diego, CA: Academic Press.

Smith, C. A., & Ellsworth, P. C. (1985). Patterns of cognitive appraisal in emotion. *Journal of Personality and Social Psychology, 48,* 813–838.

Spencer-Rogers, J., Hamilton, D. L., & Sherman, S. J. (2007). The central role of entitativity in stereotypes of social categories and task groups. *Journal of Personality and Social Psychology, 92,* 369–388.

Spini, D., Elcheroth, G., & Fasel, R. (2008). The impact of groups norms and generalization of risks on judgments of war behavior. *Political Psychology, 29*, 919–941.

Stearns, P. N., & Stearns, C. Z. (1985). Emotionology: Clarifying the history of emotions and emotional standards. *The American Historical Review, 90*(4), 813–836.

Stone, P. J., Dunphy, D. C., Smith, M. S., & Oglivie, D. M. (1966). *The general inquirer: A computer approach transcripts.* Mahwah, NJ: Erlbaum.

Szalai, K. (2010). *Az ágencia nyelvi jegyei: az aktív és passzív igék szerepe a narratívumokban* [*Lingusitic markers of agency. The role of active and passive verbs in narratives*]. Unpublished doctoral dissertation.

Tajfel, H. (Ed.). (1978). *Differentiation between social groups.* London, England: Academic Press.

Tajfel, H. (1981). *Human groups and social categories: Studies in social psychology.* Cambridge, England: Cambridge University Press.

Tajfel, H., & Turner, J. C. (1979). An integrative theory of intergroup conflict. In W. G. Austin & S. Worchel (Eds.), *The social psychology of intergroup relations* (pp. 33–47). Monterey, CA: Brooks Cole.

Turnbull, W. (1994). Thematic structure of descriptions of violent events influences perceptions of responsibility: A thematic structure effect. *Journal of Language and Social Psychology, 13*(2), 132–157.

Turner, J. C. (1999). Some current issues in research on social identity and self categorization theories. In N. Ellemers, R. Spears, & B. Doosje (Eds.), *Social identity: Context, commitment, content* (pp. 6–34). Oxford, England: Wiley-Blackwell.

Turner, J. C., Hogg, M. A., Oakes, P. J., Reicher, S. D., & Wetherell, M. (1987). *Rediscovering the social group: A self-categorization theory.* Oxford, England: Blackwell.

Uspensky, B. A. (1974). *The poetics of composition: Structure of the artistic text and the typology of compositional form.* Berkeley: University of California Press.

Vincze, O., & László, J. (2011). *Narrative means of intergroup relations: Cognitive states and their role in reducing or increasing intergroup conflict.* Paper presented at the 16th general meeting of the European Association of Social Psychology.

Vincze, O. & Rein, (2011). Narrative means of intergroup relations: cognitive states and their role in reducing or increasing intergroup conflict. General meeting of EASP 2012, Stockholm.

Vincze, O., Tóth, J., & László, J. (2007). Representations of the Austro-Hungarian monarchy in the history books of two nations. *Empirical Text and Culture Research, 3*, 62–71.

Wertsch, J. V. (2002). *Voices of collective remembering.* Cambridge, England: Cambridge University Press.

White, H. (1981). The value of narrativity in the representation of reality. In W. J. T. Mitchell (Ed.), *On narrative* (pp. 1–23). Chicago, IL: University of Chicago Press.

Wigboldus, D. H. J., Semin, G. R., & Spears, R. (2000). How do we communicate stereotypes? Linguistic bases and inferential consequences. *Journal of Personality and Social Psychology, 78*(1), 5–18.

Wojciszke, B., & Abele, A. E. (2008). The primacy of communion over agency and its reversal sine valuations. *European Journal of Social Psychology, 38*, 1139–1147.

# 13

# The Role of Narrative Perspective in the Elaboration of Individual and Historical Traumas

ORSOLYA VINCZE, BARBARA ILG, AND TIBOR PÓLYA

## THE FUNCTIONS OF LIFE NARRATIVES AND GROUP NARRATIVES

Narratives are everyday forms of communication. At the same time, they are a particular mode of knowing (Bruner, 1986) and the organizing principle of our knowledge about our life history and about the history of our groups. Following Antonovsky (1987), Erikson (1959), László (2003, 2008, 2011), László and Ehmann (Chapter 12, this volume), Liu and László (2007), and McAdams (1985) have argued that individual life narratives and group narratives are the building blocks of personal and group identity, respectively. By their power to construct reality (Bruner, 1986), narratives compose the significant life events in a manner to support the construction of an adaptive identity. Narratives facilitate historical continuity on both individual and group levels and also have a function in coping with the effects of threatening events (see Chapter 12, this volume). They do not merely account for past events but construct identity in a sense that they define who we are, where are we from, how we deal with conflicts, and what are our relations to significant others. Narratives have several structural-compositional features each having correlates with the identity organization and identity state of the narrator. To map these structural-compositional features, a content analytic program NarrCat has been developed that measures configurations or patterns of words instead of word frequency. NarrCat, by using advanced grammar that assigns these contents to the narrator or to each character, places psychological contents (e.g., emotions, evaluations, cognitions, or agency) into identity relevant interpersonal and intergroup context (see László, 2008; Chapter 12, this volume).

## DEFINITION OF NARRATIVE PERSPECTIVE

Narrative perspective can be defined as a technical term. In this sense, the narrative perspective is a relational concept. It refers to the fact that story events are related from a position, sometimes called point of view or vantage point. As a relational concept, the narrative perspective performs a modulator role in perception. It shapes perception and meaning of the narrative by encouraging a particular reading of the story. There are several dimensions to relate the event and the position to each other (Bal, 1985; Cohn, 1978; Uspensky, 1974). We deal in this chapter with *spatiotemporal perspective* and *psychological perspective* in more detail.

Whereas narrative perspective has been discussed primarily by literary narratologists as a narrative device that modulates literary reception, László, Ehmann, Péley, and Pólya (2002) suggest that spatiotemporal perspective be considered an identity marker in life narratives. Similarly, adopting psychological perspective in historical narratives has been suggested as an indicator of group identity (Vincze, Tóth, & László, 2007; Pólya, Vincze, Fülöp, & Ferenczhalmy, 2007). This chapter examines how spatiotemporal and psychological perspectives relate to personal and group identity, particularly to coping with traumatic events.

## SPATIOTEMPORAL PERSPECTIVE AND COPING WITH IDENTITY THREATS

Spatiotemporal perspective is performed by locating both the events and the narrator's position in time and space. It has three forms (Pólya, 2007). The retrospective form of narrative perspective locates position in the present of narration, whereas the events are located in the past (e.g., *I was living with my mother.*). However, the position and the events can be located in the same way either to the past (e.g., *Come in mum!*) or to the present (e.g., *I remember well.*). These two forms are called *experiencing* and *metanarrative* forms, respectively.

Although spatiotemporal perspective is an essential feature of the narrative structure, there are only a limited number of studies on this feature. However, studies on verb tense are informative about the spatiotemporal perspective, because the verb tense is systematically related to it. For example, Pennebaker, Mayne, and Francis (1997) have found that the use of past tense predicts positive state after the loss of partners. Most interesting, they have not found the reverse relation between present verb time and negative state. This might be explained by considering that both experiencing and metanarrative forms use present time, but these two present times are different. The experiencing form uses the historical present time, whereas the metanarrative form uses present time to refer to the here and now of the narration.

Our studies have investigated the role of spatiotemporal perspective in coping with identity threats. Results from four studies are reviewed here.

In the first study (Pólya, 2007), 20 homosexual men and 20 women participated in in vivo fertilization treatment. Their social identities were under threat because being homosexual is valued negatively. Similarly, not being able to be a mother is also negatively valued at least for women who put up with the consequences of going through an in vivo fertilization treatment. Participants were asked to tell the story of how they accommodated their homosexual identity or how they protect themselves from the stigma of not being able to be a mother. Three components of their experiences related to the sexual identity category were measured by questionnaires. The cognitive component was measured by the Purpose to Life Scale, short version (Antonovsky, 1987); the emotional component was assessed by the Profile of Mood States (McNair, Lorr, & Droppleman, 1971); and the self-esteem component was reflected by the State Self-Esteem Scale (Heatherton & Polivy, 1991).

Results revealed that the spatiotemporal perspective forms used in the life stories reflect the effectiveness of coping with threats. The frequent use of the retrospective form is indicative on the successful coping. Those narrators use frequently this perspective form who tended to have high self-esteem and who are not depressed. The frequent use of the retrospective form is also predicted by emotional noninvolvement in the experiences. This result can be explained as showing a detached way to managing those experiences that are related to their sexual identity category.

The frequent use of experiencing form is indicative of a failure in coping. This perspective form is used frequently by those narrators with low self-esteem and who are stressed. The low level of sense of coherence also predicts the frequent use of the experiencing form.

Finally, the frequent use of the metanarrative form was predicted by more severe failures in coping. The difficulties in coping were revealed by low scores on self-esteem and high scores on emotional embarrassment.

The second study (Pólya, László, & Forgas, 2005) explored the same relationships between coping with threats and spatiotemporal perspective but approached from a different angle. This study investigated the effects of spatiotemporal perspective on readers of short stories that describe significant life events. The significant life events were chosen from narrative interviews. Two events had been chosen from the first study—a homosexual man's coming out for his parents and a woman who had learned about the failure of her in vivo fertilization. A third significant event was chosen from interviews on Jewish ethnic social identity. This story was about a boy learning about his Jewish ethnic origin.

Participants read short stories with manipulated spatiotemporal perspective. This study considered the retrospective and the experiencing forms but omitted the metanarrative form. The reason behind this exclusion was that in this study it was important to minimalize the differences in content between story variants, and the metanarrative form hardly meets this condition. The results of this study have revealed that the spatiotemporal perspective influences the perception of how narrators did cope with threats on their social identity.

More specific, narrators of the stories that use the retrospective form were perceived to have coped successfully with threats. They were perceived as more mentally adjusted, and they were more positively evaluated socially than narrators of the stories with the experiencing form. On the contrary, narrators who take the experiencing form were perceived as not coping successfully with threats, because they were perceived as more anxious than the narrators of stories with retrospective form.

The third study (Pólya, Kis, Naszódi, & László, 2007) examined the contribution of the spatiotemporal perspective to the process of emotion regulation. Eighty-two participants were asked about important life events such as a great achievement, a good and a bad episode, with an important person. The emotion regulation was measured with questionnaires. The coherence of emotion regulation was measured by administering the clarity factor of the trait meta-mood scale (Salovey, Mayer, Goldman, Turvey, & Palfai, 1995), which reflects on how clearly a person sees his or her feelings. The purpose to life scale (Antonovsky, 1987) was again used to measure the sense of coherence construct. Stability of emotion regulation was reflected by administering the emotion stability factor of the Big Five Questionnaire (Caprara, Barbaranelli, Borgogni, & Perugini, 1993). This factor consists of two subfactors. The emotional control subfactor measures the capacity for coping with anxiety and emotions. The impulse control subfactor measures the capacity for managing irritability, discontent, and anger.

Associations were found only in stories about negative episodes that confirm the relation between successful coping and the use of the retrospective form. Results also are in line with the hypothesized relation between problems in coping and the use of the experiencing form. People who used this form frequently had less clear experiences, were more reluctant to be involved emotionally in the search for coherence in experiences, and were less efficient in controlling impulses. The strongest association was found between the use of the metanarrative form and emotion regulation measures.

Finally, the fourth study (Pólya& Kovács, 2011; Pólya, submitted) focused on the spatiotemporal perspective on the elaboration process. Thirty-five participants were asked to tell about everyday emotional episodes by cue words. The elaboration process was reflected by administering the Affective Grid (Russell, Weiss, & Mendelsohn, 1989) with two instructions: How they did feel in the past? and how they did feel during narration? The elaboration process was reflected by the difference between past and present scores of the Affective Grid.

Type of elaboration had an effect on only one form of perspective, namely on metanarrative. In line with the earlier results on the poor coping associated with the use of the metanarrative form, it was found that frequent use of this perspective indicates low elaboration of emotional experiences.

These studies show that spatiotemporal perspective is informative about the coping process in an individual setting. The use of the retrospective form reflects the progress of the elaboration process, whereas the use of the experiencing and the metanarrative forms reflect difficulties of the elaboration process.

## PSYCHOLOGICAL PERSPECTIVE

Psychological perspective or inner focalization (Genette, 1980) takes place when events are presented from the character's point of view by citing her mental states. It is often performed by using verbs referring to cognitive and emotional processes (e.g., thinks or feels). The effect of psychological perspective on shaping meaning is well known in experimental social psychology in relation to empathy and attribution studies where psychological perspective or inner focalization is often used either as an independent or dependent variable. Concerning empathy, researchers agreed on the two components of empathy: cognitive and emotional (Davis, 2006; Gladstein, 1983; Hoffman, 1984). Cognitive empathy is usually regarded as perspective-taking, an effortful process (Gilbert, Pelham & Krull, 1988) by which the observer suppresses her own egocentric perspective and rather focuses on the actor's thoughts, feelings, and the situational factors (Batson, Early, & Salvarini, 1997; Davis, Conklin, Smith, & Luce, 1996; Stephan & Finaly, 1999). By this means the observer adjusts to the actor on the level of emotional and cognitive understanding. This consequence of perspective-taking was also found in attribution research where a perspective-taking instruction eliminates actor-observer bias (Regan & Totten, 1975) hence transforming dispositional attributions to situational ones in behavioral explanations (Davis et al., 1996; Fiske & Taylor, 1991; Regan & Totten, 1975) and creating more positive evaluations of the target (Batson et al., 1997). A commonly held explanation of this phenomenon is that perspective-taking produces an overlap of an observer's own self concept and the mental representations of a target (Aron, Aron, Tudor, & Nelson, 1991; Batson, 1994; Davis et al., 1996). That is, the target's representation held by an observer becomes more similar to the observer's self-constructions.

Merging the self and the other's mental representation is also assumed to be the cognitive basis of group identification (Smith & Henry, 1996; Turner, Hogg, Oakes, Reicher, & Wetherell, 1987; Tropp & Wright 2001). In our self-definition, we often use attributes we share with members of the in-group (Kuhn & McPartland, 1954). Self-categorization theory (Turner et al., 1987) introduced the concept of depersonalization, which accounts for several intragroup and intergroup processes such as in-group favoritism or stereotyping. Recent research demonstrates that overlap of selfin-group representations do not merely extend to trait ascription (Otten & Epstude, 2006; Smith & Henry, 1996; Tropp & Wright, 2001) but also to in-group attitudes (Coats, Smith, Claypool, & Banner, 2000). Moreover, the degree of this merging goes together with a stronger in-group perspective and positively correlates with ethnocentric responses (Cadinu & Rothbart, 1996; Smith & Henry, 1996). Substantial evidence has shown that changing self-perspective of a group member and shifting her focus toward an out-group target's point of view is a promising technique of decreasing out-group stereotyping and prejudice (Galinsky & Ku, 2004; Galinsky & Moskowitz, 2000; Pettigrew, 1997; Vescio, Sechrist, & Paolucci, 2003) leading to a more positive view of the out-group (Batson et al., 1997; Stephan & Finaly, 1999).

## PSYCHOLOGICAL PERSPECTIVE AND EMPATHY IN NARRATIVES

In narratives, modulation of empathy is partly performed by psychological perspective—that is, presenting the character's mentally executed actions carried out by emotional and cognitive stateverbs and phrases. Presenting feeling and thoughts of a character in a narrative makes the psychological perspective directly accessible. It is not necessary to infer the inner cognitive and emotional states of a character because they are already visible. Narrative empathy is usually considered as a group-based empathy (Gerrig, 1990; Keen, 2006). This means that in the course of reception, the reader conjoins the character and a group based on some trait or value similarities. This approach to group-based empathy held by narratologists implies the same processes underlying group identification established by self in-group representational overlap (Otten & Epstude, 2006; Smith & Henry, 1996). Hogan (2001) takes a similar standpoint when he holds group-based empathy as empathy with characters matching a reader's group identity. This *quick-match categorical empathy* easily allows for biases (i.e., ethnocentrism or exclusionary thinking based on reader's group identity; Keen, 2006, p. 218). In this respect, psychological perspective can be considered as a pragmatic tool serving different transmitting purposes of group history. On the one hand, presenting the psychological perspective of in-group provides a vicarious experience tempting the reader to identification with the in-group (Bruner, 1990). On the other hand, introducing the inner states of the out-group at the same time enables the reader to enlarge this empathic circle, including the out-group. Although the former way of presentation can easily lead to an exclusionary view of the events, in the latter case, a much more detached view prevails by gaining access to the out-group's point of view (i.e., by taking the perspective of the out-group).

The process of reception is substantial in group narratives, particularly in the case of those events that are already part of the cultural memory. The manner narratives of group history depict the events (e.g., ascribing psychological perspective exclusively or mutually to in-group and out-group) has an important effect on meaning formation.

## PROPOSITIONAL CONTENT OF COGNITIVE PROCESSES

However, the mere presence of out-group's psychological perspective is not sufficient for being empathic with or taking the perspective of the out-group. As mentioned above, narrative psychological perspective is carried out by mental phrases of the characters (i.e., emotional and cognitive stateverbs). Among mental states, cognitive stateverbs usually do not stand alone in a sentence but are followed with propositional contents, which represent the subjectmatter of beliefs (e.g., The Austrians believed *in reconciliations of Hungarians*). Propositional contents are often referred as an attitudinal or valuing position. Valence of the propositional contents following cognitive stateverbs can affect the evaluation of the actor in relation to the outcome of the behavior. To test the effect of propositional contents (Vincze, Rein, & László, 2011), we provided subjects with different versions of a brief story about British colonization. Each version of the stories contained six cognitive sentences (cognitive verb + propositional content) related to the British differing only in valence of their propositional contents—except the control story, which does not present cognitive phrases at all. Valence of the propositional contents was previously rated by another group of subjects. Applying the paradigm of Vescio et al. (2003), after presenting the story, subjects were asked to rate the relative importance of the situational and the dispositional causal factors and the degree of responsibility attributed to British colonizers. Finally, a semantic bipolar scale (Hunyady, 1996) was used to measure intergroup attitudes. The results show that the more positive the propositional contents, the less responsibility attributed to the British. Moreover, the positive propositional contents increased the likelihood of using situational attributions and the subjects to evaluate more positively the target group. Interesting and opposite to our expectations, negative propositional contents did not significantly increase the responsibility comparing with the control story, which means that narratives without cognitivism behave in a manner similar to narratives presenting cognitive verbs with negative propositional contents. Although in the experimental settings the observer is free to use her own mental representations as an anchor-point during mental attribution processes induced by perspective-taking in narratives, it is strictly guided by cognitive stateverbs and their propositional contents. For that reason, it matters whose point of view and whose belief will prevail, especially concerning the valence of their propositional content. On the other hand, the same intergroup distribution of cognitive phrases with positive propositional content strengthens in-group identity, and at the same time, it allows the reader to form an entire picture of the event including the out-group point of view. It leads the reader to overcome her previously held out-group stereotypes and revalues the intergroup relation in question. Enhancing of the out-group's cognitive considerations with negative contents can be regarded as a narrative tool of emphasizing their responsibility.

## COGNITIVE PROCESSES IN TRAUMA ELABORATION

Demands for preserving group past (i.e., for having a sense of continuity with the past) is a fundamental requirement of group identity. It does not mean a simple conservation of past events, but retaining it in an acceptable way for the group (i.e., endowing their members with positive social identity). Constructing history this way provides an internal coherence of the past, which in turn strengthens the group's integration. Collective traumas, like individual traumas, disrupt this sense of continuity and impede the development of an adaptive group identity. Pennebaker and his colleagues (Pennebaker & Gonzales, 2009; Pennebaker & Harber, 1993) have developed a three-stage model of collective trauma elaboration. The core concept of this model is social sharing. That is, talking and changing point of views promotes cognitive and emotional elaboration of upsetting experiences (Davis & Nolen-Hoeksema, & Larson, 1998; Pennebaker & Harber, 1993; Pennebaker, Mehl, & Niederhoffer, 2003). It also emerges from these studies that although talking promotes cognitive assimilation, retaining memory of the event decreases at the same time (Crow & Pennebaker, 1996; Pennebaker, Páez, & Rimé, 1997). In other words, once a traumatic event is elaborated, there is no need for it to be remembered in detail. The effect of cognitive activity concerning health improvement was also demonstrated in personal disclosive writing. Those who wrote about traumas using a high number of cognitive words were more likely to elaborate them (Pennebaker, 1997; Pennebaker & Francis, 1996). Based on these results, the authors suggest that cognitive activity plays a significant role in narrative construction, advancing a coherent organization of the events. As a consequence, they are indicators of trauma elaboration. For elaborating group traumas, however, cognitive processes and states in historical narratives do not necessarily indicate elaboration. In historical texts, not only the narrator and the in-group but also the out-groups can be and are endowed with cognitive states, and it is the distribution of cognitive states between in-groups and out-groups, rather than the total amount of cognitive processes and states that indicates the stage of trauma elaboration. Therefore, we suggest the term *perspective composition.* Moreover, the propositional content of the cognitive processes also matters. If only positive propositional content leads to more favorable attributions for out-groups as Vincze, Rein, and László (2011) suggest, then using out-groups' perspective in historical narratives reflects trauma elaboration in the sense of decreasing emotional turbulence and hostility toward perpetrator out-groups only when cognitive processes contain positive propositional content. In other cases, when out-groups' thoughts and intentions have primarily negative content, it suggests truncation of the elaboration process.

Having in mind these considerations, we conducted content analytic studies on three text corpora, each dealing with the Trianon Peace Treaty, a major historical trauma of Hungarians. The Trianon Peace Treaty was the peace agreement between the Allied powers and Hungary at the end of World War I (July 4, 1920). This event represents a landmark in national history because the agreement reduced the territory and population of Hungary by about two-thirds.

Intergroup distribution of cognitive verbs and phrases with their propositional contents were analyzed in schoolbooks published between 1920 and 2000 (sample texts selected from 22 school history books, 17,884 words), in contemporary folk histories (brief narratives on the Trianon Peace Treaty collected form a stratified sample of 500 subjects, 8,441 words), and newspaper articles published between 1920 and 2010 ($N$= 354, 142,492 words). Content analysis was performed with NarrCat's cognitive algorithm. Each hit was subjected to secondary manual content analysis performed by three independent coders, so as to decide on the valence of the propositional content.

## TRIANON PEACE TREATY AND TRAUMA ELABORATION IN SCHOOLBOOKS AND IN FOLK HISTORY

The results showed that the pattern of assigning cognitive phrases varies in different periods. During the two decades after the event, schoolbooks show a very low level of cognitivization both for in-group and out-groups. These results are in accord with the assumption that the Peace Treaty exerted a traumatic effect indeed—see Figure 13.1.

After World War II, there is a considerable displacement in attribution of the psychological perspective showing high frequencies of cognitive verbs with negative propositional content assigned to the out-group (83% of the cognitive verbs belong to out-groups in the 1970s). This presentation of the event in the first postwar decades suggests a failure of elaboration. Shortly after World War II, a communist dictatorship prevailed in Hungary, whose internationalist ideology prevented public discussion of national traumas. Schoolbooks were not devoid of reference to the Peace Treaty, but placing imperialist hegemonic ambitions at the forefront served the legitimacy needs of the ruling communist elite. In the 1980s and particularly after the system's change (1989), the out-group's perspective has also been emphasized, but in this case, cognitive verbs attributed to out-groups are related to positive propositional contents (76% in 2000). This way of presentation allows readers to inspect the broad context of events, and readers become enabled to familiarize with the considerations of

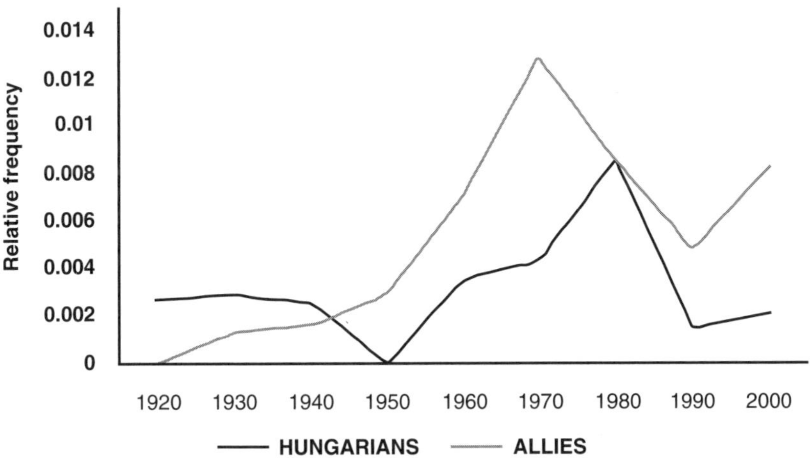


Figure 13.1 Intergroup distribution of cognitive verbs and phrases in schoolbooks (in relative frequency)

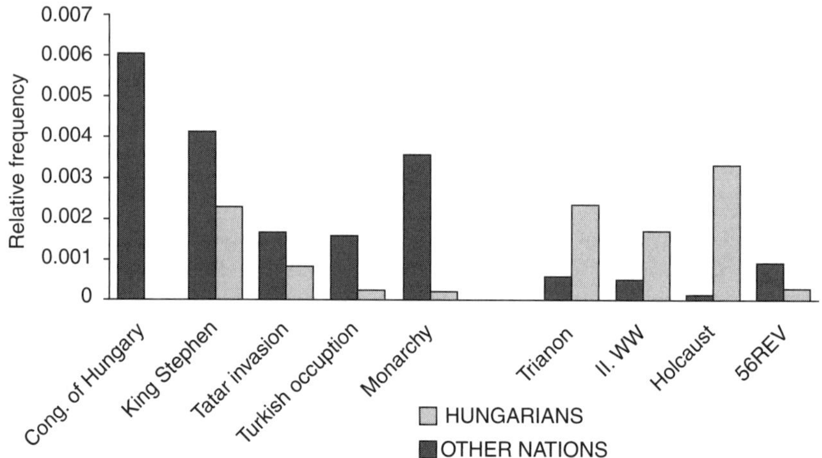


Figure 13.2 Intergroup distribution of cognitive verbs and phrases in contemporary folk history narratives

out-groups. As compared with schoolbooks, folk narratives, with expressions of the communicative memory of the society (Assmann, 1992), show a different picture.

Although perspectivization through cognitive processes and the propositional content of the cognitive processes show elaboration attempts in the beginning of the 21st century in schoolbooks, the high frequency of out-group's cognitive states or processes with negative propositional content (78%) found in folk history suggests that laypeople remain bound to the traumatic experience of Trianon—see Figure 13.2.

## TRIANON PEACE TREATY AND TRAUMA ELABORATION IN NEWSPAPERS

Media is a primary forum of public memory; therefore, it seems to be particularly apt for tracing changes in remembering historical events. Although there are differences between newspapers having left-wing or right-wing ideological orientations, for a rough analysis we collapsed all media texts—see Figure 13.3. As far as the in-group cognitive processes are concerned, they reach a relatively high level immediately after the Peace Treaty (revolving around the opportunities for revision), but they decrease in the subsequent decades and show an ascending tendency only in the recent decade. It is important to note that during the communist dictatorship, the Trianon Treaty was a taboo in public talk, and newspapers were forbidden to talk about it. There was much more pressure for silence than the local governmental expectation in Dallas for not speaking about the Kennedy assassination described by Pennebaker and Banasik (1997); as a consequence, it thwarted the trauma elaboration process to a greater extent.

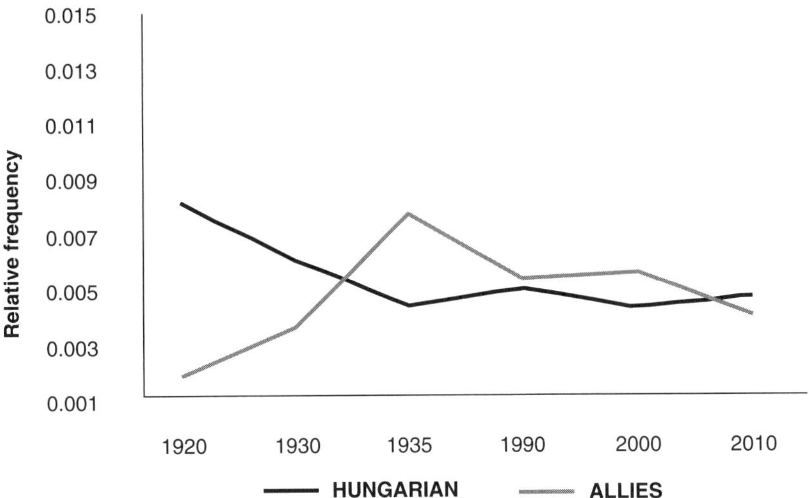


Figure 13.3 Intergroup distribution of cognitive verbs and phrases in newspapers

Out-group cognitivizations show an increasing tendency until World War II, but their almost exclusively negative content (76% in 1930) still reflects a deep absorption in the traumatic experience. This out-group's inner considerations rather represent their self-serving interests in the events. The demand for revision continues in the newspapers published in 1935. From the existing negative cognitivization of out-group only, those nations' considerations (e.g., the United States and Italy) are presented with positive contents (32% in 1935), who also protested against this peace condition. Presenting their supportive point of view confirms the belief that the peace was unjust.

From the system's change (1989), a balanced intergroup distribution of cognitive verbs appears. The appearance of a mutual intergroup cognitive perspective represents a need for a new sense making process, reorganizing the event based upon the documents coming to light (Ormos, 1983). Even though this sense making process continues today, the decreasing tendency of the out-group's perspective and its dominantly negative propositional content (62% in 2010), particularly in contemporary newspapers, imply a slowdown in trauma elaboration due to the political-ideological orientation of the current Hungarian government that is reflected also in the media.

## CONCLUSIONS

In this chapter, we have tried to build a close connection between coping with identity threats and identity traumas on the one hand and narrative language on the other. For coping with individual identity threats, we have shown that the spatiotemporal perspective that is expressed in a configuration of the linguistic markers can give a more differentiated picture of a person's identity state than simple past tense indicators. For tracing the elaboration of group traumas, we adopted the concept of psychological perspective and introduced the concept of perspective composition of historical narratives, which involves not only in-group but also out-group perspectives and differentiates between them. We used cognitive states and processes for linguistically operationalizing psychological perspective and also considered their propositional content when inferring the stages of the elaboration process.

Significant group events have a long lasting effect on the group life. It is particularly true for the traumatic events that disrupt the sense of continuity and impede the development of an adaptive group identity. Studies on collective trauma elaboration have demonstrated the relevance of sense making and reorganization process (Pennebaker & Gonzales, 2009). These studies also pointed out the linguistic forms of elaboration assuming that these linguistic markers (i.e., cognitive activity, the frequency, and quality of emotional states) facilitate a coherent and acceptable narrative about the event (Pennebaker & Francis, 1996). Narrative construction is considered as basis in scientific narrative psychology (László, 2008), which takes the relation between language and psychology seriously and stresses that structural-compositional qualities of narratives reveal psychological qualities of identity states. The present study, in accord with other narrative psychological investigations (e.g., Chapter 14, this volume), focuses on the narrative-linguistic indicators of trauma elaboration. Besides the presence of the character's mental processes indicated by the frequency of cognitive states, we have also demonstrated the relevance of the propositional contents in trauma elaboration. The exclusive expression of the in-group's cognitivizations and the presence of out-group's considerations with negative contents are considered as low level trauma elaboration. Although the former prevents the extension of the interpretational context to points of view of the in-group, the latter enhances out-group's responsibility, thus inhibiting reconciliation. According to the findings on trauma elaboration (Pennebaker & Harber, 1993), initial intensive emotional involvement is usually followed by cognitive processes that help to reorganize the event. Our results with contemporary newspapers and particularly with folk stories, consistent with the study by Fülöp and her colleagues (Chapter 14, this volume), show a moderate cognitivization with a strong emotional impregnation, which indicates that the Trianon trauma in the Hungarian collective memory is far from being resolved.

The changing pattern of intergroup distribution of cognitivization concerning Trianon shows that trauma elaboration is not merely a question of time. Group history is a dynamic narrative genre, which has constructional power to modify the frame of reference of the event without root-changes in facts (White, 1981). According to Ricoeur (2006) elaboration of collective traumas proceed in the public sphere. Thus, the elaboration process is subjected to the political-ideological demands of a given period which, by prescribing particular interpretational contexts rule the public sphere and may thwart or accelerate the process.

## REFERENCES

Antonovsky, A. (1987). *Unravelling the mystery of health. How people manage stress and stay well.* San Francisco, CA: Jossey-Bass.

Aron, A., Aron, E. N., Tudor, M., & Nelson, G. (1991). Close relationships as including other in the self. *Journal of Personality and Social Psychology, 60,* 241–253.

Assmann, J. (1992). *Das kulturelle Gedachtnis.* Munich, Germany: C. H. Beck.

Bal, M. (1985). *Narratology. Introduction to the theory of narrative.* Toronto, Canada: University of Toronto Press.

Batson, C. D. (1994). Prosocial motivation: Why do we help others? In A. Tesser (Ed.), *Advanced social psychology* (pp. 333–381). Boston, MA: McGraw-Hill.

Batson, C. D., Early, S., & Salvarini, G. (1997). Perspective-taking: Imagining how another feels versus imagining how you would feel. *Personality and Social Psychology Bulletin, 23*(7), 751–758.

Bruner, J. (1986). *Actual minds, possible worlds.* Cambridge, MA: Harvard University Press.

Bruner, J. (1990). *Acts of meaning.* Cambridge, MA: Harvard University Press.

Cadinu, M. R., & Rothbart, M. (1996). Self-anchoring and differentiation processes in the minimal group setting. *Journal of Personality and Social Psychology, 70,* 661–677.

Caprara, G. V., Barbaranelli, C., Borgogni, L., & Perugini, M. (1993). The Big 5 questionnaire. A new questionnaire to assess the 5 factor model. *Personality and Individual Differences, 15*(3), 281–288.

Carr, D. (1986). Narrative and the Real World: An Argument for Continuity. *History and Theory, 25,* 2, 117–131.

Coats, S., Smith, E. R., Claypool, H. M., & Banner, M. J. (2000). Overlapping mental representations of self and in-group: Reaction time evidence and its relationship with explicit measures of group identification. *Journal of Experimental Social Psychology, 36,* 304–315.

Cohn, D. (1978). *Transparent minds: Narrative modes for presenting consciousness in fiction.* Princeton, NJ: Princeton University Press.

Crow, D. M., & Pennebaker, J. W. (1996). *The Persian Gulf War: The forgetting of an emotionally important event.* Manuscript submitted for publication.

Davis, C. G., Nolen-Hoeksema, S., & Larson, J. (1998). Making sense of loss and growing from the experience: Two construals of meaning. *Journal of Personality and Social Psychology, 75,* 561–574.

Davis, M. H. (2006). Empathy. In J. Stets & J. Turner (Eds.), *The handbook of the sociology of emotions.* New York, NY: Springer.

Davis, M. H., Conklin, L., Smith, A., & Luce, C. (1996). Effect of perspective-taking on the cognitive representation of persons: A merging of self and other. *Journal of Personality and Social Psychology, 70,* 713–726.

Erikson, E. H. (1959). *Identity and the life cycle: Selected papers.* New York, NY: International Universities Press.

Fiske, S. T., & Taylor, S. E. (1991). *Social cognition.* New York, NY: McGraw-Hill.

Galinsky, A. D., & Ku, G. (2004). The effects of perspective-taking on prejudice: The moderating role of self-evaluation. *Personality and Social Psychology, 30*(5), 594–604.

Galinsky, A. D., & Moskowitz, G. B. (2000). Perspective-taking: Decreasing stereotype expression, stereotype accessibility, and in-group favoritism. *Journal of Personality and Social Psychology, 78,* 708–724.

Genette, G. (1980). *Narrative discourse.* Oxford, England: Blackwell.

Gerrig, R. J. (1990). The construction of literary character: A view from cognitive psychology. *Style, 24,* 380–392.

Gilbert, D. T., Pelham, B. W., & Krull, D. S. (1988). On cognitive busyness: When person perceivers meet persons perceived. *Journal of Personality and Social Psychology, 54,* 733–740.

Gladstein, G. A. (1983). Understanding empathy: Integrating counseling, developmental, and social psychology perspectives. *Journal of Counseling Psychology, 30,* 467–482.

Heatherton, T. F., & Polivy, J. (1991). Development and validation of a scale for measuring state self-esteem. *Journal of Personality and Social Psychology, 60*(6), 895–910.

Hoffman, M. L. (1984). Interaction of affect and cognition in empathy. In C. E. Izard, J. Kagan, & R. B. Zajonc (Eds.), *Emotion, cognition, and behavior* (pp. 103–131). Cambridge, England: Cambridge University Press.

Hogan, P. C. (2001). The epilogue of suffering: Heroism, empathy, ethics. *SubStance, 30,* 119–143.

Hunyady, G. (1996). *Sztereotípiák a változó közgondolkodásban.* Budapest, Hungary: Akadémiai Kiadó.

Keen, S. (2006). A theory of narrative empathy. *Narrative, 14*(3), 207–236.

Kuhn, M. H., & McPartland, T. S. (1954). An empirical investigation of self-attitude. *American Sociological Review, 19,* 68–76.

László, J. (2003). History, identity and narratives. In J. László & W. Wagner (Eds.), *Theories and controversies in societal psychology.* Budapest, Hungary: New Mandate.

László, J. (2008). *The science of stories: An introduction to narrative psychology.* London, England: Routledge.

László, J., Ehmann, B., Péley, B., & Pólya, T. (2002). Narrative psychology and narrative psychological content analysis. In J. László & W. Stainton Rogers (Eds.), *Narrative approaches in social psychology.* Budapest, Hungary: New Mandate.

László, J. (2011). Narrative Psychology, in *Daniel Christie: The Encyclopedia of Peace Psychology*. San Francisco: Wiley-Blackwell, 2011. pp. 687–691.

Liu, J. H., & László, J. (2007). A narrative theory of history and identity: Social identity, social representations, society and the individual. In G. Moloney & I. Walker (Eds.), *Social representations and history* (pp. 85–107). New York, NY: Palgrave-Macmillan.

McAdams, D. P. (1985). *Power, intimacy and the life story: Personological inquiries into identity.* New York, NY: Guilford Press.

McNair, D. M., Lorr, M., & Droppleman, L. F. (1971). *Manual: Profile of mood states.* San Diego, CA: Educational and Industrial Testing Service.

Ormos, M. (1983). *Padovától Trianonig, 1918–1920.* Budapest, Hungary: Kossuth.

Otten, S., & Epstude, K. (2006). Overlapping mental representations of self, ingroup, and outgroup: Unraveling self-stereotyping and self-anchoring. *Personality and Social Psychology Bulletin, 32*(7), 957–969.

Pennebaker, J. W. (1997). Writing about emotional experiences as a therapeutic process. *Psychological Science, 8,* 162–166.

Pennebaker, J., & Francis, M. (1996). Cognitive, emotional, and language processes in disclosure. *Cognition & Emotion, 10*(6), 601–626.

Pennebaker, J., Mehl, M., & Niederhoffer, K. (2003). Psychological aspects of natural language use: Our words, our selves. *Annual Review of Psychology, 54*(1), 547–577.

Pennebaker, J. W., & Banasik, B. (1997). On the creation and maintenance of collective memories: History as social psychology. In J. W. Pennebaker, D. Paez, & B. Rime (Eds.), *Collective memory of political events: Social psychological perspectives* (pp. 3–19). Mahwah, NJ: Erlbaum.

Pennebaker, J. W., & Gonzales, A. L. (2009). Making history: Social and psychological processes underlying collective memory. In P. Boyer & J. V. Wertsch (Eds.), *Memory in mind and culture* (pp. 171–193). New York, NY: Cambridge University Press.
Pennebaker, J. W., & Harber, K. D. (1993). A social stage model of collective coping: The Loma Prieta earthquake and the Persian Gulf War. *Journal of Social Issues, 49,* 125–145.
Pennebaker, J. W., Mayne, T. J., & Francis, M. E. (1997). Linguistic predictors of adaptive bereavement. *Journal of Personality and Social Psychology, 72*(4), 863–871.
Pennebaker, J., Paez, D., & Rimé, B. (Eds.). (1997). *Collective memories of political events: Social psychological perspectives.* Hillsdale, NJ: Erlbaum.
Pettigrew, F. T. (1979). The ultimate attribution error: Extending Allport's cognitive analysis of prejudice. *Personality and Social Psychology Bulletin, 5*(4), 461–476.
Pólya, T. (2007). *Identitás az elbeszélésben. Szociális identitás és narratív perspektíva.* Budapest, Hungary: Új Mandátum Kiadó.
Pólya, T. (submitted). Emotional experiences and stories: Reliving or elaboration.
Pólya, T., & Kovács, I. (2011). Történetszerkezet és érzelmi intenzitás. *Pszichológia, 31*(3), 273–294.
Pólya, T., Kis, B., Naszódi, M., & László, J. (2007). Narrative perspective and the emotion regulation of a narrating person. *Empirical Text and Culture Research, 7*(3), 50–61.
Pólya, T., László, J., & Forgas, J. P. (2005). Making sense of life stories: The role of narrative perspective in communicating hidden information about social identity. *European Journal of Social Psychology, 35*(6), 785–796.
Pólya, T., Vincze, O., Fülöp, É., & Ferenczhalmy, R. (2007). A pszichológiai perspektíva el fordulása történelem tankönyvi szövegekben. *V. Magyar Számítógépes Nyelvészeti Konferencia* (pp. 235–241). Szeged, Hungary: Szegedi Tudományegyetem Informatikai Tanszékcsoport.
Regan, D. T., & Totten, J. (1975). Empathy and attribution: Turning observers into actors. *Journal of Personality and Social Psychology, 32*(5), 850–856.
Ricoeur, P. (2006). *Memory, history, forgetting.* Chicago, IL: University of Chicago Press.
Russell, J. A., Weiss, A., & Mendelsohn, G. A. (1989). Affect grid: A single—item scale of pleasure and arousal. *Journal of Personality and Social Psychology, 57*(3), 493–502.
Salovey, P., Mayer, J. D., Goldman, S. L., Turvey, C., & Palfai, T. P. (1995). Emotional attention, clarity, and repair: Exploring emotional intelligence using the trait meta-mood scale. In J. W. Pennebaker (Ed.), *Emotion, disclosure, and health* (pp. 125–154). Washington, DC: American Psychological Association.
Smith, E. R., & Henry, S. (1996). An in-group becomes part of the self: Response time evidence. *Personality and Social Psychology Bulletin, 22,* 635–642.
Stephan, W. G., & Finlay, K. (1999). The role of empathy in improving intergroup relations. *Journal of Social Issues, 55*(4), 729–743.
Tropp, L. R., & Wright, S. C. (2001). Ingroup identification as inclusion of ingroup in the self. *Personality and Social Psychology Bulletin, 27,* 585–600.
Turner, J. C., Hogg, M. A., Oakes, P. J., Reicher, S. D., & Wetherell, M. S. (1987). *Rediscovering the social group: A self-categorization theory.* New York, NY: Blackwell.
Uspensky, B. A. (1974). *The poetics of composition: Structure of the artistic text and the typology of compositional form.* Berkeley: University of California Press.
Vescio, T. K., Sechrist, G., & Paolucci, M. P. (2003). Perspective-taking and prejudice reduction: The mediational role of empathy arousal and situational attributions. *European Journal of Social Psychology, 33,* 455–472.
Vincze, O., Rein, G., & László, J. (2011). Narrative means of intergroup relations: Cognitive states and their role in reducing or increasing intergroup conflict. In *EASP 2012—17th European Association of social psychology general meeting,* Stockholm, Sweden.

Vincze, O., Tóth, J., & László, J. (2007). Representations of the Austro-Hungarian monarchy in the history books of the two nations. *Empirical Text and Culture Research, 3*, 62–71.

White, H. (1981). The value of narrativity in the representation of reality. In W. J. T. Mitchell (Ed.), *On narrative.* Chicago, IL: University of Chicago Press.

Wright, C. S., Aron, A., & Tropp, R. L. (2001). Including others (and their groups) in the self: Self-expansion and intergroup relations. In P. J. Forgas & D. W. Kipling (Eds.), *The social self: Cognitive, interpersonal and intergroup perspectives*. New York, NY: Psychology Press.

# 14

# Emotional Elaboration of Collective Traumas in Historical Narratives

ÉVA FÜLÖP, ISTVÁN CSERTŐ, BARBARA ILG, ZSOLT SZABÓ, BEN SLUGOSKI, AND JÁNOS LÁSZLÓ

Narratives and narrative language are targets of social psychological inquiry for at least two related reasons. First, because they are means of constructing both personal and group identity, they can reveal actual or more permanent states and characteristics of identity (László, 2003, 2008; László & Fülöp, 2010; Liu & László, 2007; Chapter 12, this volume). Second, because they are means of communicating and thereby transmitting representations of the past through generations, they render possible studying the elaboration of individual and historical traumas in their natural context (Bar-Tal, Halperin & de Rivera; László, 2008, 2011; Pennebaker & Harber, 1993; Vincze & László, 2010; Chapter 13, this volume). Narrative social psychology claims that states and characteristics of group identity that govern people's behavior when they act as group members, as well as elaboration of traumatic experiences that affect the group as a whole, can be traced objectively—that is, empirically in the narrative composition and narrative language of different forms of group histories (see Chapter 12, this volume). In this chapter, we deal with the emotional basis of the Hungarian national identity as it is expressed in different forms of historical narratives and with the collective elaboration of a major historical trauma in narratives.

However, historical representations of a group necessarily manifest in variable ways, due to being influenced by ideological and individual differences. Some factors of these differences (e.g., identification with the nation, collective guilt orientation, etc.) are also investigated in this chapter.

## EMOTIONAL BASIS OF THE HUNGARIAN NATIONAL IDENTITY

Narrative psychology presumes a strong interrelation between narrative and identity, and correspondences between narrative organization and psychological organization of representations of events. Scientific narrative psychology serves as a means of identification of inner states and representations of social relations by connecting narrative compositions to psychological processes either in individuals and groups. Group identity is assumed to be constructed by a genuinely narrative group history. We have proposed that not only individuals have a *life trajectory*, which sequentially represents the positively or negatively evaluated events of their lives (see e.g., Gergen & Gergen, 1988), but this evaluative sequence of salient historical events as *historical trajectory* is also characteristic of the identity of nations, including their emotional life (László, 2008).

Historical trajectory resembles identity narratives of collective memory proposed by Wertsch (2002). Wertsch has reconstructed the Russian *heroic* narrative from several Russian historical accounts all suggesting that Russians after vicissitudes and sufferings eventually overcome the troubles. In similar vein, MacAdams (2006) described the American *redemption* story, and Garagozov (2008) presented the Armenian *faithfulness* narrative. Each of these narratives clearly has emotional entailments.

In the Hungarian collective memory, positively evaluated events belong to the medieval period. Those having occurred in later centuries, for example, local victories against the Ottoman Empire, wars of freedom, and revolutions against the Habsburg Empire and the Soviet Union (1703, 1848, 1956), were always followed by defeats and repression. The pattern reoccurred in the world wars and is preserved in collective memory in this form (László, Ehmann, & Imre, 2002).

Fülöp and László (Fülöp, Péley, & László, 2011; László & Fülöp, 2010, 2011a) attempted to operationalize the theoretical concept of historical trajectory and to test empirically the emotional attributions and reactions of participants in a series of studies applying narrative psychological content analyses to the Hungarian historical trajectory. Narrative content analyses of historical narratives were performed using the NarrCat content analysis (see narrativpszichologia.pte.hu/).

László and Ehmann (Chapter 12, this volume) argue that national identity construction has three main channels. Historiography anchors one pole of the dimension of accuracy, providing the most canonized form of historical experiences by attempting to ascertain objective facts of events and to diminish ambiguities, whereas collective memory (e.g., diaries, family accounts, oral histories), on the other hand, tends to represent history in a biased, group-serving way from the perspective of the ingroup. History textbooks and historical novels represent transitional forms of memory between historiography and collective memory because in these narratives concrete acts of history are saturated with psychological aspects of episodes (e.g., intentions, perspectives, evaluations, emotions, agency, etc.). In the next section, we present results of three studies, which aimed to empirically operationalize the concept of historical trajectory and to explore emotional aspects of national identity through a narrative analysis of emotional entailments of the Hungarian historical trajectory.

## EMOTIONS EXPRESSED IN HUNGARIAN HISTORICAL NARRATIVES

László and Fülöp (2010) studied collective emotional representations of historical events in history textbooks and in folk history narratives. The analyzed text corpora included of the 10 most important episodes of the Hungarian history from primary and secondary schoolbooks and lay stories from 500 persons about the same events served as material for our analyses. An emotional pattern of *fear, hope, enthusiasm, sadness, and disappointment* was to prevail in the self-representation of the nation in both history books and folk narratives—see Tables 14.1 and 14.2. Nearly half of the emotions assigned to the Hungarian group or to Hungarian characters in history books, and more than two-thirds in folk narratives, belong to this set of emotions and appear significantly more frequently related to Hungarians than to other nations. This configuration of emotions was labeled as *historical trajectory emotions*. Beside on overwhelming appearance of historical trajectory emotions, there were two other symptomatic features of the Hungarian emotions. On the one hand, some affective responses occurred in incongruous situations (e.g., sadness related to positive events or hope related to negative events). On the other, outgroups were mostly endowed with hostile, negative emotions. These results suggest that the national self-representation is organized around mistrust, bitterness, and dissatisfaction due to unfulfilled aspirations.

TABLE 14.1 Frequency of Attributed Emotions to Ingroup and Outgroup in Hungarian History Textbooks (in Proportion to Text Length: Frequency of Expressions/Overall Words × 10,000)

| | Ingroup (463) | Outgroup (161) |
|---|---|---|
| Sadness | **5.39**** | 0.62 |
| Hope | **14.68*** | 6.83 |
| Respect | 1.94 | **7.45***** |
| Sympathy | 0.86 | **4.96**** |
| Trust | 3.02 | **7.45*** |
| Indignation | 1.29 | **4.34*** |
| Contempt | 0 | **1.86**** |
| Historical Trajectory Emotions | **44.92**** | 24.22 |

*Note:* Absolute frequencies are in brackets. The table shows normalized relative frequencies. *$p < .05$; **$p < .01$; ***$p < .001$.

TABLE 14.2 Frequency of Attributed Emotions to Ingroup and Outgroup in Hungarian in Folk Narratives (in Proportion to Text Length: Frequency of Expressions/Overall Words × 10,000)

| | Ingroup (187) | Outgroup (107) |
|---|---|---|
| Sadness | **17.11*** | 6.54 |
| Enthusiasm | **8.02**** | 0.93 |
| Hope | 6.41 | 1.86 |
| Respect | 3.21 | **12.14**** |
| Hatred | 3.21 | **20.56***** |
| Historical Trajectory Emotions | **34.22***** | 12.14 |

*Note*: Absolute frequencies are in brackets. The table shows normalized relative frequencies. $^{*}p < .05$; $^{**}p < .01$; $^{***}p < .001$.

In historical novels, characters of stories convey identity patterns (e.g., Bar-Tal & Antebi, 1992; László & Vincze, 2004; Nencini, 2007; this volume). Based on this assumption, the second study (Fülöp, Péley, & László, 2011) dealt with emotional representations in literary works. Four popular Hungarian novels were selected containing different significant events or periods of the nation's history. Emotional representation in these historical novels showed partial overlap with the results of the analyses of history textbooks and folk narratives. The historical trajectory related emotions assigned to Hungarian characters were less salient; however, within the range of historical trajectory emotions, emotional dynamics of the Hungarians was represented with much more depressive emotions (sadness, disappointment) than that of other nations in all historical novels—independently of the given historical situation or intergroup relation. Self-critical (guilt, shame) emotions were also attributed rather to the ingroup whereas outgroup characters were depicted with more hostile emotions (anger, hatred, disgust).

Historical trajectory emotions were also tested in an experimental setting (László & Fülöp, 2011a). Hungarian participants were presented 12 stories in relation to different outgroups from various periods of the Hungarian history. The participants attributed emotions to the ingroup and to the outgroups and to themselves. In half of the stories, the Hungarians were victims, and in the other half, they were perpetrators. The self-representations of the national group and the images of the enemy were highly similar to those found in previous narrative studies: Historical trajectory-related emotions belonged to the ingroup, whereas outgroups were characterized by hostile emotions. Although the contemporary subjects' self-attributed emotions corresponded with attributed ingroup emotions, emotions of self-criticism and anger were more prevalent in their emotional repertoire—see Tables 14.3 and 14.4.

What implications do the above results convey on the emotional dynamics of the Hungarian national identity? Our results can best be interpreted in terms of an identity form, which has been called collective victimhood by Bar-Tal, Chernyak-Hai, Schori, and Gundar (2009).

TABLE 14.3 Frequency of Attributed Emotions to the Ingroup and to the Outgroups Related to Narratives about Historical Intergroup Conflicts where Hungarians Were Perpetrators of the Atrocities

| Perpetrator | Fear | Hope | Disappointment | Enthusiasm | Anger | Hated | Satisfaction | Disgust | Guilt | Shame | Forgiveness | Pride | Sadness | Happiness | Relief | Gratification |
|---|---|---|---|---|---|---|---|---|---|---|---|---|---|---|---|---|
| Ingroup | 0.25 | 0.26** | 0.15*** | 0.65* | 0.52 | 0.38 | 0.87 | 0.04 | 0.4*** | 0.24*** | 0.02 | 0.86 | 0.15* | 0.3 | 0.17 | 0.73 |
| Outgroup | 0.17 | 0.12 | 0.03 | 0.32 | 0.3 | 0.5 | 1.4*** | 0.05 | 0.11 | 0.03 | 0 | 0.83 | 0.05 | 0.25 | 0.25 | 1.2*** |

*Note:* Two-tailed $t$-tests were run between the ingroup and outgroup for each emotion and for victim and perpetrator positions separately. $^{*}p < .05$; $^{**}p < .01$; $^{***}p < .001$

TABLE 14.4 Frequency of Attributed Emotions to the Ingroup and to the Outgroups Related to Narratives about Historical Intergroup Conflicts where Hungarians Were Victims of the Atrocities

| Victim | Fear | Hope | Disappointment | Enthusiasm | Anger | Hated | Satisfaction | Disgust | Guilt | Shame | Forgiveness | Pride | Sadness | Happiness | Relief | Gratification |
|---|---|---|---|---|---|---|---|---|---|---|---|---|---|---|---|---|
| Ingroup | 1.4 *** | 0.11 | 1.08*** | 0.1* | 0.91 | 0.93 | 0 | 0.17 | 0.05 | 0.23 | 0 | 0.07 | 0.86*** | 0 | 0 | 0.01 |
| Outgroup | 0.9 | 0.07 | 0.7 | 0.02 | 1.5*** | 0.93 | 0.04 | 0.35* | 0.04 | 0.23 | 0.02 | 0.11 | 0.5 | 0.02 | 0.01 | 0.02 |

*Note:* Two-tailed $t$-tests were run between the ingroup and outgroup for each emotion and for victim and perpetrator positions separately. $^{*}p < .05$; $^{**}p < .01$; $^{***}p < .001$

## GROUP IDENTITY OF COLLECTIVE VICTIMHOOD AS AN INTERPRETIVE FRAMEWORK FOR THE HUNGARIAN NATIONAL IDENTITY

Victimization in the history of a group can cause substantive changes in group identity. Bar-Tal et al. (2009) have proposed the idea of self-perceived collective sense of victimhood, which describes the identity state arising as a consequence of recurrent or prolonged victimization. They define collective victimhood as a mindset of members of collectives that is based on the sense of being victim of a harm intentionally committed by another group. This harm is perceived as undeserved, unjust, and immoral. It has important consequences on the regulation of intergroup relations, particularly in the management of intergroup conflicts. Collective victimhood is more likely to arise when people feel the sense of victimhood not because of the harm experienced by themselves but because of the loss or suffering of their group. The self-categorization theory (Turner, Hogg, Oakes, Reicher, & Wetherell, 1987) describes certain underlying psychological processes of these shared beliefs and emotions. Individuals identifying with a social group see themselves in group-related events as interchangeable members of the group, and as a consequence of the actualization of social identity, they assimilate to the norms, beliefs, emotions, and acts of the group. These processes underlie the sense of collective victimhood as well. Being a victim of repeated traumas, losses, repressions, and failures threatens the positive identity of the group, because they are opposed to the essential beliefs that the group is competent, strong, and capable for resolving conflicts more difficult to maintain. Moreover, they may threaten the integrity or survival of the collective. At the same time, the sense of collective victimhood may have certain identity-serving functions as well. It provides explanation for threatening events. Through sense-making, it helps the group cope with stress induced by a conflict, it gives moral justification and a feeling of superiority, it prepares the society for future harms, it enhances ingroup solidarity, it motivates patriotism, and it can potentially gain international support. Thus, collectives are motivated to maintain this status. By providing a scheme for interpreting subsequent intergroup events, assuming the victim position can become permanent. These *syndromes of victimhood* may become a very dominant part of the repertoire of collective reactions, being transmitted through generations in channels of social communication and societal institutions (e.g., educational system, public, and political discourses, traditions, rites, cultural products).

The notion of *emotional orientation* (Bar-Tal, Halperin & de Rivera, 2007) refers to the tendency of the society to express a certain emotion or set of emotions. This emotional orientation attunes members of the group to some cues and signals of social situations. Collective victimhood is also reflected in the emotional orientation of the group. Social construction of reality including the emotional orientations of a society can be influenced by the current political, economic, or cultural factors. However, when a society is affected by events as a nation, or ethnic categorizations become salient, history and historical representations come to the forefront and will determine emotional orientation of the group. The history of the group through recurring experiences makes collectives more sensitive to certain emotions, and as a consequence, every nation has its own characteristic emotion repertoire and norms of emotion expression.

Results of the previous studies on the emotional representation of the Hungarian history indicate a marked convergence of emotional responses which comprise the characteristic emotional pattern of national identity. The very fact that collective memory splits history into a glorious distant past and a subsequent series of defeats and losses with occasional heroic revolutions, represented as starting with celebrated victories but ending with subjugation and suppression, suggest that this historical trajectory is not a favorable ground so as to build an emotionally stable identity around. The Hungarian social scientist, István Bibó (2004) traced back the state of mind he called *political hysteria* to the historical evolution of nation-states in the Central-European region. Our results empirically show that the concept of political history can be defined by the emotions stemming from the historical trajectory. These emotions are fear, sadness, disappointment, enthusiasm, and hope.

## TESTING THE COLLECTIVE VICTIMHOOD HYPOTHESIS

To test the interpretation based on the collective victimhood hypothesis, we conducted an experiment in which we varied the victim and perpetrator roles in different historical situations. As in the previous study (László & Fülöp, 2011b), narratives about historical events were exposed to participants, and they attributed emotions to the ingroup and to themselves from a selected range of emotions. Concerning emotional attributions and reactions of subjects, a high overlap was expected between affective responses in victim and perpetrator context that would indicate that one determining reaction tendency directs emotional processes in intergroup situations independently of situational factors of the conflict. More specific, the dominance of those emotions also in perpetrator situations that normally emerge in victim situations (e.g., depressive and hostile emotions), also appearing in perpetrator situations, suggest an identity structure that is organized around victimhood. Similarity of perpetrator and victim emotions was significant in case of historical trajectory and hostile emotions—see Figures 14.1 and 14.2. (Cramer's V: $C = 0.457$, $p = 0.01$; $C = 0.678$, $p < 0.05$, respectively). In the present study, participants in both victim and perpetrator situations reported hostile emotions (disgust, hatred, anger) and emotions of bitterness (disappointment, sadness) whereas the frequency of self-critical emotions (shame, guilt, forgiveness) related to responsibility and elaboration was considerable, although it did not reach the frequency of the former sets.

Collective victimhood involves an emotional functioning where emotions, which are adequate in victim situations, occupy the group also in perpetrator roles, and group members feel negatively toward other groups, are unable to face their own sins, and show signs of regret. As Bar-Tal et al. (2009) notes,

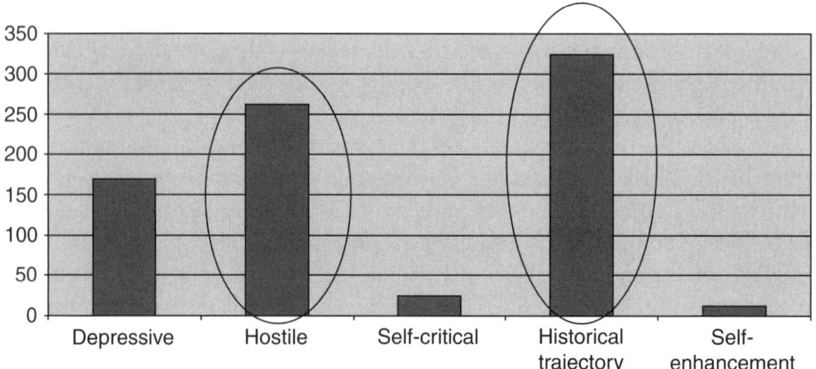


Figure 14.1 Frequency of attribution emotions to the ingroup according to emotion categories related to narratives where Hungarians were victims of the historical atrocities

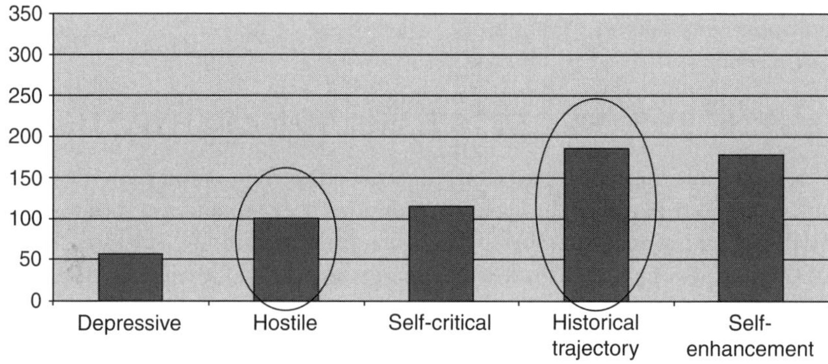


Figure 14.2 Frequency of attribution emotions to the ingroup according to emotion categories related to narratives where Hungarians were perpetrators of the historical atrocities

the groups which perceive intergroup events from the perspective of the victim, tend to feel fear, anger, and self-pity. These are exactly the same emotions that we obtained in our historical trajectory emotions studies, and what is more important, we obtained them not only in the stories of ingroup victimhood but in the perpetrator narratives as well. Considering the emotional dynamics of collective victimhood, this indicates an attitude such that we are entitled to feel self-enhancing and other critical emotions also when we commit harm because we are right, and we are essentially the victims. Emotions that seem incongruent in a given role (e.g., feeling pride when being a victim or forgiveness as perpetrator) or, in general, the overrepresentation of negative emotions in perpetrator role, can be interpreted in the conceptual framework of a historically evolved pattern of emotional reactions, namely, collective victimhood.

There are at least three features of experiences that can contribute to the emergence of collective victimhood in a given society. *Prolongation* of suffering as in the case of an intractable conflict consolidates emergency states and hostility, and maintains the victim role continuously. *Recurrence* of losses and damages focuses reactions on failures and prevents the complete reparation and reconciliation. *Extremity* of events strains coping potentials very intensively and threatens the survival of the victimized by shattering the core of the self. Traumatic experiences, as extreme negative events in this approach, are special incidents of victimhood.

## TRAUMA AND TRAUMA ELABORATION

Psychological trauma is an emotional shock that challenges a person's relation to reality. Freud (1914), in his paper on trauma repetition, argues that until the person who suffers from trauma manages to elaborate it, this experience compulsively recurs in dreams, fantasies, and misdeeds (*trauma reexperiencing*) and seriously endangers the person's psychological well-being and his or her adaptation to reality. Similarly, Freud (1917) describes the process of grief as a form of elaboration of traumatic object loss.

Contemporary psychopathology devotes substantial attention to mechanisms and consequences of individual traumatization. DSM IV classifies these consequences under the diagnostic category of posttraumatic stress disorders: such as serious injury, threatened physical or psychological integrity of the self with intense sense of fear and helplessness, persistent reexperience of the traumatic event, persistent avoidance of stimuli associated with the trauma, and persistent symptoms of increased arousal.

In psychoanalytic tradition, process models have been developed both for trauma elaboration (e.g., Laub & Auerhahn, 1993) and grief (Kübler-Ross, 1969). Until recently, however, relatively less attention has been paid to processes of mass traumatization—that is, to cases when not individual but group identity is threatened. Philosophers and historians, such as LaCarpa, (2001), Novick, (1999), Ricoeur (2006), or Rüsen (2004), have attempted to draw parallels between individual and collective traumatization and to describe the phenomena of transgenerational traumatization, mostly focusing on the Holocaust as the most extreme traumatization of the 20th century. Ricoeur (2006, p. 78.) carries the issue of collective trauma elaboration even to the opportunities of therapy. He claims that the role of the psychotherapists in collective trauma elaboration should be taken by critical thinkers, who assist society to cope with its traumas in the public sphere of open debates.

In individual personality development, creative resolution of a crisis or successful elaboration of a trauma may strengthen a person's ego. The term posttraumatic growth refers to a positive psychological change experienced as a result of the struggle with highly challenging life circumstances (Calhoun & Tedeschi, 1999, 2001). Posttraumatic growth involves better coping capacities and a higher level of stress tolerance. Similar phenomena can be observed at a group level. However, there are other ways of dealing with traumatic experiences. In certain historical contexts, collective remembering is organized around collective traumas that are destructive or harmful to group identity. Volkan (1997) describes the phenomenon of *chosen trauma* when ethnic groups or nations stick to their heroic defeats without being able to elaborate or mourn the loss.

A serious problem of the parallel between individual and collective traumas is that, whereas loss of a beloved person by death is final and unchangeable, territorial or prestige losses of ethnic or national groups will never seem to be irreversible. A further difficulty is that in several cases, compatriots, that is ingroup members, remain in the lost territory whose persisting situation keep the trauma alive, not to mention the historical experience of *shuttling* territories between ethnic groups or states. Nevertheless, the emotional shock of traumatic defeats and losses of territory and prestige should be elaborated at a group level even if without a proper *remembrance formation* (Volkan, 1990).

The process of group level elaboration in history and collective memory has rarely been studied. An empirically grounded stage model of social sharing after traumatic experiences has been developed by Pennebaker and Harber (1993; see also Pennebaker & Gonzales, 2008). This stage model emphasizes dynamic aspects of group traumatization deriving from changes of the social environment of trauma elaboration over time. The first 2 or 3 weeks after the trauma is the time of social sharing of experiences and social bonding. In this *emergency stage*, people seek help together to cope with the emotional shock. This exaggerated social activity is followed after a couple of months by the stage of *inhibition* with a decreased level of communication about the event. Although people speak less about the trauma, an increasing rate of illnesses, trauma-related dreams, and assaults can be observed. Last, in the final *adaptation stage*, people are no more engaged in the event, they continue their normal lives.

Although this model helps to predict people's reactions to traumatic events, the ways in which nations may cognitively and emotionally cope with past traumas and how they accept and integrate defeats and losses into their identity, have not yet been explored.

Historical narratives, as written accounts of past experiences, are available sources of collective memory representations that make them a valuable tool for identification while also enabling the empirical analysis of linguistic markers of trauma elaboration. Based partly on theoretical models of trauma elaboration (e.g., Freud, 1914 Laub & Auerhahn, 1993) and partly on previous experimental evidences (Pólya, László, & Forgas, 2005), it is expected that weak trauma elaboration will manifest in the following narrative structural and content characteristics: (a) reexperiencing of trauma: *present time narration, interjections*, (b) high emotional involvement reflected in a high number of emotional expressions: *explicit emotions, emotional evaluations and extreme words* instead of cognitive words, (c) regressive functioning: primitive defense mechanisms, such as *denial*, splitting (devaluation and idealization) in *extreme evaluations*, distortion in *biased perception*, and self-serving interpretation of events, projection of negative intentions, and feelings in *hostile enemy representations (hostile emotion attribution)*, (d) narrow perceptual field: *inability to change perspectives*,

(e) paralysis: perseverance of *cognitive and emotional patterns,* and (f) a sense of losing agency and control: *transmission of causal focus* and responsibility to others. Additional markers in the case of group trauma: polemic representations instead of hegemonic representations (see Moscovici, 1988) and intense occupation with the topic in social discourses, active communication, and need for sharing: *constant rate of trauma-related narratives.*

In the previous, we have dealt with emotional aspects of the Hungarian historical trajectory. In the next two studies, we focus on a single but highly traumatic event of this historical trajectory, the Treaty of Trianon that ended World War 1. These two studies were performed on longitudinally sampled text corpora, thereby providing opportunity for examining the *process of trauma elaborations* in its dynamic nature.

## THE ELABORATION PROCESS OF THE TRAUMATIC CONSEQUENCES OF THE DEFEAT IN WORLD WAR I

One of the most significant events in 20th-century Hungarian national history was the collective trauma of the Treaty of Trianon in 1920. The treaty ending World War I for Hungary approved the detachment of approximately two-thirds of its territory with 3.3 million Hungarian inhabitants, assigning the territory to neighboring enemy countries. Although till the end of World War II, there were temporary chances for the revision of the treaty, in 1947 it was ultimately affirmed that meant retraumatization for the nation.

Following the notion in Ricouer (2006) that elaboration of group traumas proceed in the public sphere, we analyzed narratives of the daily press about the Treaty of Trianon. Newspaper articles such as news, reports, interviews, and readers' opinions are parts of collective memory. Polemic representations of divergent ideologies emerge in those scripts in a transparent way. Subjective comments, evaluations of narrators, are permissible; papers with different political orientations represent historical events from different perspectives with different motives fitting their present goals and needs.

Articles were chosen from the period ranging from the year of the treaty (1920) to our days (2010) in five year intervals. The sample included right-wing, left-wing, and centrist papers. However, there is no data from the era of communism (1950–1990) because in that period, the issue of the Treaty of Trianon was excluded from political discourses. The obtained patterns of overall emotions and each emotion category (positive, negative, self-critical, other-critical, self-enhancement, and historical trajectory) indicate that from the beginning of the narration, a decline can be observed to the 1940s and then the frequency of emotional reactions rises from the 1990s again—see Figure 14.3. Results show that an initial period of refusal of the national losses until the end of World War II was followed by a period of ideological repression by the communist rule that prevented the thematization of the trauma, and after the democratic political system change in 1989, the narratives partly returned to the initial narrative representation implying the refusal of the loss.

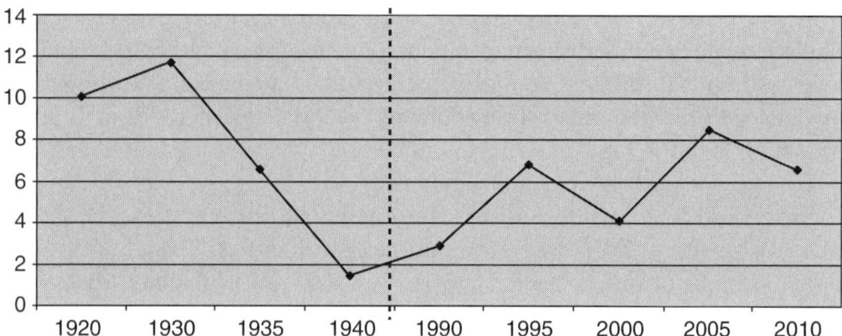


Figure 14.3 Frequency of emotions in newspaper articles about the national trauma of treaty of trianon (in proportion to text length: frequency of expressions/overall words × 10,000)

Certain lexical elements may carry particularly powerful psychological impact (see Chapters 2 and 3, this volume). We call these lexical elements extreme words. The tendency of extreme words (expressions with high emotional connotation) provides support for this suggestion. Using these linguistic categories rate of expressions remains constant over time—see Figure 14.4. These representational patterns with recurrently increasing or constant frequency of emotions implies a very weak emotional elaboration of the trauma. Consistent with our preliminary expectations, the articles of the right-wing press are in every period more emotional than those of the left-winged newspapers, considering especially negative emotions. Contrary to the findings reported by Pennebaker (1997) and Pennebaker and Francis (1996), where emotional words decreased and cognitive processes replaced them during the elaboration process of a significant emotionally straining event, these results represent an emotionally unresolved situation.

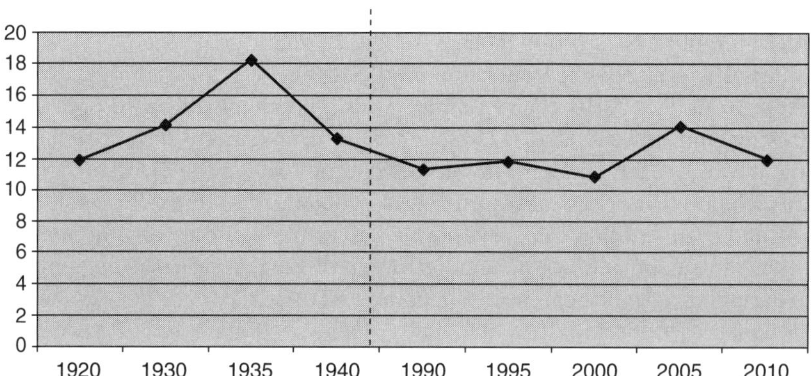


Figure 14.4 Frequency of extreme words in newspaper articles about the national trauma of treaty of trianon (in proportion to text length: frequency of expressions/overall words × 10,000)

## INTERRELATION OF THE INDIVIDUAL AND COLLECTIVE PROCESSES

Baram and Klar (2011) note that descendants' commitment to a consensual ingroup narrative mediates between the identification with the ingroup and their action tendencies to change the existing narrative templates. People who are more committed to ingroup narrative tend to reconstruct conflict-related events in a biased way. This suggestion raises the issue of interrelation between individual and collective processes.

In a content analytic study, we investigated whether individual differences in the significance of collective guilt and identification with the nation play an important role in the elaboration of traumatic national historical memories.

Collective guilt, on the one hand, was associated with acceptance of group responsibility and to be linked to the willingness to perform compensatory actions (Branscombe, Slugoski, & Kappen, 2004). Legitimization strategies, on the other hand, can be used to protect the group from disturbing effects of facing their own past misdeeds (Doosje, Branscombe, Spears, & Manstead, 1998).

Participants' collective guilt was measured with the collective guilt scale (Branscombe, Slugoski, & Kappen, 2004; Slugoski, Branscombe, & Kappen, 2002) that was developed to reflect a person's views on the impact of one's group's past harmful actions on others, as well as to predict entailments in the domains of social action (e.g., apology, restitution, revenge, etc.) In the present study, the scale was used to predict the effects of different views on collective guilt on the ways of narrative construction of significant group historical events. The 20-item collective guilt scale (Branscombe et al., 2004; Slugoski et al., 2002) composes of four relatively homogeneous subscales of five items each: *collective guilt acceptance, collective guilt assignment, whole group accountability,* and *acceptance of collective responsibility*. The adaptation of the collective guilt scale to Hungarian (Csertő, Szabó, & Slugoski, 2012) showed that the Hungarian version of the collective guilt scale is a multidimensional scale and consists of the same four factors as the original one.

Identification seems to be an important factor in taking responsibility and feeling emotions of self-criticism such as collective guilt. Participants' identification with Hungarians was measured with the identification with the nation scale developed by Szabó and László (2012). Following Roccas, Klar, and Liviatan's (2006) categories, the identification with the nation scale distinguishes between two modes of identification: *attachment to the nation* (e.g., *I am linked to Hungarians by strong bonds*) and *glorification of the nation* (e.g., *Hungarians always acted in their history more morally than other nations*). These two modes do not exclude one another but together give the overall measure of identification. Previous studies (Roccas, Klar, & Liviatan, 2006; Szabó & László, 2012) showed that attachment to the ingroup relates to the willingness to accept the negative aspects of the ingroup image and to the experience of group-based guilt, whereas glorification relates to the rejection of the ingroup's responsibility and therefore to a lack of experience of self-critical emotions.

After having filled in the collective guilt scale and then the identification with the nation scale, one-half of the subjects were asked to write a story about the Treaty of Trianon, and one-half of them were asked to write about the Jewish Holocaust in Hungary. The topic of the Treaty of Trianon provided the context in which Hungary was the victim of a trauma, whereas in the Holocaust, Hungary played the role of the perpetrator as an ally of Nazi Germany—actively cooperating in the deportations. Linguistic markers of evaluation were analyzed with the NarrCat content analytic tool, and then the object and subject references of the evaluations were coded. The concept of narrative intergroup evaluation refers to a set of linguistic instruments by which explicit social judgments are made on the characters of a narrative, either by the narrator or by the characters themselves. Correlations among the collective guilt scale and subscales, the type and level of identification, and the indicators of narrative evaluation were tested. In the narratives about Trianon, significant negative correlation was found between the *no denial of responsibility for group* subscale of the collective guilt scale and the rate of narrator's evaluations (in the percentage of overall word count; $r = -0.313$, $p < .05$). The *no denial* scale indirectly assesses the measure of acceptance of responsibility for the harm caused by the ingroup. Earlier results showed that a relatively high rate of narrator's evaluations in the case of Trianon indicates a lower level of elaboration (Csertő, Slugoski & László, in preparation). Thus, the more one can accept collective responsibility, the fewer direct (narrator's) evaluations used in the narrative about Trianon—that is, the more psychological distance taken from the event. It is assumable that those who generally consider the role of the ingroup's own actions in the outgroup's harmful actions against them, can more easily construct or accept a narrative that assigns an active role to Hungary in the events leading to the peace treaty, instead of the role of a victim without any chance to influence its fortune (e.g., Hungary mistreated its ethnic minorities, thus they strived for national autonomy). This way the consequences of the harmful event are more acceptable emotionally, and the experience can be integrated into an acceptable national identity. In the stories about the Holocaust, the *whole group accountability* scale significantly correlated with the rate of negative evaluations on the outgroup ($r = 0.384$, $p < .05$) and with the rate of narrator's evaluations ($r = .365$, $p < .05$). It seems that the more one assigns importance to collective responsibility in general, the more he or she is emotionally affected by the trauma (narrator's evaluations), and the more he or she externalizes the responsibility for the Holocaust (negative evaluations on the outgroup). These results suggest that Hungarian people are far not open yet to accept Hungary's responsibility for the Holocaust, as opposed to the Trianon Peace Treaty, which can be accounted for by such circumstances as the smaller temporal distance from the events and Germany's leading role in the genocide. Considering the identification with the nation scale, significant correlations were obtained between the rate of negative evaluations on an unspecified object and each of the glorification subscale and the overall measure of identification with the nation ($r = -0.404$, $p < .05$ and $r = -0.341$, $p < .05$, respectively). These results indicate that those strongly identifying with the nation and especially glorifiers tend to avoid the use of unspecified object references that do not distinguish between the actions of the outgroup and the ingroup in relation to events of an unacceptable inhuman nature. Negative evaluations on such unclear references in the context of the Jewish Holocaust in Hungary leave the way open to easily relate them to Hungarians, and this implicit connection between the generally evaluated harmful events and Hungarians threatens the positive distinction of the ingroup that glorifiers are concerned in, thus they eliminate these implicit indicators of responsibility.

The results of this study imply that the tendency to hold entire groups accountable enables the recovery of national identity in the sense that it balances the biased perspective of the victim that maintains the experience of helplessness, depression, and hostility.

## CONCLUSIONS

The presented studies show a remarkable convergence of shared beliefs and emotions in collective memory representations of national historical events. Narrative analysis of these representations provides insight into emotional contents of the Hungarian national identity from the perspective of elaboration of historical conflicts. Collective victimhood seems to be an integrated part of national identity. The pervasive occurrence of fear, depression, and hostility found empirically in history books, novels, and contemporary narratives corresponds to the emotional dynamics of collective victimhood suggested in theoretical descriptions. In this mostly depressive emotional functioning, temporary emotions of enthusiasm occur in situations where they are incongruent and occur parallel to a perceived lack of self-agency, so they rarely manifest in constructive actions. The sense of victimhood expands to all intergroup situations, and the victim perspective is maintained even in perpetrator role. Although these studies indicate a universal presence of collective victimhood in the society, the individual quality of identification and the inclination to feel collective guilt seem to be important mediator factors of national identity templates. It seems that those who are prone to accept the responsibility of the ingroup for past misdeeds are more likely to process the events of the past emotionally. In studies on the collective guilt scale, correlation of collective guilt acceptance and complex temporal attribution (see Fletcher, Danilovics, Fernandez, Peterson, & Reeder, 1986 for attributional complexity scale) was revealed. It raises the idea that people who perceive history in a more complex way, as a trajectory of causally connected successive events, and consider more antecedents of a certain negative event, will more easily accept the ingroup's responsibility and will be able to accept the unchangeable past. Further studies may confirm that.

Collective victimhood has an inhibitory effect on the emotional elaboration of a trauma as well. Extremely negative experiences such as traumas do not diminish automatically over time; elaboration requires active and constructive mobilization of coping potentials. Facing our own misdeeds and undertaking responsibility for them, mourning of losses, ventilation of sufferings, forgiving and forgetting past harms, and fading of intense emotions are crucial conditions of trauma elaboration. Stagnation in the position of the victim obstructs the process of healing processes. Experiences of loss of control, lack of outer support, exaggeration, and repetition of trials, divergence of inner interests, or failures of sharing can contribute to the psychological state of being traumatized. All of them pervaded the Hungarian history. Even so, the Treaty of Trianon represents an extreme trauma in this victimhood narrative. Not only did the detachment of two-thirds of the territory of the country generate a very serious injury of the integrity and a threat to the survival of the group, but the issues of the transborder Hungarian population remain to be resolved and have become regular topics of political discourses. The emphasis put on the irreversibility of the losses keeps it on the agenda. Unresolved issues of transborder Hungarians mean a real challenge for removing the past and leaving the victim role, because being subject to political provisions and casual discriminations, they are still real victims on the ground of their nationality. Obviously, this situation has consequences for the identity of the whole nation. This state can be considered identical with other intractable conflicts in respect of its sociopsychological conditions (see Bar-Tal, Chernyak-Hai, Score & Gundar, 2009) and preserves a sense of collective victimhood, although in these situations conflicts of interests occurs not at the level of wars but at the level of diplomacy and political conflicts.

High emotional involvement in, and some divergence of representations of, the Treaty of Trianon in newspapers with different political orientations originates from the long-term repression of sharing and the emergence of different political interests after the change of regime. Elaboration entails a process of collective meaning construction through narratives and traumatization involving the experience that victims are unable to organize events in a reasonable and meaningful narrative. Victim identity helps this meaning construction because it offers a coherent perspective that is on halfway between a constructive coping and a total disintegration. Despite its advantages, the sense of victimhood can never be satisfying because of its consequences: *Rejection of responsibility, inhibition of elaboration, and prolongation of reconciliation* can facilitate the emergence of alternative discourses. Victimhood becomes tradition, and the trauma remains unresolved.

## REFERENCES


Baram, H., & Klar, Y. (2011). *Commitment to the ingroup narrative (CIN) and the burden of hearing the narrative of the other.* Paper presented at the annual meeting of the ISPP 34th Annual Scientific Meeting, Bilgi University, Istanbul, Turkey.

Bar-Tal, D., & Antebi, D. (1992). Beliefs about negative intentions of the world: A study of the Israeli siege mentality. *Political Psychology*, *13*, 633–645.

Bar-Tal, D., Chernyak-Hai, L., Schori, N., & Gundar, A. (2009). A sense of self-perceived collective victimhood in intractable conflicts. *International Red Cross Review*, *91*, 229–277.

Bar-Tal, D., Halperin, E., & De Rivera, J. (2007). Collective emotions in conflict situations: Societal implications. *Journal of Social Issues*, *63*(2), 441–460.

Bibó, I. (2004). *Selected studies*. Budapest, Hungary: Magvet Kiadó.

Branscombe, N. R., Slugoski, B., & Kappen, D. M. (2004). The measurement of collective guilt. What it is and what it is not. In N. R. Branscombe & B. Doosje (Eds.), *Collective guilt. International perspectives* (pp. 16–34). Cambridge, England: Cambridge University Press.

Calhoun, L. G., & Tedeschi, R. G. (1999). *Facilitating posttraumatic growth: A clinician's guide.* Mahwah, NJ: Erlbaum.

Calhoun, L. G., & Tedeschi, R. G. (2001). Posttraumatic growth: The positive lessons of loss. In R. A. Neirneyer (Ed.), *Meaning reconstruction and the experience of loss* (pp. 157–172). Washington, DC: American Psychological Association.

Csertő, I., Szabó, Zs., & Slugoski, B. (2012). The Hungarian standard of the collective guilt scale. Manuscript in preparation.

Csertő, I., Slugoski, B., László, J. (in preparation): Dealing with collective guilt through history: dynamics of intergroup evaluation in collective memory processes of national historical traumas

Doosje, B., Branscombe, N. R., Spears, R., & Manstead, A. S. R. (1998). Guilty by association: When one's group has a negative history. *Journal of Personality and Social Psychology, 75,* 872–886.

Fletcher, G. J. O., Danilovics, P., Fernandez, G., Peterson, D., & Reeder, G. D. (1986). Attributional complexity: An individual differences measure. *Journal of Personality and Social Psychology, 51,* 875–884.

Freud, S. (1914). Errinern, Wiederholen und Durcharbeiten (Weitere Ratschläge zur Technik der Psychoanalyse, II). *Internationale Zeitschrift für ärtztliche Psychoanalyse, 2,* 485–491. Freud, S. (1917). Mourning and melancholia. In *The standard edition of the complete psychological works of Sigmund Freud, volume XIV (1914–1916): On the history of the psycho-analytic movement. Papers on metapsychology and other works* (pp. 237–258).

Fülöp, É., Péley, B., & László, J. (2011). Historical trajectory emotions in historical novels. *Pszichológia, 31*(1), 47–61.

Garagozov, R. (2008). Characteristics of collective memory, ethnic conflicts, historiography, and the "politics of memory." *Journal of Russian and East European Psychology, 46*(2), 58–95.

Gergen, K. J., & Gergen, M. M. (1988). Narrative and the self as relationship. In L. Berkowitz (Ed.), *Advances in experimental social psychology* (p. 21). San Diego, CA: Academic Press.

Kübler-Ross, E. (1969). *On death and dying.* New York, NY: Macmillan.

LaCarpa, D. (2001). *Writing history, writing trauma.* Baltimore, MD: The Johns Hopkins University Press.

László, J. (2003). History, identity and narratives. In J. László & W. Wagner (Eds.),
*Theories and controversies in societal psychology* (pp. 180–192). Budapest, Hungary: New Mandate.

László, J. (2008). *The science of stories: An introduction to narrative psychology.* London, England: Routledge.

László, J. (2011). Scientific narrative psychological content analysis and traditions of psychological content analysis. *Pszichológia, 31*(1), 3–15.

László, J., Ehmann, B., & Imre, O. (2002). Les représentations sociales de l'histoire: La narration populaire historique et l'identité nationale. In S. Laurens & N. Roussiau (Eds.), *La mémoire sociale. Identités et représentations sociales* (pp. 187–198). Rennes, France: Université Rennes.

László, J., & Fülöp, É. (2010). Emotional representation of history in history textbooks and lay narratives in *Történelemtanítás—Online történelemdidaktikai folyóirat* (XLV.) I/3.

László, J., & Fülöp, É. (2011a). Emotions in real-life intergroup conflicts, group-based emotions are historically anchored. *Magyar Pszichológiai Szemle, 66*(3), 467–485.

László, J., & Fülöp, É. (2011b). National identity and collective victimhood. *Pszichológia, 31*(3), 295–315.
László, J., & Vincze, O. (2004). Coping with historical tasks. The role of historical novels in transmitting psychological patterns of national identity. *Spiel, 21*(1), 76–88.
Laub, D., & Auerhahn, N. C. (1993). Knowing and not knowing massive trauma: Forms of traumatic memory. *International Journal of Psychoanalysis, 74,* 287–302.
Liu, J. H., & László, J. (2007). A narrative theory of history and identity: Social identity, social representations, society and the individual. In G. Moloney & I. Walker (Eds.), *Social representations and history* (pp. 85–107). New York, NY: Palgrave Macmillan.
McAdams, D. P. (2006). *The redemptive self: Stories Americans live by.* Oxford, England: Oxford University Press.
Moscovici, S. (1988). Notes towards a description of social representations. Journal of European Social, *Psychology*, 18 (3), 211–250.
Nencini, A. (2007). The reader at work: The role of the text and text-receiver in the construction of the protagonist of a novel. *Empirical Studies of the Arts, 1,* 97–115.
Novick, P. (1999). *The Holocaust in American life*. New York, NY: Mariner Books.
Pennebaker, J. W. (1997). Writing about emotional experiences as a therapeutic process. *Psychological Science, 8,* 162–166.
Pennebaker, J., & Francis, M. (1996). Cognitive, emotional, and language processes in disclosure. *Cognition & Emotion, 10*(6), 601–626.
Pennebaker, J. W., & Gonzales, A. (2008). Making history: Social and psychological processes underlying collective memory. In J. V. Wertsch & P. Boyer (Eds.), *Collective memory* (pp. 110–129). New York, NY: Cambridge University Press.
Pennebaker, J. W., & Harber, K. D. (1993). A social stage model of collective coping: The Loma Prieta earthquake and the Persian Gulf War. *Journal of Social Issues, 49,* 125–145.
Pólya T, László J, Forgas J P (2005) Making sense of life stories: The role of narrative perspective in communicating hidden information about social identity and personality *European Journal of Social Psychology 35,* 785–796
Ricoeur, P. (2006). *Memory, history, forgetting*. Chicago, IL: Chicago University Press.
Roccas, S., Klar, Y., & Liviatan, I. (2006). The paradox of group-based guilt: Modes of national identification, conflict vehemence, and reactions to the ingroup's moral violations. *Journal of Personality and Social Psychology, 91,* 698–711.
Rüsen, J. (2004). Trauma and mourning in historical thinking. *Journal of Interdisciplinary Studies in History and Archeology, 1*(1), 10–21.
Slugoski, B. R., Branscombe, N. R., & Kappen, D. M. (2002). *Development and validation of the collective guilt scale (CGS).* Paper presented at the 31st annual meeting of the Society of Australian Social Psychologist, Adelaide, Australia.
Szabó, Zs., & László, J. (2012). The Hungarian identification with the nation scale (INS). *Magyar Pszichológiai Szemle* (accepted).
Turner, J. C., Hogg, M. A., Oakes, P. J., Reicher, S. D., & Wetherell, M. S. (1987). *Rediscovering the social group: A self-categorization theory.* Oxford, England: Blackwell.
Vincze, O., & László, J. (2010). Role of narrative perspective in history textbooks. *Magyar Pszichológiai Szemle, 65*(4), 571–595.
Volkan, V.(1990). An overview of psychological concepts pertinent to interethnic and/or international relationships. In The Psychodynamics of International Relationships: Concepts and Theories, Volume I, eds. V. Volkan D. Julius, and J. Montville, 31–46. Lexington, MA: Lexington Books.
Volkan, V.(1997). *Blood lines: From ethnic pride to ethnic terrorism*. Boulder, CO: Westview Press.
Wertsch, J. W. (2002). *Voices of collective remembering.* Cambridge, England: Cambridge University Press.

# 15

# Narrative Constructions of Italian Identity

## *An Investigation through Literary Texts over Time*

ALESSIO NENCINI

## THE RELEVANCE OF NARRATIVES IN EVERYDAY LIFE INTERACTIONS

The origin of the label *narrative psychology* is usually traced back to the work of Theodor Sarbin (1986) and the almost contemporary theoretical shift proposed by Jerome Bruner (1986, 1990), who stressed the increasing focus on information processing and the corresponding lesser degree of attention given to the construction of meaning in social psychology. According to Bruner, the so-called second cognitive revolution embodied individual mental processes into wider cultural and social processes, which fundamentally regard the social construction of meaning (László, 2004). Following Sarbin (1986), narratives play a fundamental function in structuring and giving meaning to human realities. In other words, the way in which people construct and communicate necessarily assumes the form of a narrative.

According to Bruner (1991), narratives can be considered as a conscious perception of reality, a deep-rooted quality of human thinking. Distinguishing *folk psychology* from *scientific psychology*, Bruner (1990) stressed the differentiation between a narrative way of thinking, which is characterized by a collective organization of meaning aimed at preserving, transmitting, and making available functional social patterns, and a paradigmatic thinking, which is regulated by formal language and logic causality, and that is proper for that particular narrative genre called *science*. Through folk psychology, the cultural features of a group are organized in coherent stories that function as a reference for all its members, even in the future. Every culture has its folk psychology—that is, its common way of thinking, its *mentality*: It covers more or less complex narratives about the members of a particular culture, their functioning, their way of thinking and acting, and the reasons why they do what they do. The goal of folk psychology is to provide not only a well-organized representation of a phenomenon or an event as *it is*, but to indicate how it could or should be. Thanks to the capability of connecting ordinary elements to exceptional categories, narratives give meaning to potential deviations from common norms and everyday beliefs, transforming the *unknown* into a story that can be told.

## NARRATIVE FEATURES

The study of narratives as basic forms of human thinking and acting has concentrated mainly on the fundamental and irreducible features of stories. Starting from the work by the Russian formalists (Propp, 1968), the study of narratives revealed some common elements or features.

Many scholars emphasized the prominent role played by the temporal structure and the causal coherence in narrative accounts (Labov & Waletzky, 1997). Time and coherence structure events in such a way that they express, "first, a connectedness, and second, a sense of movement or direction through time" (Gergen & Gergen, 1986, p. 25).

As stated by Sarbin (1986), "a story is a symbolized account of actions of human beings that has a temporal dimension" (p. 3). Sequentiality of two elements, or even their co-presence *at the same time,* imposes to any form of narrative to be temporally organized. To say it through the words of Ricoeur (1980), "I take temporality to be that structure of existence that reaches language in narrativity and narrativity to be the language structure that has temporality as its ultimate referent. Their relationship is therefore reciprocal" (p. 169). The different use of time in narratives has been largely investigated. Without entering too much into details, the way through which events are placed on the temporal dimension—analogously as the numberless combinations of different nucleotides on a DNA segment—generates different patterns of narrative forms that are associated to different psychological states and configurations of reality.

Every narrative action implies also an attribution of intentional stances. Narrative coherence is maintained by the perception of causal linkages of two or more events. In other terms, narrative coherence indicates the principle according to which each event furnishes some elements that are used to understand how the next event occurs (Gergen & Gergen, 1986).

At this regard, for instance, Gergen and Gergen (1983) have suggested the existence of three prototypical narrative forms that arrange a sequence of events on the basis of the extent to which they are able to achieve a particular goal: stability (narratives in which no change occurs), progression (narratives in which progress toward the goal is enhanced), and regression (narratives in which the progress toward the goal is hindered).

The combination of time and coherence concurs in providing different patterns of stories, or narrative canons (László, 2008). A story will then reflect recognizable human sentiments, goals, purposes, valuations, and judgments. The plot will influence the flow of action of the constructed narrative figures (Sarbin, 1986). For each cultural context, some canons are more easily available. These canons collect and provide individuals with a shared structure for storytelling—that is, the situated reality that is communicated. Highly shared plots represent the metastructure of what is acceptable, plausible, and meaningful. Examples of relevant plots in the Mediterranean culture can be found in Homeric epics (Martindale, 1987). The recurrent structure of the story comprehends a hero, who is provided with extraordinary qualities and capacities and who needs to undertake hard actions to prove his or her value and to fulfill him- or herself. Then, a preparation-initiation phase comes, followed by some difficulties that the hero encounters, which bring doubts about his or her capacities and chances of success. Eventually, thanks also to divine or superior interventions, the hero succeeds in the venture, thus completing his or her heroic identity. This kind of plot is extremely well-rooted in culture, to the point that it works as organizing structure also in therapeutic narratives (Epston, Morris, & Maisel, 1995).

Beyond time and coherence, narratives can be decomposed in other structural features such as perspective (Polya, László, & Forgas, 2005; see also Chapter 13, this volume), goals (Gergen & Gergen, 1983), roles (Parker-Oliver, 2000), characters' agency (László, Ferenczhalmy, & Szalai, 2010), evaluation (Bigazzi & Nencini, 2008; Stephenson, Laszlo, Ehmann, Lefever, & Lefever, 1997) and interpersonal relationships. In particular, the latter can be used to deepen the study of collective identity as a relational, interactive construct.

The relationship feature of a narrative regards to the way in which interpersonal bonds between individuals are legitimated and become meaningful within a cultural group. The number, frequency, and value of relationships contribute to generate a psychological reality that defines what a group is, in all its different typologies, such as, family, work, nation.

The relationship pattern also contributes to embed and diffuse the most frequent and functional ways of human interaction in narratives. In this sense, the relationship pattern, together with the *evaluation* feature, concur in providing a narrative with a normative, often implicit, system that differentiates what *is* from what *is not*, what *is possible* from what *should not be*.

The study of relational attributes in narratives has received less attention as compared with time and coherence, but nevertheless, it is possible to find some illuminating examples and suggestions. For example, Propp (1968), in his renowned study of Russian folktales, showed how stories are composed by a combination of a limited number of functions or narrative units. Functions are considered generalizations of characters' actions, loaded with intentionality and emotional value. The composition of such functions itself is regulated by patterns that determine the final plot or global style. Without entering too much into details, it is important to stress that the functions studied by Propp are not considered objective characteristics of the text, but rather they are deep-rooted modalities in which language is used over time in a given cultural context. Therefore, they constitute actual ways of reality construction.

The intersubjective patterns of relationality sustain and transform narratives over time. The relational pattern provides public narratives with cultural and institutional intersubjective networks that can be found in local or macrostories. These stories range from the narratives of one's family, to those of the workplace, church, government, and nation (Somers, 1994), providing strong metaphorical structures for how relationships are meaningful in a given society.

## NARRATIVES AND IDENTITY

The prominent focus on the process of co-construction under the narrative coherence principle requires that identity becomes an individual (or group) story in which events and experiences are placed along a temporal line: Each element assumes valued connotations in the story, which is always told from a particular perspective. What is called *identity* is the story that structures and organizes past and present experiences to anticipate the future (Bruner, 1987), or to say it in different words, identity is the result of a constant reconstruction of one's own biography (Ricoeur, 1980). Past elements join with present experiences and future purposes, in a continuous process of reorganization that aims to give coherence and continuity to the group.

Ricoeur (1991) sustains that the essential feature of identity, that is the self-perception of continuity as the *same* individual, notwithstanding the multiple variations in the way of being and behaving, is based on the narrative structure that attributes the form of a life story to these perceptions. In the same way, group identity can be considered as a set of stories about the group itself, which are more or less shared and available to its members. In these stories, it is easy to find the connection to Bruner's folk psychology. For instance, László, Ehmann, and Imre (2002) have emphasized the link between individual and group stories, showing that these narratives are mainly constituted by some patterns that recursively come back across history and everyday life. More specific, the authors illustrated how narratives about relevant events in the Hungarian national history can be traced back to a limited number of patterns in which the moral and evaluative process remains constant; the acknowledgment of the good qualities of the Hungarian in-group leads to a first phase characterized by victory or partial success, often followed by a painful and bitter defeat that lingers on depressive collective memories (see also Chapter 12, this volume). Another example is advanced by Thorne and McLean (2003), who collected accounts of traumatic events provided by American adolescents. The analysis of recurrent narrative patterns among the different stories allowed to illustrate three narrative models of emotional positions: the *John Wayne* narrative, defined by a focus on action and on courage; a *vulnerability* narrative, which emphasized one's own fear, sadness, and helplessness in the face of the traumatic event;

and a *Florence Nightingale* narrative, characterized by care and concern for the feelings of others.

To this regard, Hammack (2008) focuses on the relationship between *master* narratives and personal identity. According to the author, a master narrative can be intended as a cultural script that is continuously accessible to the members of a given group, may this be a nation, an ethnic group, or a community group. Within this narrative, each individual may find his or her own personal positioning—that is, a plot that organizes one's individual experiences in a coherent story (also) as a member of the group, a story enriched by values, meaning, explanations, and possibilities of the future. In this sense, identity becomes a construct that connects the self, the group, and the societal level through narratives that give meaning to social categories.

## TOWARD A RELATIONAL VISION OF NATIONAL IDENTITY

It is largely accepted that the *nation* is a relatively recent product if confronted with the human phylogenesis. The birth of the nation is usually traced back to the second half of the 18th century, after the crisis of the traditional empires (Hobsbawm, 1994). In opposition to the essentialist vision of a nation, which considered the origins of the national group and some specific characteristics (language, national character, land . . .) as indicators of the *true essence* of it (Guibernau, 1996), some authors, and in particular, Benedict Anderson (1983), stressed that the nation can be considered as an imagined community held by a series of symbolic relationships among its members. Anderson drew on the label *imagined community* from the French philosopher Renan (1990) and described the factors that brought to the birth of modern nationalisms and to the development of the current national structures from an historical and modernist perspective. According to Anderson, a nation is an imagined community because the content of the relational bond among its members is necessarily symbolic, related to all the potential interpersonal relationships that can be imagined even without concrete interactions. The nation is also "imagined as both inherently limited and sovereign" (Anderson, 1983, p. 6). It is limited because every nation is represented with borders, which separate a nation from another and who is in-group from who is out-group. It is sovereign because, according to the author, the nation was constructed in the illuminist period, where freedom was considered one of the highest ideals. And finally, a nation is a community because, notwithstanding the inequities that usually occur, a nation is always experienced with affective involvement formed by "deep, horizontal comradeship" (Anderson, 1983, p. 7).

The imagined community described by Anderson is a macrosocial symbolic entity that is mainly constituted by sense of belonging and intentions to act with reference to it, rather than a clear object made of concrete elements that can be *objectively* described and measured. In this perspective, relationships assume a privileged position. A nation has to be considered a cultural construction—as any other anthropological construct such as *kinship* and *religion*—that is, strongly structured along the symbolic connections between members that generate complex systems that respond to individual and social needs.

In other, more social psychological words, it is possible to affirm that a nation—and, as a consequence, the story of living one's life as being part of it (i.e., national identity)—assumes the traits of a particularly *thick* social construction, widely diffused through numerous collective narratives over time. At the basis of the construction of a nation, we can identify the everyday interactions of those who use this construct and, through discourses and actions, concur in assembling the normative narrative structure of what a nation is, what a particular nation means, how one should behave with reference to his or her nation, how one should interact as member of his or her nation, and who are the members of one's nation.

## NARRATIVES OF NATIONAL IDENTITY

Mainstream social psychology has studied and studies national identity referring mainly to the social identity theory (Tajfel, 1981) and to the self categorization theory (Turner, Hogg, Oakes, Reicher, & Wetherell, 1987). The nation is considered a social category equal to others and, as a consequence, it is subjected to the processes typical of intergroup relations (categorization, identification, social comparison). Within this framework, national identity has been studied mostly as an independent variable and, consequently, research has looked at its effects on other psychological variables or intentions to act (Cinnirella, 2007; Doosje, Branscombe, Spears, & Manstead, 1998, 2006). However, national identity risks to be used as an ontological reference to the nation category, which is, as we discussed earlier, far from being a defined and clearly identifiable element.

Following a narrative approach to the study of identity as social representation (László, 1997), national identity can be conceived as a series of stories concerning the national group that are more or less shared and available to its members (László, 2008).

The usual correspondence between a nation and its land is studied for its capacity of generating meaningful stories of membership and territorial settlement (Reicher & Hopkins, 2001). National identity is shaped in relation to other memberships connected to relevant symbolic places (Breakwell, 1986, 1992; Twigger-Ross, Bonaiuto, & Breakwell, 2003). Through the use of geographical labels, whenever individuals represent their membership, they refer to different territorial levels (local, regional, national, supranational . . . ). Therefore, national identity can be considered a fluid construct: Representations of national identity are composed of narrative elements that can be found also in more local territorial levels.

These narratives are not neutral. On the contrary, they are filled with judgments, values, evaluations, and beliefs. They are actual common sense theories that can be used by community members in a specific context. As a consequence, representations of national identity are structured as a series of *stories* about past meaningful experiences, which constitute functional models available to individuals every time a territorial reference to identity is salient.

Following a narrative perspective, the narrative construction of Hungarian national identity has been studied focusing on the cultural artifacts that are perceived as relevant for the diffusion of collective knowledge, such as history textbooks (Vincze, Tóth, & László, 2007; see also Chapter 14, this volume) and successful historical novels (László, Vincze, & Somogyvári, 2003). Both types of material contain and make available fundamental narrative elements—such as characters, goals, moral evaluations, relationships—that are necessary for the organization and transmission of identity content. The final product contributes to the formation of narrative-organized representations (László, 1997) of the past, the present, and the future of the national group.

## LITERARY TEXTS AS WELL-ORGANIZED REPRESENTATIONS OF SOCIAL REALITIES

The relationship between psychology and literature has been characterized by numerous exchanges and reciprocal contaminations (Moghaddam, 2004), although criticisms and skepticism toward the scientific nature of this collaboration has always been there. Novelists, dramatists, and poets—storytellers all—have continued to provide insights about human motives and actions, even during the years in which human conduct has been studied by scientific psychology (Sarbin, 1986). The distinction proposed by Bruner (1986) about the nature of narrative psychology finds a good objectification in the differentiation concerning the realm of *reality* to which both psychology and literature refer to. However, referring to a social constructionist framework, social realities are intersubjective products that are generated through social interactions. From this perspective, the distinction between the object of psychological research and the object of literary representations becomes thinner and thinner, to the point that it can be transposed to the perception of coherence between what is told and what is experienced by social actors. Thus, literary texts can be used as relevant social artifacts as much as other psychological theories, the former being distinguished from the latter for their communicative registry and their goals, but not for their domain of reference. Novels and fiction constitute different ways of representing human experiences and, at the same time, means through which to act on the social world as active elements in the collective discourse. Voices of writers and scholars are important in contemporary societies as expression, on the one hand, and as proposal, on the other hand, of debated issues and generative views of the world (Gergen, 1989).

Every text is made of both shared, culturally available elements and original, peculiar qualities (Nencini, 2011). Relevant literary texts are able to depict plausible fictional worlds, so that the reader can accept the described reality as *real* and recognize some relevant patterns for his or her own life in what is narrated (Contarello, 2008). This type of text usually responds to criteria of success (i.e., the capacity to encounter and fulfill social needs), diffusion (i.e., the possibility to reach a large number of individuals and, consequently, feed the collective debate), and authoritativeness (i.e., the writer's ability to reproduce relational, emotional, and cognitive aspects of human experience that are able to resonate with the readers' personal experiences; see Larsen & Seilman, 1988). Regardless of the domain of the described reality, a well-organized literary text that fulfills the aforementioned criteria draws on plausible and shared elements that refer to the world of the author and to the one of the readers.

Literary texts can thus be used also as research material. Specifically, successful novels that are narrated by "those with well-honed language skills" (Gergen, 1989, p.76)—professionals in storytelling with particular sensibility in describing and communicating—and that have a particular social-historical impact, can be investigated as real exemplification of possible social worlds.

## NARRATIVE REPRESENTATIONS OF ITALIAN NATIONAL IDENTITY

The aforementioned theoretical considerations were used as guidelines in the studies presented here. They aimed to explore the content and the narrative structure of representations of national identity from a historical perspective. The main goal of the project was to search for common and divergent elements in the historical evolution of different levels of national identity, with particular attention to the macrocontexts *north* and *south* of Italy. To this purpose, narrative patterns of Italian national identity were researched in successful literary works. Novels written and set in different periods of national history were analyzed to explore the representations of relevant social *realities* they provide. Analyses were aimed at investigating many aspects concerning Italian national identity—the way in which different levels of territorial identity are constructed and negotiated, the structure of social relations, and the evaluations used by characters in the text, the main themes on which characters define their territorial identity. For the scope of this chapter, the focus is mainly on the results related to the relationship feature.

The choice of the *social realities*—the novels—to be investigated is a relevant part of the research itself, because the criteria through which a researcher selects the particular portion of the world to investigate, inevitably direct the possibilities of the results that will be obtained. Because one of the aims was to study the representations of national identity over time, three relevant periods of Italian recent history were chosen: the 1930s to 1940s (Italy between the two World Wars); the 1960s (the Italian economic boom); and the 1990s to 2000s (contemporary Italy). For each period, two novels were selected, one written by a southern author and set in southern Italy and the other written by a northern author and set in northern Italy. Then, to fulfill the criteria of diffusion, success, and authoritativeness, the novels had to:

- be published and set in the historical period of reference (i.e., novels have to narrate the present of the described social *reality*);
- be successful and popular at the time of publication;

- meet with approval of the present critics (i.e., considered relevant texts from a social and historical point of view);
- have similar length; and
- be narrated in first person (by the protagonist).

At the end of a long collaborative procedure of evaluation that involved other colleagues and two schoolteachers, the six novels were selected.[1]

Novels were analyzed for their contents related to characters, evaluations between characters, and references to national identity (and other levels of territorial identities). Content analysis was performed through two different techniques: a manual thematic content analysis (TCA) and an automatic analysis of evaluations (AAE). TCA was conducted with the aid of QSR Nud.Ist.4 (Richards & Richards, 1998).

Each novel was first divided into text units (each corresponding to a sentence), and then text units were coded on the basis of their contents related to interpersonal relationships and evaluations. The coding of relationships was further divided into *agent*—the character who gives an evaluation—and *coagent*—the character/group who receives an evaluation. Evaluation included the content of attributes and actions used to denote the other. Finally, references to the territory used by characters to define themselves and their salient social environment were also coded.

The AAE (Bigazzi & Nencini, 2008) consisted of a linguistic analysis conducted through the aid of the software Nooj (Koeva, Maurel, & Silberztein, 2007) and by means of specific grammars created on purpose by the author of the present chapter, and aimed at automatically extracting interpersonal and intergroup evaluations from the texts.

Through the TCA, a series of copresence matrixes was created: Each matrix extracted the frequency and the content of every interaction between two characters (agent and coagent), thus allowing to recreate a relational network of the novel (illustrated in the next paragraph), qualitatively and quantitatively weighted.

The AAE provided support to the TCA by automatically extracting the evaluative expression of interpersonal interchanges and giving the opportunity to explore the most frequent evaluative dimensions used in the text. Also, combining evaluations with the character who was the object of that particular expression, we extracted a series of *models of individuals* that were made available through the novels.

## CONTENTS AND STRUCTURE OF RELATIONSHIPS OVER TIME

The analysis of the evaluations between characters allowed to quantify the number of interrelations and to qualify the most frequent contents for each interpersonal relationship.

To construct a visual structure of the relationship patterns underlying the texts, characters of each novel were connected by arrows as in a classic sociogram, where the thicker the line is, the more frequent the interrelation is (i.e., the number of evaluations between characters). Globally, as shown in the figures below, texts written and set in northern Italy show a relational pattern in which an independent self prevails, an individual who autonomously moves in the society in search of the fulfillment of individual needs, desires, and choice. From the analysis of the novels set in southern Italy, on the contrary, a more crowded and complex relational pattern seems to emerge. Relationships are more frequent and broad, connecting a larger number of characters. The individual identity is composed of a number of others who enter, sometimes forcedly, the life narrative of the single individual.

From a historical perspective, the relational pattern is intertwined with the most relevant territorial references. In the 1930s and 1940s, where the territorial borders of the perceived relevant group is limited to the village, and the family is central in everyday discourses and practices. In contrast, in the 1990s, the relational pattern is connected with a wider territorial reference, which probably enlarges the possibility of interchange, and thus of self-definition, relying on a more widely shared narrative of the individual.

In the 1930s and 1940s, the antinomy between Sicilians and others (Figure 15.1—left) is opposed to the one between townsmen and countrymen (Figure 15.1—right). The role of the family is central in both novels, although with some differences between north and south. In *Conversations in Sicily*, the family represents the core of the characters' identity, clearly differentiated from the other Sicilians. Although narrated in first-person perspective by Silvestro (the protagonist), the relational pattern shows numerous connections also between secondary characters. In *Your Villages*, relations between characters are fewer, even among members of the peasant family. Relationships are centered on Berto (the narrator) and rarely show bidirectional connections. Here, the family constitutes, even geographically, the privileged place where everyday interpersonal relationships, workplace, and intimacy overlap, representing a microuniverse that the individual can hardly leave.

The most salient territorial identity in both novels is the local one, coinciding with the island in Vittorini's novel ("and Sicily or World was the same thing"[2]), and with the village in which the characters live, in Pavese's. Sicilians are described as poor people, and they are represented mostly through attributes of sadness and compassion ("the boat was full of third-class little Sicilians, hungry and quiet in getting cold, without any coat, with their hands in the pocket of their trousers"). Other non-Sicilian characters are addressed with exclusion and differentiation, without peculiar, explicit evaluations.

Countrymen are presented through awkwardness and stupidity ("One from the country is like a drunk. He's too stupid to let someone make a fool of him."), but also through cunning and naughtiness (especially men). Townsmen (and in particular townswomen) are evaluated as naughty and ungrateful. ("Up the stairs, she asks me if she was the first woman I came to see. And she says, 'What

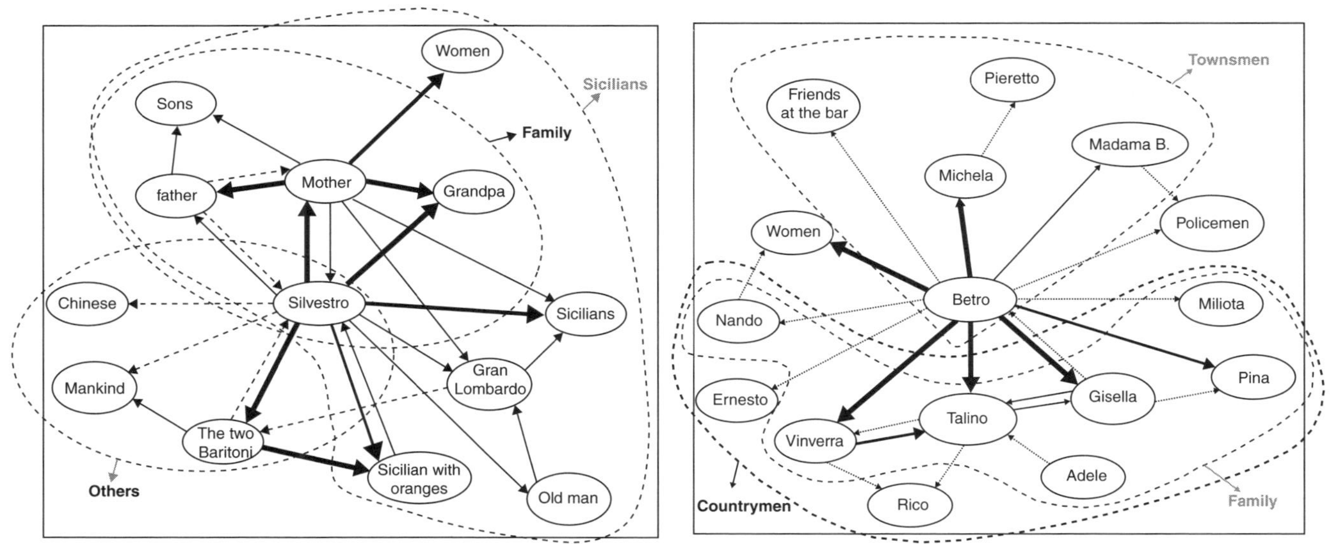


Figure 15.1 On the left: *conversations in sicily* (1941)—south; on the right: *your villages* (1941)— north

would Pieretto say if he knew it!'—He would say you are always the same, I think.")

In the 1960s, although both novels are set in an historical moment characterized by economic growth at the national level, local territorial identities are still the most salient. The relational pattern remains substantially the same as the one emerged in the 1930s and 1940s. In *To Each His Own* (Figure 15.2—left), an intricate web of evaluative relations is shown, where the families are again nuclear elements. ("Once the police commissioner was convinced, the girl had to convince the entire village, 7,500 people, her family members included.") In *La Vita Agra* (Figure 15.2—right), relationships are concentrated mostly from the protagonist to the other characters, showing a strong individualist conception of the self, oriented toward self-fulfillment and success.

Available models of individuals appear to be rooted in the spirit of the historical period (Jossa, 2006). There are successful characters, who behave functionally with respect to the social environment in which they live, but who are not exactly honest or virtuous. ("Mister Fernaspe usually arrived around ten, grave and breathless; he called one of us in his room and gave him an article to pass or a title to compose. [ . . . ] The Fernaspe got on the telephone and we heard him shout insults while we continued to cut and add.") And there are traditional characters, who are depicted as appreciable persons but who are defeated and bypassed at the end of the story, and thus are considered weak or naive. ("Yes, my son. . . . He was intelligent: but a quiet, slow intelligence.")

Sicilians are again described through negative traits, characterized by decay and self-pity. ("A Sicilian on the contrary sees the killed dead and the murderer, and the alive one who needs to be helped is precisely the murderer.") Families are mainly described through virtuousness, which is connected to honor and respectability, and evaluations of sorrow and unpleasantness. The specific use of an evaluation is related to processes of in-group favoritism in intra- and inter-familiar relations.

In *La Vita Agra*, the antinomy is between citizens (of Milan) and those who come from (everywhere) outside the city. Townsmen are represented as restlessness, surly persons—if they are bosses—or good and poor people—if they are workers. ("Mrs. De Sio did not protest, because she was a good and tolerant woman.") Strangers are depicted mainly as worried and ingenuous persons. ("I urged to get out and have a coffee, so I sneaked out of the sheets, so softly not to wake Anna up, this irresponsible, sleepy woman. Nobody would ever steal her eight-hours sleep. As long as she had to typing, nothing worried her.")

The 1990s are years of rising globalization, especially at the European level. The relational pattern shows a wider correspondence between the two macro-regional contexts. References to a broader, global identity are frequent, whereas local identifications, as well as the family, lose their centrality in the description of the social reality narrated in the texts. In *Involuntary Witness*, a more individualist pattern emerges, in which individuals are represented principally as separate entities. In *Techniques of Seduction*, the Milanese characters are separate and detached from each other, whereas those from Rome are joined by

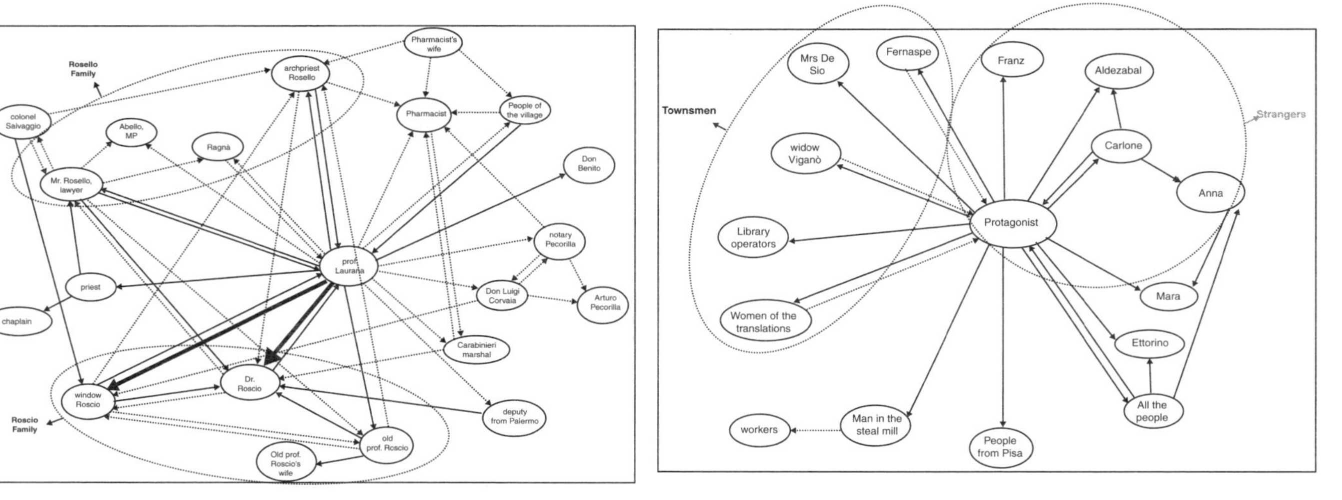


Figure 15.2 On the left: *to each his own* (1966)—south; on the right: *la vita agra* (1962)—north

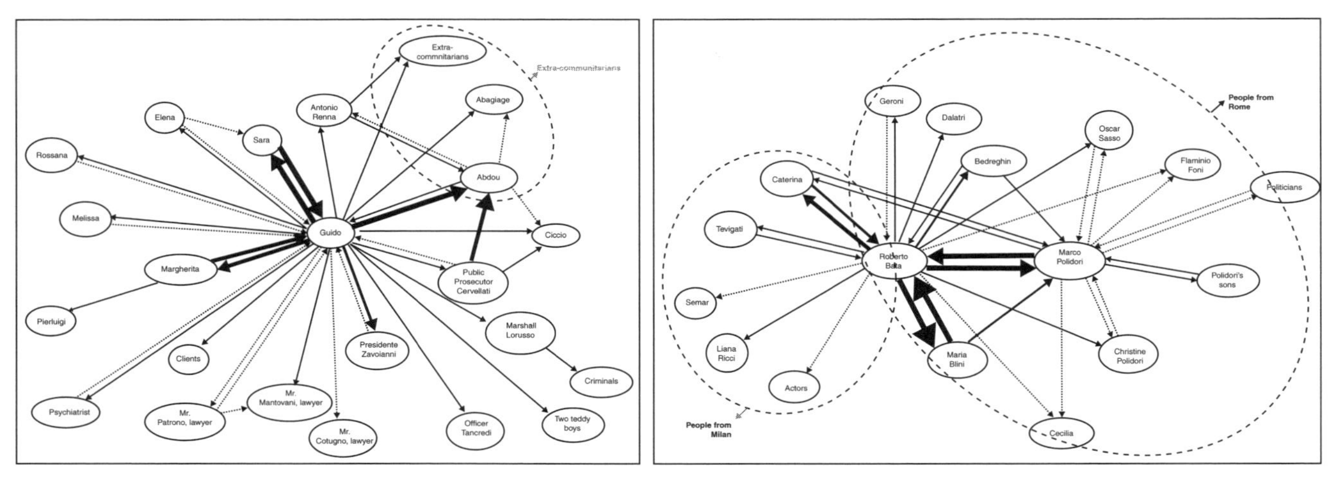


Figure 15.3 On the left: *involuntary witness* (2002)—south; on the right: *techniques of seduction* (1991)—north

a higher number of interrelations, although sometimes fake and instrumental. Thus, the Roman context results to be more likely oriented to a wide and collective interpersonal network.

In *Involuntary Witness,* identities become more relevant at a supranational level, due to intergroup relation between the protagonist (Italian, European, White) and the other main characters (Senegalese, African, Black). Italians are described mostly as pleasant and good people opposed to extra-communitarians that are evaluated as unpleasant and criminal. ("The first stereotype suggested me the following sequence: African, remanded in custody, drug. Africans are frequently arrested for this reason.") In *Techniques of Seduction,* evaluations are organized along a dimension of *openness* versus *closeness* toward the others: People from Milan are described as close, breathless individuals, whereas people living in Rome are evaluated as hypocritical but also as more calm, open, and smiling. ("Inside and in front of bars, people from the offices ate and drank and smoked and chatted without any trace of the distressing hurry that, in Milan, drives bunches of clerks to gulp something down in a few minutes and then rush back to the workplace, with the food sat heavily on their stomach.")

## CONCLUSIONS

The analysis of the literary texts, here briefly presented, describes a series of narrative representations that constitute privileged outlooks on social *realities*. These fictional narratives collect and organize available everyday life elements in meaningful stories that, at the same time, play a key role in proposing and diffusing functional patterns of sociality (Contarello, 2008). Exploring in depth the contents and the relational structure of the representations of national identity—or more widely, the representations of different territorial identities—it is possible to map out a sort of invisible line—another narrative!—that temporally connects historical moments, social contexts, and different social psychological dynamics.

Taken together, results show some points of discontinuity in relation to the representation of national identity, in particular with regards to the most salient territorial levels for each historical period and to the relational pattern that structures the story. The evolution of the narrative representation of identity at the national level appears substantially shared and coherent in its core elements, although with some interesting and peculiar differences over time and across the two macrocontexts.

From a temporal point of view, local identity is more salient in the past (especially in the 1930s and 1940s), starting from family identity. The representation is characterized by differentiation and isolation. In the 1990s, a global and supranational representation can be observed, which appears to be more open to the others. Families are less important for defining the individual identity, and the whole territorial representation is held principally by individualism. In all three periods, references to a common national identity are scarce.

From a contextual point of view, some relational patterns seem to be available and diffused in different ways in the two macrocontexts. In southern Italy, the relational network is thick and the public dimension prevails on the individual one. Membership to a small group (familiar, mostly, but also local and regional in relation with the nation) is extremely relevant for self-definition. On the contrary, in northern Italy a more individualistic organization of relationships emerges. Individuals are more oriented to self-enhancement rather than to the good of the community. For the individual, concrete relations are less relevant, whereas symbolic relations related to social identities (as a worker, for example) are more significant.

From a theoretical point of view, the present paper aims to suggest that relational patterns provide a structure for those types of human interchanges that give meaning to a group. From a social constructionist perspective that sees social realities as the product of relational co-constructions, the relational patterns constitute important narrative elements for the configurations of reality that will be generated under the form of stories (Gergen & Gergen, 1986). In a certain social context then, narratives that organize forms of knowledge, practices, and values of a group contain relational structures that provide indications regarding the way in which memberships and social relationships are meaningful and functional in that particular group. The relational pattern gives to a social narrative the *ground layer* that regulates, even normatively, the social interchanges. This objectifies not only who is part of the group and who is not, but also which role one has in the group, which relationships are significant for the group's goals and well-being, and which practices are associated to those who are part of the relational network of the group.

## NOTES

1. The novels are: from the 1930s to 1940s, *Conversations in Sicily* by Elio Vittorini (south) and *Your Villages* by Cesare Pavese (north); from the 1960s, *To Each His Own* by Leonardo Sciascia and *La Vita Agra. It's a Hard Life* by Luciano Bianciardi (north); and finally, from the 1990s to 2000s, *Involuntary Witness* by Gianrico Carofiglio (south) and *Techniques of Seduction* by Andrea De Carlo (north).
2. This excerpt, as well as the others that follow, were translated by the author of the present chapter because text analyses were conducted in the original language (Italian).

## REFERENCES

Anderson, B. (1983). *Imagined communities*. London, England: Verso.

Bigazzi, S., & Nencini, A. (2008). How evaluations construct identities: The psycholinguistic model of evaluation. In O. Vincze & S. Bigazzi (Eds.), *Élmény, Történetek, a Történetek Élménye* (pp. 91–105). Budapest, Hungary: UMK.

Breakwell, G. M. (1986). *Coping with threatened identities*. London, England: Methuen.

Breakwell, G. M. (1992). *Social psychology of identity and self concept*. San Diego, CA: Academic Press.

Bruner, J. (1986). *Actual minds, possible worlds*. Cambridge, England: Harvard University Press.

Bruner, J. (1987). Life as narrative. *Social Research, 54,* 11–32.

Bruner, J. (1990). *Acts of meaning*. Cambridge, England: Harvard University Press.

Bruner, J. (1991). The narrative construction of reality. *Critical Inquiry, 18,* 1–21.

Cinnirella, M. (2007). National identification, type and specificity of comparison and their effects on descriptions. *European Journal of Social Psychology, 37,* 672–691.

Contarello, A. (2008). Social psychology and literature: Toward possible correspondence. In T. Sugiman, K. J. Gergen, W. Wagner, & Y. Yamada (Eds.), *Meaning in action: Constructions, Narratives, and Representations* (pp. 303–325). New York, NY: Springer-Verlag.

Doosje, B., Branscombe, N. R., Spears, R., & Manstead, A. S. R. (1998). Guilty by association: When one's group has a negative history. *Journal of Personality and Social Psychology, 75*(4), 872–886.

Doosje, B., Branscombe, N. R., Spears, R., & Manstead, A. S. R. (2006). Antecedents and consequences of group-based guilt: The effects of ingroup identification. *Group Processes & Intergroup Relations, 9*(3), 325–338.

Epston, D., Morris, F., & Maisel, R. (1995). A narrative approach to so-called anorexia/bulimia. *Journal of Feminist Family Therapy, 7*(1–2), 69–96.

Gergen, K. J. (1989). Warranting voice and the elaboration of the self. In J. Shotter & K. J. Gergen (Eds.), *Texts of identity. Inquiries in social construction series* (pp. 70–81). London, England: Sage.

Gergen, K. J., & Gergen, M. M. (1983). Narratives of the self. In T. R. Sarbin & K. E. Scheibe (Eds.), *Studies in social identity* (pp. 254–273). New York, NY: Praeger.

Gergen, K. J., & Gergen, M. M. (1986). Narrative form and the construction of psychological science. In T. R. Sarbin (Ed.), *Narrative psychology: The storied nature of human conduct* (pp. 22–44). New York, NY: Praeger.

Guibernau, M. (1996). *Nationalism: The nation-state and nationalism in the twentieth century*. Cambridge, England: Polity Press.

Hammack, P. L. (2008). Narrative and the cultural psychology of identity. *Personality and Social Psychology Review, 12*(3), 222–247.

Hobsbawm, E. (1994). *Age of extremis*. London, England: Michael Joseph.

Jossa, S. (2006). *L'Italia letteraria*. Bologna, Italy: Il Mulino.

Koeva, S., Maurel, D., & Silberztein, M. (2007). *Formaliser les langues avec l'ordinateur: de INTEX à NooJ*. Besançon, France: Presses Universitaires de Franche- Comté.

Labov, W., & Waletzky, J. (1997). Narrative analysis: Oral versions of personal experience. *Journal of Narrative and Life History, 7*(1–4), 3–38.

Larsen, S. F., & Seilman, U. (1988). Personal remindings while reading literature. *Text, 8,* 411–429.

László, J. (1997). Narrative organisation of social representations. *Papers on Social Representations, 6*(2), 155–172.

László, J. (2004). Narrative psychology's contribution to the second cognitive revolution. *Journal of Cultural and Evolutionary Psychology, 2*(3), 337–354.

László, J. (2008). *The science of stories: An introduction to narrative psychology*. London, England: Routledge.

László, J., Ehmann, B., & Imre, O. (2002). Les représentations sociales de l'histoire: La narration populaire historique et l'identité nationals. In S. Laurens & N. Roussiau (Eds.), *La mémoire sociale. Identités et représentations sociales*. Rennes, France: Université Rennes.

László, J., Ferenczhalmy, R., & Szalai, K. (2010). Role of agency in social representations of history. *Societal and Political Psychology International Review, 1,* 31–43.

László, J., Vincze, O., & Somogyvári, I. K. (2003). Representation of national identity in successful historical novels. *Empirical Studies of the Arts, 21*(1), 69–80.

Martindale, C. (1987). Narrative pattern analysis: A quantitative method for inferring the symbolic meaning of narratives. In L. Halasz (Ed.), *Literary discourse: Aspects of cognitive and social psychological approaches* (pp. 167–181). Berlin, Germany: de Gruyter.

Moghaddam, F. M. (2004). From "psychology in literature" to "psychology is literature": An exploration of boundaries and relationships. *Theory & Psychology, 14*(4), 505–525.

Nencini, A. (2011). A matter of shared knowledge. *PSYART: A Hyperlink Journal for the Psychological Study of the Arts*. Retrieved from http://www.psyartjournal.com/article/show/nencini-a_matter_of_shared_knowledge

Parker-Oliver, D. (2000). The social construction of the "dying role" and the hospice drama. *Omega, 40*(4), 493–512.

Polya, T., László, J., & Forgas, J. P. (2005). Making sense of life stories: The role of narrative perspective in perceiving hidden information about social identity. *European Journal of Social Psychology, 35*(6), 785–796.

Propp, V. (1968). *The morphology of folk tales*. Austin, TX: University of Texas Press.

Reicher, S., & Hopkins, N. (2001). *Self and nation*. London, England: Sage.

Renan, E. (1990). What is a nation? In H. K. Bhabha (Ed.), *Nation and narration* (pp. 8–22). London, England: Routledge.

Richards, L., & Richards, T. J. (1998). *QSR NUD.IST*. Melbourne, Australia: Qualitative Solutions and Research Pty.

Ricoeur, P. (1980). Narrative time. *Critical Inquiry, 7*(1), 169–190.

Ricoeur, P. (1991). Narrative identity. *Philosophy Today, 35*(1), 73–81.

Sarbin, T. R. (1986). *Narrative psychology: The storied nature of human conduct*. New York, NY: Praeger.

Somers, M. R. (1994). The narrative constitution of identity: A relational and network approach. *Theory and Society, 23*(5), 605–649.

Stephenson, G. M., Laszlo, J., Ehmann, B., Lefever, R. M. H., & Lefever, R. (1997). Diaries of significant events: Socio-linguistic correlates of therapeutic outcomes in patients with addiction problems. *Journal of Community & Applied Social Psychology, 7*(5), 389–411.

Tajfel, H. (1981). *Human groups and social categories*. Cambridge, England: Cambridge University Press.

Thorne, A., & McLean, K. C. (2003). Telling traumatic events in adolescence: A study of master narrative positioning. In R. Fivush & C. Haden (Eds.), *Connecting culture and memory: The development of an autobiographical self* (pp. 169–185). Mahwah, NJ: Erlbaum.

Turner, J. C., Hogg, M. A., Oakes, P. J., Reicher, S., & Wetherell, M. (1987). *Rediscovering the social group: A self-categorization theory*. Oxford, England: Blackwell.

Twigger-Ross, C. L., Bonaiuto, M., & Breakwell, G. M. (2003). Identity theories and environmental psychology. In M. Bonnes, T. Lee, & M. Bonaiuto (Eds.), *Psychological theories for environmental issues* (pp. 203–235). Aldershot, England: Ashgate.

Vincze, O., Tóth, J., & László, J. (2007). Representations of the Austro-Hungarian monarchy in the history books of the two nations. *Empirical Text and Culture Research, 3*, 62–71.

# Part 4

# The Political and Social Consequences of Communication and Cognition

# 16

# Political Communication, Social Cognitive Processes, and Voters' Judgments

PATRIZIA CATELLANI AND MAURO BERTOLOTTI

How do our opinions of politicians depend on what politicians say and what other people tell about them or to them? In the present paper, we focus on the relations between some subtle and indirect (but widely employed) forms of political communication and the effects they may have on the perception of political candidates. We especially focus on attack and defense communication and on the possibility that using a subtle and indirect communicative strategy such as counterfactual statements (i.e., "If only . . .") may increase the effectiveness of communication. After taking into account some pragmatic features of political communication and its links with impression formation, we briefly review the sociocognitive processes that previous research has shown to be connected to the generation of counterfactual thoughts. We then examine how the use of counterfactuals in attack and defense messages may affect receivers' judgments in the political context.

## POLITICAL COMMUNICATION AND IMPRESSION FORMATION

Political communication has been widely investigated in terms of form, content, and discursive function (e.g., Kaid & Holtz-Bacha, 2008). Political attitudes, their formation, change, and effects have also been investigated, as well as several individual and social factors affecting them (e.g., Kuklinski, 2001). The effects of political communication on political attitudes, however, have been scarcely explored so far (but see McGraw, 2003). In particular, we have little knowledge of the subtle and complex processes through which the media and politicians can influence citizens' judgments and decisions, including voting choice.

Something similar has happened in the wider field of social psychology. Research on social cognition, intergroup processes, and decision making has rarely come in touch with research on communication and language. As discussed by Fiedler (2007), a wide range of fundamental psychosocial processes such as attribution (Maass, Salvi, Arcuri, & Semin, 1989; Semin & Fiedler, 1988), conflict, stereotype formation, and maintenance (Beukeboom, Finkenauer, & Wigboldus, 2010; Wigboldus, Semin, & Spears, 2000, 2006), or self- and other-presentation (Douglas & Sutton, 2003; Douglas, Sutton, & Wilkin, 2008) can be better understood by focusing on their communicational and linguistic basis. Actually, people may more or less purposely exploit the subtle mechanisms linking communication and cognition to influence receivers to their own advantage.

The relevance of language and communication in impression formation and decision making is possibly further enhanced in the political field. Rarely do citizens have direct access to political and economic facts. Several different political agents such as incumbent government officials, members of the opposition, journalists, pundits, and commentators present and explain those facts to voters. For instance, when facing a financial crisis or economic downturn, citizens may not be able to fully realize the extent or the consequences of the situation, and they get most of the information from what is said in the political debate on the topic (Gomez & Wilson, 2001).

Besides being an essential source of information for citizens' decision making, political communication is a form of persuasive communication. In fact, politicians do not simply provide citizens information, but they do it with a purpose (e.g., increasing their own chances of being voted). Such persuasive function of political communication is often very evident, but sometimes it can be more subtle and less easy to discern from the actual informational content. Analyzing the functions of political communication is therefore vital to an understanding of the speakers' communicative intentions and their intended (and actual) effects.

## ATTACKS AND DEFENSES IN POLITICAL COMMUNICATION

In their functional theory of political discourse, Benoit and Hartcock (1999) defined three main functions of political messages: acclaiming, attacking, and defending. First, candidates use acclaims to praise their accomplishments, policy stances, or personal qualities. Second, candidates attack their opponents on personal, party, or policy issues. Third, when attacked by an opponent or the media, candidates defend themselves, responding to external criticism.

Attacks and defenses are not only dialectic exchanges between political actors, but they involve a third and most important actor: the audience. This introduces a further layer of complexity in the pragmatics of political communication, making it the main channel through which impression management is performed (McGraw, 2003), with both positive and negative results. For example, attacks can sometimes backfire, resulting in more negative judgments of the source rather than of the target of attacks (Carraro, Gawronski, & Castelli, 2010; Haddock & Zanna, 1997; Hill, 1989; Roese & Sande, 1993). When exposed to a political attack, such as negative advertising, or criticism during a debate, people do not just ponder over the negative information about the target provided by the source of the attack. They also try to figure out the intent of such negative comment, whether it is an honest opinion or a malicious attempt at putting one's adversary in a negative light. Thereby, they adjust their attitudes toward not only the target, but also the source.

A similar process may turn up when politicians defend themselves from attacks. Research on defensive accounts both in the political and organizational fields (see Kim, Dirks, Cooper, & Ferrin, 2006; McGraw, 1991) indicates that blame avoidance can sometimes backfire and expose the defending speaker as irresponsible, unreliable, and ultimately untrustworthy. This is especially the case when politicians devote most of their time to responding to other candidates' statements and therefore risk being seen as excessively defensive and reactive.

Social psychological research has shown that receivers are often able to infer the speaker's motivations from several contextual and conversational cues (Hornsey, Robson, Smith, Esposo, & Sutton, 2008; Wänke, 2007), including subtle ones such as linguistic abstraction (Douglas & Sutton, 2006). Speakers, in turn, can actively adjust their language to make those cues less evident to receivers, thus reducing the probability of negative backlash (for further examples, see the linguistic strategies analyzed by Chapter 3, this volume).

In the political domain citizens are aware, to some extent, of politicians' communicative purposes, and they consequently weigh politicians' words depending on the issue they are dealing with. As found by McGraw, Lodge, and Jones (2002), suspicion of further motives is an important factor in the appraisal and elaboration of political communication, triggered by both stable individual factors (e.g., political trust and knowledge) and situational ones (e.g., policy disagreement, congruence between the speaker's and the audience's position, and even the mere fact of the speaker being a politician). When these conditions are met, receivers engage in more critical and intense scrutiny of politicians' communication, leaving their prior attitudes largely unaffected by the persuasive attempt. This process may also result in a less positive evaluation of the speaker. Going back to the previously cited example of a nation facing an economic downturn, citizens can judge a member of the opposition criticizing the current economic outlook as being genuinely concerned for the state of the economy. However, they can also attribute those complaints to a more selfish motivation, such as putting the incumbent government and its current policy in a negative light.

Research on political communication investigated politicians' attempts to use language for their persuasive goals. When facing predicaments that might endanger their reputation or credibility, for example, politicians often resort to indirect or noncommittal discourse (Bavelas, Black, Bryson, & Mullett, 1988; Bull, 2008). By doing so, they use several different discursive and communicative strategies (Bull, 2000; Bull & Mayer, 1993) to avoid conflict and to present themselves positively to the audience.

## COUNTERFACTUAL COMMUNICATION

Counterfactuals are one of the subtle communication strategies that politicians widely employ in their discourse (Catellani, 2011). Counterfactuals consist in the simulation of alternatives to actual scenarios or events, based on the modification of one or more elements in them (Roese, 1997). They are usually expressed through conditional propositions of the "if . . . then" type (e.g., "If you had taken effective measures to save the country's economy, citizens would be more satisfied with your government"). Counterfactuals may be also conveyed in other linguistic forms that may be brought back to the "if . . . then" type proposition. In this case, they are signaled by the presence of linguistic markers alluding to scenarios that never occurred in reality (e.g., *otherwise*, *though*) or to expectations that have not been met (e.g., *even*, *instead*; Catellani & Milesi, 2001; Davis, Lehman, Wortman, Silver, & Thompson, 1995; Sanna & Turley-Ames, 2000).

People spontaneously engage in counterfactual thinking when unexpected or undesired events occur. In these cases, they mentally simulate how the final result could have been better (or worse) if some prior event had gone differently. Research on counterfactual thinking showed that the events that are more likely to be counterfactually mutated are those deviating from the subjective *norm* (Kahneman & Miller, 1986), that is a routine or common course of action, such as leaving work at the same time every day or following the usual route to go back home. When something goes wrong (e.g., when a traffic jam or a car accident occurs), routine-breaking behaviors are easily detected, and counterfactual thinking is used to hypothetically restore the *normal* pattern to the desired outcome (e.g., "If I had taken the usual route home, I would not have had a car accident"). Perceived violations of a *social norm* are also likely to trigger counterfactual thinking. Stereotypical expectations about individuals or social groups and their behavior (e.g., gender roles) can become salient when generating hypothetical alternatives to an undesired event (Catellani, Alberici, & Milesi, 2004; Catellani & Milesi, 2005).

By focusing on norm-deviating behaviors and events, people also tend to overestimate their importance, ignoring or undervaluing other possible factors that contributed to the actual outcome. Several studies in social and cognitive psychology have demonstrated that counterfactual thinking is associated to event explanation and responsibility attribution (Markman & Tetlock, 2000; Nario-Redmond & Branscombe, 1996; Wells & Gavanski, 1989), as well as evaluations, emotions, and attitudes toward past events (Branscombe, Wohl, Owen, Allison, & N'gbala, 2003; Mandel & Dhami, 2005; Sevdalis & Kokkinaki, 2006; Van Dijk & Zeelenberg, 2005). In the study of these phenomena, two characteristics of counterfactuals assume special relevance, namely, their target and their direction. The *counterfactual target* is the individual or collective actor whose actions are mutated in the counterfactual antecedent (e.g., "If the *prime minister* had been more efficient . . ." or "If the *opposition* had kept its stance . . ."). The *counterfactual direction* has instead to do with the outcome of the hypothetically mutated antecedent. Such an outcome can be either more positive than the real outcome in *upward counterfactuals* (e.g., "our country would be in a *better* condition now") or more negative than the real outcome in *downward counterfactuals* (e.g., "our country would be in a *worse* condition now").

Past research has shown that the generation of upward counterfactuals leads to perceive the real event as more negative whereas the generation of downward counterfactuals leads to perceive the real event as less negative (Jones & Davis, 1965; Markman, Gavanski, Sherman, & McMullen, 1993; Medvec, Madey, & Gilovich, 1995; Sanna, Turley-Ames, & Meier, 1999). Besides, when a person is the target of upward counterfactuals, the same person is more likely to be perceived as responsible of the real event as compared with other actors involved in the event (Markman & Tetlock, 2000; Nario-Redmond & Branscombe, 1996; Wells & Gavanski, 1989). The generation of downward counterfactuals is instead associated with positive emotions (Markman et al., 1993; McMullen & Markman, 2000; Medvec et al., 1995; Sanna et al., 1999). When thinking about how things could have gone worse than they did, people usually feel comforted and reassured about their skill and ability to deal with negative situations (a "positive contrast effect"; McMullen, 1997; Roese, 1994).

If these are the consequences of counterfactual thoughts, one may figure out that counterfactuals can be effectively evoked in communication to attack other people and to defend oneself. Using counterfactual communication speakers can provide their audience with an easy and familiar way of explaining complex events (Kahneman & Tversky, 1982), and this may enhance the probability of such an explanation to be understood and agreed upon. As a matter of fact, however, studies on counterfactuals embedded in a communicative context and their effects on receivers' judgments have been scarce so far (Catellani et al., 2004; Tal-Or, Boninger, Poran, & Gleicher, 2004; Wong, 2010). To fill this gap, we carried out a series of studies to investigate the effects of counterfactuals when they are employed in attack and defense communication in the political context.

## THE EFFECTS OF COUNTERFACTUAL ATTACKS AND DEFENSES

### *Factual and Counterfactual Attacks*

Counterfactual communication can have some advantages over factual communication. For example, being a form of indirect communication, it may reduce the probability of backlash effect when used in an attack message. Besides, being formulated as hypothetical, counterfactual communication allows speakers to express their point of view without having to demonstrate its empirical foundations. An opposition leader could say "If the government had cut down on taxes, the national economy would be in a better condition," thus indirectly attacking the government, without going into a detailed explanation of how a proposed policy (i.e., cutting down on taxes) would have led to the desired outcome (i.e., improving the national economy).

In a series of studies (Catellani & Bertolotti, 2013a), we investigated the effect of factual and counterfactual attacks against a politician in an interview scenario. We created several versions of a fictional interview by a journalist to an incumbent prime minister. The interview dealt with the government's interventions on national economy and ended with a final critical statement by the journalist, varying as to attack style and attack dimension. As to the *attack style,* the journalist used either a *factual attack* or a *counterfactual attack*. In the former case, the attack was expressed in a very blunt and straightforward manner (e.g., "You acted incorrectly on the fiscal problem"). In the latter case, the attack was instead expressed in a more subtle manner, stating how things might have been better if the politician had acted in a different way (e.g., "If you had acted correctly on the fiscal problem, our country would be in a better condition today"). As to the *attack dimension,* both factual and counterfactual attacks were either against the politician's *leadership* (e.g., "You shied away from the fiscal problem") or against the politician's *morality* (e.g., "You misrepresented the problem of taxation burdens"). After reading the interview, participants were asked to evaluate both the politician and the journalist, as well as to judge the journalist's attack indicating how convincing, relevant, intelligent, and polite they found it.

In the case of morality attacks, factual attacks yielded a more negative evaluation of the journalist as compared with counterfactual attacks. Evidently, factual attacks were attributed to the attack source being biased against the politician and ended up with backfiring on the source (see also Carraro et al., 2010; Haddock & Zanna, 1997; Hill, 1989; Roese & Sande, 1993). Counterfactual attacks, on the other hand, did not trigger such negative reaction against the source and succeeded in negatively affecting the evaluation of the target politician. As already discussed in this volume (see Chapters 10 and 11), when evaluating others, people tend to focus on the morality dimension. This is true also in the political domain (Cislak & Wojciszke, 2008), where citizens are understandably concerned about their representatives' reliability and trustworthiness. Consistently, we found morality-based attacks to have a stronger effect than leadership-attacks, but only when they were made in indirect, counterfactual terms.

These results provide some insight on how citizens perceive attacks against politicians. Negative information about politicians seems to prompt receivers to make inferences about the source's intentions, even when the source is allegedly neutral such as in the case of a journalist. This prevents the more straightforward attacks against politicians to negatively influence receivers' attitudes toward them. Although in principle counterfactual attacks are less conclusive than direct attacks, as they are formulated in "if . . . then" conditional clauses, they turn out to be more effective. Thanks to their indirectness, they more easily avoid the backlash commonly elicited by attacks.

### Factual and Counterfactual Defenses

Like attacks, defenses may also be expressed in a more or less direct way. In another series of studies (Catellani & Bertolotti, 2013b), we investigated the effect of factual and counterfactual statements used by politicians to defend themselves. We created different versions of an interview scenario similar to the one used in studies quoted above. The text consisted in a one-page exchange between a journalist and a former prime minister running for reelection, discussing the current state of the economy. After a couple of negative comments by the journalist, the politician made a final defensive statement, which varied across the conditions of the various studies. After the participants had read the text, we asked their evaluation of the politician and their responsibility attribution for the negative economic conditions discussed in the interview. We expected these judgments to vary depending on the politician's defense.

In one of the studies, we tested two opposite defensive scenarios. In one case, the politician blamed the opposition for the government's alleged insufficient results, a defense that may be defined as *denial-attack* (based on McGraw's [1990] typology of political defensive statements). In the other case, the politician admitted that the government's results were not positive, a defense that may be defined as *concession*. Both factual and counterfactual formulations of the two defensive strategies were used, thus providing participants in the different experimental conditions with factual denial-attack (e.g., "The opposition did not revise its ideological stance and it did not keep members of its extreme wing under control"), counterfactual denial-attack (e.g., "Things would have been better, if the opposition had revised its ideological stance and if it had kept members of its extreme wing under control"), factual concession (e.g., "I did not state my position firmly enough and I did not fully implement my own ideas"), or counterfactual concession (e.g., "Things would have been better, if I had stated my position firmly enough and if I had fully implemented my own ideas").

On the one hand, one would expect a concession to be hardly an effective way of defending from criticism. On the other hand, politicians who openly blame others for their poor results risk being perceived as more interested in promoting themselves than working for their country's good. In both cases, our expectation was that politicians using counterfactual statements would defend themselves more effectively than politicians using factual statements.

Results showed that, compared with participants in the factual defense conditions, participants in the counterfactual defense conditions attributed less responsibility for the bad economic results to the politician and overall evaluated the politician better. This was particularly evident in the case of denial-attacks. Focusing counterfactuals on the opposition effectively shifted responsibility attribution away from the defending politician, inducing receivers to think of how things might have been better if someone else (the opposition, in this case) had behaved differently. These findings indicate that counterfactual communication may adequately serve the aim of shifting responsibility for a negative event or outcome on to someone else, as compared with more explicit modes of communication. As in the case of attacks, also in the case of denial-attacks, receivers are not likely to accept argumentations coming from a source too blatantly blaming other people for their faults. Counterfactuals may help disguising the speaker's communicative intention, thus making receivers less vigilant and, potentially, more easily persuadable (Brehm, 2000; see also Chapter 3, this volume).

### Upward and Downward Counterfactual Defenses

In a further study, we varied the direction of the counterfactual defense and compared self-focused *upward* counterfactuals (e.g., "Things would have been *better*, if I had stated my position firmly enough and if I had fully implemented my own ideas") with self-focused *downward* counterfactuals (e.g., "Things would have been *worse*, if I had hesitated to state my position firmly enough and if I had not fully implemented my own ideas"). According to McGraw's (1990) typology of defensive statements, we thus compared a *concession*, in which the person partially admits responsibility for the negative event, with a *justification*, in which the person tries to reduce the seriousness of the event.

As mentioned above, whereas the generation of upward counterfactuals increases the perceived negativity of the actual event, the generation of downward counterfactuals decreases it (Jones & Davis, 1965; Markman et al., 1993; Medvec et al., 1995; Sanna et al., 1999). When used as a defense, comparing an actual negative outcome with an even more negative hypothetical one can presumably put the actual outcome in a more positive light, through a contrast effect. In other words, downward, self-focused defenses can be used to provide the audience a negative, albeit purely hypothetical, comparison term. This would in turn induce the audience to be somewhat indulgent toward the actual results one is accounting for, as a more negative element is made salient.

We therefore expected downward counterfactuals to be a useful defensive strategy and our results confirmed that self-focused downward counterfactuals lead to a better evaluation of the defending politician than self-focused upward counterfactuals. A defense based on downward counterfactuals successfully directs receivers' attention to a worse scenario, thus making the actual scenario comparatively less negative. This in turn leads to a more positive evaluation of the person held responsible for it.

### Individual Differences

One may wonder whether the effectiveness of indirect messages in political communication varies according to some characteristics of the receiver. In our analysis, we took into account two characteristics of the receivers that might interfere with political communication, namely, ideology and political sophistication. The first may vary receivers' motivation to listen and accept what politicians say, whereas the second may vary receivers' ability to understand politicians and interpret their purposes.

In some of our studies on counterfactual attacks and defenses, we manipulated the ideology of politicians being attacked or defending themselves and measured the ideology of the participants (Catellani & Bertolotti, 2013a, 2013b). Consistent with the widespread phenomenon of *partisan bias* (see Bartels, 2002), we found that participants gave a better evaluation of politicians sharing their ideology. However, no interaction with either attack or defense style was found. For example, downward counterfactual defenses turned out to be more effective than upward ones regardless of the ideological similarity or dissimilarity between participants and the politician.

We also investigated (Bertolotti, Catellani, Douglas, & Sutton, 2013) the potential moderating effect of political sophistication, intended as a composite of political interest, knowledge, and media use (Luskin, 1990). Research on political information processing indicates that political sophistication can alter the way people evaluate information about political events, the degree of scrutiny in the elaboration of persuasive messages (McGraw et al., 2002), and the way they perceive and evaluate political candidates (Funk, 1997). In our studies, we found that political sophistication moderated the effects of upward and downward counterfactual defenses on the perception of one personality dimension in particular, that is, the morality of politicians. Participants with a low level of political sophistication attributed higher morality to the politician employing a downward counterfactual defense ("Things would have been worse, if I . . ."), whereas participants with a high level of political sophistication attributed higher morality to the politician employing an upward counterfactual defense ("Things would have been better, if I . . ."). More generally, less sophisticated participants found downward comparison convincing in restoring both the politician's leadership and the politician's morality. Things were partially different for more sophisticated participants. They attributed higher leadership to the politician using downward comparison, but attributed higher morality to the politician using upward comparison.

The communicative intention attributed to the politician mediated the positive effect of upward counterfactuals and, conversely, the negative effect of downward ones among highly sophisticated participants. Upward counterfactuals, stating how things might have been better if the politician had acted differently, were seen as a form of responsibility taking, an intention denoting some degree of morality. Downward counterfactuals, focusing on how things might have been even worse, on the other hand, were seen as a form of deceptiveness and negatively regarded in terms of morality.

These findings bring us back to the already mentioned issue of receivers' pragmatic inferences about communication. The less sophisticated tend to take the message at face value and let the politician reduce the negativity of the current events with strategically crafted downward comparisons. On the contrary, the more sophisticated base their assessment of politicians' morality on a more complex examination of defensive messages. Despite being less persuading per se, an upward counterfactual defense is recognized as not having a deceptive intent and indicates that the politician is more willing to take responsibility for past actions. Sophisticated citizens, in other words, base their judgments not only on how politicians present their results, but also on their understanding of politicians' communicative intention in presenting them.

## CONCLUSIONS

Results from our research contribute to an understanding of how the use of subtle linguistic strategies in political communication may influence citizens' judgments and attributions. We focused on the effects of counterfactual attacks and defenses, which prove *useful* for politicians in two ways. On the one hand, they allow them to avoid full commitment in their statements, and this may prove to be an advantage especially in the case of less socially accepted statements, such as attacking adversaries or blaming them for their failures. On the other hand, they can be used as an effective argumentation to influence citizens' responsibility attributions, as well as the explanation of actual events and situations.

Our results suggest that the effectiveness of indirect language employed by politicians is not reduced by otherwise strong and pervasive evaluative biases such as partisan bias. It is, however, moderated by the political sophistication of the receivers. We found that receivers with a high level of political sophistication are able to make complex inferences based on politicians' communication. They recognize the persuasive purpose of politicians' messages and accordingly make leadership and morality attributions. Receivers with a lower level of political sophistication are less capable to do so. This finding indicates that people with lower understanding of the subtle dynamics of political communication make less accurate judgments about politicians, which may bias their voting decisions. As it is the case for any kind of communication exchange, a sound political communication needs a common ground being shared by politicians and citizens. When this common ground is missing (e.g., when citizens lack familiarity with political communication rules), politicians are able to pursue their communicative agendas without citizens being fully aware of them. Doing so, they can break the rules of the collaborative inference games that provide meaning and context to communication, driving citizens toward the desired attributions and judgments (Fiedler, 2007).

These results also contribute to our understanding of the social factors influencing epistemic vigilance in communication (see also Chapter 8, this volume). In general, political communication has little effect on people's beliefs (and therefore on their attitudes), as citizens approach it with caution or even suspicion. Counterfactual communication may be used to bypass such preemptive filter, as its "if . . . then" formulation does not explicitly request receivers to believe the content of a statement. Receivers may perceive counterfactual communication coming from politicians as a harmless invitation to engage in hypothetical considerations, rather than a socially intrusive persuasive attempt.

Future research may investigate whether the same effects of counterfactual attacks and defenses can be found also beyond the political realm taken into account here. As we stated in the introduction, attacks and defenses play a particularly relevant role in political impression formation and management. However, accounting for one's past behavior, presenting oneself in a positive light (or conversely presenting someone else in a negative light), and more generally, trying to exert an influence on other peoples' impressions are common communicative tasks in a range of social contexts and situations. We could reasonably expect the features of counterfactual communication we analyzed in the political context to have at least partially similar effects in other contexts. At the same time, the pragmatic constraints that differentiate the political context from other contexts should be taken into account because they may influence the cognitive and social processes triggered by counterfactual communication. For example, although a counterfactual defense based on denial of responsibility by shifting it on to the adversaries was evidently effective in the context of political public speaking, it might not be equally effective in more informal, interpersonal communication. To conclude, thanks to the present and possible future developments, the study of counterfactual communication can contribute to expanding our knowledge of the complex and multifaceted relations between communication, individual cognitive processes, and the social context.

## REFERENCES

Bartels, L. M. (2002). Beyond the running tally: Partisan bias in political perceptions. *Political Behavior, 24,* 117–150.

Bavelas, J. B., Black, A., Bryson, L., & Mullett, J. (1988). Political equivocation: A situational explanation. *Journal of Language and Social Psychology, 7,* 137–145.

Benoit, W. L., & Hartcock, A. (1999). Functions of the great debates: Acclaims, attacks, and defense in the 1960 presidential debates. *Communication Monographs, 66,* 341–357.

Bertolotti, M., Catellani, P., Douglas, K., & Sutton, R. M. (2013). The "big two" in political communication: The effects of attacking and defending politicians' leadership and morality. *Social Psychology, 44,* 117–128.

Beukeboom, C. J., Finkenauer, C., & Wigboldus, H. J. (2010). The negation bias: When negations signal stereotypic expectancies. *Journal of Personality and Social Psychology, 99,* 978–992.

Branscombe, N. R., Wohl, M. J., Owen, S., Allison, J. A., & N'gbala, A. (2003). Counterfactual thinking, blame assignment, and well-being in rape victims. *Basic and Applied Social Psychology, 25,* 265–273.

Brehm, J. W. (2000). Reactance. In A. E. Kazdin (Ed.), *Encyclopedia of psychology* (Vol. 7, pp. 10–12). Washington, DC: American Psychological Association.

Bull, P. E. (2000). Equivocation and the rhetoric of modernization: An analysis of televised interviews with Tony Blair in the 1997 British General Election. *Journal of Language and Social Psychology, 19,* 222–247.

Bull, P. E. (2008). Slipperiness, evasion and ambiguity. Equivocation and facework in noncommittal political discourse. *Journal of Language and Social Psychology, 27,* 333–344.

Bull P. E., & Mayer, K. (1993). How not to answer questions in political interviews. *Political Psychology, 14,* 651–666.

Carraro, L., Gawronski, B., & Castelli, L. (2010). Losing on all fronts: The effects of negative versus positive person-based campaigns on implicit and explicit evaluations of political candidates. *British Journal of Social Psychology, 49,* 453–470.

Catellani, P. (2011). Counterfactuals in the social context: The case of political interviews and their effects. In D. Birke, M. Butter, & T. Koeppe (Eds.), *Counterfactual thinking-counterfactual writing* (pp. 81–94). Berlin, Germany: De Gruyter.

Catellani, P., Alberici, A. I., & Milesi, P. (2004). Counterfactual thinking and stereotypes: The nonconformity effect. *European Journal of Social Psychology, 34,* 421–436.

Catellani, P., & Bertolotti, M. (2013a). *The effects of factual and counterfactual attacks on morality: The case of politicians.* Manuscript submitted for publication.

Catellani, P., & Bertolotti, M. (2013b). *The effects of counterfactual defences.* Manuscript under review.

Catellani, P., & Milesi, P. (2001). Counterfactuals and roles: Mock victims' and perpetrators' accounts of judicial cases. *European Journal of Social Psychology, 31,* 247–264.

Catellani, P., & Milesi, P. (2005). When the social context frames the case: Counterfactuals in the courtroom. In D. Mandel, D. Hilton, & P. Catellani (Eds.), *The psychology of counterfactual thinking* (pp. 183–198). London, England: Routledge.

Cislak, A., & Wojciszke, B. (2008). Agency and communion are inferred from actions serving interests of self or others. *European Journal of Social Psychology, 37,* 1103–1110.

Davis, C. G., Lehman, D. R., Wortman, C. B., Silver, R. C., & Thompson, S. C. (1995). The undoing of traumatic life events. *Personality and Social Psychology Bulletin, 21,* 109–124.

Douglas, K. M., & Sutton, R. M. (2003). Effects of communication goals and expectancies on language abstraction. *Journal of Personality and Social Psychology, 84,* 682–696.

Douglas, K. M., & Sutton, R. M. (2006). When what you say about others says something about you: Language abstraction and inferences about describers' attitudes and goals. *Journal of Experimental Social Psychology, 42,* 500–508.

Douglas, K. M., Sutton, R. M., & Wilkin, K. (2008). Could you mind your language? An investigation of communicators' ability to inhibit linguistic bias. *Journal of Language and Social Psychology, 27,* 123–139.

Fiedler, K. (2007). *Social communication.* New York, NY: Psychology Press.

Funk, C. L. (1997). Implications of political expertise in candidate trait evaluations. *Political Research Quarterly, 50,* 675–697.

Gomez, B. T., & Wilson, J. M. (2001). Political sophistication and economic voting in the American electorate: A theory of heterogeneous attribution. *American Journal of Political Science, 45,* 899–914.

Haddock, G., & Zanna, M. (1997). Impact of negative advertising on evaluations of political candidates: The 1993 Canadian federal election. *Basic and Applied Social Psychology, 19,* 205–223.

Hill, R. P. (1989). An exploration of voter responses to political advertisements. *Journal of Advertising, 18,* 14–22.

Hornsey, M. J., Robson, E., Smith, J., Esposo, S., & Sutton, R. M. (2008). Sugaring the pill: Assessing rhetorical strategies designed to minimize defensive reactions to group criticism. *Human Communication Research, 34,* 70–98.

Jones, E. E., & Davis, K. E. (1965). From acts to dispositions: The attribution process in person perception. In L. Berkowitz (Ed.), *Advances in experimental social psychology* (Vol. 2, pp. 219–266). New York, NY: Academic Press.

Kahneman, D., & Miller, D. T. (1986). Norm theory: Comparing reality to its alternatives. *Psychological Review, 93,* 136–153.

Kahneman, D., & Tversky, A. (1982). The simulation heuristic. In D. Kahneman, P. Slovic, & A. Tversky (Eds.), *Judgment under uncertainty: Heuristics and biases* (pp. 201–208). New York, NY: Cambridge University Press.

Kaid, L. L., & Holtz-Bacha, C. (Eds.). (2008). *The encyclopedia of political communication.* Thousand Oaks, CA: Sage.

Kim, P., Dirks, K., Cooper, C., & Ferrin, D. (2006). When more blame is better than less: The implications of internal vs. external attributions for the repair of trust after a competence- vs. integrity-based trust violation. *Organizational Behavior and Human Decision Processes, 99,* 49–65.

Kuklinski, J. (Ed.). (2001). *Citizens and politics. Perspectives from political psychology.* Cambridge, England: Cambridge University Press.

Luskin, R. (1990). Explaining political sophistication. *Political Behavior, 12,* 331–361.

Maass, A., Salvi, D., Arcuri, L., & Semin, G. R. (1989). Language use in intergroup contexts: The linguistic intergroup bias. *Journal of Personality and Social Psychology, 57,* 981–993.

Mandel, D., & Dhami, M. (2005). "What I did" versus "what I might have done": Effect of factual versus counterfactual thinking on blame, guilt, and shame in prisoners. *Journal of Experimental Social Psychology, 41,* 627–635.

Markman, K. D., Gavanski, I., Sherman, S. J., & McMullen, M. N. (1993). The mental simulation of better and worse possible worlds. *Journal of Experimental Social Psychology, 29,* 87–109.

Markman, K. D., & Tetlock, P. E. (2000). 'I couldn't have known': Accountability, foreseeability and counterfactual denials of responsibility. *British Journal of Social Psychology, 39,* 313–325.

McGraw, K. M. (1990). Avoiding blame: An experimental investigation of political excuses and justifications. *British Journal of Political Science, 20,* 119–131.

McGraw, K. M. (1991). Managing blame: An experimental test of the effects of political accounts. *The American Political Science Review, 85,* 1133–1157.

McGraw, K. M. (2003). Political impressions. In D. O. Sears, L. Huddy, & R. Jervis (Eds.), *Oxford handbook of political psychology.* New York, NY: Oxford University Press.

McGraw, K. M., Lodge, M., & Jones, J. (2002). The pandering politicians of suspicious minds. *Journal of Politics, 64,* 362–383.

McMullen, M. N. (1997). Affective contrast and assimilation in counterfactual thinking. *Journal of Experimental Social Psychology, 33,* 77–100.

McMullen, M. N., & Markman, K. D. (2000). Downward counterfactuals and motivation: The wake-up call and the pangloss effect. *Personality and Social Psychology Bulletin, 26,* 575–584.

Medvec, V. H., Madey, S. F., & Gilovich, T. (1995). When less is more: Counterfactual thinking and satisfaction among Olympic medalists. *Journal of Personality and Social Psychology, 69,* 603–610.

Nario-Redmond, M., & Branscombe, N. (1996). It could have been better or it might have been worse: Implications for blame assignment in rape cases. *Basic and Applied Social Psychology, 18,* 347–366.

Roese, N. J. (1994). The functional basis of counterfactual thinking. *Journal of Personality and Social Psychology, 66,* 805–818.

Roese, N. J. (1997). Counterfactual thinking. *Psychological Bulletin, 121,* 133–148.

Roese, N. J., & Sande, G. N. (1993). Backlash effect in attack politics. *Journal of Applied Social Psychology, 23,* 632–653.

Sanna, L. J., & Turley-Ames, K. J. (2000). Counterfactual intensity. *European Journal of Social Psychology, 30,* 273–296.

Sanna, L. J., Turley-Ames, K. J., & Meier, S. (1999). Mood, self-esteem, and simulated alternatives: Thought-provoking affective influences on counterfactual direction. *Journal of Personality and Social Psychology, 76,* 543–558.

Semin, G. R., & Fiedler, K. (1988). The cognitive functions of linguistic categories in describing persons: Social cognition and language. *Journal of Personality and Social Psychology, 54,* 558–568.

Sevdalis, N., & Kokkinaki, F. (2006). The differential effect of realistic and unrealistic counterfactual thinking on regret. *Acta Psychologica, 122,* 111–128.

Tal-Or, N., Boninger, D. S., Poran, A., & Gleicher, F. (2004). Counterfactual thinking as a mechanism in narrative persuasion. *Human Communication Research, 30,* 301–328.

Van Dijk, E., & Zeelenberg, M. (2005). On the psychology of 'if only': Regret and the comparison between factual and counterfactual outcomes. *Organizational Behavior and Human Decision Processes, 97,* 152–160.

Wänke, M. (2007). What is said and what is meant: Conversational implicatures in natural conversations, research settings, media, and advertising. In K. Fiedler (Ed.), *Social communication* (pp. 223–256). New York, NY: Psychology Press.

Wells, G. L., & Gavanski, I. (1989). Mental simulation of causality. *Journal of Personality and Social Psychology, 56,* 161–169.

Wigboldus, D. H. J., Semin, G. R., & Spears, R. (2000). How do we communicate stereotypes? Linguistic bases and inferential consequences. *Journal of Personality and Social Psychology, 78,* 5–18.

Wigboldus, D. H. J., Semin, G. R., & Spears, R. (2006). Communicating expectancies about others. *European Journal of Social Psychology, 36,* 815–824.

Wong, E. M. (2010). It could have been better: The effects of counterfactual communication on impression formation. *European Journal of Social Psychology, 40,* 1251–1260.

# 17

# Social Factors That Affect the Processing of Minority-Sourced Persuasive Communications

WILLIAM D. CRANO AND EUSEBIO M. ALVARO

It is through the process of verbal communication and persuasion that cultures progress and historical inventions exert their inexorable force on society. Remarkably, such profound historical change often occurs as a result of persuasive messages received from minorities that exert their influence through their persistence and the power and truth of their arguments. As several chapters in the volume illustrate, historical narratives play a powerful role in shaping the way entire cultures and subgroups within those cultures view themselves (see also Chapters 12, 13, 14, 15, and 16, this volume). Linking these narratives to the role of minority groups as agents of social change is the goal of this chapter.

It is commonplace for historians of science to acknowledge the near inescapable conclusion that the adoption of a scientific mindset was a fundamental ingredient in the social, political, and intellectual ascent of the West. These *Whig-centric* historic accounts, as they have been characterized, reach their apogee in the writings of Timothy Ferris, who viewed the rise of the scientific method in the West not as an effect of the Enlightenment, but as the necessary cause of social progress and the growth of freedom and human dignity that characterized this period of incredible ferment (Ferris, 2010). He contended the standard account, in which the Renaissance gave rise to the scientific revolution, which ultimately resulted in the Enlightenment, was shortsighted and causally backward. Rather, pride of place belonged to the scientists and protoscientists whose insights, which grew out of an elemental break in the ways in which the world was understood, at least in the West, made the Renaissance possible. The transformation of Western science was made possible by the more ready availability of books and translations, communication in short, which served as a continuing stimulus to new visions, despite the efforts of the establishment to reign-in or control it. Western democracies and the recognition of inalienable human rights did not emerge magically through an aberrant conjunction of humanistic and scientific thought; rather, science gave rise to the possibility of the Renaissance, the Enlightenment, and all that followed.[1]

Ferris consistently emphasized the primacy of the experiment, because the logic and openness of the experiment, with its insistence on data-constrained feedback rather than preordained authority, fostered an unyielding and unremitting reliance on objective evidence in defining truth (Crano & Lac, 2012). The experiment's nonnegotiable and obstinate requirement of a *special* kind of knowledge of truth unprivileged by hereditary succession, divine right, or other forms of authority was resisted by the often incompetent and always self-interested leaders of societies engineered to maintain established positions of wealth and power.

## *Persuasion and Human Progress*

If the experiment is the essential precondition of enlightenment, and science the mother of all good things (liberty, fraternity, equality), then persuasion is the necessary and irreplaceable engine of human progress, the indispensable implement of human social development; for without persuasion, it is unlikely that the common person could be induced willingly to abandon the security of the known for the unknown, to give up the comfort of blind faith for the tempered conclusions of science. Arguably, it was through communication and persuasive speech, the power of words, (Chapters 2 and 3, this volume) founded on logic and reason, and replicated empirical results that the West ascended from the Dark Ages. There is no doubt that social revolutions are not won by rhetoric alone—although at one point in his life, Robespierre might have begged to differ—but they may be begun and sustained by persuasive communication that carries the necessary appeal for radical change, encouraging and maintaining the new orthodoxy (Chapter 14, this volume).

Given the importance of communication and persuasion as fundamental to much of what we hold dear, it is useful to understand something about the process. As persuasion is the central defining feature of social psychology, it is reasonable that we take a stab at its characterization (Crano, 2000a; Crano & Prislin, 2008). The process of persuasion is neither good nor evil in and of itself, it is merely a tool. As such, it is not usefully judged in moral terms, although certainly the results of the persuasion process may, and should be. Leni Riefenstahl's *Triumph of the Will,* a blatantly propagandistic film glorifying the Nazi Party at its 1934 rally in Nuremberg, served wholly immoral ends, but one can only judge as brilliant the communication processes she brought to bear in the work. The persuasive methods used in the film helped reinforce a hateful, immoral group of unadulterated thugs, but the process itself was morally neutral. The same persuasive processes could be used to encourage organ donation or to prevent illicit drug use—admiral goals, but as before, even in these circumstances the processes themselves cannot be judged as good or evil.

### *Persuasion and Attitudes*

To attain a better grip on the processes of communication and persuasion, it is important to consider their focus, namely, attitudes. Hundreds of definitions of attitude may be found in the psychological literature, and this is as it should be, as it reflects the centrality of the construct to the field (Campbell, 1963; McGuire, 1985). In Crano and Prislin's (2006) terms, an attitude is "an integration of cognitions and affects experienced in relation to an object" (p. 347). An attitude is a complex cognitive structure, an evaluation that involves knowledge of an object and a judgment of the goodness (or badness) of the object conditioned by that knowledge. The evaluative nature of attitudes is central to this view, as it was at the beginning, when Thurstone (1931) laid out the techniques used to define them objectively. This view suggests that to effect change, one must alter either the knowledge associated with an attitude object or the perceived evaluation of the implications of that knowledge.

Persuasion refers to the act of inducing another to adopt a belief that is different from an established one. This definition requires that the proffered attitude or belief is different from that held by the persuasion target. This requirement distinguishes persuasion from other forms of influence. It constrains the focus of our discussion so as to exclude considerations of conditioning, evaluative or otherwise, which are considered by many as methods of attitude formation rather than change (Cacioppo, Marshall-Goodell, Tassinary, & Petty, 1992). Further, we are primarily concerned with message-based persuasion, although acknowledging that many other methods of changing beliefs are available to the skillful persuader.

## MINORITY INFLUENCE AND SOCIAL CHANGE

Our focus on persuasion as the engine of enlightened thought calls our attention to the persuasive power of minority groups. Societies in which all members are happy and satisfied are stagnant, unlikely to change, and probably nonexistent. Societies in which the discontent of the citizenry reaches a critical mass will change, even if blood must be spilled to do so. Any situation in which the ruling power is overthrown, peaceably or otherwise, may be considered an example of minority influence at work, even if the minority far outnumbers the ruling class, the power majority (Crano, 2012). Without minority discontent, it is difficult to envision the means by which social progress would occur. Systems in which the minority is denied a voice typically involve coercion and lack of due process. It is for this reason that in all of the research in social psychology devoted to the investigation of persuasion, studies focused on minority influence are most relevant to the furtherance of a free society. The impetus for social change begins with an idea contrary to that held, and often suppressed by the majority. The existence of such a process of minority-inspired social change and the diffusion of knowledge necessary to foster it is a hallmark of a democratizing society, although the minority's medicine often proves worse than the old majority's disease (Prislin, Sawicki, & Williams, 2011). It logically follows that the study of social change and social progress may be served best by understanding the processes by which minorities gain persuasive traction, and that is the goal of this work.

Serge Moscovici is primarily responsible for contemporary interest in the scientific study of minority influence. He claimed that minorities were the source of all social innovation. In his studies of minority group influence, Moscovici found that minority positions could prevail, but only if the minority was consistent, persistent, and unanimous when presenting its position (Moscovici, 1985; Moscovici, Lage, & Naffrechoux, 1969). Although the majority always has the upper hand in the influence game and usually can force compliance if it chooses to do so, its influence often (but not always) is fleeting (Crano, 2001; Crano & Alvaro, 1998a). Minority influence, on the other hand, although rarely direct, often may be observed on beliefs associated with, but distinguishable from, the target or focus of its persuasive message (Pérez & Mugny, 1987). When direct minority influence is found, it usually appears only after some time has passed (Crano & Chen, 1998; Wood, Lundgren, Ouellette, Busceme, & Blackstone, 1994), or on issues on which the majority has no vested interest (Crano & Hannula-Bral, 1994). The unusual pattern of immediate but indirect influence, and delayed direct (or focal) persuasion, is rarely found in majority-based influence research. The theoretical models proposed in the early days of minority research to explain this curious influence pattern succeeded in painting only part of the picture.

## THE LENIENCY CONTRACT MODEL

To make sense of the curious processes involved in minority influence, Crano and Alvaro (1998a) proposed a theoretical model that not only was consistent with the pattern of results found in earlier majority and minority influence studies, but also proffered predictions that anticipated the range of outcomes that might occur in studies in which various features of the minority and its actions varied. The overall predictive device, the context/comparison model (CCM), integrated features of social categorization theory (Abrams, 1999), inter- and intragroup relations (Crano & Hemovich, 2011; Tajfel, 1978, 1979), and classic persuasion theory (Hovland, Janis, & Kelley, 1963). It was designed to detail the circumstances in which the majority's attempts at influence would succeed and persist, succeed fleetingly, or fail entirely. It also laid out the conditions under which a minority would have an immediate direct or indirect effect, and conditions under which delayed focal effects would arise.

This chapter is an extension of the leniency contract, a central component of the CCM that is concerned with minority influence. We revisit our consideration of attitudinal associative networks, extend the model in adopting this perspective, and conceptualize attitude change as a process that unfolds over time in response to multiple persuasive messages. Moscovici (1985) critiqued attitude change research as being the study of the majority on hapless majorities, while ignoring the possibility of minority influence. A parallel critique can be leveled at the practice of studying attitudes in isolation and attitude change in response to a single persuasive communication. The dominant paradigm in attitude research with few exceptions has involved observation of the effects of a single treatment on change of an isolated attitude. Minority influence research suggests the need to address multiple associated attitudes, a suggestion that if followed could lead to important advances in understanding.

Considering indirect attitude change suggests the desirability of a broader conceptualization of the attitude change process, one that includes study of the effects of multiple messages on a focal issue and on the attitudes related to it. The minority influence research context provides a fertile venue for serious consideration of societal attitude change over time and may prove valuable in development of general and encompassing principles of social change. Our proposed extension of the CCM/leniency contract involves consideration of change as a process unfolding over time, in response to multiple messages. It proceeds from the view of attitudes as evaluations enmeshed in a complex structural network of associated evaluations.

The CCM relies heavily on the near-axiomatic proposition that attitudes, like knowledge, are interconnected in associative networks (Collins & Loftus, 1975; Fazio, Sanbonmatsu, Powell, & Kardes, 1986) typified by nodes interlinked via associative paths that vary in strength (Anderson, 1983; Fazio, 1986; Forgas, 2001; Greene, 1984; Smith, 1994; see also Chapter 4, this volume). This network is engaged upon the activation of a specific node (Anderson, 1983), and this initial activation spreads to other nodes within the network (Smith, 1998).[2] Although the strength of associative paths has been the subject of considerable theoretical and investigative work, the concept of node strength has been the subject of less study—especially in research on attitudes. An exception is found in the work of Pfau and colleagues in research on resistance to persuasion (Pfau et al., 2003, 2005). They contend that increased node strength enhances resistance to persuasion and stronger nodes exert greater influence in attitude networks.

## THE LENIENCY CONTRACT

A central component of the CCM, the leniency contract, provides a useful means of conceptualizing the processes by which a minority influences the majority, and not incidentally, the ways the majority wields influence (Alvaro & Crano, 1996, 1997; Crano, 2001, 2010; Crano & Alvaro, 1998a, 1998b; Crano & Hemovich, 2011; Crano & Seyranian, 2007, 2009).[3] We begin with the common situation in which a person or group holding an opinion at odds with that of the majority advances an idea and seeks to influence the opposition. From the perspective of the majority group members, this is not an unusual occurrence. Disagreements within groups, even highly entitative groups, are commonplace (Abrams & Hogg, 1999; Guinote, 2004; Hogg, 2012), but the question that springs to the mind of the majority group members in these contexts concerns the identity of the deviant information source. Is the aberrant position promoted by a fellow group member or by an outsider (in our terms, an out-group member)? The answer has much to do with the majority group's response, but the question is more complicated than it appears.

**Out-group minorities.** Obviously, minorities can be either in- or out-group, and the difference matters (Crano & Seyranian, 2007; David & Turner, 2001). Most minority influence research has implicitly cast minority sources as in-group, thus rendering results most applicable to intragroup influence contexts. When minorities are considered out-group, the insights drawn from theories on intergroup relations become more relevant. We have taken advantage of this possibility in our discussion of in- and out-group minorities. The danger of implicitly assuming the minority is in-group, as much research has done, is that this supposition masks strong differences that reside in the persuasive potential of one or another form of minority group. In-group minorities can prevail, and often do. Out-group minorities are not likely to do so, because unless they pose a serious threat to the in-group, they usually are dismissed, their views judged unimportant. If the out-group does pose a threat, the majority's response can be severe. In most circumstances, the out-group is not capable of threatening the viability of the majority, and as such, it generally will have little, if any influence on the majority (Alvaro & Crano, 1997; Clark & Maass, 1988a, 1988b).

**Judgmental considerations.** In some admittedly rare circumstances, an out-group minority can communicate in a way that persuades the majority to consider its position and accept its recommendations. These circumstances involve issues on which members of the majority believe there is an objective solution to a question that is at issue, and that the minority has (or can) provided that solution. In these cases, the opinion of the minority can prevail. Laughlin and Ellis (1986) referred such issues or tasks as *intellective*, "problems or decisions for which there exists a demonstrably correct answer" (p. 177). With questions having a "demonstrably correct answer," the in-group or out-group status of the minority will not affect the majority's acceptance of the proffered answer, *assuming* the majority does not recast the problem or decision as involving subjective preferences rather than objective reality. This would not seem a high bar, but research has shown that recasting an obviously objective issue as subjective is not difficult (Crano & Hannula-Bral, 1994; Gorenflo & Crano, 1989), so the out-group's job may be considerably harder than it might appear at first glance.

The upshot of this integration of in-group/out-group minority status with the subjective or objective nature of the issue is that out-group minorities can have influence, if conditions are right. Out-groups can move the majority, but only if the issue admits to a clear solution that the majority to that point had failed to find. The *eureka* effect supplies a useful example of such context. These circumstances are rare, however, and the minority's communicative influence can be upended by the majority's recasting the issue as involving subjective preference, or as working against the vested interests of the group. In those situations, the out-group's persuasive power is lost. Neglect of the subjective or objective nature of the persuasion context, or the in-group or out-group nature of the minority probably is partly responsible for the sometimes uneven and confusing results found in the literature on minority group influence.

**The in-group minority's tests.** In-group minorities have an easier time influencing the majority, but this is not to say that their road is simple, even though they are accepted by the majority as part of the larger collective (Chapter 6, this volume). If the in-group minority is to move the majority to its position, it must pass a series of tests, the first of which—is the minority in- or out-group?—has been considered. The second test has to do with the implications of the minority's message for the majority group's viability. If the minority's position promotes the decline or demise of the group, the majority will reject it. In-group minorities advocating a position that threatens the core group identity will elicit strong defense motivation from in-group majority members. Attitudes at the core of a group's identity are strong (Petty & Krosnick, 1995) and well-embedded in an attitudinal network. As such, the in-group majority influence targets will not yield, and will forcefully reject the advocated position—along with those advocating the position. In effect, this response relegates an ostensible in-group minority to out-group status, subject to devaluation and the constraints imposed on out-group members (Marques & Yzerbyt, 1988; Marques, Yzerbyt, & Leyens, 1988; Meindl & Lerner, 1984; see also Chapters 4 and 18, this volume). Majority members enjoy many benefits as a consequence of their position and are unlikely to accept positions that require them to surrender them.

There remain tests to pass even after the minority has persuaded the majority that its position is not so self-interested that its acceptance threatens the group's existence (see Chapter 19, this volume). The next test has to do with the quality of the minority's message. Research by Martin and Hewstone indicates that message quality is a key determinant of a minority's success, because relevant in-group minority communications are likely to be highly elaborated (Martin & Hewstone, 2001, 2008). A minority is unlikely to prevail, even if it passes all these tests, if it does not deliver a strong and persuasive message. A position conveyed in a weak message will not be persuasive under conditions of high elaboration, and the minority's influence will be forfeit (Petty & Cacioppo, 1986).

The leniency model mandates strong messages if the minority is to make a dent in the majority's armor, but even with strong messages, the likelihood of finding a direct association between the minority's appeal and the majority's response is minimal, unless the situation involves issues on which the majority has not developed a firm position on the issue. Usually, these involve issues of norm or attitude formation rather than attitude change (Crano & Hannula-Bral, 1994). In these circumstances, the minority can have an immediate and direct impact, but it should be understood that the issue must be one on which the majority has no position and does not see its interests at risk. In most other cases, the majority will not succumb directly to the minority's persuasive appeals.

## ATTITUDE CHANGE

What, then, of the prototypical persuasion scenario in which an established belief is targeted for change? Moscovici observed that majority group members were reluctant to respond favorably to minority appeals, for to do so suggests they had moved to the minority group. In the in-group minority case, the leniency contract demurs, as in-group minorities *are* part of the larger majority. Rather than being reluctant to identify with a minority in-group member, the contract suggests that majority group members are reluctant to be identified with a position that may be censured. Thus, the leniency model fosters the prediction that the most likely immediate outcome of a persuasive minority group that has passed all of the tests is an accommodation by the majority on an issue (or issues) related, but not identical to the focal issue. This avoids identification with a counter normative position while preserving the minority's membership in the group. An interesting example from earlier research showed that an opinion minority that argued for a liberalization of abortion laws apparently failed to persuade a staunchly pro-life audience; however, the audience was significantly more amenable to contraception than were those of a group that had heard the identical pro-abortion message attributed to either an out-group minority or the majority (Pérez & Mugny, 1987), despite the minority's message never having mentioned contraception. This result was replicated and extended by Alvaro and Crano (1997) and Crano and Chen (1998). In the earlier study, Alvaro and Crano (1997) showed the *apparent* or *perceived* relatedness of the issues was unnecessary to observe this cross-over of influence effect. They demonstrated that a strong in-group minority message arguing against allowing gay people to serve in the U.S. military, a position strongly opposed by the respondents, had very little effect. However, as predicted, it significantly affected subjects' attitudes toward gun control, an issue established in preliminary research as strongly associated with the focal issue. The impressive feature of this result is that participants themselves did not realize the two attitudes were linked in their associative networks, despite strong empirical evidence that this was the case. Reversing the focal and indirect issues in a follow-on study produced results that replicated the earlier findings.

Crano and Chen (1998) extended these results. Using different attitude objects, they demonstrated indirect majority attitude change in response to an in-group minority's persuasive communication. Focal change was notably absent. However, when revisited two weeks later, they found that the participants whose indirect attitudes had changed the most showed significant delayed focal change, even though the issue was not reinstated in the delayed measurement session. This result implies that the delayed focal change found in many earlier studies (Wood et al., 1994) might have been associated with the magnitude of immediate indirect attitude change.

The leniency interpretation of these studies—which show an immediate, but indirect change in response to a minority's persuasive message, sometimes followed by a delayed focal change—holds that majority members resist being identified with a minority-espoused position, because doing so puts them at the same risk as the minority—of becoming a target of a negative majority reaction. It is a mistake to interpret majority group members' reluctance to accept the minority's message because acceptance suggests identification with the minority. As in-group members, the minority and majority factions share a common identity. Majority group members *are* identified with the in-group minority.

The indirect changes found in these contexts occur because the majority, to maintain entitativity, rejects strong measures against a minority group that has passed the earlier tests. Majority members will elaborate the minority's message without strong counter argumentation or derogation, but the price to be paid for this open-minded response is the implicit agreement that no changes will ensue. The minority is allowed to state its case, the majority listens and elaborates, but stasis prevails. However, the open-minded elaboration of a strong counter attitudinal message is bound to have an effect, which is manifest in a change in related attitudes in the associative network. These changes ultimately unbalance the network and may result in focal change if the imbalance is sufficient. This accommodation requires time, and this is why focal change, when it occurs in response to minority influence, almost always is delayed.[4]

## CONSIDERATIONS OF MULTIPLE MESSAGES AND CHANGE OVER TIME

Crano and Chen's (1998) results provided some insights into the nature of the delayed change effect often reported in response to minority influence (Alvaro & Crano, 1996; Crano, 2000b; David & Turner, 1996, 1999; Gardikiotis, 2011; Mugny & Pérez, 1988). We now consider more thoroughly the impact of initial attitude change on subsequent outcomes. First, change is a process unfolding over time, likely subject to multiple messages advocating multiple (complementary) positions. Besides the potential for new discoveries inherent in this orientation, it comports with the reality of social change initiated by minority social actors and movements. Moreover, examining influence over time can revitalize minority influence research by taking a somewhat ironic step back via consideration of factors initially serving as the impetus for this research (Moscovici, 1985).

New social movements advance novel ideas. Over time, these ideas can become consensual and widely shared. What does theory and research in minority influence have to say about minority influence over time and via the use of multiple messages? Considerations of decay or persistence of initial change as well as of the impact of multiple messages are logical starting points. The former issue has garnered some serious, albeit sporadic, attention since the 1980s; the latter has seen more recent and increasing interest in the minority influence literature (Martin & Hewstone, 2008; Tormala, DeSensi, & Petty, 2007). Both issues benefit from an associative network perspective, as well as consideration of the roles of both direct and indirect attitudes subject to multiple messages.

A CCM-based view of the impact of multiple messages over time benefits from research on attitude stability and resistance following minority advocacy. The work of Martin and colleagues (Martin & Hewstone, 2001; Martin, Hewstone, & Martin, 2008) and that of Tormala and his coinvestigators (Tormala et al., 2007) recognizes the value of the resistance to change paradigm for investigating minority influence. Given the CCM's reliance on an associative network view of attitudes, Pfau and colleagues' work on inoculation to persuasion (Ivanov, Pfau, & Parker, 2009a, 2009b; Pfau et al., 2003, 2005), although not conducted in a minority influence context, sheds light on how attitude structure may influence responses to multiple messages.

## OVERCOMING RESISTANCE

An attitude network perspective can account for attitude certainty and articulates with recent research on resistance to persuasion (Tormala et al., 2007). Instability or uncertainty is introduced into the network as a result of indirect change. Inconsistencies among associated beliefs are sources of discomfort and uncertainty, and the stronger the associations among beliefs, the greater the uncertainty. More than five decades of research has convincingly shown that cognitive or attitudinal uncertainty is a state that most prefer to avoid (Festinger, 1957), so it stands to reason that conflicting attitudes linked in a network would prove an ideal matrix for uncertainty. Attitudes are particularly vulnerable to change when doubts are cast on certainties (Crano, Gorenflo, & Shackelford, 1988; Crano & Sivacek, 1984). When an attitude is changed, linked attitudes become more tentative, and this uncertainty renders these attitudes unstable and susceptible to change. If the minority's message is later recalled in this context of attitudinal uncertainty, it is likely to have a strong effect, especially if the communication source is dissociated from its message (Kelman & Hovland, 1953).

In this sense, *uncertainty* may be indicative of imbalance in the attitudinal network. Taking a positive frame uncertainly may also be an early signal of openness to seeing an issue in a different light—perhaps a precursor to Nemeth's divergent thinking (Nemeth & Kwan, 1985, 1987). We have held that indirect change engenders a destabilizing pressure that may rearrange interattitudinal relationships; uncertainty may be one manifestation of such pressure, as well as a precursor to subsequent delayed change on the focal attitude.

Considering uncertainty via an associative network orientation also may facilitate understanding of change by examining the role of individual node (attitude) strength as well as the strength of links between nodes (Pfau et al., 2005). As certainty has long been a proxy for attitude strength, it is logical to assume that introducing uncertainty into a node would result in a *weakened* node (or attitude) open to modification. Perhaps by introducing increasingly greater uncertainty into the various nodes in an attitudinal network, true and lasting change (conversion) is achieved. This also would seem to be a key process in *cognitive reorganization*, a long-discussed but under-explicated and little-investigated phenomenon that has played an explanatory role in many important consistency theories in social psychology (e.g., balance theory, cognitive dissonance, etc.).

The effects of minority influence, considered from an attitudinal network perspective, can be varied, distinct, and disparate. A minority-sourced message that is weak or delivered by an out-group will not persuade because it will not introduce uncertainty into the network. A moderately strong message attributed to an in-group minority may stimulate immediate and discernible change in an attitude (or attitudes) linked to the focus of the persuasion message, but the change might not be sufficient to cause a realignment of the associative network. In this case, no focal influence would be evident, and the indirect change itself would be ephemeral. Ultimately, the inertia of the belief system would pull the aberrant attitude back to its original position in the structure to reestablish equilibrium. Alternatively, the in-group minority may deliver a strong message capable of withstanding strong counterargumentation. Even in this circumstance, immediate direct (focal) change is unlikely. However, change in associated attitudes is common, and if it is of sufficient magnitude, will destabilize the focal attitude.

## CONCLUSIONS

The leniency contract predicts different outcomes of out-group minority influence when subjective or objective (or intellective) judgments are involved. Its predictions are more complex when the minority influence source is in-group. In research involving these subgroups, all possible outcomes can be predicted and have been obtained. In this chapter, we have attempted to support the model by considering the cognitive underpinnings of the unusual patterns of findings that characterize minority group influence research. The model outlined here is plausible and grounded in strong social and cognitive theories. The integration of an associationistic network orientation with a social group emphasis borrows from the strongest areas of social psychology and communication science, and facilitates development of a theoretical device of considerable explanatory power. We assume further research on the CCM will result in refinement and modification of the model, as all good research is designed to do, but believe that the general outlines of this predictive device will remain relatively intact.

Considerations outlined in the expanded CCM, besides being grounded in a diverse body of theory and research ranging from the macro (intra- and intergroup processes) to the micro (attitude networks), have the additional benefit of providing a theoretical perspective that comports with the observable reality of social change made in response to rising social movements. Social change—decidedly a persuasion outcome—is not a result of a stand-alone message delivered by a minority source to a recalcitrant privileged majority. Such a message may serve as the impetus for change and a galvanizing force that coalesces people around a common position, but it is through repeated interactions between a minority and its influence targets—interactions involving the delivery of multiple messages—that change occurs. The change that results from this process often becomes so imbedded and integrated that in retrospect, it seems difficult to believe that the newly arrived-at status quo is novel. This macrolevel integration reflects, and is rooted in, the more intraindividual interconnections among beliefs found within individual members of a collective. The expanded model of minority influence provides a theoretical basis from which macrolevel social changes can be extrapolated and explained.

Social change is inevitable, whether it is brought about by social upheaval invigorated by the power of an idea once whispered furtively but passionately in secret meeting rooms, or via more palatable democratic processes ideally typifying progressive societies. Given the centrality of minority discontent as the engine of social progress, we believe the study of minority influence is crucial if we seek to expand the possibility of achieving a society characterized by the ideals of freedom tempered with equality.

## NOTES

1. The basis of the budding scientific work found in the Renaissance was to be found in earlier writings from the Islamic Golden Age (AD 8th–15th centuries), whose translations formed the foundation for rapid scientific advance (Crano & Lac, 2012).
2. Although the strength of associate paths has been the subject of considerable theoretical debate and investigative research, the concept of node strength has been subject to considerably less consideration—especially in the study of attitudes. One exception is the work of Pfau and colleagues, which addressed resistance to persuasion. They contend that node strength is positively related to attitude durability (resistance) and that stronger nodes exert a greater impact within attitudinal networks (Pfau et al., 2003, 2005).
3. We are concerned here with minority influence, but for a description of differences in the processes activated in successful majority and minority influence, see Crano (2012).
4. If the indirect change is not great, the imbalance introduced into the network is not sufficient to cause a radical restructuring, and the indirectly changed attitude is likely to snap back to its original value (Crano & Chen, 1998).

## REFERENCES


Abrams, D. (1999). Social identity, social cognition, and the self: The flexibility and stability of self-categorization. In D. Abrams & M. A. Hogg (Eds.), *Social identity and social cognition* (pp. 197–229). Malden, MA: Blackwell.

Abrams, D., & Hogg, M. A. (1999). *Social identity and social cognition.* Malden, MA: Blackwell.

Alvaro, E. M., & Crano, W. D. (1996). Cognitive responses to minority- or majority-based communications: Factors that underlie minority influence. *British Journal of Social Psychology,* 35(1), 105–121.

Alvaro, E. M., & Crano, W. D. (1997). Indirect minority influence: Evidence for leniency in source evaluation and counterargumentation. *Journal of Personality and Social Psychology, 72,* 949–964.

Anderson, J. R. (1983). *The architecture of cognition.* Hillsdale, NJ: Erlbaum.

Cacioppo, J. T., Marshall-Goodell, B. S., Tassinary, L. G., & Petty, R. E. (1992). Rudimentary determinants of attitudes: Classical conditioning is more effective when

prior knowledge about the attitude stimulus is low than high. *Journal of Experimental Social Psychology, 28,* 207–233.
Campbell, D. T. (1963). Social attitudes and other acquired behavioral dispositions. In S. Koch (Ed.), *Psychology: A study of a science. Study II. Empirical substructure and relations with other sciences. Volume 6. Investigations of man as socius: Their place in psychology and the social sciences* (pp. 94–172). New York, NY: McGraw-Hill.
Clark, R. D., & Maass, A. (1988a). The role of social categorization and perceived source credibility in minority influence. *European Journal of Social Psychology, 18,* 381–394.
Clark, R. D., & Maass, A. (1988b). Social categorization in minority influence: The case of homosexuality. *European Journal of Social Psychology, 18,* 347–364.
Collins, A. M., & Loftus, E. (1975). A spreading activation theory of semantic memory. *Psychological Review, 82,* 407–428.
Crano, W. D. (2000a). Milestones in the psychological analysis of social influence. *Group Dynamics: Theory, Research, and Practice, 4,* 68–80.
Crano, W. D. (2000b). Social influence: Effects of leniency on majority- and minority-induced focal and indirect attitude change. *Revue Internationale de Psychologie Sociale, 13*(3), 89–121.
Crano, W. D. (2001). Social influence, social identity, and ingroup leniency. In C. K. W. De Dreu & N. K. De Vries (Eds.), *Group consensus and minority influence: Implications for innovation* (pp. 122–143). Malden, MA: Blackwell.
Crano, W. D. (2010). Majority and minority influence in attitude formation and attitude change: Context/categorization—leniency contract theory. In R. Martin & M. Hewstone (Eds.), *Minority influence and innovation: Antecedents, processes and consequences* (pp. 53–77). New York, NY: Psychology Press.
Crano, W. D. (2012). *The rules of influence.* New York, NY: St. Martin's Press.
Crano, W. D., & Alvaro, E. M. (1998a). The context/comparison model of social influence: Mechanisms, structure, and linkages that underlie indirect attitude change. In W. Stroebe & M. Hewstone (Eds.), *European review of social psychology* (Vol. 8, pp. 175–202). Hoboken, NJ: Wiley.
Crano, W. D., & Alvaro, E. M. (1998b). Indirect minority influence: The leniency contract revisited. *Group Processes & Intergroup Relations, 1*(2), 99–115.
Crano, W. D., & Chen, X. (1998). The leniency contract and persistence of majority and minority influence. *Journal of Personality and Social Psychology, 74,* 1437–1450.
Crano, W. D., Gorenflo, D. W., & Shackelford, S. L. (1988). Overjustification, assumed consensus, and attitude change: Further investigation of the incentive-aroused ambivalence hypothesis. *Journal of Personality and Social Psychology, 55*(1), 12–22.
Crano, W. D., & Hannula-Bral, K. A. (1994). Context/categorization model of social influence: Minority and majority influence in the formation of a novel response norm. *Journal of Experimental Social Psychology, 30,* 247–276.
Crano, W. D., & Hemovich, V. (2011). Intergroup relations and majority or minority group influence. In R. M. Kramer, G. J. Leonardelli, & R. W. Livingston (Eds.), *Social cognition, social identity, and intergroup relations: A Festschrift in honor of Marilynn B. Brewer* (pp. 221–246). New York, NY: Psychology Press.
Crano, W. D., & Lac, A. (2012). The evolution of research methodologies in (social) psychology. In A. Kruglanski & W. Stroebe (Eds.), *Handbook of the history of social psychology*. New York, NY: Psychology Press.
Crano, W. D., & Prislin, R. (2006). Attitudes and persuasion. *Annual Review of Psychology, 57,* 345–374.
Crano, W. D., & Prislin, R. (2008). *Attitudes and attitude change.* New York, NY: Psychology Press.
Crano, W. D., & Seyranian, V. (2007). Majority and minority influence. *Social and Personality Psychology Compass, 1,* 572–589.

Crano, W. D., & Seyranian, V. (2009). How minorities prevail: The context/comparison-leniency contract model. *Journal of Social Issues, 65*, 335–363.

Crano, W. D., & Sivacek, J. (1984). The influence of incentive-arousal ambivalence on overjustification effects in attitude change. *Journal of Experimental Social Psychology, 20*(2), 137–158.

David, B., & Turner, J. C. (1996). Studies in self-categorization and minority conversion: Is being a member of the out-group an advantage? *British Journal of Social Psychology, 35*(1), 179–199.

David, B., & Turner, J. C. (1999). Studies in self-categorization and minority conversion: The in-group minority in intragroup and intergroup contexts. *British Journal of Social Psychology, 38*(2), 115–134.

David, B., & Turner, J. C. (2001). Majority and minority influence: A single process self-categorization analysis. In C. K. W. De Dreu & N. K. De Vries (Eds.), *Group consensus and minority influence: Implications for innovation* (pp. 91–121). Malden, MA: Blackwell.

Fazio, R. H. (1986). How do attitudes guide behavior? In R. M. Sorrentino & E. T. Higgins (Eds.), *The handbook of motivation and cognition: Foundations of social behavior* (pp. 204–243).

Fazio, R. H., Sanbonmatsu, D. M., Powell, M. C., & Kardes, F. R. (1986). On the automatic activation of attitudes. *Journal of Personality and Social Psychology, 50*, 229–238.

Ferris, T. (2010). *The science of liberty: Democracy, reason, and the laws of nature.* New York, NY: HarperCollins.

Festinger, L. (1957). *A theory of cognitive dissonance:* Stanford, CA: Stanford University Press.

Forgas, J. P. (2001). Introduction: The role of affect in social cognition. In J. P. Forgas (Ed.), *Feeling and thinking: The role of affect in social cognition* (pp. 1–28).

Gardikiotis, A. (2011). Minority influence. *Social and Personality Psychology Compass, 5*(9), 679–693.

Gorenflo, D. W., & Crano, W. D. (1989). Judgmental subjectivity/objectivity and locus of choice in social comparison. *Journal of Personality and Social Psychology, 57*, 605–614.

Greene, J. O. (1984). A cognitive approach to human communication: An action assembly theory. *Communication Monographs, 51*, 289–306.

Guinote, A. (2004). Group size, outcome dependency, and power: Effects on perceived and objective group variability. In V. Yzerbyt, C. M. Judd, & O. Corneille (Eds.), *The psychology of group perception: Perceived variability, entitativity, and essentialism* (pp. 221–236). New York, NY: Psychology Press.

Hogg, M. A. (2012). Uncertainty-identity theory. In P. A. M. Van Lange, A. W. Kruglanski, & E. T. Higgins (Eds.), *Handbook of theories of social psychology* (Vol. 2, pp. 62–80). Thousand Oaks, CA: Sage.

Hovland, C. I., Janis, I. L., & Kelley, H. H. (1963). *Communication and persuasion.* Oxford, England: Yale University Press.

Ivanov, B., Pfau, M., & Parker, K. A. (2009a). The attitude base as a moderator of the effectiveness of inoculation strategy. *Communication Monographs, 76*(1), 47–72.

Ivanov, B., Pfau, M., & Parker, K. A. (2009b). Can inoculation withstand multiple attacks? An examination of the effectiveness of the inoculation strategy compared to the supportive and restoration strategies. *Communication Research, 36*(5), 655–676.

Kelman, H. C., & Hovland, C. I. (1953). 'Reinstatement' of the communicator in delayed measurement of opinion change. *The Journal of Abnormal and Social Psychology, 48*(3), 327–335.

Laughlin, P. R., & Ellis, A. L. (1986). Demonstrability and social combination processes on mathematical intellective tasks. *Journal of Experimental Social Psychology, 22*, 177–189.

Marques, J. M., & Yzerbyt, V. Y. (1988). The black sheep effect: Judgmental extremity towards ingroup members in inter- and intra-group situations. *European Journal of Social Psychology, 18*(3), 287–292.

Marques, J. M., Yzerbyt, V. Y., & Leyens, J.-P. (1988). The 'black sheep effect': Extremity of judgments towards ingroup members as a function of group identification. *European Journal of Social Psychology, 18*(1), 1–16.

Martin, R., & Hewstone, M. (2001). Determinants and consequences of cognitive processes in majority and minority influence. In J. P. Forgas & K. D. Williams (Eds.), *Social influence: Direct and indirect processes* (pp. 315–330). New York, NY: Psychology Press.

Martin, R., & Hewstone, M. (2008). Majority versus minority influence, message processing and attitude change: The source-context-elaboration model. In M. P. Zanna (Ed.), *Advances in experimental social psychology* (Vol. 49, pp. 238–326). New York, NY: Academic Press.

Martin, R., Hewstone, M., & Martin, P. Y. (2008). Majority versus minority influence: The role of message processing in determining resistance to counter-persuasion. *European Journal of Social Psychology, 38*(1), 16–34.

McGuire, W. J. (1985). Attitudes and attitude change. In G. Lindzey & E. Aronson (Eds.), *Handbook of social psychology* (3rd ed., Vol. 3, pp. 233–346). New York, NY: Random House.

Meindl, J. R., & Lerner, M. J. (1984). Exacerbation of extreme responses to an out-group. *Journal of Personality and Social Psychology, 47*(1), 71–84.

Moscovici, S. (1985). Social influence and conformity. In G. Lindzey & E. Aronson (Eds.), *Handbook of social psychology* (3rd ed., Vol. 2, pp. 347–412). New York, NY: Random House.

Moscovici, S., Lage, E., & Naffrechoux, M. (1969). Influence of a consistent minority on the responses of a majority in a color perception task. *Sociometry, 32,* 365–380.

Mugny, G., & Pérez, J. A. (1988). Conflicto intergrupal, validación e influencia minoritaria inmediata y diferida. *Revista de Psicología Social, 3*(1), 23–36.

Nemeth, C. J., & Kwan, J. L. (1985). Originality of word associations as a function of majority vs. minority influence. *Social Psychology Quarterly, 48*(3), 277–282.

Nemeth, C. J., & Kwan, J. L. (1987). Minority influence, divergent thinking and detection of correct solutions. *Journal of Applied Social Psychology, 17*(9), 788–799.

Pérez, J. A., & Mugny, G. (1987). Paradoxical effects of categorization in minority influence: When being an outgroup is an advantage. *European Journal of Social Psychology, 17,* 157–169.

Petty, R. E., & Cacioppo, J. T. (1986). *Communication and persuasion: Central and peripheral routes to attitude change.* New York, NY: Springer-Verlag.

Petty, R. E., & Krosnick, J. A. (1995). *Attitude strength: Antecedents and consequences.* Mahwah, NJ: Erlbaum.

Petty, R. E., Wegener, D. T., Fabrigar, L. R., Priester, J. R., & Cacioppo, J. T. (1993). Conceptual and methodological issues in the elaboration likelihood model of persuasion: A reply to the Michigan State critics. *Communication Theory, 3,* 336–362.

Pfau, M., Ivanov, B., Houston, B., Haigh, M., Sims, J., Gilchrist, E., . . . Richert, N. (2005). Inoculation and mental processing: The instrumental role of associative networks in the process of resistance to counterattitudinal influence. *Communication Monographs, 72,* 414–441.

Pfau, M., Roskos-Ewoldsen, D., Wood, M., Yin, S., Cho, J., Lu, K.-H., & Shen, L. (2003). Attitude accessibility as an alternative explanation for how inoculation confers resistance. *Communication Monographs, 70,* 39–51.

Prislin, R., Sawicki, V., & Williams, K. (2011). New majorities' abuse of power: Effects of perceived control and social support. *Group Processes & Intergroup Relations, 14,* 489–504.

Smith, E. R. (1994). Procedural knowledge and processing strategies in social cognition. In R. S. Wyer, Jr. & T. K. Srull (Eds.), *Basic processes* (Vol. 1, pp. 99–151).

Smith, E. R. (1998). Mental representation and memory. In D. T. Gilbert, S. T. Fiske, & G. Lindzey (Eds.), *The handbook of social psychology* (pp. 391–445).

Stiff, J. B., & Boster, F. J. (1987). Cognitive processing: Additional thoughts, and a reply to Petty, Kasmer, Haugtvedt, and Cacioppo. *Communication Monographs, 54,* 250–256.

Tajfel, H. (1978). *Differentiation between social groups: Studies in the social psychology of intergroup relations.* Oxford, England: Academic Press.

Tajfel, H. (1979). The exit of social mobility and the voice of social change: Notes on the social psychology of intergroup relations. *Przegl d Psychologiczny, 22,* 17–38.

Thurstone, L. L. (1931). The measurement of social attitudes. *The Journal of Abnormal and Social Psychology, 26,* 249–269.

Tormala, Z. L., DeSensi, V. L., & Petty, R. E. (2007). Resisting persuasion by illegitimate means: A metacognitive perspective on minority influence. *Personality and Social Psychology Bulletin, 33,* 354–367.

Wood, W., Lundgren, S., Ouellette, J. A., Busceme, S., & Blackstone, T. (1994). Minority influence: A meta-analytic review of social influence processes. *Psychological Bulletin, 115,* 323–345.

# 18

# Mechanisms of Linguistic Bias

## *How Words Reflect and Maintain Stereotypic Expectancies*

CAMIEL J. BEUKEBOOM

Stereotypes about people are widespread and play a crucial role in social perception and interaction. An important question is how stereotypic expectancies about social categories are transmitted and maintained interpersonally. Although stereotypes and prejudice may be shared explicitly (e.g., racist speech, derogatory group labels; Leets & Giles, 1997; Simon & Greenberg, 1996), most people disapprove of the explicit expression of stereotypes and especially racism (Castelli, Vanzetto, Sherman, & Arcuri, 2001; Monteith, 1993), and it appears that stereotypes are predominantly shared at a largely implicit level (see also Chapter 6, this volume). Research on linguistic bias has revealed a number of subtle systematic variations in language use that not only reflect stereotypic expectancies, but may also strengthen them in both sender and recipients. Research on this topic, however, has predominantly—and rather narrowly—focused on one linguistic aspect (i.e., language abstraction), where knowledge on other linguistic biases is scarce and scattered in the literature. This chapter reviews and aims to integrate the knowledge on the role of linguistic bias in stereotyping. It first reviews existing evidence for linguistic biases and the effects they have on recipients, the sender, and the collective. Subsequently, it discusses potential underlying mechanisms that these biases (may) have in common and explores future areas of research.

## EVIDENCE FOR LINGUISTIC BIAS: SYSTEMATIC VARIATIONS IN LANGUAGE USE

The area of language use in relation to stereotypes deals specifically with language used when describing people and their behavior. Stereotypic beliefs about the targets of these descriptions surface in subtle linguistic biases. A linguistic bias can be defined as a systematic asymmetry in word choice as a function of the social category to which the target belongs. It should be noted that it is not necessarily harmful, nor evidence of discrimination and prejudice when expectancies about people are reflected in language use. Linguistic biases result from, and facilitate the transmission of essentialist beliefs about social categories. Essentialist beliefs denote that members of a social category share a deep, underlying, inherent nature (*essence*), causing them to be fundamentally similar to one another and across situations (Carnaghi et al., 2008; Rhodes, Leslie, & Tworek, in press). To have—and share—such stable expectancies about people and social categories is often highly functional (Moskowitz, 2005). Yet, it may promote prejudice and discrimination when individuals are described and prejudged on (negative) stereotypic, rather than available individuating information. In this chapter, the term *bias* refers to all instances—harmful or not—in which language use is colored by existing stereotypic beliefs, where unbiased language is devoid of such influence. I distinguish between research on the use of labels to refer to social categories and their individual members, and on language used to describe their behavior.

### *Category Labels*

One area of research on linguistic bias focuses on the labels used to refer to (members of) social categories. Research on sexist language, for instance, is concerned with asymmetries in references to female and male persons as a function of gender stereotypes. In such references, a systematic bias in *markedness* has been observed, wherein expectancy inconsistent individuals are more explicitly marked or noted (Stahlberg, Braun, Irmen, & Sczesny, 2007; Romaine, 2001). More specific, when referring to female and male persons, who are in a role or occupation that is inconsistent with the stereotypically expected role for his or her gender, people tend to add an explicit mention of the person's sex (e.g., female surgeon, male nurse), where this does not occur when the person's sex fits the respective gender role.

The tendency to explicitly mark unexpected gender roles appears to be even reflected in lexical gaps. In these cases, the lexicon contains terms for stereotypically unexpected gender roles, but not for the expected (Stahlberg et al., 2007). For instance, the male term *family man* exists, but a female equivalent is lacking. Likewise, the label *career woman* has no male equivalent. Apparently taking care of the family is stereotypically unexpected for men, but self-evident for women. Having a career, in contrast, is unexpected for women, but expected for men (Romaine, 2001). Thus, the unexpected roles are marked, whereas their equivalent expressions (family woman, career man) are seemingly redundant as they refer to stereotypically expected and obvious situations.

A comparable asymmetry has been found in the use of more narrow labels for individuals who do not fit with general social category expectations. Individuals showing behavior that violates the general stereotype are referred to with labels that create a subcategory or subtype for the unexpected group (Devine & Baker, 1991). For example, with labels like *a nice Moroccan, a tough woman,* or *African-American businessman,* exceptions to the rule are placed in a new category that is narrower than the broad group (i.e., Moroccans, women, businessmen). For expectancy consistent individuals, however, the broad label is used.

Another systematic variation pertains the use of nouns compared with adjectives to describe a person. Nouns and adjectives can be exceedingly similar (e.g. being a Jew versus Jewish). Nevertheless, Carnaghi et al. (2008, Study 6) showed that the use of nouns (compared with adjectives) increased when participants believed that a described characteristic resulted from a stable genetically determined aspect of the target (increased essentialism), rather than a transient, situationally determined property. Although these studies did not explicitly test the link with stereotypes, the findings strongly suggest that nouns are likely used to communicate stable stereotypic beliefs about a person. Carnaghi et al. (2008), suggested that persons exhibiting stereotypically expected characteristics of a social category are more likely referred to with a noun than adjective (e.g., Paul is *a* homosexual versus is homosexual), because nouns better reflect the belief that it is an enduring and essentialist aspect of the person's personality.

In the above variations of referential terms, senders reveal their stereotypic expectancies about the targets and communicate these to recipients. Moreover, these biases may allow people to defend and maintain stereotypic knowledge (Devine & Baker, 1991). By specifically marking and mentioning the unexpected, and by creating subtypes, inconsistent information is compartmentalized, allowing the general rule to remain inviolate. A label like a nice Moroccan creates a narrow subtype that allows for the maintenance of a more general belief that *most* Moroccans are not nice. Information that fits the general expectation, in contrast, is unmarked or described with general category labels (e.g., noun).

### *Descriptions of Behaviors*

The previous section showed how stereotypic expectancies are reflected in referential labels. Comparable linguistic biases have been observed in descriptions of others' behaviors. Most research on this topic followed from the LCM (for linguistic category model; Semin, 2011; Semin & Fiedler, 1988, 1992; Wigboldus & Douglas, 2007).

The LCM distinguishes four different word categories that vary on a concrete-abstract dimension. Most concrete are descriptive action verbs. These describe single, observable actions (e.g., Jack talks to Sue) and preserve perceptual features of the event. Most abstract are adjectives (Jack is flirtatious) that describe only the subject, show no reference to context or to specific acts, and thus generalize across specific events and objects. Relative to concrete descriptions, abstract descriptions give more information about the stable dispositional qualities of the actor and less about the specific situation or context in which the actor finds himself (Semin & Fiedler, 1988, 1992; see also Chapter 3, this volume).

The LCM formed the basis for a major contribution to the linguistic mechanism underlying the communication of stereotypes; the LIB (for linguistic intergroup bias; Maass, Salvi, Arcuri, & Semin, 1989). The LIB refers to the hypothesis that desirable behaviors of in-group members and undesirable behaviors of out-group members are described at a relatively high level of language abstraction (e.g., the in-group member is helpful; the out-group member is aggressive). In contrast, to describe an *out*-group member showing desirable behavior and an *in*-group member showing undesirable behavior, relatively low levels of language abstraction are used (e.g., the in-group member hits somebody; the out-group member opens the door for someone; Maass et al., 1989). Because the different LCM categories elicit different cognitive inferences, the implicit meaning that is communicated varies as a function of level of abstraction. By describing desirable behavior of in-group members and undesirable behavior of out-group members abstractly, these behaviors are portrayed as stable and highly diagnostic traits. Undesirable behavior of in-group members and desirable behavior of out-group members, in contrast, are portrayed as situationally determined and exceptions to the rule.

Research demonstrated that the LIB mechanism also operates outside an intergroup context and may result from general expectancies (Maass, Ceccarelli, & Rudin, 1996; Maass, Milesi, Zabbini, & Stahlberg, 1995). Given that expected behavior is considered to be more stable, diagnostic, and typical than unexpected behavior, it is more appropriately described with abstract terms. Wigboldus, Semin, and Spears (2000) demonstrated that stereotypic expectancies give rise to differences in language abstraction and termed this phenomenon the linguistic expectancy bias (LEB). For example, to describe behavior that is inconsistent with the male stereotype (e.g., crying), people use relatively more concrete language (e.g., he has tears in his eyes). In contrast, when describing a woman demonstrating the same—but female stereotype consistent—behavior, people tend to use more abstract language (e.g., she is emotional).

Another linguistic bias focusing on behavior descriptions is the stereotypic explanatory bias (SEB; Sekaquaptewa, Espinoza, Thompson, Vargas, & Von Hippel, 2003). SEB pertains to the tendency to provide relatively more explanations in descriptions of stereotype inconsistent, compared with consistent behavior. Learning about stereotype incongruent behaviors instigate explanatory processing, which is reflected in an explanation to make sense of the incongruity. Sekaquaptewa et al. (2003) demonstrated that the tendency to engage in SEB was related to prejudiced behavior. The more external, situational explanations White participants provided to explain stereotype inconsistent behavior of Black individuals (e.g., Marcellus got a job at Microsoft, because he knew someone there), the more negative behavior they showed toward a Black partner in an interracial interaction.

A recent extension to the linguistic bias literature pertains to the use of negations. The negation bias (Beukeboom, Finkenauer, & Wigboldus, 2010)

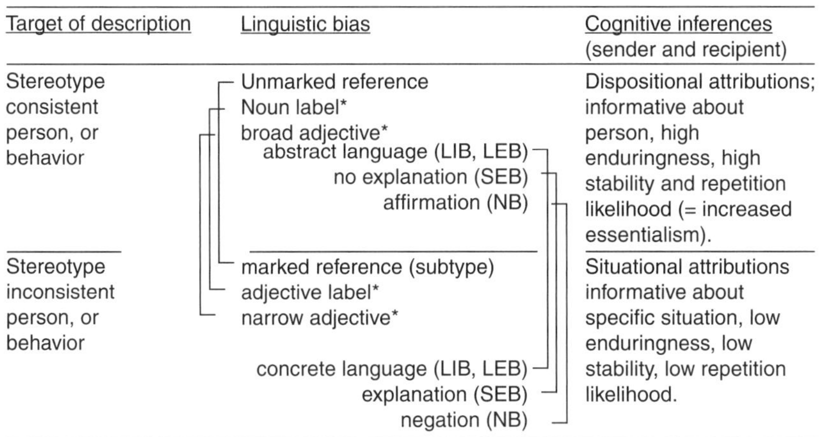


Figure 18.1 Overview of different linguistic biases and the cognitive inferences they induce

(Note: LIB / LEB = Linguistic intergroup / expectancy bias, SEB = Stereotypic explanatory bias, NB = Negation bias. *Not empirically demonstrated with respect to stereotypes.)

entails that the use of negations (e.g., *not stupid,* rather than *smart*) is more pronounced in descriptions of stereotype inconsistent compared with stereotype consistent behaviors. For example, if a sender's stereotypic expectancy dictates that garbage men are stupid, but a particular garbage man violates this expectancy by showing highly intelligent behavior, the sender is likely to reveal his prior expectancy by using a negation like *The garbage man was not stupid.* In contrast, for stereotype consistent behavior (e.g., The garbage man was stupid; The professor was smart), the use of negations is less likely.

In sum, the different linguistic biases described above demonstrate that people reveal their stereotypic expectancies in a number of subtle ways in their choice of words—see Figure 18.1. It appears that stereotype inconsistent information is in general described with relatively more narrow, specific or concrete terms than stereotype consistent information. This is shown in increased markedness and subtyping in reference to stereotype inconsistent individuals, in more concrete language (LIB, LEB), and more frequent specific situational explanations (SEB) in descriptions of stereotype inconsistent behaviors. The use of adjectives versus nouns and negations versus affirmations (negation biases) also appears to fit this general pattern, particularly when looking at the cognitive inferences that the different linguistic devices induce. This is what is focused on in the next section.

## EFFECTS OF LINGUISTIC BIAS

The previous section showed that stereotypic expectancies of senders surface in subtle variations in language use. The significance of these linguistic biases lies in the fact that they implicitly communicate these stereotypes to message recipients, and thereby contribute to the transmission and maintenance of socially shared stereotypes. These effects occur mainly by influencing the cognitive inferences of recipients of biased messages, but may also affect the sender and the collective (Holtgraves & Kashima, 2008). More important, the inferences that recipients draw from biased descriptions tend to be consistent with the sender's stereotypic expectancies (Maass et al., 1989; Wigboldus et al., 2000), and as a consequence, the stereotypic view about the described actor is transmitted.

### *Recipient Inferences*

The type of term used to refer to a person clearly has a strong effect on the impressions recipients form (see Chapter 19, this volume). Verbal category labels activate categorical representations containing additional information that the observed target itself does not convey. Derogatory group labels (e.g., fag, nigger) activate a different, more negative representation than neutral labels (e.g., gay, Afro-American; Carnaghi & Maass, 2007). Where recipients may intentionally regulate negative reactions to such explicit derogatory ethnic labels, because of egalitarian social norms (Simon & Greenberg, 1996), these corrections are unlikely when stereotypes surface in the above reviewed subtle implicit biases. As a consequence, seemingly harmless differences in labels can exert significant effects on the impressions that recipients draw.

A recent study (Foroni & Rothbart, 2011) showed that observers, in estimating the weight of persons, are influenced by the labels presented with the targets, even when these labels are self-generated. Participants judged silhouette drawings of body types, presented either without labels, with weak category labels (below-average; average; above-average) or with strong labels (anorexic; normal; obese). By looking at the judged similarity and the estimated weight of body types, it was shown that the presence of a label reduced perceived differences between members of the same category (assimilation), whereas exaggerating the differences between members of different categories (contrast). These categorization effects were stronger for strong labels, but even weak labels showed significant differences compared with unlabeled conditions.

These findings are largely in line with the previously described difference between nouns (that would constitute a strong label) and adjectives (Carnaghi et al., 2008). This research showed that nouns (e.g., a Jew) have a more powerful impact on impression formation than adjectives (e.g., Jewish). Compared with adjectives, nouns more strongly induce stereotype congruent inferences about the target (e.g., always goes to the Synagogue) and simultaneously inhibit counterstereotypical inferences (e.g., always goes to church). Furthermore, nouns inhibit alternative classifications. A person described with a noun (e.g., an athlete) rather than adjective (e.g., athletic) is less likely categorized in alternative categories (e.g., an artist; Carnaghi et al., 2008). Moreover, nouns induce stronger essentialist attributions; the relevant characteristic is seen as a more profound and unchangeable behavior tendency, as more informative about the person, to have a higher enduringness and higher likelihood of future repetition (Carnaghi et al., 2008).

It appears then that labels used to refer to stereotype consistent individuals (i.e., nouns and unmarked labels) induce more stereotype confirming inferences, as compared with labels used to refer to stereotype *in*consistent individuals (i.e., marked and subtyped reference). The *strong*—stereotype consistent—labels induce recipients to (a) more strongly categorize the individual, (b) more strongly activate the associated stereotypic expectancies with the category, and (c) to infer that the characteristic is more essentialist, profound, and enduring.

The inferences that recipients draw from biased behavior descriptions (LIB and LEB) show a comparable pattern. It has consistently been shown that the relatively concrete language used in stereotype inconsistent messages causes recipients to infer that the behavior is unexpected, is an exception to the rule, and more likely caused by situational circumstances than by dispositional factors. In contrast, the more abstract language used in stereotype consistent messages implies that the behavior is expected, more likely caused by the actor's stable dispositional characteristics, and thus more likely to be repeated and to generalize across situations (Maass et al., 1989; Wigboldus et al., 2000). This pattern of inferences shows that higher abstraction implies greater essentialism. Likewise, generic (versus specific) statements about social categories (e.g., "Italians love pasta") have been shown to induce more essentialist stereotypic beliefs (Rhodes et al., in press).

Although recipient inferences to descriptions containing explanations (SEB; Sekaquaptewa et al., 2003) have to my knowledge not been specifically tested, it seems apparent that they should induce lower essentialist inferences. That is, the explanations people tend to give for stereotype inconsistent behavior provide an external situational attribution, which by definition suggest it is a transient behavior caused by situational rather than stable dispositional factors.

A similar pattern is observed with respect to the negation bias (Beukeboom et al., 2010). Negations (e.g., not stupid), compared with affirmations (e.g., smart), were shown to induce lower dispositional than situational attribution in recipients and a lower repetition likelihood. Recipients also inferred from negations that the sender had an opposite prior expectancy. Thus again, the language used to describe stereotype inconsistent behavior implies reduced essentialism for the target.

With respect to negations, two additional effects can be mentioned. First, when a negation rather than affirmative antonym is used to describe stereotype inconsistent behavior, stereotype consistent concepts are introduced to the discourse. Research suggests that negations make associations with the negated concept more accessible and, as a consequence, may activate the opposite of the message content in recipients (Giora, Fein, Aschkenazi, & Alkabets-Zlozover, 2007; Grant, Malaviya, & Sternthal, 2004; Mayo, Schul, & Burnstein, 2004). Thus, when negations are used to describe stereotype inconsistent behavior (e.g., the garbage man is not stupid), stereotype consistent associations are activated and reinforced in a recipient. Second, by introducing information via negation, senders convey a mitigated, more neutral version of the described event (see Fraenkel & Schul, 2008; Giora, Fein, Ganzi, & Alkeslassy, 2005). When intelligent behavior of a garbage man is described as *not stupid,* this activates negative associations, it communicates that the positive performance is unexpected and inessential, and conveys a less positive meaning than the positive behavior allows. Thus by means of negations, senders share negative (or positive) prior expectancies with recipients.

In sum, the different linguistic biases are comparable in the pattern of inferences they induce (see Figure 18.1). More important, the induced inferences are congruent with the stereotypic expectancies that induce the biased word choice in the first place. Senders choose other linguistic devices to describe stereotype consistent versus inconsistent behaviors and actors. By means of these linguistic devises, senders reveal and activate their stereotypic beliefs in recipients.

## *Effects on the Sender*

Although this has not been studied extensively, based on other research, it seems likely that biased language use also has a stereotype confirming effect on the sender. The influence of verbal communication on subsequent cognition of the sender is well established. The classic demonstration probably being the *saying-is-believing* effect (Higgins & Rholes, 1978), which shows that communicators end up believing and remembering what they said rather than what they originally learned about a target. Subsequent research has confirmed that people's mental representations of an experience can be profoundly shaped by how they verbally describe it (for reviews McCann & Higgins, 1990; Marsh, 2007).

In the context of linguistic bias, research by Karpinski and Von Hippel (1996) is particularly relevant. They studied whether the LEB helps people maintain their expectancies in the face of incongruency. They experimentally manipulated an initial expectancy (positive versus negative) of a target person Scott. Subsequently, participants rated a number of target person descriptions that varied in language abstraction, after which the extent to which the initial expectancy was maintained was determined. Their results replicated the LEB effect; expectancy congruent (versus incongruent) behaviors were preferably described more abstractly. More important, the more participants displayed the LEB in their descriptions, the more their initial expectancy was maintained. This effect was especially the case for behaviors of moderate valence (Karpinski & Von Hippel, 1996).

In sum, it appears that people not only communicate information to others in a subtly biased fashion, the sender's linguistic choices also appear to reverberate on the sender. The act of verbalizing a stereotypic expectancy in language, albeit in a subtly biased manner, may reconfirm and strengthen existing stereotypes in the sender. The sender is, just as a recipient, prone to activate stereotype confirming inferences.

### Collective Effects

Moreover, the social cognitive implications of biased language use go beyond the senders' and recipients' individual cognitions (Holtgraves & Kashima, 2008; see also Chapter 11, this volume). People usually talk about other people and their behavior in interpersonal conversations. In such conversations, conversation partners create a shared view in a dynamic collaborative process. Research (Echterhoff, Higgins, & Groll, 2005, Hellmann, Kopietz, & Echterhoff, 2007; Kopietz, Hellmann, Higgins, & Echterhoff, 2010) has demonstrated that the saying-is-believing effect (Higgins & Rholes, 1978) mainly occurs when sender and recipient create a shared reality and mutually recognize that they have reached understanding about a target person (i.e., Hardin & Higgins, 1996). Kashima et al. (2010) showed that the act of communicating about characteristics of a novel social category induced stronger dispositional attributions and stronger beliefs that this was an immutable essence of the category. This increased essentialism occurred especially when the senders' descriptions were elaborately grounded (i.e., accepted by the conversation partner; Clark, 1996).

The biases described above reveal how stereotype consistent and inconsistent information is confirmed and strengthened through linguistic biases. It explains why stereotypical views are difficult to disconfirm and resistant to change (Biernat & Ma, 2005; Rothbart & Park, 1986). They perpetuate, even when stereotype inconsistent behavior is being described.

## UNDERLYING MECHANISMS OF LINGUISTIC BIAS

Most research on potential underlying mechanisms of linguistic biases has been done with respect to the LIB and LEB. Maass et al. (1995) distinguished two independent mechanisms that give rise to the LIB. One mechanism is argued to arise from implicit cognitive associations and expectancies, the other from motivational or strategic factors (Wigboldus & Douglas, 2007). Although these mechanisms are linked to the LIB and LEB, it is plausible that both mechanisms are in operation to produce the other linguistic bias effects. The following two sections successively elaborate on these initially proposed mechanisms and subsequently propose a third mechanism.

### Cognitive Mechanism: Spontaneous Reflection of Cognitive Expectancies

This first mechanism pertains to the idea that linguistic biases are the result of intrapersonal cognitive processes. The words that people choose when describing the behavior of individuals belonging to different social categories unintentionally reflect existing associations and expectancies. In studies on the underlying mechanisms of the LIB, Maass et al. (1995) and Maas et al. (1996) demonstrated that expectancy consistent behaviors based on stereotypes about northern and southern Italians are described at a higher level of abstraction than expectancy inconsistent behavior. This effect was shown to be independent of the desirability of behavior and the in- versus out-group membership of the participant. As described above, further research confirmed this mechanism in research on the LEB (Karpinski & Von Hippel, 1996; Wenneker, Wigboldus, & Spears, 2005; Wigboldus et al., 2000).

Likewise, the negation bias (Beukeboom et al., 2010) is argued to result from existing stereotypic associations. The stereotype literature suggests that, upon perceiving (or reading about) the behavior of an actor, people automatically activate the mental representations associated with the social category to which the person belongs (Devine, 1989; Fiske, 1998; Lepore & Brown, 1997). For example, the category label professor activates stereotype consistent trait terms such as *smart* and inhibits stereotype inconsistent trait terms such as *stupid* (Dijksterhuis & Van Knippenberg, 1996). This should make the use of terms that are stereotype consistent with the activated social category more probable in descriptions of category members. Because of the decreased accessibility of stereotype inconsistent terms, their use will be less likely. These differences in accessibility may explain why the description of unexpected dim behavior of a professor is relatively likely to contain a negation (e.g., not smart), whereas the same behavior is described with an affirmation when it is consistent with expectations (e.g., the garbage man is stupid).

Perhaps like most linguistic choices, the reflection of stereotypic beliefs in language use typically occurs unintentionally and operates outside of people's awareness (Franco & Maass, 1996; Maass, 1999). As a consequence, the effects of stereotypic expectations on linguistic choices appear to be difficult to inhibit (Franco & Maass, 1996; Douglas, Sutton, & Wilkin; 2008). Hence, the LIB/LEB (Von Hippel, Sekaquaptewa, & Vargas, 1997) and SEB (Sekaquaptewa et al., 2003) have been used as implicit measures of prejudice. It seems reasonable to assume that the choice for a noun or adjective (Carnaghi et al., 2008) and markedness in reference occurs largely outside awareness, and results from implicit cognitive processes. When a person's characteristics are encoded as consistent with an activated category, the person will subsequently be more likely referred to using a noun and unmarked reference.

It thus seems that people's linguistic choices automatically reflect existing social knowledge. However, such linguistic choices may also be driven by a fundamental need to maintain existing beliefs. When people are confronted with inconsistencies, they have been shown to attempt to defend and maintain their stereotypic knowledge and adopt a variety of cognitive strategies that allow them to keep the general stereotype inviolate (e.g., Kunda & Oleson, 1995; Yzerbyt, Coull, & Rocher, 1999; Zoe & Hewstone, 2001). Exactly these cognitive strategies may be reflected in linguistic biases. When people are confronted with stereotype inconsistent events they tend to (a) compartmentalize it (i.e., marking, subtyping), (b) to perceive it as a transient property that is under the influence of situational factors rather than stable dispositional factors (LIB, LEB, negation bias), (c) to explain the inconsistency (SEB), (d) to mitigate the valence of the event, and simultaneously connect it to concepts that fit the stereotype (negation bias). In contrast, consistent information is processed such that it allows one to reconfirm existing stereotypes, (e) by using strong category labels (nouns) and more abstract language (LIB, LEB) implying stability and essentialism.

### *Motivational Mechanism: Communication Goals and Strategic Language Use*

The second mechanism that has been proposed to give rise to linguistic bias is motivational in nature. Utterances obviously do not merely express privately held beliefs; they are tailored to suit communication goals (Higgins, 1992). Senders may want to achieve something in a recipient (e.g., persuade, derogate, ingratiate), and they need to take into account the recipient's level of understanding and acceptance (Clark & Brennan, 1991; Clark & Krych, 2004; Krauss & Fussell, 1991). Thus, when formulating an utterance, people adapt their language on the basis of what they intend or need to achieve interpersonally in a recipient.

Research on the LIB demonstrated that the use of predicates of different abstraction may be driven by a motivation to protect one's social identity (Maass et al., 1995; Maas et al., 1996; Wigboldus & Douglas, 2007). It was demonstrated that the LIB was more pronounced in intergroup settings wherein the in-group was threatened (e.g., hostility between northern and southern Italians). The LIB allows a sender to convince oneself or recipients of one's positive essentialist group identity.

Other research confirmed that motivational factors and interpersonal communication goals have an important effect on linguistic bias. Douglas and Sutton (2003) showed that explicit communication goals have a strong effect on the use of language abstraction. When someone has the intent to favorably portray a person, he or she adopts abstract predicates to describe positive behaviors and concrete predicates to describe negative behaviors. Such motivations to portray a person or social group in a positive or negative light may result from one's social role. For instance, prosecution and defense attorneys have been shown to strategically adopt different levels of abstraction to imply guilt and innocence of defendants (Schmid & Fiedler, 1998; Schmid, Fiedler, Englich, Ehrenberger, & Semin, 1996).

Likewise, negations may be used strategically. That is, one is likely to use a negation when one wants to change a (assumed) recipient's view about a target (e.g., I am not stupid!). One may also use negations to mitigate the valence of a description (Giora et al. 2007; Fraenkel & Schul, 2008) and thus strategically describe someone's behavior in a more neutral manner. That is, to say that someone is *not smart* (compared with stupid) yields a weaker face threat and is more polite (Brown & Levinson, 1987).

In sum, the above mechanisms suggest that linguistic biases may result from implicit cognitive processes, or from interpersonal goals to portray a target in a particular way. These mechanisms, at least with respect to the LIB and LEB, have been shown to operate independently of each other (Maass et al., 1995; Maass et al., 1996; Wigboldus & Douglas, 2007), although communication goals tend to largely overrule the effects of existing expectancies (Douglas & Sutton, 2003). Based on other literature, a third mechanism is proposed.

### *Interpersonal Context and Interactive Processes*

A third mechanism that likely determines biased message formulations arises from the interpersonal context and the interaction between individuals. The characteristics of recipients, and the sender's and recipient's relation to each other and the target, will determine whether linguistic biases occur (Freytag, 2008).

First, the communicative context may determine whether relevant stereotypes are activated. Wigboldus, Spears, and Semin (2005) suggested that in an intragroup context (e.g., when females talk to females about females), a target's category membership (e.g., gender) is less likely to become salient. As a consequence, stereotypic expectancies with this category are not activated, thus rendering it unlikely that linguistic biases occur. In an intergroup context, however (i.e., when either target or recipient is an out-group member), a required category activation is more likely and linguistic bias is expected.

Second, senders tend to tune their formulations to recipients (Higgins & Rholes, 1978) and linguistic bias may thus arise from the assumed beliefs of a recipient. Carnaghi and Yzerbyt (2006, 2007), for instance, showed that participants showed stronger subtyping of a target person when they anticipated communicating their impression to an audience they thought had an opposing stereotype. This suggests that biased language use may even arise in unprejudiced senders when they communicate to (assumed) prejudiced recipients. However, the perceived expectancies in recipients might also induce a sender to either conceal one's own expectancies (and show less linguistic bias), or instead a motivation to argue against the beliefs of the recipient. A motivation to explain, teach, or interpret a behavioral event in a description toward a recipient with an opposing attitude may result in a reversal of, for instance, the LEB effect (Fiedler, Bluemke, Friese, & Hofmann, 2003).

A particularly interesting situation occurs when the target of a behavior description is also the recipient. Variations in language can be employed strategically to put someone in a positive or negative light, to praise or denigrate the other. In these cases, the nature of the interaction is likely to affect the goal, and thus the occurrence of a linguistic bias effect. Semin, Gil de Montes, and Valencia (2003) showed that when senders expected to cooperate with a partner, the regular LIB pattern emerged; positive behaviors of the partner were described at a higher level of abstraction than negative behavior. When senders expected to compete with a partner, however, the LIB pattern was reversed. This pattern only emerged when senders were told that their message would be passed on to their partner, suggesting that a goal to influence the relation with the partner determined the LIB effect.

In sum, the interpersonal context may determine whether or not stereotypes become activated (Carnaghi & Yzerbyt, 2006, 2007; Wigboldus et al., 2005) and may evoke particular communication goals, either aimed at explaining something or convincing a recipient (Fiedler et al., 2003), or at strategically influencing interpersonal relations (Semin et al., 2003). As described above, contextually induced communication goals may overrule effects of activated stereotypic expectancies (Douglas & Sutton, 2003) and can, consequently, completely reverse linguistic biases.

## CONCLUSIONS

This chapter reviewed research on linguistic bias in communications about stereotype relevant information. Different linguistic biases show that people tend to systematically vary their language in communications about stereotype inconsistent information as compared with stereotype consistent information. The reviewed linguistic biases suggest that stereotype inconsistent information is, in general, reflected in relatively more specific and concrete linguistic predicates than stereotype consistent information. This is in line with the idea that stereotype inconsistent information demands elaboration. People tend to explain inconsistencies, by compartmentalizing and attributing it as information separate from the general stereotype. These cognitive efforts occur at an intrapersonal level but surface in language use and interpersonal conversations. The biased descriptions induce different cognitive inferences in both senders and recipients, implying that stereotype inconsistent (as compared with consistent) characteristics and behaviors are relatively less enduring, stable, and dispositional. In other words, the descriptions used for stereotype inconsistent persons and behaviors imply lower essentialism (see Figure 18.1). This pattern of inferences is stereotype confirming and maintains the stereotypic expectancies that instigate the biased descriptions.

The research described in this chapter shows that *how* people talk about stereotypic information is an important factor in stereotype maintenance. A complementary area of research focuses on *what* people tend to talk about in stereotype relevant communications. Research demonstrated that people are more likely to talk about information they share with other people (Fast, Heath, & Wu, 2009), and that stereotype consistent information gets advantage over stereotype inconsistent information (Clark & Kashima, 2007; Kashima, Klein, & Clark, 2007). The linguistic biases discussed in this chapter show that even when stereotype inconsistent information is introduced in communication, it is formulated in such a way that stereotypic knowledge remains intact. Even in the face of stereotype inconsistent information, stereotypes are continuously reconfirmed or strengthened. Communicating about stereotype relevant information allows one to verify stereotypes, and reaching acceptance of recipients may even strengthen one's privately held convictions about social categories. As a consequence, when people communicate about stereotype relevant information they are more likely to essentialize category information, than when they simply memorize it (Kashima et al., 2010).

Stereotype confirming effects of linguistic biases are mainly expected when sender and recipient have common ground and share the same stereotypic expectancies about a target (Kashima et al., 2007; Ruscher & Duval, 1998). In these cases, provided that the relevant stereotypic expectancies are activated, a senders language will both reflect his or her own stereotypic expectancies and will concurrently be tuned to the perceived corresponding expectancies of recipients. By producing and receiving biased language, and by obtaining mutual agreement, both sender and recipient will reconfirm and strengthen their stereotypes. When common ground is lacking, however, effects may reverse. In these cases, a sender may employ the same linguistic tools to explain or convince a recipient about stereotypic expectancies to establish common ground (Fiedler et al. 2003). Future research may shed more light on the intra- and interpersonal mechanisms underlying linguistic biases.

The integrative approach adopted in this chapter enables predictions about the mechanisms and effects of different biases. An integrative methodological approach may be adopted to study how these different biases combine in spontaneous language use. Do they co-occur or does the use of one type of bias diminish the use of another? Future research may also reveal other biases in language use that undoubtedly exist (e.g., syntactic agency bias; Chapter 12, this volume). In line with the biases described in the present chapter, such other biases in language use may vary along a concrete- abstract dimension. For instance, a bias may exist within the use of different adjectives distinguished in breadth versus narrowness (Karpinski, Steinberg, Versek, & Alloy, 2007; Karpinski & Von Hippel, 1996). Broad adjectives subsume more distinct behaviors (e.g., talented) than narrow adjectives (e.g., musical), rendering broad adjectives more abstract than narrow adjectives. Most interesting, this may correspond to differences between *concrete* adjectives derived from action verbs (IAV; help-helpful), versus state verbs (SV; like-likable) and *abstract* adjectives not derived from verbs (e.g., kind, generous). It has been suggested that differences between these adjectives should mirror the differences between the corresponding verbs (Semin, 1994; Semin & Fiedler, 1988). As a consequence, there may be an expectancy maintenance mechanism relying upon adjective breadth (Hamilton, Gibbons, Stroessner, & Sherman, 1992), meaning that stereotype consistent (versus inconsistent) manners are more likely described with broad rather than narrow adjectives.

Another extension may lie in several distinct word categories defined in the LIWC for linguistic inquiry and word count (Pennebaker, Booth, & Francis, 2007, see also Chapter 2, this volume). A recent study (Beukeboom, Tanis, & Vermeulen, in press) revealed a number of significant correlations between language abstraction as defined by the LCM and LIWC variables in descriptions of social events. Particularly, an increased concreteness in language covaried with the use of articles, numbers, and specific references to humans.

To conclude, research has revealed how seemingly harmless subtleties in language use can have a major impact in the maintenance of stereotypic representations. By revealing the mechanisms of these biases, people may become more aware of biased word choices and prevent potentially negative effects.

## REFERENCES

Beukeboom, C. J., Finkenauer, C., & Wigboldus, D. H. J. (2010). The negation bias: When negations signal stereotypic expectancies. *Journal of Personality and Social Psychology, 99*(6), 978–992.

Beukeboom, C. J., Tanis, M. A., & Vermeulen, I. (in press). The language of extraversion: Extraverted people talk more abstractly, introverts are more concrete. *Journal of Language and Social Psychology.*

Biernat, M., & Ma, J. E. (2005). Stereotypes and the confirmability of trait concepts. *Personality and Social Psychology Bulletin, 31,* 483–495.

Brown, P., & Levinson, S. (1987). *Politeness.* Cambridge, England: Cambridge University Press.

Carnaghi, A., & Maass, A. (2007). In-group and out-group perspectives in the use of derogatory group labels: Gay versus fag. *Journal of Language and Social Psychology, 26,* 142–156.

Carnaghi, A., Maass, A., Gresta, S., Bianchi, M., Cadinu, M., & Arcuri, L. (2008). Nomina sunt omina: On the inductive potential of nouns and adjectives in person perception. *Journal of Personality and Social Psychology, 94,* 839–859.

Carnaghi, A., & Yzerbyt, V. Y. (2006). Social consensus and the encoding of consistent and inconsistent information: When one's future audience orients information processing. *European Journal of Social Psychology, 36,* 199–210.

Carnaghi, A., & Yzerbyt, V. Y. (2007). Subtyping and social consensus: The role of the audience in the maintenance of stereotypic beliefs. *European Journal of Social Psychology, 37,* 902–922.

Castelli, L., Vanzetto, K., Sherman, S. J., & Arcuri, L. (2001). The explicit and implicit perception of ingroup members who use stereotypes: Blatant rejection but subtle conformity. *Journal of Experimental Social Psychology, 37,* 419–426.

Clark, A. E., & Kashima, Y. (2007). Stereotypes help people connect with others in the community: A situated functional analysis of the stereotype consistency bias in communication. *Journal of Personality and Social Psychology, 93,* 1028–1039.

Clark, H. H. (1996). *Using language.* Cambridge, England: Cambridge University Press.

Clark, H. H., & Brennan, S. E. (1991). Grounding in communication. In L. B. Resnick, J. M. Levine, & S. D. Teasley (Eds.), *Perspectives on socially shared cognition* (pp. 127–149). Washington, DC: American Psychological Association.

Clark, H. H., & Krych, M. A. (2004). Speaking while monitoring addressees for understanding. *Journal of Memory and Language, 50,* 62–81.

Devine, P. G. (1989). Stereotypes and prejudice: Their automatic and controlled components. *Journal of Personality and Social Psychology, 56,* 5–18.

Devine, P. G., & Baker, S. M. (1991). Measurement of racial stereotypes subtyping. *Personality and Social Psychology Bulletin, 17,* 44–50.

Dijksterhuis, A., & Van Knippenberg, A. (1996). The knife that cuts both ways: Facilitated and inhibited access to traits as a result of stereotype activation. *Journal of Experimental Social Psychology, 32,* 271–288.

Douglas, K. M., & Sutton, R. M. (2003). Effects of communication goals and expectancies on language abstraction. *Journal of Personality and Social Psychology, 84,* 682–696.

Douglas, K. M., Sutton, R. M. & Wilkin, K. (2008) Could you mind your language? An investigation of communicators' ability to inhibit linguistic bias. *Journal of Language and Social Psychology, 27* (2). pp. 123–139.

Echterhoff, G., Higgins, E. T., & Groll, S. (2005). Audience-tuning effects on memory: The role of shared reality. *Journal of Language and Social Psychology, 89* (3), 257–276.

Fast, N. J., Heath, C., & Wu, G. (2009). Common ground and cultural prominence: How conversation reinforces culture. *Psychological Science, 20,* 904–911.

Fiedler, K., Bluemke, M., Friese, M., & Hofmann, W. (2003). On the different uses of linguistic abstractness: From LIB to LEB and beyond. *European Journal of Social Psychology, 33,* 441–453.

Fiske, S. T. (1998). Stereotyping, prejudice, and discrimination. In D. T. Gilbert, S. T. Fiske, & G. Lindzey (Eds.), *The handbook of social psychology* (4th ed., pp. 357–411). New York, NY: McGraw-Hill.

Foroni, F., & Rothbart, M. (2011). Category boundaries and category labels: When does a category name influence the perceived similarity of category members? *Social Cognition, 29,* 547–576.

Fraenkel, T., & Schul, Y. (2008). The meaning of negated adjectives. *Intercultural Pragmatics, 5,* 517–540.

Franco, F. M., & Maass, A. (1996). Implicit vs. explicit strategies of outgroup discrimination: The role of intentional control in biased language use and reward allocation. *Journal of Language and Social Psychology, 15,* 335–359.

Freytag, P. (2008). Sender-receiver constellations as a moderator of linguistic abstraction bias. In Y. Kashima, K. Fiedler, & P. Freytag (Eds.), *Stereotype dynamics: Language-based approaches to stereotype formation, maintenance, and transformation* (pp. 213–237). Mahwah, NJ: Erlbaum.

Giora, R., Fein, O., Aschkenazi, K., & Alkabets-Zlozover, I. (2007). Negation in context: A functional approach to suppression. *Discourse Processes, 43,* 153–172.

Giora, R., Fein, O., Ganzi, J., & Alkeslassy Levi, N. (2005). On negation as mitigation: The case of negative irony. Discourse Processes, *39,* 81–100.

Grant, S. J., Malaviya, P., & Sternthal, B. (2004). The influence of negation on product evaluations. *Journal of Consumer Research, 31,* 583–591.

Hamilton, D. L., Gibbons, P. A., Stroessner, S. J., & Sherman, J. W. (1992). Stereotypes and language use. In G. R. Semin & K. Fiedler (Eds.), *Language, interaction and social cognition* (pp. 102–128). London, England: Sage.

Hardin, C. D., & Higgins, E. T. (1996). Shared reality: How social verification makes the subjective objective. In R. M. Sorrentino & E. T. Higgins (Eds.), *Handbook of motivation and cognition, Vol. 3: The interpersonal context* (pp. 28–84). New York, NY: Guilford Press.

Hellmann, J. H., Kopietz, R., & Echterhoff, G. (2007). Shared memories, shared beliefs: The formation and use of joint representations in social interaction. *European Bulletin of Social Psychology, 19,* 40–46.

Higgins, E. T. (1992). Achieving "shared reality" in the communication game: A social action that creates meaning. *Journal of Language and Social Psychology, 11,* 107–125.

Higgins, E. T., & Rholes, W. S. (1978). "Saying is believing": Effects of message modification on memory and liking for the person described. *Journal of Experimental Social Psychology, 14,* 363–378.

Holtgraves, T., & Kashima, Y. (2008). Language, meaning, and social cognition. *Personality and Social Psychology Review, 12,* 73–94.

Karpinski, A., Steinberg, J. A., Versek, B., & Alloy, L. B. (2007). The breadth–based adjective rating task (BART) as an indirect measure of self–esteem. *Social Cognition, 25*(6), 778–818.

Karpinski, A., & Von Hippel, W. (1996). The role of the linguistic intergroup bias in expectancy-maintenance. *Social Cognition, 14,* 141–163.

Kashima, Y., Kashima, E. S., Bain, P., Lyons, A., Tindale, R. S., Robins, G., Vears, C., & Whelan, J. (2010). Communication and essentialism: Grounding the shared reality of a social category. *Social Cognition, 28*(3), 306–328.

Kashima, Y., Klein, O., & Clark, A. E. (2007). Grounding: Sharing information in social interaction. In K. Fiedler (Ed.), *Social communication* (pp. 27–77). New York, NY: Psychology Press.

Kopietz, R., Hellmann, J. H., Higgins, E. T., & Echterhoff, G. (2010). Shared-reality effects on memory: Communicating to fulfill epistemic needs. Social Cognition, 28, 353–378.

Krauss, R. M., & Fussell, S. R. (1991). Perspective-taking in communication: Representations of others' knowledge in reference. *Social Cognition, 9,* 2–24.

Kunda, Z., & Oleson, K. C. (1995). Maintaining stereotypes in the face of disconfirmation: Constructing grounds for subtyping deviants. *Journal of Personality and Social Psychology, 68,* 565–579.

Leets, L., & Giles, H. (1997). Words as weapons: When do they wound? Investigations of harmful speech. *Human Communication Research, 24,* 260–301.

Lepore, L., & Brown, R. (1997). Category and stereotype activation: Is prejudice inevitable? *Journal of Personality and Social Psychology, 61,* 164–176.

Maass, A. (1999). Linguistic intergroup bias: Stereotype perpetuation through language. In M. P. Zanna (Ed.), *Advances in experimental social psychology* (Vol. 31, pp. 79–121). San Diego, CA: Academic Press.

Maass, A., Ceccarelli, R., & Rudin, S. (1996). Linguistic intergroup bias: Evidence for in-group protective motivation. *Journal of Personality and Social Psychology, 71,* 512–526.

Maass, A., Milesi, A., Zabbini, S., & Stahlberg, D. (1995). The linguistic intergroup bias: Differential expectancies or in-group protection? *Journal of Personality and Social Psychology, 68,* 116–126.

Maass, A., Salvi, D., Arcuri, L., & Semin, G. R. (1989). Language use in intergroup contexts: The linguistic intergroup bias. *Journal of Personality and Social Psychology, 57,* 981–993.

Marsh, E. J. (2007). Retelling is not the same as recalling: Implications for memory. *Current Directions in Psychological Science, 16,* 16–20.

Mayo, R., Schul, Y., & Burnstein, E. (2004). "I am not guilty" vs. "I am innocent": Successful negation may depend on the schema used for its encoding. *Journal of Experimental Social Psychology, 40,* 433–449.

McCann, C. D., & Higgins, E. T. (1990). Social cognition and communication. In H. Giles & W. P. Robinson (Eds.), *Handbook of language and social psychology* (pp. 13–32). Oxford, England: Wiley.

Monteith, M. J. (1993). Self-regulation of prejudiced responses: Implication for progress in prejudice-reduction efforts. *Journal of Personality and Social Psychology, 65,* 469–485.

Moskowitz, G. B. (2005). *Social cognition: Understanding self and others*. New York, NY: Guilford Press.

Pennebaker, J. W., Booth, R. J., & Francis, M. E. (2007). Linguistic Inquiry and Word Count: LIWC 2007. [Computer software]. Austin, TX: LIWC.

Rhodes, M., Leslie, S.-J., & Tworek, C. (in press). The cultural transmission of social essentialism. Proceedings of the National Academy of Science.

Romaine, S. (2001). A corpus-based view of gender in British and American English. In M. Hellinger & H. Bussmann (Eds.), *Gender across languages: The linguistic representation of women and men*. Amsterdam, The Netherlands: John Benjamins.

Rothbart, M., & Park, B. (1986). On the confirmability and disconfirmability of trait concepts. *Journal of Personality and Social Psychology, 50,* 131–142.

Ruscher, J. B., & Duval, L. L. (1998). Multiple communicators with unique target information transmit less stereotypical impressions. *Journal of Personality and Social Psychology, 74,* 329–344.

Schmid, J., & Fiedler, K. (1998). The backbone of closing speeches: The impact of prosecution versus defense language on judicial attributions. *Journal of Applied Social Psychology, 28,* 1140–1172.

Schmid, J., Fiedler, K., Englich, B., Ehrenberger, T., & Semin, G. R. (1996). Taking sides with the defendant: Grammatical choice and the influence of implicit attributions in prosecution and defense speeches. *International Journal of Psycholinguistics, 12,* 127–148.

Sekaquaptewa, D., Espinoza, P., Thompson, M., Vargas, P., & Von Hippel, W. (2003). Stereotypic explanatory bias: Implicit stereotyping as a predictor of discrimination. *Journal of Experimental Social Psychology, 39,* 75–82.

Semin, G. R. (1994). The linguistic category model and personality language. In J. Siegfried (Ed.), *The status of common sense in psychology* (pp. 305–321). Norwood, NJ: Ablex.

Semin, G. R. (2011). The linguistic category model. In P. A. M. Van Lange, A. Kruglanski, & E. T. Higgins (Eds.), *Handbook of theories of social psychology*. London, England: Sage.

Semin, G. R., & Fiedler, K. (1988). The cognitive functions of linguistic categories in describing persons: Social cognition and language. *Journal of Personality and Social Psychology, 54,* 558–568.

Semin, G. R., & Fiedler, K. (1992). The inferential properties of interpersonal verbs. In G. R. Semin & K. Fiedler (Eds.), *Language, interaction and social cognition* (pp. 58–78). Newbury Park, CA: Sage.

Semin, G. R., Gil de Montes, L., & Valencia, J. F. (2003). Communication constraints on the linguistic intergroup bias. *Journal of Experimental Social Psychology, 39,* 142–148.

Simon, L., & Greenberg, J. (1996). Further progress in understanding the effects of derogatory ethnic labels: The role of preexisting attitudes toward the targeted group. *Personality and Social Psychology Bulletin, 12,* 1195–1204.

Stahlberg, D., Braun, F., Irmen, L., & Sczesny, S. (2007). Representation of the sexes in language. In K. Fiedler (Ed.), *Social communication* (pp. 163–187). New York, NY: Psychology Press.

Von Hippel, W., Sekaquaptewa, D., & Vargas, P. (1997). The linguistic intergroup bias as an implicit indicator of prejudice. *Journal of Experimental Social Psychology, 33,* 490–509.

Wenneker, C. P. J., Wigboldus, D. H. J., & Spears, R. (2005). Biased language use in stereotype maintenance: The role of encoding and goals. Journal of Personality and Social Psychology, 89, 504–516.

Wigboldus, D., & Douglas, K. (2007). Language, stereotypes, and intergroup relations. In K. Fiedler (Ed.), *Social communication* (pp. 79–106). New York, NY: Psychology Press.

Wigboldus, D. H. J., Semin, G. R., & Spears, R. (2000). How do we communicate stereotypes? Linguistic bases and inferential consequences. *Journal of Personality and Social Psychology, 78,* 5–18.

Wigboldus, D. H. J., Spears, R., & Semin, G. R. (2005). When do we communicate stereotypes? Influence of the social context on the linguistic expectancy bias. *Group Processes and Intergroup Relations, 8,* 215–230.

Yzerbyt, V. Y., Coull, A., & Rocher, S. J. (1999). Fencing off the deviant: The role of cognitive resources in the maintenance of stereotypes. *Journal of Personality and Social Psychology, 77,* 449–462.

Zoe, R., & Hewstone, M. (2001). Subtyping and subgrouping: Processes for prevention and promotion of stereotype change. *Personality and Social Psychology Review,* 5(1), 52–73.

# 19

# Does Political Correctness Make (Social) Sense?

ANNE MAASS, CATERINA SUITNER, AND ELISA MERKEL

Most countries in Northern America and Europe have laws and regulations that define what is appropriate or inappropriate language. Political correctness[1] embraces many different speech codes and refers to a wide variety of speech acts, ranging from blatantly offensive speech or *hate speech* to more subtle forms of discrimination such as the generic use of the masculine forms (e.g., *fireman*) or of nouns rather than adjectives to describe social groups. In many countries, blatantly abusive language or hate speech is regulated by national laws, whereas the softer forms of discriminatory speech are generally subject to rules and regulations of organizations, such as political institutions (parliament, city governments), educational institutions (schools and universities), industry, media organizations, and professional organizations (such as the American Psychological Association, APA). Political correctness norms primarily aim at *preventing* abusive or discriminatory language, but in case of severe violations, individuals may face lawsuits and/or disciplinary actions.

An example of political correctness rules of a professional organization is the *APA Publication Manual* (2009) that most readers are likely to be familiar with. APA provides precise guidelines for authors, including the avoidance of pejorative and biased language. As a general rule, APA suggests to avoid language that could cause *offense* and to use designations that the target group would prefer to be called by. Also, APA suggests that authors use *inclusive* language. Although this rule applies, in principle, to any social group it has mainly been discussed with respect to gender-inclusive language (e.g., *native language* rather than *mother tongue, police officers* rather than *policemen, humans* rather than *men* to refer to human beings). Another rule is to avoid *asymmetrical* language that implies different status (such as *man and wife* or *Mr.* and *Miss*) or in which one group becomes the standard against which other groups are compared. Finally, APA suggests to avoid *essentializing* language that equates persons with their condition (*the depressive, the schizophrenic, the epileptic*) and that implies that the physical or psychological condition is the very essence of the person. The recommendation is to use alternative language forms that put the individual at the center and treat the disease as one out of many attributes. One possible way to avoid essentializing implications is to use adjectives rather than nouns (*depressive individuals*); the other is to follow the *person-first* principle (*patients diagnosed with depression*). Thus, APA rules include at least four important principles, namely the avoidance of offensive, exclusive, asymmetrical, and essentializing language.

## THE POLITICAL CORRECTNESS CONTROVERSY

Although common in many organizations, political correctness norms are highly controversial and have been subject to political and philosophical debate for decades (see overviews in Hughes, 2010; Wilson, 1995). The main argument in favor of politically correct speech is that language not only reflects, but also channels thought. How messages are framed significantly affects how they are interpreted, processed, and remembered. Thus, if democratic societies prohibit discrimination on the basis of ethnicity, gender, age, disability, religion, beliefs, etc., then this same principle should hold not only for behaviors, but also for speech acts, assuming that speech acts are one type of behavior.

However, critics have been very vocal by raising a number of arguments against political correctness rules. First, political correctness is seen as violating the principle of free speech. In fact, many opponents of political correctness have argued that speech should not be censored or suppressed on any grounds, at times equating political correctness with *thought police, totalitarianism,* or *McCarthyism of the left.* Second, many critics claim that political correctness rules interfere with the natural flow of speech production as speakers have to monitor consciously what they are saying. This argument holds particular in earlier stages of a language reform, whereas most political correctness expressions are likely to become automatic over time, much like seat-belt use initially required conscious monitoring but became automatic shortly after the introduction of seat belt laws. Third, some political correctness rules (such as gender-fair language) are seen as complicated and as destroying the natural beauty of language. As a case in point, in the 1990s, the feminization of occupational nouns in French language was strongly supported by the Quebec government, whereas the *Académie Française* in Paris thought that this constituted an affront to the logic and beauty of the French language. Although the judgment of what constitutes *beauty* in language is largely subjective, it has been used as an argument against political correctness rules.

Finally, many opponents believe that political correctness is an unlikely tool to create equality, as it introduces a superficial and hypocritical correction unable to hide the speaker's true attitude. In fact, at times, political correctness forms appear exaggerated and illogical such as when groups are described by what they are not or by what they are lacking. In Italian, blind people are often called *non vedenti* (non-seeing), and people in wheelchairs or on crutches are referred to a *non-deambulanti* (non-deambulating), whereas the organizations representing these groups often use the more common term, for instance defining themselves as *blind.* Moreover, when substituting offensive group labels (e.g., *Negroe*) with new, politically correct labels (e.g., *Black*), any new term will soon take on the negative connotation of former expressions (Pinker, 2007). This argument, known as *euphemism treadmill,* refers to the fact that politically correct substitutes for offensive terms may quickly loose their positive connotation, creating the need for repeated replacements. Examples for this process are terms describing mental disability (*moron, mentally retarded, mentally challenged, with an intellectual disability, learning difficulties,* and *special needs*) or race (*Nigger, Negroe, Black, Afro-American,* and *African-American*). An interesting exception to this process of repeated replacement is the term *gay* that has maintained its positive or neutral valence since the 1920s, when it was coined by the gay community.

The above list of arguments illustrates that political correctness has been criticized on very different grounds and for very different reasons, some of which are best addressed by other sciences. For instance, the subordination of free speech versus politically correct speech (or vice versa) is mainly a philosophical and legal matter, whereas the *beauty-of-language* argument is best judged by linguists. However, the question of the effectiveness of political correctness is an empirical question that falls into the realm of competence of psychological research. But what evidence is there that speaks to the effectiveness or ineffectiveness of political correctness norms? In the subsequent sections, we review the existing literature, together with some unpublished studies, addressing the main political correctness strategies. We report evidence that political correctness language affects cognition and behavior and that it does mostly (but not exclusively) in the intended direction. Following the main suggestions included in the *APA Manual* on how to avoid linguistic biases, we briefly review the literature on the four main principles, namely the avoidance of (a) exclusive language, (b) essentializing labels, (c) asymmetrical, and (d) offensive language.

## EXCLUSIVE LANGUAGE

As far as exclusive language is concerned, professional organizations such as APA are encouraging writers and speakers to pay attention to expressions that make some social categories salient and others invisible, or that exclude individuals or entire categories. An example are the terms referring to people's first language that, in the past, were described as *mother tongue (in English), Muttersprache (in German),* or *lingua madre (in Italian),* as if children were to learn language exclusively from mothers while their fathers apparently kept silent for about three years. In most languages in North America and Europe, these terms have now been replaced by more inclusive ones, such as *native language (in English), Erstsprache (in German),* and *lingua nativa* or *prima lingua (in*

*Italian*). Also, questions or response alternatives (e.g., *single, married, divorced*) are often framed so as to exclude unmarried heterosexual partners or same-sex couples (especially in countries or states in which homosexual marriage is still prohibited). Unless researchers are specifically interested in the legal status of their participants, more inclusive questions about *partnership* or *cohabitation* are better able to capture different forms of partnership.

Undoubtedly, the most extensive line of research on inclusive language refers to gender-fair language, especially in grammatical gender languages where the explication of gender is mandatory (see Stahlberg, Braun, Irmen, & Sczesny, 2007, for an overview of the literature on gender-fair language). This research has shown that women tend to be overlooked when masculine forms are used, whereas politically correct neutralizations and splitting-forms, naming both women and men, increase the social visibility of women. Stahlberg, Sczesny, and Braun (2001) conducted a survey-type research in which German participants were asked to indicate their favorite writer, actor, musician, or athlete. The linguistic form was varied so that the question was either framed in the masculine form (e.g., *Athlet* [m]) or in one of two inclusive political correctness forms (neutralization or splitting-form, e.g., *Athlet* [m] *oder Athletin* [f]). As expected, participants named more women when inclusive language was used, suggesting that the masculine form inhibits access to female exemplars stored in memory. Also reading time experiments conducted in German confirmed this bias (Irmen & Roßberg, 2004). When perceiving incongruence between a person's sex and the language form they are described with, participants' reading times slowed down (e.g., congruent phrase: *Artists* [m] *can be very moody. This is sometimes difficult for their wives;* incongruent phrase: *Artists* [m] *can be very moody. This is sometimes difficult for their husbands*). This indicates that women were not mentally included when the masculine form was used. Irmen and Roßberg (2004), moreover, found evidence that gender-stereotypicality of professions influences mental representations. Stereotypically masculine professions (e.g., *Astronaut*) resulted in longer reading times in the incongruent condition than stereotypically feminine professions (e.g., *Kindergarten teacher*). That gender-stereotypicality is inherent in role nouns, was also found in other languages, such as Italian, Spanish, English, and French (Cacciari & Padovani, 2007; Carreiras, Garnham, Oakhill, & Cain, 1996; Gabriel, Gygax, Sarrasin, Garnham, & Oakhill, 2008).

The practical implications of these linguistic biases have been shown in various fields of applications. For instance, Hamilton, Hunter, and Stuart-Smith (1992) found that the masculine form penalizes women in court decisions and Stahlberg and Sczesny (2001) reported similar results for public opinion polls. Also workplace decisions are highly influenced by language. Bem and Bem (1973) demonstrated that women perceived a lack of fit when reading job ads in the masculine form and, subsequently, were less willing to apply for the offered position. Prewitt-Freilino, Caswell, and Laasko (2011) argued that language is closely associated to economic and social gender equality. Their findings suggest a greater gender gap in countries with grammatical gender languages than in those with other language systems, and this remained consistent even after controlling for other relevant factors such as religion and type of political system. Despite the overwhelming empirical evidence, there are still many voices arguing against gender-fair, inclusive language. Slovenko (2007) calls gender-fair language "an absurdity and a distraction from serious social issues" and refers to it as a "loony idea promoted by ideologically deranged feminists" (p. 96). Along the same lines, Kreeft (2005) states that turning to gender-fair forms would mean to give up one's *linguistic sanity* (p. 36).

Given that empirical results convincingly demonstrate the importance of gender-fair language, public policy seems nevertheless moving towards gender-fair language use. For example, derogatory feminine suffices such as *-ess* in *Quakeress, Actress,* or *Jewess* have almost been abolished from today's English (Miller & Swift, 2001), and many associations have adopted gender-inclusive language rules (e.g., American Medical Association, National Council of Teachers of English). Language guidelines released by political institutions (such as the European Parliament) are generally in favor of gender-fair language use. For instance, the UNESCO Guidelines for Gender-Neutral Language (UNESCO, 1999), which were approved by its 193 member states, have become one of the most established commonly cited guidelines with regard to gender-fair language for the English language. The UNESCO aimed at establishing guidelines in order "to transform behavior and attitudes that legitimize and perpetuate the moral and social exclusion of women" (p. 3) under the premise that current language usage was "exclusionist to women and girls" (see Moser, Sato, Chiarini, Dmitrow-Devold, & Kuhn, 2011, for an overview of the gender-fair language guidelines).

## ESSENTIALIZING LABELS

The second rule imposed by APA regards the politically correct labeling of people. The linguistic guidelines suggest avoiding categorizations whose framing essentializes people's membership and reduces their individuality and personhood. In particular, individuals should not be equated with their conditions. There are different linguistic strategies to put the individual person at the center, namely (a) to use adjectives (*depressive individuals, older people*) rather than nouns (*the depressives, the elderly*) and (b) to add report on the condition after having provided individualizing information (*individuals with depression, a person with hearing impairment*).

By the age of two, children are able to distinguish different word classes, recognizing that nouns refer to objects, adjectives to properties, and verbs to actions. As investigated from several theoretical perspectives, the use of these linguistic elements in describing a person strongly affects the information conveyed about the person (e.g., Carnaghi, Maass, Gresta, Bianchi, Cadinu, & Arcuri, 2008; Semin & Fiedler, 1988). Nouns are the primary linguistic instrument used to describe a person's social membership and, compared with other forms, nouns tend to enhance the essentialism and the permanence of this membership (Markman, 1989). Nouns are the grammatical form used to indicate objects and, hence their application to human beings, may promote an object-like perception. For instance, referring to somebody as *the depressive* may prevent listeners from noting other characteristics of the person. A chair is defined by specific properties and functions (e.g., *it is used to sit on and is part of the furniture*), and any irrelevant information (e.g., *whether it can also be used for cooking or be part of sport gear*) is prevented by that definition. As we do for objects, when we label a person using a noun, we depersonalize him or her, thus equating the person with his or her conditions or group membership. To avoid these implications, APA suggests two alternatives to nouns, namely adjectives (*depressive individuals*) or the *person-first* strategy (*individual diagnosed with depression*), in which the condition or membership is defined as a characteristic owned by the target rather than being equated with his or her identity.

To our knowledge, the first evidence regarding the impact of nouns and adjectives in people's descriptions was provided by Markman and Smith (as cited in Markman, 1989). In one study, the authors presented two descriptions of targets to undergraduate students. One of the descriptions used a noun (e.g., *John is a sexist*) and the other an adjective (e.g., *John is sexist*). The two descriptions were pretested to check their semantic similarity and to assure that they referred to the same class of people. The presentation order of the two descriptions was counterbalanced. Participants were asked to choose which description was in their opinion the more powerful statement about the target and to justify their choice. Noun descriptions were selected more frequently (68%) as the most powerful statement because participants thought that nouns were more informative about the target and referred to more central and stable features of the person. In another study, participants were either presented with statements presenting several targets using nouns (e.g., *Suppose the person is an intellectual*) or adjectives (e.g., *Suppose the person is intellectual*) and then asked to list other properties of the targets. When the target was presented with a noun, it triggered more additional attributes than when it was presented with an adjective. Therefore, nouns are more powerful and trigger more inferences than adjectives.

Similar findings have also been reported by Carnaghi et al. (2008) who had participants draw inferences from simple statements such as *Mark is homosexual* versus *Mark is a homosexual.* In line with hypotheses, Carnaghi and colleagues found that nouns (versus adjectives) facilitate stereotype-congruent inferences but inhibit incongruent ones. Also, in the case of nouns, the relevant characteristic (e.g., *being intelligent or athletic*) is perceived as more essentialistic and, indeed, takes on a quasigenetic quality, whereas the same property described by adjectives is perceived as a less stable and less enduring feature of the individual. Finally, and most important, this research shows that alternative classifications are inhibited when nouns rather than adjectives are used. Thus, once a person has been labeled by a noun, it becomes difficult to imagine the same person along different social dimensions.

An unpublished study by Maass, Lindenthal, and Carnaghi (in preparation) has extended this reasoning to the clinical realm, presenting psychiatric patients either under a noun (*a schizophrenic*) or an adjective label (*schizophrenic*). After reading the case descriptions, clinical students in their last year of training attributed the causes of the disorder more to genetic and less to environmental reasons and were less optimistic about the prognosis when noun labels were used. Most important, however, this was true only in German where differences between nouns and adjectives are very marked (adjective *schizophren* versus noun *ein Schizophrener*), but not in Italian where the difference lies only in the absence or presence of the article (adjective *schizofrenico* versus noun *uno schizofrenico*). On one side, this study confirms that nouns are more essentializing than adjectives; on the other side, it also suggests that the magnitude of the difference between nouns and adjectives depends on the grammatical features of a given language. Together, the above studies allow us to conclude that adjectives are indeed the more politically correct form compared with nouns, because adjectives safeguard the personhood of the target individual by reducing the strength, essentialism, and stability of the ascribed membership.

The second strategy proposed by APA to avoid labeling people is to use the person-first strategy, namely to first introduce the person and then use a descriptive clause indicating the relevant characteristic. The additional description usually requires the use of a verb, which makes the information more context-dependent and less permanent and pervasive (e.g., *individuals diagnosed with attention deficit hyperactivity disorder*). The role of verbs in social cognition has been introduced by the LCM (for linguistic category model; Semin & Fiedler, 1988) according to which verbs define a situation in a more concrete way, whereas adjectives are more abstract. In comparison with adjectives (e.g., *being aggressive*), verbs (e.g., *acting aggressively*) imply greater context-dependence and lesser stability over time. This characteristic of linguistic abstraction has been applied to the context of intergroup relations, and several studies have shown that linguistic abstraction can be strategically used to affirm positive characteristics of the in-group (*we are friendly*) and negative characteristics of the out-group (*they are aggressive*). At the same time, the stability of negative information about the in-group (*we have insulted that person*) and positive information about the out-group (*they have helped that person*) is reduced by using a concrete language (see Maass, Salvi, Arcuri, & Semin, 1989).

Gelman and Heyman (1999) compared nouns and verbs in relation to attitude inferences. They asked five- and seven-year-old children to rate the strength of the characteristic of a person described using a noun (e.g., *Marc is a carrot eater*) or a verb (e.g., *Marc eats carrots whenever he can*) and showed that the attitude inferred by a noun-description was perceived as stronger compared with the attitude inferred by a description using a verb. Walton and Banaji (2004) replicated these findings with adults and confirmed that the perception of the strength of the attitude was based on the grammatical form rather than on the content. In two additional studies, the authors showed that also own attitudes were affected by the linguistic structure of the sentence in which an attitude was described. When the description involved a noun as the key word for communicating the attitude (e.g., *I am a Shakespeare reader*), the attitude was subsequently rated as more essential compared with when the attitude was described using a verb as a key word (e.g., *I read Shakespeare a lot*) (Walton & Banaji, 2004, Studies 2 and 3). It is, therefore, clear that the strength, stability, and resilience of the information communicated by nouns are stronger than the semantically corresponding information communicated by verbs.

Whether verbs are also better suited than adjectives is an issue that needs to be further examined. According to the previously described LCM (for detailed analyses on linguistic abstractedness and its consequences in communication see also Chapters 3 and 18, this volume), verbs represent the most concrete level of an ideal linguistic abstraction line, and therefore verbal descriptions should be the least essentializing structure to describe a person. In line with this idea, Wigboldus, Semin, and Spears (2000) showed that when a target person is defined with an adjective (e.g., *Sandra is emotional*), the dispositional inferences are stronger compared with those triggered by a corresponding verb description (e.g., *Sandra brushes away a tear from her eyes*).

The most direct test of APA's rule to avoid essentializing expressions comes from a set of studies of Reynaert and Gelman (2007) who compared the implication of three wording strategies (i.e., noun labels, adjectives, and verbs) on the perception of illness. The authors presented participants with three wordings of imaginary illnesses (e.g., *he has baxtermia, he is baxtermic, he is a baxtermic*) and asked which wording made the illness seem to be more permanent over time and showed that the noun form conveys the higher level of permanence, the verb form the lowest and the adjective form occupying an intermediate position.

Together the studies reported here confirm that noun labels (e.g., *Mark is a paralytic*) equate the condition with the person's identity, leaving little space to other possible identities or to changes over time. Adjectives (e.g., *Mark is paralytic*) improve the situation, but still the ascribed characteristics are thought to be relatively context-independent and relatively enduring. The most correct wording to define a person is by using a sentence that puts the person first and then describes the possession of a characteristic (e.g., *Mark has been diagnosed with paralysis* or *Mark has a paralysis*).

## ASYMMETRICAL COMPARISONS

A third important suggestion advanced by the *APA Manual* to reduce linguistic biases is to pay attention to social comparisons. When two (or more) social groups or individuals are compared, it is desirable to avoid the use of one group or person as the normal or standard, especially if that group or person is the higher status representative. Biased comparisons can take many different forms, some of them are rather transparent (e.g., *men and girls, borderline versus normal, lesbians versus normal women*), others are very subtle such as when the order of mentioning favors one group over the other, implicitly making the first mentioned group the standard against which the other is compared. Hegarty, Watson, Fletcher, and McQueen (2011) investigated the order of romantic partners' names and showed that speakers spontaneously tend to mention first the partner possessing more stereotypically masculine traits. The same bias is found in graphs, given that both scientists and laypeople place the bar representing men or powerful group members to the left (i.e., before, in a left-to-right writing system) of women or of powerless group members (Hegarty & Buechel, 2006; Hegarty, Lemieux, & McQueen, 2010). In this way, we subtly confirm the social bias that maleness comes before femaleness.

Choosing one group as the norm to which others are compared has deep social roots and important consequences. Pratto, Korchmaros, and Hegarty (2007) showed that powerful groups are typically used as the standard against which powerless groups are compared. Similarly, Bruckmüller and Abele (2010) found that the group that was used as the norm of a comparison was perceived as higher in status, more agentic, and more powerful, despite the fact that a previous pretest had attested to the similarity of the groups (for a discussion on agency and power ascription to groups and self see Chapter 10, this volume). Finally, Bruckmüller, Hegarty, and Abele (2012) showed that when gender differences in status were linguistically framed proposing men as referent group (e.g., *Compared to males, females are . . .* ), these differences were perceived as larger and more legitimate. How we frame social comparisons has important consequences for how we perceive social groups and for how legitimate we believe the social difference is. Thus, language and cognition are part of a self-perpetuating cycle in which linguistic bias derives from the stereotypical status ascribed to groups and reinforces and legitimates it, contributing to the maintenance of the status quo.

## OFFENSIVE LANGUAGE

The fourth and most obvious violation of political correctness is the use of offensive language. In extreme cases, the offense is so blatant that there is little doubt about the derogatory intent of the speaker such as when racial or ethnic slurs are used. Even overhearing such terms or being subliminally exposed to them induces a shift in evaluations of the target group. For instance, studies comparing exposure to offensive (e.g., *fag*) versus politically correct language (e.g., *gay* or *homosexual*) have consistently shown that offensive language induces more negative attitudes and more discriminatory behaviors toward the targeted minority group than politically correct language (see Carnaghi & Maass, 2007, for an overview).

However, often labels are not clearly derogatory but have a vaguely negative connotation. For instance, the suffix *-ess* in English (*actress*) or *-essa* in Italian (*professoressa, avvocatessa*) often conveys lesser status than alternative forms (e.g., *professora, avvocata*; see Merkel, Maass, & Frommelt, 2012). These subtle forms make it more difficult for listeners to discover the discriminatory nature of discourse and are therefore an important target of language reforms and speech codes. For instance, in many languages the professional noun for *garbage collector* has been substituted by new terms that give greater dignity to the professional collecting waste. The English *garbage collector* turned into a *sanitation worker* and the Italian *spazzino* became an *operatore ecologico*. Such transformations are generally ridiculed by opponents of political correctness language rules. But are these new political correctness labels able to change the image of those performing the profession? Many professional labels, especially those of low-status professions (janitor, garbage collector) have undergone changes in labeling, yet it remains unclear whether such changes also led to shifts in the public image of the professions and in the perceived hierarchy within organizations. For instance, if school principal and janitor are now called head teacher and school custodian, will this change the perceived distance between the two professional roles? Will it ultimately affect the interaction between school principals and janitors?

To investigate this question, we have recently conducted a set of studies in which dated professional labels were compared with novel, politically correct labels (Maass, Barbiero, & Suitner, in preparation). As a first step (pilot study), we identified work settings in which linguistic labels for specific pairs of high versus low status jobs had undergone a clear change over the past 30 years. This was done on the basis of legal documents and on interviews, which led to the selection of four professional role pairs, referring respectively to school, hospital, factory, and company settings. For each pair, one role was subordinate to the other in the organizational hierarchy, and both roles had undergone a change in language over the past decades. For instance, in the case of the school setting, the roles can roughly be translated into principal versus janitor in the case of the dated labels and as head of school versus school attendant or school custodian in the case of current labels. The current labels correspond to those now used in job advertisements and in legal documents. Some of the new labels have already entered the popular vocabulary, whereas in other cases the old labels are still used in informal discourse, as in the case of the *school attendant* who is still referred to as *janitor* or of the *health operator*, who is still referred to as *nurse* in everyday speech.

The aim of the first study was to test whether different professional role labels would suggest different degrees of interpersonal and institutional distance. A pilot study allowed the identification of work settings in which a high and low status worker were labeled with well-known, dated, and current words. Participants were exposed either to dated or to current (politically correct) labels and asked to indicate the perceived interpersonal and institutional distance between the professional roles of each pair (indicated by drawing a symbolic vertical line, similar to the one used in organizational charts) as well as the degree of overlap between the roles (indicated by choosing the degree of overlap of two circles symbolically representing the two workers). They also were asked to provide estimates of the likely income and of the relative prestige and autonomy.

Findings were consistent across variables. Current politically correct labels made observers believe that the interpersonal and institutional distance was significantly smaller than when dated labels were used. Similarly, the professional overlap between the two roles was judged greater, and the perceived difference in prestige and autonomy smaller when professions were described by politically correct labels. Also, differences in salary were judged somewhat greater for the dated (€2,290.70) than for the current label (€2,041.57) labels, although this difference was nonsignificant, probably due to the fact that participants found it difficult to estimate the salaries, resulting in considerable variance in estimates. Together, these findings illustrate a strong effect of linguistic label on how distant professional roles are perceived, with modern labels implying a much smaller distance between superior and subordinate roles. Although confirming our expectations, the findings of Study 1 only refer to perceptions of external observers but provide little insight into the way in which linguistic labels channel the actual behavior of those to whom the labels refer. If professional role labels are as powerful as Study 1 suggests, then they may also affect the way in which people enact their respective roles.

This question was investigated in a subsequent study, which used a role-play methodology in which an interaction between high and low status professionals was simulated by pairs of participants. We selected two of the four work settings from Study 1, namely school and company, in which pairs of participants either simulated an interaction between a school principal and a janitor at a school or between a manager and an employee at a company. Within pairs, participants were randomly assigned to either the high or the low status role and had to perform a number of tasks, some of which constituted individual, others collective dependent measures.

The most important individual measure was leadership style (corrected for preexperimental leadership style assessed a few weeks before the study). Overall, people claimed more leadership abilities when politically correct rather than dated labels were used, but this was entirely due to those assigned to low status professions. Thus, lower (but not higher) status professionals claimed greater leadership capacities in the recent label condition, rather than in the dated label condition.

The remaining measures represent collective responses regarding funding allocation, a salary bonus, and the construction of a hypothetical organization chart. We had expected that, collectively, participants in the current (versus dated) label condition would distribute funds and salary bonus in a more egalitarian way and that they would represent their roles as less distant on a hypothetical organization chart. With the exception of the salary bonus, these predictions were born out. When negotiating how to distribute funds that would mainly favor one or the other professional role, resources were indeed assigned more fairly when politically correct new labels were used. It is interesting to note that an exactly opposite trend emerged for the collective decision on how to distribute a salary bonus to be divided between the two roles. Here, a greater salary bonus was assigned to the low (rather than high) status role in the dated label condition. Presumably, participants considered the low status person more needy of salary compensation when the dated (rather than current) labels were used.

The last collective task consisted of the construction of a hypothetical organizational chart. Participants were provided with a number of possible roles (e.g., teacher, lab technician, gardener), including their own roles, and asked to jointly develop an organizational chart of their organization as they envisaged it. This allowed us to calculate two measures, namely the relative distance between high versus low status role and the number of intermediate positions. As predicted, the distance between the two professional roles in the organizational chart was greater when dated than when recent labels were used. A similar pattern emerged when looking at the number of intermediate ranks, which was greater when dated, than when the recent label was used. Together, our research suggests that political correctness labels are by no means irrelevant in organizational settings and may effect both the perception of external observers and the individual and collective behaviors of actors within the organization.

## CONCLUSIONS

Together, the small but growing psychological literature on political correctness language suggests that rules such as those of APA may have tangible effects on the listener, the reader, and sometimes even on the speaker. To a large degree, these effects are in line with the nondiscrimination goals of political correctness policies, thus illustrating their effectiveness. Professional role labels may even affect those enacting these roles, although more research is needed to assure that this also holds for real work settings. Indeed, with the possible exception of research on gender-fair language, empirical research is not only sparse, but also mainly limited to controlled experiments, whereas only few attempts have been made to test the effects of political correctness rules in the field. The limited amount of empirical investigation is quite in contrast to the lively and often heated debate surrounding political correctness, where proponents and opponents take rigid positions on purely ideological grounds. In practice, political correctness rules are often grounded in idealistic and wishful intuition rather than being guided by solid empirical evidence.

The current overview shows that political correctness language rules do have concrete and multifaceted consequences that are likely to be driven by a multitude of processes. Language guides our attention, making groups salient or invisible, as in the case of the *generic* masculine forms. It also affects our inferences by creating links between people and the groups they belong to or by suggesting that a given feature is an essential, deeply rooted aspect of an individual, as in the case of essentializing language.

Language also channels interpretation as in the case where one group—according to a simple criterion of temporal or spatial ordering—is taken as the standard with which the other is being compared. Such asymmetries are created not only through language but also through seemingly objective tools such as graphs. Finally, language affects our affective reactions toward individuals and groups, as in the case of offensive language, and it creates or reduces status hierarchies, as in the case of professional role labels. Adjusting to others and accommodating our communication style to the social situation we are facing is a critical factor in promoting positive interactions (see Chapter 9, this volume). The functions reviewed here are by no means exhaustive but illustrate the multitude of effects that language can have on our cognition. Most of these language tools are very subtle and, hence, difficult to control, although extensive experience with language reforms around the world suggests that people are able to learn new language rules that are likely to become automatic and to sound *natural* after short periods of practice. Our review suggests that such practice may be worth the effort if one wants to create more inclusive, symmetrical, and democratic organizations.

## NOTES

1. Although political correctness embraces many other aspects (behavior, economic, and social policies, etc.) aimed at reducing offense on the basis of gender, race, occupation, ethnicity, religion, sexual orientation, disability, age, beliefs, etc., in this chapter, we exclusively focus on *language*.

## REFERENCES

American Psychological Association. (2009). *Publication manual of the American Psychological Association* (6th ed.). Washington, DC: Author.

Bem, S. L., & Bem, D. J. (1973). Does sex-biased job advertising "aid and abet" sex discrimination? *Journal of Applied Social Psychology, 3,* 6–18.

Bruckmüller, S., & Abele, A. E. (2010). Comparison focus in intergroup comparisons: Who we compare to whom influences who we see as powerful and agentic. *Personality and Social Psychology Bulletin, 36,* 1424–1435.

Bruckmüller, S., Hegarty, P., & Abele, A. E. (2012). Framing gender differences: Linguistic normativity affects perceptions of gendered power and gender stereotypes. *European Journal of Social Psychology, 42,* 210–218.

Cacciari, C., & Padovani, R. (2007). Further evidence of gender stereotype priming in language: Semantic facilitation and inhibition in Italian role nouns. *Applied Psycholinguistics, 28,* 277–293.

Carnaghi, A., & Maass, A. (2007). Derogatory language in intergroup context: Are "gay" and "fag" synonymous? In Y. Kashima, K. Fiedler, & P. Freytag (Eds.), *Stereotype dynamics: Language based approaches to stereotype formation, maintenance, and transformation.* Mahwah, NJ: Erlbaum.

Carnaghi, A., Maass, A., Gresta, S., Bianchi, M., Cadinu, M., & Arcuri, L. (2008). Nomina sunt omina: On the inductive potential of nouns and adjectives in person perception. *Journal of Personality and Social Psychology, 94,* 839–859.

Carreiras, M., Garnham, A., Oakhill, J., & Cain, K. (1996). The use of stereotypical gender information in constructing a mental model: Evidence from English and Spanish. *The Quarterly Journal of Experimental Psychology, 49A,* 639–663.

Gabriel, U., Gygax, P., Sarrasin, O., Garnham, A., & Oakhill, J. (2008). Au pairs are rarely male: Norms on the gender perception of role names across English, French, and German. *Behavior Research Methods, 40*(1), 206–212.

Gelman, S. A., & Heyman, G. D. (1999). Carrot-eaters and creature-believers: The effects of lexicalization on children's inferences about social categories. *Psychological Science, 10,* 489–493.

Hamilton, M. C., Hunter, B., & Stuart-Smith, S. (1992). Jury instructions worded in the masculine generic: Can a woman claim self-defence when "he" is threatened? In J. C. Christer & D. Howard (Eds.), *New directions in feminist psychology: Practice, theory and research* (pp. 169–178). New York, NY: Springer.

Hegarty, P., & Buechel, C. (2006) Androcentric reporting of gender differences in APA journals: 1965–2004. *Review of General Psychology, 10,* 377–389.

Hegarty, P. J., Lemieux, A., & McQueen, G. (2010). Graphing the order of the sexes: Constructing, recalling, interpreting, and putting the self in gender difference graphs. *Journal of Personality and Social Psychology, 98,* 375–391.

Hegarty, P. J., Watson, N., Fletcher, L., & McQueen, G. (2011). When gentlemen are first and ladies are last: Effects of gender stereotypes on the order of romantic partners' names. *British Journal of Social Psychology, 50,* 21–35.

Hughes, G. (2010). Political correctness: A history of semantics and culture. Malden, MA: Wiley-Blackwell.

Irmen, L., & Roßberg, N. (2004). Gender markedness of language: The impact of grammatical and nonlinguistic information on the mental representation of person information. *Journal of Language and Social Psychology, 23,* 272–307.

Kreeft, P. (2005). *Socratic logic.* South Bend, IN: St. Augustin Press.

Maass, A., Barbiero, E., & Suitner, C. (in preparation). *The power of linguistic labels: Professional role denominations affect perception and enactment.*

Maass, A., Salvi, D., Arcuri, L., & Semin, G. (1989). Language use in intergroup contexts: The linguistic intergroup bias. *Journal of Personality and Social Psychology, 57,* 981–993.

Markman, E. M. (1989). Categorization and naming in children: Problems of induction. Cambridge, MA: MIT Press.

Merkel, E., Maass, A., & Frommelt, L. (in press). Shielding women against status loss. The masculine form and its alternatives in Italian. *Journal of Language and Social Psychology,* 31, 311–320.

Miller, C., & Swift, K. (2001). *The handbook of nonsexist writing* (2nd ed.). Bloomington, IN: iUniverse.

Moser, F., Sato, S., Chiarini, T., Dmitrow-Devold, K., & Kuhn, E. (2011). *Comparative analysis of existing guidelines for gender-fair language within the ITN LCG Network.* Marie Curie Initial Training Network: Language, Cognition and Gender (ITN LCG).

Pinker, P. (2007). *The stuff of thought: Language as a window into human nature.* New York, NY: Penguin.

Pratto, F., Korchmaros, J. D., & Hegarty, P. (2007). When race and gender go without saying. *Social Cognition, 25*(2), 221–247.

Prewitt-Freilino, J. L., Caswell, T. A., & Laakso, E. K. (2011). The gendering of language: A comparison of gender equality in countries with gendered, natural gender, and genderless languages. *Sex Roles,* 1–14.

Reynaert, C. C., & Gelman, S. A. (2007). The influence of language form and conventional wording on judgments of illness. *Journal of Psycholinguistic research, 36,* 273–295.

Semin, G. R., & Fiedler, K. (1988). The cognitive functions of linguistic categories in describing persons: Social cognition and language. *Journal of Personality and Social Psychology, 54,* 558–568.

Slovenko, R. (2007). Nonsexist language—empowering women, dethroning men. *The Journal of Psychiatry & Law, 35,* 77–104.

Stahlberg, D., Braun, F., Irmen, L., & Sczesny, S. (2007). Representation of the sexes in language. In K. Fiedler (Ed.), *Social communication. A volume in the series Frontiers of Social Psychology* (pp. 163–187). New York, NY: Psychology Press.

Stahlberg, D., & Sczesny, S. (2001). Effekte des generischen Maskulinums und alternativer. *Psychologische Rundschau, 52*(1), 131–140.

Stahlberg, D., Sczesny, S., & Braun, F. (2001). Name your favorite musician: Effects of masculine generics and of their alternatives in German. *Journal of Language and Social Psychology, 20*(4), 464–469.

UNESCO. (1999). Guidelines for gender-neutral language.
Walton, G. M., & Banaji, M. R. (2004). Being what you say: The effect of essentialist linguistic labels on preferences. *Social Cognition, 22,* 193–213.
Wigboldus, D., Semin, G. R., & Spears, R. (2000). How do we communicate stereotypes? Linguistic bases and inferential consequences. *Journal of Personality and Social Psychology, 78,* 5–18.
Wilson, J. K. (1995). *The myth of political correctness: The conservative attack on higher education.* Durham, NC: Duke University Press.

# Index